Adobe®
PHOTOSHOP® ELEMENTS 4
COLLECTION

New Riders

Scott Kelby

ADOBE PHOTOSHOP® ELEMENTS 4 COLLECTION

PUBLISHED BY
New Riders
1249 Eighth Street, Berkeley, CA 94710
800-283-9444 • 510-524-2178 • 510-524-2221 (fax)

New Riders is an imprint of Peachpit, a division of Pearson Education.

FIRST EDITION: December 2005

Composed in Cronos, Helvetica, and Apple Garamond Light by NAPP Publishing

Trademarks
All terms mentioned in this book that are known to be trademarks or service marks have been appropriately capitalized. New Riders cannot attest to the accuracy of this information. Use of a term in the book should not be regarded as affecting the validity of any trademark or service mark.

Photoshop is a registered trademark of Adobe Systems, Inc.
Windows is a registered trademark of Microsoft Corporation.

Warning and Disclaimer
This book is designed to provide information about Photoshop Elements. Every effort has been made to make this book as complete and as accurate as possible, but no warranty of fitness is implied. The information is provided on an as-is basis. The authors and New Riders shall have neither liability nor responsibility to any person or entity with respect to any loss or damages arising from the information contained in this book or from the use of the discs or programs that may accompany it.

ISBN 0-321-37460-6

Note: This edition is a collection of *The Photoshop Elements 4 Book for Digital Photographers* and *Photoshop Elements Down & Dirty Tricks*

9 8 7 6 5 4 3 2

Printed and bound in the United States of America

www.newriders.com
www.peachpit.com
www.scottkelbybooks.com

ABOUT THIS COMBINED BOOK

Thank you for purchasing the *Adobe Photoshop Elements 4 Collection*. By combining two books into one, you save money and learn the best techniques and effects for Photoshop Elements.

The Photoshop Elements 4 Book for Digital Photographers is the first book in this combined volume, with the index for the book following immediately after the text. This is followed by *Photoshop Elements Down & Dirty Tricks*, with its index following immediately after the text, as well.

the photoshop
elements 4
book

for digital photographers

Scott Kelby

The Photoshop Elements 4 Book for Digital Photographers Team

CREATIVE DIRECTOR
Felix Nelson

TECHNICAL EDITORS
Polly Reincheld
Cindy Snyder
Kim Doty

PRODUCTION EDITOR
Kim Gabriel

PRODUCTION MANAGER
Dave Damstra

COVER DESIGNED BY
Felix Nelson

COVER PHOTOS COURTESY OF
iStockphoto.com
Scott Kelby

Published by
New Riders

Composed in Cronos, Helvetica, and Apple Garamond Light by NAPP Publishing

ISBN 0-321-38483-0

9 8 7 6 5 4 3 2 1

Printed and bound in the United States of America

www.newriders.com
www.scottkelbybooks.com

ACKNOWLEDGMENTS

First, I want to thank my amazing wife Kalebra. As I'm writing this, she's lying on the couch across from me reading a book (not one of mine, sadly), but I have to say that just looking at her makes my heart skip a beat, and again reminds me how much I adore her, how genuinely beautiful she is, and how I couldn't live without her. She's the type of woman love songs are written for, and I am, without a doubt, the luckiest man alive to have her as my wife.

Secondly, I want to thank my 8-year-old son Jordan, who spent many afternoons with his adorable little head resting on my lap as I wrote this book. God has blessed our family with so many wonderful gifts, and I can see them all reflected in his eyes. I'm so proud of him, so thrilled to be his dad, and I dearly love watching him grow to be such a wonderful little guy, with such a tender and loving heart. (You're the greatest, little buddy.)

I also want to thank my big brother Jeffrey for being such a positive influence in my life, for always taking the high road, for always knowing the right thing to say, and just the right time to say it, and for having so much of our dad in you. I'm honored to have you as my brother and my friend.

My heartfelt thanks go to the entire team at KW Media Group, who every day redefine what teamwork and dedication are all about. They are truly a special group of people, who come together to do some really amazing things (on really scary deadlines) and they do it with class, poise, and a can-do attitude that is truly inspiring. I'm so proud to be working with you all.

Thanks to my layout and production crew. In particular, I want to thank my friend and Creative Director Felix Nelson for his limitless talent, creativity, input, cover design, overall layout, and just for his flat-out great ideas. To my way cool tech editor, Polly Reincheld for putting every technique through rigorous testing, and keeping me on my toes through the whole process. To Kim Gabriel for keeping us all on track and organized, so we could face those really scary deadlines. To Dave Damstra and his amazing crew for giving the book such a tight, clean layout.

Thanks to my compadre Dave Moser, whose tireless dedication to creating a quality product makes every project we do better than the last. Thanks to Jean A. Kendra for her support, and for keeping a lot of plates in the air while I'm writing these books. A special thanks to my Executive Assistant Kathy Siler for all her hard work and dedication, and for mentally preparing herself for the inevitable loss that her beloved Redskins will face this year as they are crushed by my Buccaneers.

Thanks to my publisher Nancy Ruenzel, and the incredibly dedicated team at Peachpit/New Riders. You are very special people doing very special things, and it's a real honor to get to work with people who really just want to make great books. Also many thanks to the awesome Rachel Tiley, Peachpit's "Secret Weapon," to Ted "Time Waits For No Man" Waitt, and to marketing maverick Scott Cowlin.

I owe a special debt of gratitude to my friends Kevin Ames and Jim DiVitale for taking the time to share their ideas, techniques, concepts, and vision for a Photoshop Elements book for digital photographers that would really make a difference. Extra special thanks to Kevin for spending hours with me sharing his retouching techniques, as well.

I want to thank all the photographers, retouchers, and Photoshop experts who've taught me so much over the years, including Jack Davis, Deke McClelland, Ben Willmore, Julieanne Kost, Robert Dennis, Helene DeLillo, Doug Gornick, Manual Obordo, Dan Margulis, Peter Bauer, Joe Glyda, and Russell Preston Brown.

Also thanks to Dave Cross and Matt Kloskowski for sharing their Elements tips and techniques with me, and for being excellent sounding boards for new Elements ideas. You guys are the best!

Thanks to my friends at Adobe Systems: Terry White, Kevin Connor, Addy Roff, Cari Gushiken, John Nack, Russell Brady, Julieanne, and Russell. Gone but not forgotten: Barbara Rice, Jill Nakashima, Bryan Lamkin, and Karen Gauthier.

Also an extra special thanks to Elements product manager Mark Dahm for taking my frantic late-night calls, and going above and beyond to help make this book a reality—and for making Elements 4.0 one kick-butt editing app.

Thanks to my mentors whose wisdom and whip-cracking have helped me immeasurably, including John Graden, Jack Lee, Dave Gales, Judy Farmer, and Douglas Poole.

Also, my personal thanks to Patrick Lor at iStockphoto.com for enabling me to use some of their wonderful photography in this book.

Most importantly, I want to thank God, and His son Jesus Christ, for leading me to the woman of my dreams, for blessing us with such a special little boy, for allowing me to make a living doing something I truly love, for always being there when I need Him, for blessing me with a wonderful, fulfilling, and happy life, and such a warm, loving family to share it with.

ABOUT THE AUTHOR

Scott Kelby

Scott is Editor and Publisher of *Photoshop User* magazine, Editor-in-Chief of Nikon's digital software magazine, Publisher of *Layers* magazine (the how-to magazine for everything Adobe), and is Executive Editor of the *Photoshop Elements Techniques* newsletter.

Scott is President and co-founder of the National Association of Photoshop Professionals (NAPP) and is President of the software training, education, and publishing firm KW Media Group.

Scott is a photographer, designer, and award-winning author of more than 30 books, including *Photoshop Elements Down & Dirty Tricks*, *The Photoshop Book for Digital Photographers*, *Photoshop Classic Effects*, and is Series Editor for the *Killer Tips* books series from New Riders. In 2004, Scott was the world's No. 1 best-selling author of all computer and technology books, across all categories.

Scott is Training Director for the Adobe Photoshop Seminar Tour and Conference Technical Chair for the Photoshop World Conference and Expo. He's featured in a series of Adobe Photoshop training DVDs and has been training Adobe Photoshop users since 1993.

For more information on Scott, visit scottkelby.com.

SCOTT KELBY PHOTOGRAPHY

I had no intentions of writing this book

(Actually, I mean the book that led to this book. Here's the story.) So here it was, about four weeks before I would be flying up to New York City to teach a one-day seminar to more than 1,200 professional Photoshop junkies. (Okay, it was more like 1,160 pros, 42 people who just wanted a paid day off from work, and one total freak who kept asking me if I'd ever been in prison. I told him unequivocally, "Not as far as you know.")

Anyway, the seminar was just four weeks away, and there was one session that I still didn't have an outline for. It was called "Correcting Photos from Digital Cameras" (which is dramatically better than my original working title for the class, "Die, Traditional Camera User, Die!").

I knew what I needed to cover in the session, because for the past 10 years I've trained thousands of traditional photographers on how to use Photoshop. Most of them either have now gone digital or are in the process of going digital, and all these digital photographers generally seem to have the same type of Photoshop questions, which I'm actually thankful for, because now I can give them the answers. If they constantly asked different questions, I'd get stumped from time to time, and then I'd have to resort to "Plan B" (providing answers that sound good, but are in reality just wild-ass guesses).

So I knew what I had to cover, but I wanted to do some research first, to see if other people in the industry were addressing these questions the same way I was, or did they have a different take on them, different techniques or ideas? So I went out and bought every single book I could find about digital photography and Photoshop. I spent nearly $1.2 million. Okay, it wasn't quite that much, but let's just say for the next few months I would have to cut out some luxuries such as running water, trash collection, heat, etc.

I started reading through all these books, and the first thing I thought I'd look up was how they dealt with digital noise (High ISO noise, Blue channel noise, color aliasing, etc.), but as I went through them, I was amazed to find out that not one single book addressed it. Not a one. Honestly, I was shocked. I get asked this question many times at every single seminar, yet not one of these books even mentioned it. So then I started looking for how they work with 16-bit photos. Nothing. Well, one book mentioned it, but they basically said, "It's not for you—it's for high-end pros with $15,000 cameras." I just couldn't believe it—I was stunned. So I kept up my search for more topics I'd been asked about again and again, with the same results.

Well, I went ahead with my New York session as planned, and by all accounts it was a big hit. I had photographer after photographer coming up to tell me, "Thank you so much—those are exactly the things I was hoping to learn." That's when I realized that there's a book missing—a book for people who already know how to shoot—they even know what they want to do in Photoshop, they just need somebody to show them how to do it. Somebody to show them how to deal with the special challenges (and amazing opportunities) of using digital photos with Photoshop. I was so excited, because I knew in my heart I could write that book.

So now I had intentions

The day after the seminar I flew home and immediately called my editor at New Riders and I said, "I know what I want my next book to be—a Photoshop book for digital photographers." There was a long uncomfortable pause, and then he politely said, "Really, a digital photography book, huh?" It was clear he wasn't nearly as excited about this concept as I was (and that's being kind). He finally said, "Ya know, there are already plenty of digital photography books out there," and I agreed with him, because I just about went broke buying them all. So now I had to convince my editor that not only was this a good idea, but that it was such a good idea that he should put our other book projects on hold so I could write this book, of which there are (as he put it) "already plenty of digital photography books out there."

continued

Here's what I told my editor what would be different about my digital photography book:

(1) It's not a digital photography book; it's a Photoshop book. There'd be no discussion of film (gasp!), f-stops, lenses, or how to frame a photo. If they don't already know how to shoot, this book just won't be for them. (*Note:* Editors hate it when you start listing the people the book won't be appropriate for. They want to hear, "It's perfect for everybody! From grandma right up to White House press photographers," but sadly, this book just isn't.)

(2) I would skip the "Here's What a Digital Camera Is" section and the "Here's Which Printer to Buy" section, because they were in all those other books that I bought. Instead, I'd start the book at the moment the photo comes into Photoshop from the camera.

(3) It would work the way digital photographers really work—in the order they work—starting with sorting and categorizing photos from the shoot, dealing with common digital photography problems, color correcting the photos, selecting areas to work, retouching critical areas, adding photographic special effects, sharpening their photos, and then preparing the photo to be output to a printer.

(4) It wouldn't be another Photoshop book that focuses on explaining every aspect of every dialog. No sirree—instead, this book would do something different—it would show them how to do it! This is what makes it different. It would show photographers step-by-step how to do all those things they keep asking at my seminars, sending me email about, and posting questions about in our forums—it would "show them how to do it!"

For example, I told my editor that about every Photoshop book out there includes info on the Unsharp Mask filter. They all talk about what the Amount, Radius, and Threshold sliders do, and how those settings affect the pixels. They all do that. But you know what they generally don't do? They don't give you any actual settings to use! Usually, not even a starting point. Some provide "numerical ranges to work within," but basically they explain how the filter works, and then leave it up to you to develop your own settings. I told him I wouldn't do that. I would flat-out give them some great Unsharp Mask filter settings—the same settings used by many professionals, even though I know some highfalutin Photoshop expert might take issue with them. I would come out and say, "Hey, use this setting when sharpening people. Use this setting to correct slightly out-of-focus photos. Use this setting on landscapes, etc." I give students in my live seminars these settings, why shouldn't I share them in my book? He agreed. I also told him that sharpening is much more than just using the Unsharp Mask filter, and it's much more important to photographers than the three or four pages every other book dedicates to it. I wanted to do an entire chapter showing all the different sharpening techniques, step-by-step, giving different solutions for different sharpening challenges.

He was starting to come on board with the idea. What he didn't want was the same thing I didn't want—another digital photography book that rehashes what every other digital photography and Photoshop book has already done. Well, he went with the idea, and thanks to him, you're holding the third Elements version of the book that I am so genuinely excited to be able to bring you. But the way the book was developed beyond that took it further than I had planned.

How the book was developed

When my editor gave me the final approval (it was more like, "Okay, but this better be good or we'll both be greeting people by saying, 'Would you like to try one of our Extra Value Meals today?'"), I sat down with two of the industry's top digital photographers—commercial product photographer Jim DiVitale and fashion photographer Kevin Ames—to get their input on the book. These two guys are amazing—they both split their time between shooting for some of the world's largest corporations, and teaching other professional digital photographers how to pull off Photoshop miracles at events such as Photoshop World, PPA/ PEI's Digital Conference, and a host of other events around the world. We spent hours hammering out which techniques would have to be included in the book, and I can't tell you how helpful and insightful their input was, and this book is far better than it would have been thanks to their contributions.

New and improved (with the same great taste!)

When we first released *The Photoshop Book for Digital Photographers*, it became a huge hit overnight, and became not only the best-selling Photoshop book, not only the best-selling digital photography book, but one of the top selling of all computer books on Amazon.com, and it's ranked as high as No. 12 of ALL books on Amazon.com. Pretty freaky!

In short—the concept worked, and that's why I knew I had to do a special version of the book for Photoshop Elements users because Elements was designed from the beginning as a tool for digital photography. Best of all, I learned a lot from writing that original book, and I've learned a lot of new techniques since I wrote it; and you're getting the benefit of both in this new version of the book just for Elements users.

This version has a secret weapon

Although Elements does offer some cool digital photography features that Photoshop CS2 doesn't even offer, obviously there are plenty of features that Photoshop CS2 has that Photoshop Elements 4.0 still doesn't have (things like Layer Masking, Channel Mixer, etc.). But here's the cool part: The single thing that I'm most proud of in this Elements book is that I've been able to figure out workarounds, cheats, and some fairly ingenious ways to replicate some of those Photoshop features from right within Elements. In some cases, it may take a few more steps to get there than it does in Photoshop CS2, but son-of-a-gun, the result looks pretty darn close, and you'll be the only one who'll know the effect was created in Elements, not in Photoshop CS2. This will test how good you are at keeping secrets.

So what's not in this book?

There are some things I intentionally didn't put in this book. Like punctuation marks (kidding). No, seriously, I tried not to put things in this book that are already in every other Photoshop Elements book out there. For example, I don't have a chapter on the Layers palette, or a chapter on the painting tools, or a chapter showing how each Elements filter looks when it's applied to the same photograph. I also didn't include a chapter on printing to your color inkjet because (a) every Photoshop book does that, and (b) every printer uses different printer driver software, and if I showed an Epson color inkjet workflow, you can bet you'd have an HP or a Canon printer (or vice versa) and then you'd just get mad at me.

Is this book for you?

I can't tell you that for sure, so let's take a simple yet amazingly accurate test that will determine without a doubt if this book is for you.

Please answer the following questions:

(1) Do you now, or will you soon have a digital camera?

(2) Do you now, or will you soon have Photoshop Elements?

(3) Do you now, or will you soon have about 35 bucks (the retail price of this book)?

Scoring: If you answered "Yes" to question 3, then yes, this book is for you. If you answered yes to questions 1 or 2, that certainly is a good indicator, too.

Is this book for Windows users, Mac users, or both?

It's really just for Windows users, because at this point in time, there is no version of Elements 4.0 for Mac. Now, I say "at this point in time" because apparently that's subject to change, because a day after Adobe announced Elements 4.0 was for

continued

Windows only, then they kind of quietly said that a Mac version may be coming (it was more like a "probably, almost certainly, maybe one day, but we don't know when, but probably soon"). So I called them, and said something along the lines of: "Hey, I wrote this book based on the fact that you told me there was going to be no Macintosh version." They said something like, "Yeah, well, we're thinking now there probably will be," so I started banging my head against the wall (in joy) because my book, for the Windows-only version, was complete and ready to go to press. However, they let me know, in no uncertain terms, that the Mac version wasn't going to be ready for "a while," so that's the scoop. I have no idea if the Mac version will have the Organizer (the last Mac version didn't) or all the same features the Windows version does (the last Mac version didn't either), and I'm not certain Adobe knows which features it will have yet (maybe they do, but my head hurt so much from all the banging that I was hesitant to call them again). So, this book is for the only version available when this book was written and published—the Windows version.

How should you use this book?

You can treat this as a "jump-in-anywhere" book because I didn't write it as a "build-on-what-you-learned-in-Chapter-1" type of book. For example, if you just bought this book, and you want to learn how to whiten someone's teeth for a portrait you're retouching, you can just turn to Chapter 7, find that technique, and you'll be able to follow along and do it immediately. That's because I spell everything out. Don't let that throw you if you've been using Elements since version 1.0; I had to do it because although some of the people who will buy this book are talented traditional photographers, since they're just now "going digital," they may not know anything about Elements. I didn't want to leave them out, or make it hard for them, so I really spell things out like "Go under the Image menu, under Adjust Color, and choose Levels" rather than just writing "Open Levels." However, I did put the chapters in an order that follows a typical correction, editing, and retouching process; so you might find it useful to start with Chapter 1 and move your way through the book in sequence.

The important thing is that wherever you start, have fun with it, and even more importantly, tell your friends about it so I can recoup the millions I spent on all those digital photography books. Also, although the official name of the software is Adobe Photoshop Elements 4.0, just to keep things short and simple I usually refer to it as just "Elements 4.0" in the book.

Wait, one more thing! You can download the photos used in the book!

That's right—you can follow right along using the work of three of my favorite photographers: (1) me (2) my best buddy Dave Moser, and (3) the incredible stock photographers over at iStockphoto.com. Thanks to these three groups of photographers, most of the photos used in this book are available for you to download from the book's companion website at **www.scottkelbybooks.com/elements4photos.html.** Of course, the whole idea is that you'd use these techniques on your own photos, but if you want to practice on these, I won't tell anybody. Okay, now turn the page and get to work!

Organized Chaos
managing photos using the organizer

"Organized Chaos" is the perfect name for this chapter because not only is it a song title (by the band Benediction), it's also apparently a marketing directive put forth by a super-secret department at Adobe who, from what I gather, is charged with making simple things more complex. For example, let's take a look at the Photo Browser (for sorting images), which is basically the same as the Organizer. By adding the word "Organizer," they secured a hefty annual bonus. Now, when they introduced the Organizer (also for sorting images), the super-secret department members all got brand new company cars, because having two completely separate tools that do seemingly the same thing is a home run. But where they really cashed in was with their addition of a button called the "Photo Browser." It's the perfect scam, because there actually is no Photo Browser; it's the Organizer. So when you click it—believe it or not—it brings up the Organizer. That should be worth some extra stock options.

Saving Your Digital Negatives

I know you want to get right to organizing and editing your photos, but before we get to those "fun parts," there are a couple critically important things you'll need to do first—before you even actually open Photoshop Elements 4.0. They'll take a minute or two, but if you don't do them, you'll be sorry down the road.

Step One:
Plug your card reader (CompactFlash card, Smartcard, etc.) into your computer and the Adobe Photoshop Elements Photo Downloader dialog will appear. By default, all of your photos are marked to be imported into your computer (that's why you'll see a little checkbox marked in the bottom-right corner of each photo). If there are photos you don't want imported, just uncheck the little box next to the photos you don't want. If there are multiple photos you don't want, Control-click on these images and then click on any selected photo's checkbox, and all those images will be deselected. Now, if you want to choose a location (folder) on your hard disk in which to save these photos, click the Browse button in section 2, choose the location where you'd like these photos saved, and then click the Get Photos button in the bottom-right corner of the Photo Downloader. When you click that button, a progress dialog will appear showing that the photos are being copied to your hard disk.

Step Two:
Once your photos are imported, they're automatically loaded into the Photoshop Elements Organizer as their own separate collection. Before you start sorting and editing these photos, you need to burn these photos to a CD. Don't open the photos, adjust them, choose your favorites, and then burn them to a CD—burn them now—right off the bat. The reason this is so important is that these are your negatives—your digital negatives—which are no different than the negatives you'd get from a film lab after it's processed your film. By burning a CD now, before you start editing, you're creating a set of digital negatives that can't be accidentally erased or discarded—you'll always have these digital negatives.

Step Three:
Now, what if you don't have a CD burner? That's easy—buy one. It's that critical and such a key part of your digital setup. Luckily, burning CDs has become so fast, so inexpensive (you can buy blank writable CDs for less than 50¢ each), and so easy to do that you can't afford to skip this step. To burn the photos you just imported onto a CD, go under the Organizer's File menu and choose Backup.

Continued

Step Four:

Choosing Backup brings up the Burn/
Backup dialog. Click the Copy/Move
Files radio button to copy all the images
in your current Photo Browser window
(the ones you just imported) onto a
CD. Click the Next button to move to
the next step. (You may get a warning
dialog asking if you want to "reconnect"
your images. This dialog just verifies
that the files imported properly. It's up
to you to click Continue or Reconnect,
but reconnecting couldn't hurt.)

Step Five:

The next screen of the dialog is where
you choose to move your files, but since
you just imported your photos, you
don't want to move them from your
hard drive. So, don't turn on the Move
Files checkbox—simply click the Next
button again. *Note:* Use this option in
case you want to back up your already
edited files onto CD, removing the
actual files from your computer to free
up hard disk space. This leaves a thumbnail of your image still in the Organizer,
but the actual file will be gone.

Step Six:

In the Select Destination Drive section
at the top of the dialog, click on your
CD burner's drive in the list. Then, in
the Options section, give your CD a
name in the Name field and choose a
burn speed from the Write Speed pop-
up menu. Now, click the Done button
at the bottom of the dialog to begin
the backup process. (If you haven't
already inserted a blank CD in your
burner, Elements will prompt you to
do so.)

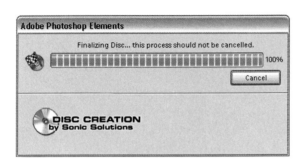

Step Seven:
A status dialog will appear while your backup disc is being burned.

Step Eight:
When it's done writing, another dialog will appear asking if you want to verify that the disc was written correctly. Since this disc contains something very important and is virtually irreplaceable, I would suggest that you *absolutely* click the Verify button. That way, you're ensured that the backup worked flawlessly.

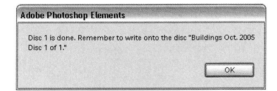

Step Nine:
When the verification process is done, you'll be greeted with a somewhat insulting dialog that reminds you to take a marker and write the name of what's on your backup disc on the backup disc itself. Think of it as the "Duh!" screen. By the way, if you're the extra-careful type (read as "paranoid"), you can burn yourself another copy to keep as a second backup. There's no loss of quality, so burn as many copies as you need to feel secure (remember, just because you're paranoid, doesn't mean they're not out to get you).

Creating a Contact Sheet for Your CD

All right, your CD of "digital negatives" is burned and it's time to get to work, but before you go any further, you can save yourself a lot of time and frustration down the road if you create a CD-jewel-box-sized contact sheet now. That way, when you pick up the CD, you'll see exactly what's on the disc before you even insert it into your computer. Luckily, if you have Adobe Acrobat, the process of creating this contact sheet is automated, but if not, you'll need to make a few decisions on how you want your contact sheet to look by "eyeing" it.

Step One:

First, open the photos you want to appear on your contact sheet in the Elements Editor, then go under the File menu and choose Print Multiple Photos (or press the keyboard shortcut Control-Alt-P). (*Note:* If you're already working in the Organizer, you can create a contact sheet from the currently open collection by going under the Organizer's File menu and choosing Print.)

Step Two:

Choosing Print Multiple Photos first brings up the Elements Organizer, and immediately after, the Print Photos dialog will appear. Along the left side of the dialog, you can drag-and-drop image thumbnails to arrange your images into the order you want them to appear on your sheet. Then, there are three categories on the right side of the dialog. Under the Select Type of Print category, choose Contact Sheet from the pop-up menu.

Step Three:

Now that you've told Elements that you want to print a contact sheet (and the preview window shows how your selected photos would look as a contact sheet on a letter-sized page, which is its default size), your next step should be to specify the size you need your contact sheet to be (in this case, one that will fit in the front of a CD jewel case). To do that, start by choosing Adobe PDF in the Select Printer pop-up menu. Then, click on the blue-and-white icon that appears to the immediate right of the Select Printer pop-up menu at the top right of the dialog. *Note:* If you don't have Adobe Acrobat, this option will not appear, in which case, skip to the Alternate Step.

Step Four:

This brings up a dialog with options for your printer (since we're printing to an Adobe PDF driver rather than printing the file out to a regular printer, you'll see the options for a PDF). Since Adobe didn't include a standard size for CD jewel cases, you're going to create one by clicking the Add button to the right of the Adobe PDF Page Size pop-up menu, which brings up the dialog shown here.

Continued

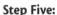

Step Five:

First, give your new paper size a name (something like "CD Jewel Case") in the Paper Names field. Then in the Paper Size section, enter 4.5 for Width and 4.5 for Height, click the Inch radio button in the Unit section, and then click the Add/Modify button to save your custom size in the Adobe PDF Page Size pop-up menu's list of presets.

Step Six:

When you click Add/Modify, it returns you to the Adobe PDF Document Properties dialog. Click on the Adobe PDF Page Size pop-up menu, and you'll see that your new custom size (CD Jewel Case) now appears in the list. Click on it to select it as your contact sheet size.

Step Seven:

When you click OK, the contact sheet preview will now display how your contact sheet thumbnail photos will appear on your CD jewel case. (*Note:* The name CD Jewel Case will appear below the preview.) If you had more than one page's worth of photos open, you'll have more than one page of thumbnails (instead of seeing page 1 of 1, it'll say something like 1 of 2, or 1 of 3, and so on). To see any additional pages, click on the right-facing arrow button below the preview.

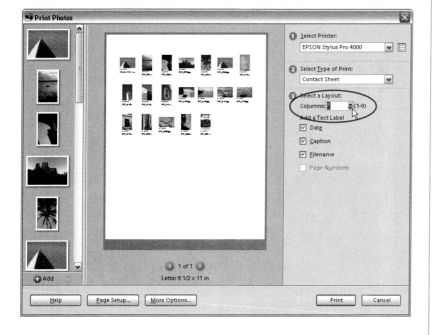

Alternate Step:

If you don't have Acrobat, there is a hokey workaround (sorry, but until Adobe adds a CD jewel case option to this dialog, which had been there in previous versions of Elements, we're stuck with a hokey workaround). Simply choose a higher amount in the Columns pop-up menu in section 3. Try 7-8 columns, and then "eye" your contact sheet using the preview in the dialog. You're trying to create a block of thumbnails that will print no larger than 4.5x4.5", so you can then cut your sheet to this size after printing. With that set, move on to Step 8.

Continued

Step Eight:

On the right side of the dialog, you can decide if you want to have Elements print the file's name below each thumbnail on your contact sheet. I strongly recommend turning this feature on because one day you may have to go back to this CD looking for a photo. The thumbnail will let you see if the photo you're looking for is on this CD (so you've narrowed your search a bit), but if there's no name below the image, you'll have to manually search through every photo on the CD to locate the exact one you saw on the cover. Believe me, it's one of those things that will keep you from ripping your hair out by the roots, one by one. Now you can click Print and your contact sheet is created in PDF format and opened in Elements. So, just go the File menu, select Print, and print your contact sheet to your printer.

Step Nine (or so you think...):

This is more like a tip than a step, but a number of photographers add a second contact sheet to make it even easier to track down the exact image they're looking for. It's based on the premise that in every roll (digital or otherwise) there are usually one or two key shots—two really good "keepers"—that will normally be the ones you'll go searching for. So what they do is make an additional contact sheet that either becomes the front cover of the jewel case (with the regular contact sheet behind it in the case) or vice versa. This additional contact sheet includes a description of the shots, to make finding the right image even easier.

©SCOTT KELBY

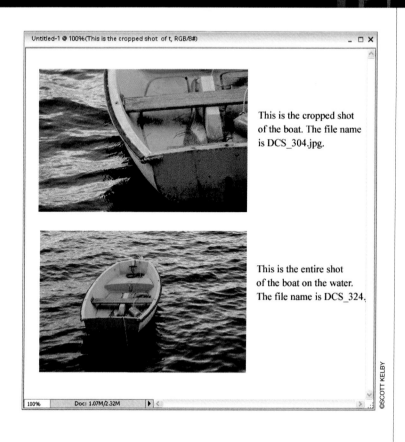

Untitled-1 @ 100%(This is the cropped shot of t, RGB/8#)

This is the cropped shot of the boat. The file name is DCS_304.jpg.

This is the entire shot of the boat on the water. The file name is DCS_324.

100%   Doc: 1.07M/2.32M

©SCOTT KELBY

Step Ten:
Here's the final result with a two-photo contact sheet for the cover of the CD jewel case, after a regular contact sheet with multiple images was printed and slid into the CD jewel case behind it. To create this contact sheet, open one or two images in the Editor and create a new document that's 4.5x4.5". Press V to get the Move tool, drag-and-drop your open images onto your new document, and then press Control-T and then Control-0 (zero) to bring up Free Transform. Resize your images on the page, and then press the letter T to switch to the Type tool and enter descriptive text next to your contact sheet thumbnail(s). Now print your new contact sheet.

Dealing with the Welcome Screen

I know, the name "Dealing with the Welcome Screen" makes the Welcome Screen sound like something obtrusive, but really it's not. At least, not at first. In fact, at first it's welcome (like the way I worked that in there?), but after you've seen it a few hundred times, if you're like most folks you'll probably want it to go away. But before you make it go away for good, there are a few things you might want to decide first. And they are...

The First Time:

The Welcome Screen that appears when you launch the program is designed to help first-time users figure out what they want. If you're holding this book, my guess is you already know what you want, so click the Edit and Enhance Photos option near the top center of the Welcome Screen, which takes you right into the Elements Editor (which, if you've used previous versions of Elements, you know simply as Photoshop Elements).

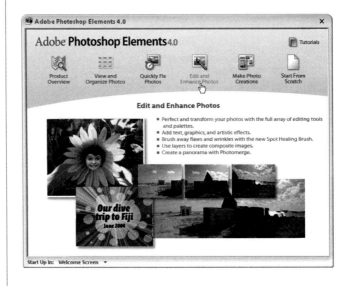

Future Uses:

You can use this Welcome Screen to decide what happens when you launch Elements 4.0 later. For example, by default it wants to show you this Welcome Screen each time you launch Elements. You may want that the first few times, but once the novelty wears off, you'll want to go straight to the Editor. So, you just need to change one thing: At the bottom left-hand corner of the Welcome Screen, where it says "Start Up In" you'll see the words "Welcome Screen." Click on Welcome Screen and choose Editor from the pop-up menu that appears. Now when you start up Elements, you'll get the Editor.

Start with Sorting:

If you'd prefer to skip the Welcome Screen and instead go right into sorting your images rather than editing them, you can go to the built-in Organizer (which used to be the standalone product Photoshop Album) by choosing Organizer from the Start Up In pop-up menu.

Welcome Back Welcome Screen:

Okay, what if you've chosen to start up in the Editor or Organizer, and then at some later date you think you'd like to get that Welcome Screen back again? It's easy—just go under the Window menu (in either the Editor or Organizer) and choose Welcome, and the screen will reappear. However, once you close it, it won't reappear at startup unless you change the Start Up In pop-up menu in the bottom-left corner to Welcome Screen.

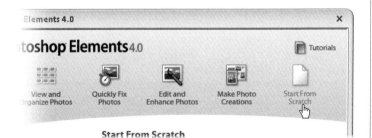

Other Options:

One last thing—just to save you some time: If you have the Welcome Screen open, there are three buttons that actually take you to the Editor—they just take you to different parts. Quickly Fix Photos opens the Editor in the Quick Fix mode; Edit and Enhance Photos just launches regular ol' Elements 4.0 (the Editor); and Start From Scratch opens the Editor too, but it thoughtfully opens the New (document) dialog for you.

Importing Photos from Your Scanner

Because this is a book for digital photographers, I imagine most of your photos will come from a digital camera (if so, see "Saving Your Digital Negatives"), but if you've been a photographer for a while now, you probably have some traditional prints lying around that you'd like to scan in, so here we'll look at importing scanned images into the Organizer.

Step One:
To scan images and have them appear in your Organizer, click the Photo Browser button in the Elements Editor's task bar (above the Options Bar) to launch the Organizer. Then in the Organizer's task bar (above the Timeline), click on the Get Photos button (it looks like a digital camera icon) and choose From Scanner. By the way, once the Organizer is open, you can use the shortcut Control-U to import photos from your scanner.

Step Two:
Once the Get Photos from Scanner dialog is open, choose your scanner from the Scanner pop-up menu. Choose a high Quality setting (I generally choose the highest quality unless the photo is for an email to my insurance company for a claim—then I'm not as concerned). Then click OK to bring in the scanned photo. See, pretty straightforward stuff.

This new feature added in Elements is a huge timesaver because it lets you choose a folder that is "watched" by the Organizer. When you drag photos into this folder, they will automatically be added to your Organizer. Here's how to set it up:

Automating the Importing of Photos by Using Watched Folders

Step One:
Go under the Organizer's File menu and choose Watch Folders.

Step Two:
When the Watch Folders dialog appears, make sure the Watch Folders and Their Sub-Folders for New Files checkbox is turned on. In the Folders to Watch section, click the Add button, and then in the resulting dialog, navigate to any folders you want the Organizer to "watch" for the addition of new photos. Select the folder you want to watch, and then click OK. Continue to click the Add button and select more folders to watch. When you've selected all your folders, they will appear in the Folders to Watch section of the Watch Folders dialog, where you have the choice of having the Organizer alert you when new photos are found in the watched folders (meaning you can choose to add them) or you can have them added automatically, which is what this feature is really all about. But if you're fussy about what gets added when (i.e., you're a control freak), at least you get an option.

Changing the Size of Your Photo Thumbnails

Thumbnails of your photos are displayed in the Organizer's Photo Browser, and luckily you have great control over what size they're displayed at.

Step One:
The size of your thumbnails is controlled by a slider at the bottom-right corner of the Photo Browser window. Drag the slider to the right to make them bigger—to the left to make them smaller. To jump to the largest possible view, just click on the Single Photo View icon to the immediate right of the slider. To jump to the smallest size, click on the Small Thumbnail Size icon to the left of the slider. To jump up one size at a time, hold the Control key and press the Plus Sign (+) key. To go down in size, press Control-Minus Sign (–).

Step Two:
Another shortcut to jump to the largest view is to just double-click on your thumbnail. At this large view, you can enter a caption directly below the photo by clicking on the placeholder text (which reads "Click here to add caption") and typing in your caption.

How about this for a view? Elements lets you see a full-screen preview of a selected thumbnail—all without leaving the Organizer. It's like an onscreen slide show of your thumbnails. Here's how it works:

Seeing Full-Screen Previews

Step One:
To see a full-screen preview of your currently selected photo(s), click on the Full Screen View icon (it looks like a tiny monitor) in the far right-hand corner of the Browser window (or just press F11).

Step Two:
This brings up the Full Screen View Options dialog with a number of presentation choices that you normally get for a slide show. Basically, that's what you'll use this Full Screen View feature for, but if you just select one photo, it shows just that one photo at full screen. So when this dialog appears, click OK and your photo will be displayed full screen. If you want to return to the Photo Browser, press the Escape key on your keyboard. By the way, once your photo(s) appears full screen, there's a floating palette at the top of the screen where you can control your viewing options—click the Play button to start it and click the Pause button to stop it. In case you want to create an actual slide show of those photos you're viewing, you can click on the Create Slide Show button on the right side of the palette.

Sorting Photos by Date

When photos are imported into the Organizer, the Organizer automatically sorts them by date. How does it know on which dates the photos were taken? The time and date are embedded into the photo by your digital camera at the moment the photo was taken (this info is called EXIF data). The Organizer reads this info and then sorts your photos automatically by date, but finding the photos by date takes a little doing on your part.

Step One:
By default, the newest photos are displayed first, so basically, the last photo you shot will be the first photo in the Organizer. Also, by default, the exact date each photograph was taken is shown directly below each photo's thumbnail. (*Note:* If you don't want this extra detail about each photo to be visible, just deselect the Details checkbox at the bottom-left side of the Browser window.)

Step Two:
If you'd prefer to see your photos in reverse order (the oldest photos up top), then choose Date (Oldest First) from the pop-up menu in the bottom-left corner of the Browser window. There you have it!

I know, I know—this is a book for "digital" photographers, but you know, and I know, that you've got a scanner. At some point you're going to scan some photos (then they'll become "digital images"), and then you'll want these images to be automatically organized in your catalog. All the scanned photos will have their "creation" date as the day you scanned them, unless you add your own date. This way, you can set the approximate date to when they were shot so they'll appear in your catalog when they were taken, rather than when they were imported.

Adding Scanned Photos? Enter the Right Time and Date

Step One:
First, get the photos from your scanner (see the "Importing Photos from Your Scanner" tutorial earlier in this chapter). Select all the photos you want to set the date for by Control-clicking each image (or Shift-clicking the first and last images if they are contiguous) in the Photo Browser window. Then, go under the Organizer's Edit menu and choose Adjust Date and Time of Selected Items (or press Control-J).

Step Two:
This brings up a dialog asking how you want to handle the date and time for these photos. For this example, select Change to a Specified Date and Time and click OK.

Step Three:
This brings up the Set Date and Time dialog, where you can use the pop-up menus to set your selected photos' date and time. Now these photos will appear sorted by the date you entered, rather than the date you imported them.

Finding Photos Fast by Their Month and Year

The method that the Organizer uses to help you find the photos you're looking for is month and year. It figures you might not know exactly when you took a group of photos, but let's say, for example, you're trying to find the photos from your last vacation. If you know you went sometime last summer—even if you can't remember whether it was June, July, or August—you can get mighty close mighty fast using the Month/Year Timeline. Here's how it works:

Step One:
We're going to assume you're trying to find vacation photos (as outlined above). You see those bars along the Timeline that look like the little bar charts from Microsoft Excel? Well, the higher the bar, the more photos that appear in that month. So click on any month in 2004 and only the photos taken in that month will appear in the Photo Browser window. As you slide your cursor to the left (or right), you'll see each month's name appear. When you get to July, only photos taken in July 2004 will appear. Take a quick look and see if any of those photos are your vacation photos. If they're not in July, scroll over on the Timeline to August, and only those photos will be visible.

Although finding your photos by month and year is fairly handy, the real power of the Organizer appears when you assign tags (keywords) to your photos. This simple step makes finding the exact photos you want very fast and very easy. The first step is to decide whether you can use the pre-made tags that Adobe puts there for you or whether you need to create your own. In this situation, you're going to create your own custom tags.

Tagging Your Photos (Tags are Keywords)

Step One:
Start by clicking on the Tags tab on the right side of the Organizer. Adobe's default set of tags will appear in a vertical list. (By the way, if you don't see the Tags and Collections tabs on the right side of the Organizer, click on the words "Organize Bin" at the bottom-right corner of the Organizer window.)

Step Two:
You'll start by creating your own custom category (in this case, we're going to create a category of all floral shots taken for your clients, who happen to own a greenhouse). Click on the New pop-up menu that appears just below the Tags tab itself and choose New Category. This brings up the Create Category dialog. Type in "Flowers." Now choose an icon from the Category Icon list and then click OK. (The icon choices are all pretty lame, but at least we can use the Flower icon.)

Continued

Step Three:

To create your own custom tag, click on the New pop-up menu again and choose New Tag. This brings up the Create Tag dialog. Choose Flowers from the Category pop-up menu (if it's not already chosen), then in the Name field, type "Close-Up Flower Shoot." If you want to add additional notes about the photo shoot, you can add them in the Note field, or you can choose a photo as an icon by clicking the Edit Icon button. Now click OK to create your tag.

Step Four:

Now you'll assign this tag to all the photos from the flower shoot. In the Photo Browser window, scroll to the photos from that shoot. We'll start by tagging just one photo, so click on the Close-Up Flower Shoot tag that appears at the bottom of your Tags list and drag-and-drop that tag on any one of the photos. That photo is now "tagged." If you have the photo's Details visible (if not, turn on the Details checkbox at the bottom-left corner of the Browser window), you'll see a small tag icon appear below the photo's thumbnail (in this case, the Flower icon).

©SCOTT KELBY

Step Five:

So at this point, we've only tagged one photo from the flower shoot. Drag-and-drop that same tag onto five more photos from the shoot so a total of six photos are tagged. Now, in the list of Tags on the right side of the Organizer, click in the small box in the column to the left of your Close-Up Flower Shoot tag (a tiny binoculars icon will appear in that box), and instantly, only the photos with that tag will appear in the Photo Browser window. To see all your photos again, click on the Back to All Photos button that appears at the top left of the Browser window.

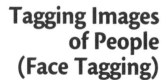

Tagging Images of People (Face Tagging)

You're either going to think this is the coolest, most advanced technology in all of Elements 4.0, or you're going to think it's creepy and very Big Brother-ish (from the book by George Orwell, not the TV show). Either way, it's here to help you tag people easier because the Organizer can now automatically find photos of people for you—as it has some sort of weird science, facial-recognition software built in (that at one point was developed for the CIA, which is all the more reason it belongs in Elements).

Step One:

Okay, let's say you went on a family vacation, and you want to quickly find all the photos that have your daughter in them, without having to search through the hundreds of images you imported. Well, first go ahead and open the Organizer, because that's where our hunt will take place. Now select the group of photos you want to search through (you can do a Control-A to select all, click on a collection, or just Control-click on as many images as you want to sort through).

Step Two:

Go under the Find menu, and at the bottom of the menu choose Find Faces for Tagging. This brings up the Face Tagging dialog. Within just a few moments (depending on how many photos you have), it will sort through your selected images and separate out the images that contain a human face.

Step Three:
Once these images appear in the Face Tagging dialog, you can Control-click on the photos of your family, and then drag-and-drop the appropriate tag from the Tags palette onto any one of the selected photos. They'll all be assigned that tag.

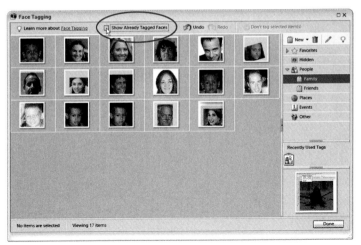

Step Four:
If you only want to see faces that haven't already been tagged, ensure the checkbox for Show Already Tagged Faces is off at the top of the Face Tagging dialog. When you're done, click Done to return to the main Organizer window.

TIP: As cool as this Face Tagging technology is, it doesn't stop there. Let's say you have a photo of a tall building, and you want to find all the similar photos that have a tall building. Just click on one of your building photos, then go under the Find menu and choose By Visual Similarity with Selected Photo(s). It will look for photos that have similar attributes (such as a building, similar colors, or orientation to what you've already chosen). Pretty *CSI Las Vegas*, dontchathink?

Tagging Multiple Photos

Okay, you've learned how to create your own custom category (Flowers), then a custom tag so you can sort one shoot from the other (Close-Up Flower Shoot), but you're dragging-and-dropping that tag onto one photo at a time (which takes too much time for an entire shoot). There are faster ways than this one-tag-at-a-time method. For example…

Step One:

To tag all the photos from your shoot at the same time, try this: First, click on any untagged photo from the shoot. Then hold the Control key and click on other photos from that particular shoot. As you click on them, they'll become selected (you'll see a thin blue box around each selected photo). Or, if all the photos are contiguous, click the first image in the series, press-and-hold the Shift key, and then click on the last image in the series to select them all.

Step Two:

Now drag-and-drop your Close-Up Flower Shoot tag on any one of those selected photos, and all of the selected photos will have that tag. If you want to see just the photos from that shoot, you can click in the box to the left of that tag and only photos with that tag will appear. By the way, if you decide you want to remove a tag from a photo, just Right-click on the photo and from the contextual menu that appears, choose Remove Tag. If you have more than one tag applied, you can choose which tag you want removed.

Okay, what if you want to assign a tag to a photo, but you also want to assign other tags (perhaps a "Client Work" tag and a "Make Prints" tag), as well? Here's how:

Assigning Multiple Tags to One Photo

Step One:
To assign multiple tags at once, first, of course, you have to create the tags you need, so go ahead and create two new tags by clicking on the New pop-up menu just below the Tags tab—naming one "Client Work" and another "Make Prints." Now you have three tags you can assign. To assign all three tags at once, just hold the Control key, then in the Tags list, click on each tag you want to assign (Close-Up Flower Shoot, Client Work, and Make Prints).

Step Two:
Now click-and-drag those selected tags, and as you drag, you'll see you're dragging three tag icons as one group. Drop them onto a photo, and all three tags will be applied at once. If you want to apply the tags to more than one photo at a time, first hold the Control key and click on all the photos you want to have all three tags. Then, go to the Tags list, hold the Control key again, and click on all the tags you want to apply. Drag those tags onto any one of the selected photos, and all the tags will be applied at once. Cool.

©SCOTT KELBY

Combining (Merging) Tags

It's easy to go "tag crazy," and if that happens (and you've got dozens of different tags applied to your photos), you may want to simplify by merging some of your tags together. For example, if you shot the Olympics, and you have tags for 100-meter dash, 400-meter dash, 600-meter dash, and a half dozen more dashes, you may want to combine all those separate tags into just one tag. Here's how:

Step One:
To combine (merge) multiple tags into just one convenient tag, start by holding the Control key and clicking on all the tags that you want to combine in the Tags list on the right side of the Organizer. Then Right-click on any of your selected tags, and from the contextual menu that appears, choose Merge Tags.

Step Two:
This brings up a dialog that asks you which of the selected tags will be the surviving tag (in other words, which tag will remain after the rest are merged into this one). Choose the tag that will remain from the list of tags, then click OK. The tags will be merged into that one. Every photo that had any one of those selected tags will now have the one combined tag.

Let's say you went to the Super Bowl with a group of photographers, and they're using Elements 4.0, too. If you've created a nice set of tags for identifying images, you can now export these tags and share them with the other photographers from that trip. That way, they can import them and start assigning tags to their Super Bowl photos without having to create tags of their own.

Sharing Your Tags (or Collections) with Others

Step One:
To export your tags to share with others, start by going to the Tags tab (on the right side of the Organizer), then click on the New pop-up menu and choose Save Tags to File.

Step Two:
When the dialog appears, you can choose to Export All Tags, or better yet, click on the Export Specified Tags radio button, and then you can choose which tags you want to export from the pop-up menu. Choose the tags you want to export, and click OK. A standard Windows Save dialog will appear, so you can choose where you want your file saved. Name your file, click Save, and now you can email your exported tags to a friend.

Step Three:
Once your friends receive your tags, tell them they can import your tags by going to the Tags tab, clicking on the New pop-up menu, and choosing From File. Now they just locate the file on their hard drive and click Open. The new tags will appear in the Tags tab.

Collections: It's How You Put Photos in Order One by One

Once you've tagged all your photos, you may want to create a collection of just the best photos (the ones you'll show to your clients). You do that by creating a "collection." An advantage of collections is that once photos are in a collection, you can put the photos in the order you want them to appear (you can't do that with tags). This is especially important when you start creating your own slide shows and albums.

Step One:

To create a collection, click on the Collections tab on the top-right side of the Organizer (it's just to the right of the Tags tab when you have the Organize Bin open). You create a new collection by clicking on the New pop-up menu, then choosing New Collection. When the Create Collection dialog appears, enter a name for your collection, and then click OK.

Step Two:

Now that your collection has been created, you can either (a) drag the Collection icon onto the photos you want in your collection, or (b) Control-click photos to select them and then drag-and-drop them onto your Collection icon in the Collections tab. Either way, the photos will be added to your collection. To see just the photos in your collection, click on the box in the column to the left of your collection and tiny binoculars will appear. Now, to put the photos in the order you want, just click on any photo and drag it into position. The Organizer automatically numbers the photos for you in each thumbnail's top-left corner, so it's easy to see what's going on as you drag. To return to all of your images, click the Back to All Photos button in the top-left corner of the Browser window.

By default, a tag or collection uses the first photo you add to that tag or collection as its icon. Unfortunately, these icons are so small that you probably can't tell what the icon represents. That's why you'll probably want to choose your own photo icons instead.

Choosing Your Own Icons for Tags and Collections

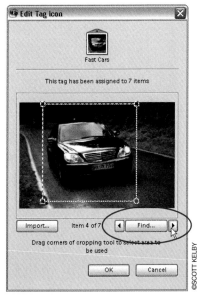

Step One:
It's easier to choose icons once you've created a tag or collection, meaning you've tagged a few photos or added some photos to a collection. Once you've done that, click on your tag or collection, then click on the Pencil icon (it's in the bar right under the tab's name). This brings up the Edit Tag (or Collection) dialog. In this dialog, click on the Edit Icon button to launch the dialog you see here.

Step Two:
You'll see the first photo in your collection in the preview window (this is why it's best to edit the icon *after* you've added tags or collections to the photos). If you don't want to use this first photo, click the arrow buttons under the bottom-right corner of the preview window to scroll through your photos. Once you find the photo you want to use, click on the little cropping border (in the preview window) to isolate part of the photo. This gives you a better close-up photo that's easier to see as an icon. Then click OK in the open dialogs and that cropped image becomes your icon.

Deleting Tags (or Collections)

If you've created a tag or a collection, and then later decide that you don't want that tag or collection, you can delete it in just three clicks.

Step One:
To delete a tag or collection, start by clicking on the tag or collection you want to delete in the Tags or Collections tab on the right side of the Organizer.

Step Two:
Once you've selected the tag or collection you want to delete, just click the Trash icon at the top of the Tags (or Collections) tab (it's found to the immediate right of the New pop-up menu). If you're deleting a tag, when you click on the Trash icon, it brings up a warning dialog letting you know that deleting the tag will remove it from all your photos. If you want to remove that tag, click OK. If you've got a collection selected when you click the Trash icon, it asks if you want to delete the collection. Click OK and it's gone. However, it does not delete these photos from your main library—it just deletes that collection.

When you take a photo with a digital camera, a host of information about that photo is embedded into the photo by the camera itself. It contains just about everything, including the make and model of the camera that took the photo, the exact time the photo was taken, what the f-stop setting was, what the focal length of the lens was, and whether or not the flash fired when you took the shot. You can view all this info (called Exchangeable Image File [EXIF] data—also known as metadata) from right within the Organizer. Here's how:

Seeing Your Photo's Metadata (EXIF Info)

Step One:
To view a photo's EXIF data, first click on the photo in the Photo Browser, and then click the Show or Hide Properties button at the bottom-left side of the Photo Browser window to show the Properties palette.

Step Two:
When the Properties palette appears in the bottom-right corner of the Organize Bin, click the Metadata button at the top of the palette (it's the fourth button from the left). This shows an abbreviated version of the photo's EXIF data (basically, the make, model, ISO, exposure, f-stop, focal length of the lens, and the status of the flash). Of course, the camera embeds much more info than this. To see the full EXIF data, under the View section at the bottom of the palette, just select Complete and you'll get more information on this file than you'd probably ever want to know. One thing that isn't displayed in the Brief section that you probably might want to know is the date and time the photo was taken, and to see that you will have to open the Complete view.

Adding Your Own Info to Photos

Although your digital camera automatically embeds information into your photos, you can also add your own info from right within the Organizer. This includes simple things like a photo caption (that can appear onscreen when you display your photos in a slide show), or you can add notes to your photos for your personal use, either of which can be used to help you search for photos later.

Step One:
First, click on the photo in the Photo Browser window you want to add your own info to and click the Show or Hide Properties button at the bottom left of the Organizer, or you can also use the keyboard shortcut by pressing Alt-Enter.

Step Two:
This brings up the Properties palette along the bottom-right corner of the Organizer. At the top of the palette are four buttons for the four different sections of your photo's properties. By default, the General section is selected. In the General section, the first field is for adding captions (I know, that's pretty self-explanatory), and then the photo's file name appears below that. It's the third field down—Notes—where you add your own personal notes about the photo.

Step Three:
If you want to see other info about your photo (for example, which tags have been added to your photos; the date when you imported the photo or when you last printed, emailed, or posted the photo on the Web; or the info embedded into the photo by your digital camera), just click on the various buttons at the top of the palette.

©SCOTT KELBY

Finding a group of photos is fairly easy using the Organizer, especially if you've tagged your images, but finding an individual photo takes a bit of work. It's not hard; it just takes some effort because you essentially have to narrow the amount of photos down to a small group (like the month or day you shot the photos). Then you scroll through the photos in that group until you find the individual photo you want. It sounds complicated, but it's really quite easy. Here are the most popular searching methods:

Finding Photos

From the Timeline:

The Timeline, which is a horizontal bar across the top of the Photo Browser, shows you all the photos in your catalog. Months and years are represented along the Timeline. The years are visible below the Timeline; the small light blue bars above the Timeline are individual months. If there is no bar visible, there are no photos stored in that month. A short blue bar means just a few photos were taken that month—a tall bar means lots of photos. If you hover your cursor over a blue bar, the month it represents will appear. To see the photos taken in that month, click on the bar and only those photos will be displayed in the Photo Browser window. Once you've clicked on a month, you can click-and-drag the locator bar to the right or left to display different months.

Using Tags:

If there's a particular shot you're looking for, and you've tagged all your shots with a particular tag, then just click on the Tags tab and click on the empty box in the column to the left of that tag. Now only shots with that tag will appear in the Photo Browser window.

Continued

By Date Ranges:

Let's say you're looking to find a particular photo you shot on vacation. If you can remember approximately when you went on vacation, you can display photos taken within a certain date range (for example, all the photos taken between June 1 and June 30, 2005). Here's how: Go under the Organizer's Find menu and choose Set Date Range. This brings up a dialog where you can enter start and end dates. Click OK and only photos taken within that time frame will be visible. Scroll through those images to see if you can find your photo.

By Caption or Note:

If you've added personal notes within tags or you've added captions to individual photos, you can search those fields to help you narrow your search. Just go under the Organizer's Find menu and choose By Caption or Note. Then in the resulting dialog, enter the word that you think may appear in the photo's caption or note, and click OK. Only photos that have that word in a caption or note will appear in the Photo Browser window.

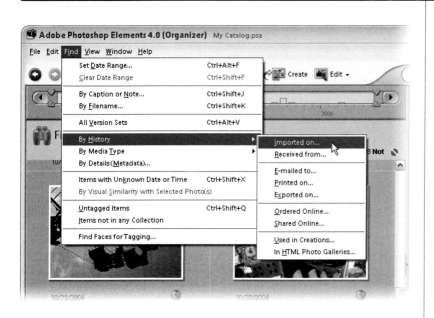

By History:

The Organizer keeps track of when you imported each photo and when you last shared it (via email, print, webpage, etc.); so if you can remember any of those dates, you're in luck. Just go under the Organizer's Find menu, under By History, and choose which attribute you want to search under in the submenu. A dialog with a list of names and dates will appear. Click on a date and name, click OK, and only photos that fit that criterion will appear in the Photo Browser window.

Finding Photos Using the Date View

Okay, I have to admit, this particular feature is probably going to be your least-used Organizer feature because it seems so...I dunno...cheesy (for lack of a better word). When you use it, you see a huge calendar, and if photos were created on a particular day in the currently visible month, you'll see a small thumbnail of one of those images on that date. Personally, when I see this view, I feel like I've just left a professional-looking application and entered a "consumer" application, so I avoid it like the plague, but just in case you dig it (hey, it's possible), here's how it works:

Step One:
To enter the Date View in the Organizer, click the Date View button at the top-right side of the Organizer window.

Step Two:
This brings up the Date View calendar window with the Month view showing by default (if you're not in Month view, click the Month button along the bottom center of the window). If you see a photo on a date, it means there are photos that were taken (or you scanned or imported) on that day. To see a photo, click on it within the calendar and a larger version will appear at the top right of the Date View window. To see the rest of the photos on this day, click the Next Item on Selected Day button found directly under this preview window. Each time you click this button, the window displays a preview of the next photo taken on that day.

©SCOTT KELBY

Step Three:
If you find the photo you're looking for (I'm assuming that if you're searching around in the Date View, you're looking for a particular photo) and you want to edit that photo, Right-click on the photo's preview and choose Go to Standard Edit (or just press Control-I). The Elements Editor will launch with your photo open and ready to edit.

Step Four:
Return to the Organizer and click the Date View button again. While we're here, I want to show you a couple of the other features. Although the Month view is shown by default, there are buttons at the bottom center of the Date View window for viewing the entire year (where days that have photos appear as solid-color blocks) or an individual day (where all the photos from that day appear in a slide-show-like window as shown here).

Step Five:
While in the Date View, you can add a Daily Note, which is a note that doesn't apply to the current photo—it applies to every photo taken on that calendar day. If you change to the Day view (by clicking the Day button at the bottom of the Date View window), fields for adding a Caption and a Daily Note to the currently displayed photo will appear along the right side of the window. Now when you're in Day view, you can not only see your caption for your photo, but you can also see the Daily Note for each photo taken on that calendar day.

Seeing an Instant Slide Show

If you want to see a quick slide show of a collection or currently selected photos in the Organizer, it's pretty much just a two-click process. Later in this book, I show you how to create rich, fully featured slide shows using an entirely different feature of Elements 4.0, but for now we'll just look at how to create a quickie slide show with minimum time and effort.

Step One:
Open the Organizer and make sure the Photo Browser window is active by clicking the Photo Browser button in the top right of the Organizer. Now hold the Control key and click on each photo you want to appear in your slide show (if the photos are contiguous, you can click on the first photo, hold the Shift key, click on the last photo, and all the photos in between will be selected). Once the photos you want are selected, click on the Full Screen View icon (it looks like a little monitor) at the bottom right of the Browser window.

Step Two:
This brings up the Full Screen View Options dialog, which contains presentation options for your slide show. You can choose music that will play during your slide show from the Background Music pop-up menu. You can also choose how long each photo will appear onscreen. By default, it assumes you want any captions included, but you can turn that off by clicking the Include Captions checkbox, and you can also have your slide show loop when it reaches the end by clicking on the Repeat Slide Show checkbox. Now click OK to begin your slide show.

Step Three:
Once you click OK, you'll enter Full Screen View mode, where you'll see a floating slide show control palette on the top-left side of your screen. Your slide show won't actually start advancing until you click the Play button (or press the shortcut F5). To stop your slide show from advancing (to pause it), click the Pause button in the control palette (the Play button toggles to the Pause button while the slides are in motion), and then to resume the slide show, just click Pause one more time.

Step Four:
Besides the standard Previous, Play, Next, and Pause buttons that appear in the control palette, you'll also see other controls on the right. These extra controls are for comparing still images and are not for use during your slide show. To hide these other controls, click on the tiny left-facing arrow on the far-right side of the control palette and it will collapse down to just display the slide show controls.

Step Five:
To quit your slide show and return to the Photo Browser, press the Escape key on your keyboard or click the Stop (X) button on the control palette.

Comparing Photos

Let's say you've just shot a bike show, and now you're looking at 14 close-up shots of the prize-winning Harley-Davidson. The Organizer has a great feature that lets you compare two images onscreen (either side by side or one above the other) to help you narrow down your choice to the best possible photo.

Step One:
Open the Organizer and make sure the Photo Browser window is active by clicking the Photo Browser button in the top right of the Organizer. To compare (or review) photos side by side, first hold the Control key and click on all the photos you want to compare. Then click the Full Screen View icon at the bottom left of the Photo Browser window (or just press the F11 key on your keyboard). This brings up the Full Screen View Options dialog, which presents options for a slide show. You can ignore those slide show options and just click OK to enter Full Screen View mode, which can be used to compare images.

Step Two:
The photo you selected first will appear in Full Screen View mode, and you'll see a floating control palette at the top-left side of your screen. Click on the Side by Side View button (it looks like two boxes), which puts the first and second photos you selected side by side onscreen. The first photo (on the left) has the number 1 in its upper-left-hand corner, and the second photo (the one being compared) is noted as number 2.

Step Three:
Now visually compare these two photos. You'll want the one that looks best to remain onscreen so you can compare other selected photos against it, right? To do that, click on the "bad" photo, and a blue highlight will appear around that photo, indicating that this is the one that will change. In this example, I thought the second photo looked better, so I clicked on photo number 1 (the one on the left).

Step Four:
Now go to the control palette, click on the Next Photo button, and the first photo will be replaced with your next photo in that series. Again, review which of these two looks the best, then click on the photo that looks worst (that way, you can replace it with another photo you want to compare). Click the Next Photo button to compare the next photo (and so on). To back up and review a previous photo, click the Previous Photo button in the control palette.

Step Five:
Besides this side-by-side mode, there's also an option that lets you see your photos stacked one on top of the other (which you might like for comparing photos in landscape orientation). To change to that mode, click on the down-facing arrow to the immediate right of the Side by Side View button, and from the pop-up menu that appears, choose Above and Below. Cycle through the images as you did before—just repeat Steps 3 and 4 until you find the photo you like best. When you're finished, press the Escape key on your keyboard or click the Stop (X) button in the control palette.

Comparing Photos by Zooming and Panning

This isn't exactly an Organizer technique, but there's also a new way to compare photos in the Elements Editor. This is a cool feature that Elements borrows from Photoshop—the ability to view multiple images at once (for comparison purposes)—but more importantly, to be able to view each one at the same magnification (even when changing zoom magnifications). You can scroll around (pan) to inspect images and have all the images pan at the same location and rate. This is one you need to try to really appreciate.

Step One:
Open the multiple photos you want to compare in the Editor. (In this instance, we'll compare four photos, so open four photos, which will appear in the Photo Bin at the bottom of the Editor window. The power of this feature will be more apparent if you open four similar images, like four portraits of the same person at one sitting, etc.)

Step Two:
Go under the Window menu, under Images, and choose Tile. This will put all your photos in their own separate windows, and then it will tile these four open windows across your screen so you can see all four photos at once.

Step Three:
Now that your photos are tiled, return to the Window menu, under Images, and choose Match Zoom. Now, press-and-hold the Shift key, press Z to switch to the Magnifying Glass tool (okay, it's called the Zoom tool, but its icon looks like a magnifying glass), and click-and-drag a selection around the person in one of the active image windows. You'll notice that all four photos jump to the same zoom. *Note:* If the Resize Windows To Fit feature is selected in the Zoom tool's Options Bar, this won't work properly.

Step Four:
Now go under the Window menu, under Images, and choose Match Location. Press H to switch to the Hand tool (it's right under the Zoom tool in the Toolbox), press-and-hold the Shift key, then click within your image and drag to pan around your photo. If you don't hold the Shift key first, it will just pan around the front-most active window. By holding Shift, all the windows pan at the same time and speed, enabling you to compare particular areas of your photos at the same time.

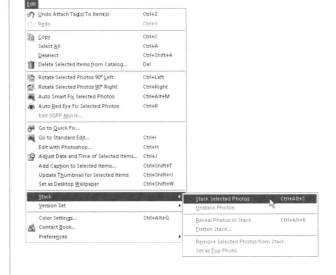

Reducing Clutter by Stacking Your Photos

This is one of my favorite features because it lets you reduce "photo clutter" and makes things more organized when working in the Photo Browser. It's called "stacking," and it lets you stack similar photos together, leaving just one photo to represent a stack of photos. So, if you took 120 shots and you've already sorted the best of the bunch into a collection, you don't have to have 120 shots cluttering up your catalog. Instead, you can have just one representative photo, and underneath it are the 120 others.

Step One:
With the Photo Browser open in the Organizer, hold the Control key on your keyboard and click on all the photos you want to add to your stack (or if the images are contiguous, simply click the first image in the series, press-and-hold the Shift key, and click on the last image in the series). Once they're all selected, go under the Organizer's Edit menu, under Stack, and choose Stack Selected Photos in the submenu.

Step Two:
No dialog appears, it just happens—your 120 photos now are stacked behind the first photo you selected (think of it as 120 layers, and on each layer is a photo, stacked one on top of another). You'll know a photo thumbnail contains a stack because a Stack icon (which looks like a little blue stack of paper) will appear in the upper-right corner of your photo.

Step Three:

Once your photos are stacked, you can view these photos at any time by clicking the photo with the Stack icon, and then going under the Edit menu, under Stack, and choosing Reveal Photos in Stack. This is like doing a "Find," where all the photos in your stack will appear in a "find results" window (called the Photos in Stack window) so you can see them without unstacking them. Then return to the Photo Browser window by clicking on the Back to All Photos button in the top-left corner of the window.

Step Four:

If you do want to unstack the photos, select the photo with the Stack icon in the Photo Browser window, then go under the Edit menu, under Stack, and choose Unstack Photos. If you decide you don't want to keep any of the photos in your stack, select the photo with the Stack icon in the Photo Browser window, go back under the Edit menu, under Stack, and choose Flatten Stack. It's like flattening your layers—all that's left is that first photo. However, when you choose Flatten, you will have the choice of deleting the photos from your hard disk or not.

Exposure: 1/4000 Focal Length: 300mm Aperture Value: *f*/2.8

Raw Hide
mastering camera raw

This is the first version of this book to have an entire chapter devoted to Camera Raw. So why a whole chapter? Three reasons: (1) Camera Raw is that important, has that many new features in Elements 4.0, and I felt I needed to cover them all; (2) I needed the extra pages to get my page count up; (3) I really didn't need the page count, but you can't be sure of that. Now, is this chapter for everybody? No. It's really only for people who shoot in RAW format (you'll know if your digital camera can shoot RAW, because the salesman who sold you the camera would've been totally naked at the time of your purchase). Okay, I'm going to get serious for just a moment (and only for a moment, so don't get excited—especially with that naked salesman around). Camera Raw isn't for everybody. For example, if you're a seasoned pro who gets the exposure dead-on every time and never has white balance issues, go ahead and shoot in a high-quality JPEG format. But for everyone else, RAW lets us fix all sorts of things after the fact, in Photoshop Elements, and because it's all happening within the data from the camera, we can tweak the exposure, white balance, and a dozen other settings to create a new, perfectly balanced "original" from our digital negative. This is very powerful stuff. Now, back to the crazy crap. See the title for this chapter, "Raw Hide"? You're thinking it's that old western TV show, right? Well, I'm thinkin' it's the theme song from that old western TV show. Come on, sing with me: "Head 'em up, move 'em out, Rawwwww Hidddeeee!" (Note to editors: Insert whip sound effect here.)

Editing Your RAW Images in Camera Raw

The RAW format is about the hottest thing happening in digital photography. There are two reasons why: (1) unmatched quality, and (2) you become the processing lab, creating your own custom originals from your digital negative (the RAW file itself, which remains unchanged). Think of it this way: With traditional film, someone at a lab processes your prints from a negative. Well, with RAW, you are the person processing the photo—with control over white balance, exposure, and more—all before your file opens in Elements 4. Oh yeah, there's another benefit—it's easier (nobody tells you that one).

Step One:

If you have a digital camera that is capable of shooting in RAW format, you may want to start shooting in RAW so you can start taking advantage of all the things we mentioned at the top of this page (if you don't shoot in RAW, you won't have access to the Camera Raw processing dialog or any of the RAW features. By the way, we call the act of editing and correcting your images in the Camera Raw dialog "processing" the image. Why processing? Because it sounds cool).

Once you've set your camera to shoot in RAW, you can open these RAW photos in one of two places:

(1) By going under Elements' File menu and choosing Open. Navigate your way to the file, click the Open button, and your file will open in the Camera Raw processing dialog (shown here).

(2) You can open RAW images from the Organizer by clicking on the thumbnail for the RAW photo and pressing Control-I on your keyboard (the shortcut to switch to Standard Edit mode). Either way you do it, Elements opens the RAW photo in the Camera Raw processing dialog.

Step Two:
Your RAW photo is displayed in the large preview area on the left side of the dialog. There are only three tools: the Zoom tool (Z) (for zooming in/out of the preview), the Hand tool (H) (for panning around when you're zoomed in), and the White Balance tool (I) (which looks like the Eyedropper used for sampling colors or reading tones). The two circular arrow icons to the right of these tools are used to rotate photos.

Step Three:
To take advantage of that large preview area, here are some quick preview short-cuts: There's a Zoom tool that works just like the one in the Elements Editor. If you double-click on it (in the top-left corner above the preview), it zooms your image to a 100% view. When you're zoomed in tight, press-and-hold the Spacebar on your keyboard to get the Hand tool, then just click-and-drag in the preview area to move around the image (as shown here). To quickly fit your entire photo in the preview area, double-click on the Hand tool above the preview or press Control-0 (zero). You can press Control–+ (Plus Sign) to zoom in and Control–- (Minus Sign) to zoom out. Also, you can rotate a photo left or right by pressing the L or R key, respectively.

Continued

Step Four:

You do your photo processing in the right column of the Camera Raw dialog. There are two tabs with different sets of controls under each, but all the basic essential adjustments are found under the Adjust tab (make sure it's visible by clicking on its tab). We'll start by adjusting the White Balance setting. When you open a photo in Camera Raw, Elements looks at the White Balance setting that was used when the photo was taken. It will display that setting in the White Balance pop-up menu (the menu will show the words "As Shot" by default). If the white balance looks good to you, you can leave it set as-is, but if the white balance wasn't set correctly in your camera (or if you just want to see if you can come up with a setting that looks better), you can apply a preset option by choosing one from the White Balance pop-up menu.

Step Five:

Besides using these preset White Balance settings, you can create your own custom white balance using the Temperature and Tint sliders. To make your white balance more blue, drag the Temperature slider to the left. To add more yellow, drag it to the right. The Tint slider basically does the same thing, just with different colors: dragging to the left brings more green into your photo and dragging to the right brings in more red. By using these two sliders, you can pretty much create whatever white balance situation you prefer (this is totally a personal preference thing).

©SCOTT KELBY

Step Six:

There's another way to set your white balance: use the White Balance tool (found at the top of the Camera Raw dialog—it looks like the regular Eyedropper tool). You just press the letter I to get that tool, then click it once in a neutral area of your photo (you don't want to click in a perfectly white area with no detail; you want an area that's off-white or light gray with some detail).

TIP: To help you find this neutral color in your images, I've included a black-and-white swatch card for you in the back of this book (it's perforated so you can tear it out). Just put this card into your RAW shot, take the shot, and when you open the RAW file in Camera Raw, you can then click the White Balance tool on the neutral gray swatch on the swatch card. When you're done, just crop the card out of the image. (See the chapter on color correction for more information on how to use this handy card.)

Step Seven:

Now, let's move on to your tonal adjustments (which are located just below the White Balance section). The top slider (and probably the most widely used slider in all of Camera Raw) is for adjusting the exposure of your photo. (You can increase the exposure up to four f-stops and decrease it up to two f-stops. So, an Exposure slider setting of +1.50 would be an increase of a stop and a half.) One way to make this adjustment is to "eye" it: Just drag the slider, then look at the preview to see how your image looks. But there are some other features to help you make more informed exposure decisions.

Continued

Step Eight:

By default, when you open a RAW image, Camera Raw tries to automatically set the Exposure, Shadows, Brightness, and Contrast settings for you. Sometimes Auto settings do a surprisingly good job of adjusting your RAW images, so it's worth seeing how your image is affected by these Auto corrections (just turn off the Preview checkbox that appears above the preview area to see what your image looks like without these Auto corrections, press Control-U to toggle them on/off, or just click on any Auto checkboxes to turn them off).

Step Nine (Exposure):

If you want to set the exposure manu-ally, you can still get some help. The method I use to set the exposure is to have Camera Raw tell me how far I can go (either increasing or decreasing the Exposure setting), so I get the best possible exposure, without clipping off any highlights or shadows. To do this, press-and-hold the Alt key and drag the Exposure slider (moving any slider auto-matically turns off the Auto checkbox for that slider). When you do this, the screen will turn black. If anything shows up in white (or red, green, or blue), that's a warning that the highlights are clipping (basically, that means there will be no detail in that area, which may actually be okay—clipping areas like a bright reflection on a car's bumper or the center of the sun isn't a problem). So, as long as important areas aren't clipped off, I keep clicking-and-dragging to the right (with Alt held down) until some real clipping starts to appear.

Step Ten (Shadows):

Now that your Exposure is set (and you protected your highlights from clipping), what about the shadows? Well, there's a slider for that too—it's called (surprisingly enough) the Shadows slider, and sliding it to the right increases the shadows in your photo. Again, there's an Auto checkbox (and you should give that a try), but you can also use the Alt-drag trick on the Shadows slider. This time, the preview will show shadow areas (with no detail) in pure black (meaning these areas are getting clipped—white areas are not clipped). If you see other colors (like red, green, or blue), they're getting clipped a bit too, but not as significantly as the overall shadows (so I'm not as concerned about a little bit of clipping in color). If there's significant clipping, drag to the left to reduce the amount of shadows. If not, drag to the right until you start getting some clipping.

TIP: Adobe added a very helpful feature to keep you from clipping either your highlights or shadows. At the top of the Camera Raw dialog, there are two checkboxes: one for Highlights, one for Shadows. When you turn them on, anytime highlight areas start getting clipped (regardless of which slider you're using), the clipped areas will appear in solid red, while clipped shadow areas will appear in blue, giving you an instant visual warning exactly where clipping is occurring. Not bad, eh?

Continued

Step Eleven (Brightness):

The next adjustment slider is Brightness. Since you've already adjusted the highlights (with Exposure) and shadows (with the Shadows slider), the Brightness slider adjusts everything else (I always relate this slider to the midtones slider in the Levels dialog, so that might help in understanding how this slider differs from Exposure or Shadows). There is an Auto checkbox for Brightness, but I'm not too crazy about this particular Auto setting, as it seems (to me anyway) to give the photo a flat look, but hey— that's just me. Turn Auto on/off to see if you agree—or just drag the slider to the right (above 50) to lighten the midtones or to the left (below 50) to darken them.

Step Twelve (Contrast):

The Contrast slider does pretty much what you'd expect it to—adds or reduces contrast (depending on which way you drag it). If you drag to the right, it increases the contrast in the image (so you can imagine you'll probably be dragging right most of the time), or if you want to reduce the contrast in your image (making it look flat), drag to the left. There's also an Auto checkbox here, but to me it never seems to add enough contrast, so I usually wind up adjusting this one myself while looking at the preview (and the histogram) as a guide.

Step Thirteen (Saturation):

The Saturation slider makes the colors in your RAW photo either more saturated and colorful (by dragging to the right) or less saturated and flat (by dragging to the left). This is my least-used slider in Camera Raw, as I normally wait until I'm in Elements, because I view adding saturation as a special effect, and not generally something I do when I'm just trying to create a nicely exposed, well-balanced image. In fact, I only adjust this setting if some of the other changes I made in Camera Raw make my colors look flat. Otherwise, I ignore that slider, but that's just me; if you want more saturated photos, go for it (I won't tell anybody). By the way, there's no Auto checkbox for Saturation. I call that an act of mercy.

TIP: I'm sure you've noticed that the Auto checkboxes are "on" by default, but what if you want to see your images without them on at all (of course you could turn off the Preview checkbox or press Control-U)? If you really want to turn them off for good, though, here's what you do: Open a RAW file, turn off all the Auto checkboxes by pressing Control-U, and then go to the Settings flyout menu (it's the right-facing arrow to the right of the Settings pop-up menu) and choose Save New Camera Raw Defaults. Now when you open a RAW image, all the Auto checkboxes will be off by default.

Noise Reduction in Camera Raw

While you're processing your image, if you notice that your image has digital noise (those annoying red-and-green spots or splotchy patches of color), you can reduce that noise—especially the color part—from right within Camera Raw.

Step One:

Open a RAW image in Camera Raw that has a digital noise issue, press Z to get the Zoom tool, and zoom in tight so the noise is easily visible. There are two types of noise you can deal with in Camera Raw: (1) high ISO noise, which often happens when you're shooting in low-light situations, especially when using a high ISO setting (hence the name); and (2) color noise, which can happen even in normal situations (this noise is more prevalent in some cameras than others).

Step Two:

Click on the Detail tab along the right side of the dialog. To decrease the amount of color noise, drag the Color Noise Reduction slider to the right. As you can see, it does a pretty fair job of removing the color noise, though it does tend to desaturate the overall color just a bit. That's why it's good to zoom out to see the preview so you don't wash out the photo. If the problem is mostly in shadow areas (high ISO noise), you can use the Luminance Smoothing slider in the same way—drag to the right to reduce the noise—but use this carefully, because it can tend to make your photo look a bit soft.

©SCOTT KELBY

Although Camera Raw enables you to sharpen your image at this early stage in the correction process, you have to decide if this is something you really want to do. I've heard arguments for sharpening at this stage, but many more against it, so like most corrections, it'll come down to your own personal preference. If you do decide to sharpen now (or if you want to turn off the sharpening that's on by default), here's how:

Sharpening within Camera Raw

Step One:
When you open an image in Camera Raw, by default it applies a small amount of sharpening to your photo. You can see how much by clicking on the Detail tab (along the right side of the dialog) and looking at the Sharpness slider. To add additional sharpness, drag the slider to the right (if you do this, first set your zoom to 100% in the pop-up menu at the bottom left of the preview so you can see the effect of sharpening).

Step Two:
Now that you know how to apply more sharpness (I hate to tell you this), I recommend setting the Sharpness slider at 0% (essentially turning it off). I recommend this for two reasons: First, because there's just one slider, you basically have to take whatever it gives you. Second, I feel sharpening should be done right before you save the file, not when you're initially creating it, so it does the minimum amount of damage to the image. If you agree (hey, it's up to you), set the Sharpness slider to 0%, then go to Camera Raw's flyout menu (it's to the right of the Settings pop-up menu) and choose Save New Camera Raw Defaults. Now when you open RAW photos, no sharpness will be applied, unless you use the slider to add it.

Bracketing with Camera Raw

If you forgot to bracket in the camera itself, you can use Camera Raw to create multiple exposures, and then open those images in Elements 4, where you can composite them together to create an image that one exposure alone couldn't capture. Here's how it's done:

Step One:
Using the Organizer, press Control-I to open the RAW image to which you want to apply a bracketing technique. In this example, the sky's exposure looks pretty decent, but the subject (my buddy and fellow photographer Dave Moser) is almost totally in the shadows. So, using Camera Raw (and the default Auto settings), create the first photo that has the proper exposure for the sky. So even though Dave's dark, as long as the sky looks good to you, click Open to create the first version of your bracketed photo in the Elements Editor.

Step Two:
In the Editor, go under the File menu and choose Duplicate to make a copy of this image. Click on the original photo and close this original image (without saving it). By doing this, we can reopen the RAW file in the next step and create a second version of this image that exposes the foreground, taking Dave out of the shadows.

Step Three:
Now, go back to the Organizer, click on the thumbnail for that same RAW photo, then press Control-I to open the RAW file again. Once the photo is open in Camera Raw, drag the Exposure slider to the right until Dave (and the foreground around him) is properly exposed. This will totally blow out the sky, but just ignore that and focus on getting a good exposure for Dave, our subject. When it looks good to you, click the Open button to create this exposed version of the photo in the Elements Editor.

Step Four:
Now you should have both versions of the image open in the Elements Editor: the brighter one exposed for the highlights (to bring out Dave) and the darker one exposed for the shadows (to bring out the sky). Arrange the windows so you can see both onscreen at the same time. Press V to get the Move tool, and with the shadow image active, press-and-hold the Shift key and drag-and-drop the darker version on top of the lighter version. The key to this part is holding down the Shift key while you drag between documents, which perfectly aligns the dark copy (that now appears on its own layer in the Layers palette) with the lighter version on the Background layer. (This exact alignment of one identical photo over another is referred to as being "pin registered.") You can now close the shadow document without saving, as both versions of the image are contained within the lighter version.

Continued

Step Five:

Go to the Layers palette, hold down the Control key, and click the Create a New Layer icon at the top of the Layers palette. This creates a new blank layer directly beneath the photo exposed for the sky. Now, in the Layers palette, click on the photo exposed for the sky (it should be the top layer), and then press Control-G. This groups your image with the blank layer, covering it so you now only see the version of the photo that's exposed for Dave (which is on the Background layer).

Step Six:

It's time to "reveal" the sky on the darker version of the photo. Here's how: First, in the Layers palette, click on the blank layer between the two image layers. Then press the letter B to get the Brush tool, and click on the down-facing arrow next to the Brush thumbnail in the Options Bar. Choose a medium-size, soft-edged brush from the Brush Picker that appears. Now, press the letter D to set your Foreground color to black, and start painting over the areas of the photo that you want to be darker (in this case, the sky). As you paint, the sky is revealed.

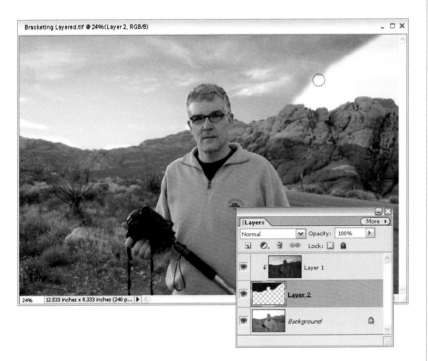

Step Seven:

Keep going until you've painted the entire sky area in, so you have an image that your digital camera couldn't possibly have captured, because in a situation like this it's going to either expose for the ground or the sky, but not both. (*Note:* If you make a mistake, press E to switch to the Eraser tool and begin erasing.) If you want this "best of both worlds," where the sky and the subject/ground are perfectly exposed, you'll have to pull it off here in Photoshop Elements, but that's not a bad thing. In fact, it totally rocks (sorry, I mean "that's fascinating"). By taking these few extra steps, you'll wind up with an image like the one shown here— one where the subject and background are perfectly exposed—it's the best of two photos combined.

Before

After

Saving RAW Files in Adobe's Digital Negative (DNG) Format

At this point in time, there's a concern with the RAW file format because there's not a single, universal format for RAW images—every digital camera manufacturer has its own. That may not seem like a problem, but what happens if one of these camera companies stops developing or supporting a format and switches to something else? Seriously, what if in a few years from now there was no easy way to open your saved RAW files? Adobe recognized this problem and created the Digital Negative (DNG) format for long-term archival storage of RAW images.

Step One:
As of the writing of this book, only a few major camera manufacturers have built in the ability to save RAW files in Adobe's DNG format (although we believe it's only a matter of time before they all do); so if your camera doesn't support DNG files yet—no sweat—you can save your RAW file to Adobe DNG format from right within the Camera Raw dialog. Just open your image in Camera Raw and hit the Save button. This brings up the Save Options dialog, which saves your RAW file to DNG by default.

Step Two:
At the bottom of this dialog, you have some additional DNG options: You can choose to embed the original RAW file into your DNG (making the file larger, but your original is embedded for safe-keeping in case you ever need to extract it—and if you have the hard disk [or CD space]—go for it!). There's a compression option (and it's "lossless," meaning you don't lose quality like you do with JPEG compression). You can also choose to include a JPEG preview with your DNG file. That's it—click Save and you've got a DNG archival-quality file that can be opened by Photoshop Elements (or the free DNG utility from Adobe).

Many high-end pro photographers want to work in 16-bit depth as much as possible because it maintains more tonal quality than 8-bit. Although Elements 4 supports opening RAW images and working in 16-bit depth, what you can do is very limited. In fact, you're basically limited to tonal adjustments because features such as layers, most filters, and a host of other cool features are not available at all when working in 16-bit—you have to convert to 8-bit to get Elements' full feature set back. Is 16-bit really that much better? It's a matter of constant debate among photographers.

Working with 16-Bit Images

Step One:
You have to start by opening an image in a "high-bit" format (like RAW) to be able to create a real 16-bit image (go to File, choose Open, and navigate to your RAW file). Opening a regular 8-bit JPEG image and then converting it to 16-bit depth won't add quality that wasn't there in the first place. You have to start with a RAW image, then you can decide whether you want to continue working in 16-bit or process the file as a regular 8-bit image. Choose your bit-depth setting from the Depth pop-up menu in the bottom-left corner of the Camera Raw dialog.

Step Two:
If you choose to process the image as a 16-bit image and click Open in the Camera Raw dialog, take a quick look under the Elements Editor's Filter menu and you'll see how few filters are available to you. Pretty much all of Elements will feel this same way—almost everything's grayed out (you can't access it). However, after you've made your tonal adjustments in 16-bit mode, you can convert to 8-bit mode by going under the Image menu, under Mode, and choosing 8 Bits/Channel.

Photo by Dave Moser   Exposure: 1/160   Focal Length: 55mm   Aperture Value: ƒ/2.8

Super Size Me
resizing and cropping

If a chapter on resizing and cropping doesn't sound exciting, really, what does? It's sad, but a good portion of our lives is spent doing just that—resizing and cropping. Why is that? It's because nothing, and I mean nothing, is ever the right size. Think about it. If everything were already the right size, there'd be no opportunity to "Super Size" it. You'd go to McDonald's, order a Value Meal, and instead of hearing, "Would you care to Super Size your order?" there would just be a long uncomfortable pause. And frankly, I'm uncomfortable enough at the McDonald's drive-thru, what with all the cropping and resizing I'm constantly doing. Anyway, although having a chapter on cropping and resizing isn't the kind of thing that sells books (though I hear books on crop circles do fairly well), both are important and necessary, especially if you ever plan on cropping or resizing things in Elements. Actually, you'll be happy to learn that I "Super Sized" the chapter with other cool techniques that honestly are probably a bit too cool to wind up in a chapter called "Resizing and Cropping," but it's the only place they'd fit. But don't let the extra techniques throw you; if this chapter seems too long to you, flip to the end of the chapter, rip out a few pages, and you have effectively cropped the chapter down to size. (And by ripping the pages out yourself, you have transformed what was originally a mere book into an "interactive experience," which thereby enhances the value of the book, making you feel like a pretty darn smart shopper.) See, it almost makes you want to read it now, doesn't it?

Cropping Photos

After you've sorted your images in the Organizer, one of the first editing tasks you'll probably undertake is cropping a photo. There are a number of different ways to crop a photo in Elements. We'll start with the basic garden-variety options, and then we'll look at some ways to make the task faster and easier.

Step One:
Open the image you want to crop in the Elements Editor, and then press the letter C to get the Crop tool (you could always select the tool directly from the Toolbox, but I only recommend doing so if you're charging by the hour).

Step Two:
Click within your photo and drag out a cropping border. The area to be cropped away will appear dimmed (shaded). You don't have to worry about getting your cropping border right when you first drag it out, because you can edit it by dragging the control handles that appear in each corner and at the center of each side.

TIP: If you don't like seeing your photo with the cropped-away areas appearing shaded (as in the previous step), you can toggle this shading feature off/on by pressing the Forward Slash key (/) on your keyboard. When you press the Forward Slash key, the border remains in place but the shading is turned off.

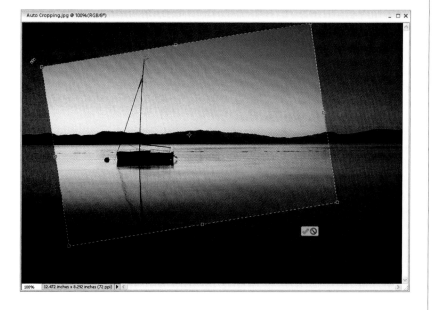

Step Three:
While you have the cropping border in place, you can rotate the entire border. Just move your cursor outside the border, and your cursor will change into a double-headed arrow. Just click-and-drag, and the cropping border will rotate in the direction that you drag. (This is a great way to save time if you have a crooked image, because it lets you crop and rotate at the same time.)

Continued

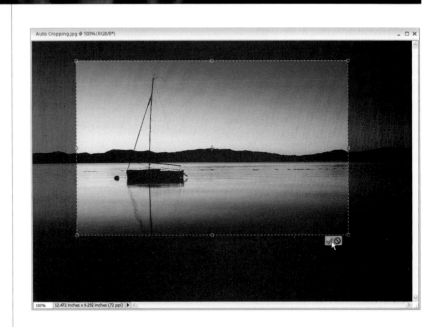

Step Four:

Once you have the cropping border where you want it, click on the green checkmark icon at the bottom-right corner of your cropping border, or just press the Enter key on your keyboard. To cancel your crop, click the red international symbol for "No Way!" at the bottom-right corner of the cropping border, or press the Escape key on your keyboard.

Before

After

The "rule of thirds" is a trick that photographers sometimes use to create more interesting compositions. Basically, you visually divide the image you see in your camera's viewfinder into thirds, and then you position your horizon so it goes along either the top imaginary horizontal line or the bottom one. Then, you position the subject (or focal point) at the center intersections of those lines. But if you didn't use the rule in the viewfinder—no sweat! Here's how to crop your image using the rule of thirds to create more appealing compositions in Elements 4.0:

Cropping Using the "Rule of Thirds"

Step One:
Open the photo to which you want to apply the rule-of-thirds cropping technique (the shot here is poorly composed, with the tree smack dab in the center of the image—it just screams "snapshot!"). Since this is a cropping technique, you realize that the dimensions of your photo are going to get smaller, right? Good. So create a new document that is somewhat smaller than the photo you want, but using the same resolution and color mode (this is very important, otherwise your image won't fit properly in this new document). In the example here, my original photo is about 12x8", so the new document I created is only 8x6"; that way, there's room to play with my cropping (you'll see how in just a moment).

Step Two:
While your new document is active, go under the Edit menu, under Preferences, and choose Grid. In the resulting dialog, enter 33.33 in the Gridline Every field, and then choose Percent from the pop-up menu on the right. In the Subdivisions field, change the default setting of 4 to just 1, and then click OK. You won't see anything in your document yet.

Continued

Step Three:
Go under the View menu and choose Grid. When you do this, the nonprinting grid you created in the previous step (the one divided into horizontal and vertical thirds) will appear in your image area as a visual representation of the rule-of-thirds grid, which you'll use for visual composition cropping.

Step Four:
Return to your image document, press V to switch to the Move tool, and click-and-drag your image onto your blank document. Here's where you create a better composition: Using the Move tool, position your image's horizon along one of the horizontal grid lines (here I used the bottom line), and be sure your focal point (the tree in this case) falls on one of the intersecting points (the top-left intersection in this example). Because your image is larger than the new document, you have plenty of room to position your photo.

Untitled-1 @ 100%(Layer 1, RGB/8#)

100% | 8 inches x 6 inches (72 ppi)

Step Five:
You can now crop away the sides of your image. Press the letter C to switch to the Crop tool and click-and-drag around your entire image. With your crop border in place, press Enter to complete your crop. Now just hide the grid lines by returning to the View menu and deselecting Grid—then enjoy your new, cropped image.

Before

After

Auto-Cropping to Standard Sizes

If you're outputting photos for clients, chances are they're going to want them in standard sizes so they can easily find frames to fit. If that's the case, here's how to crop your photos to a predetermined size (like a 5x7", 8x10", etc.).

Step One:

Open an image in the Elements Editor that you want to crop to be a perfect 5x7" (or in this case, 7x5" because our image is horizontal). Press C to get the Crop tool, then go to the Options Bar, and from the Aspect Ratio pop-up menu, click on the words "No Restriction." When the list of preset crop sizes appears, click on 5x7 in.

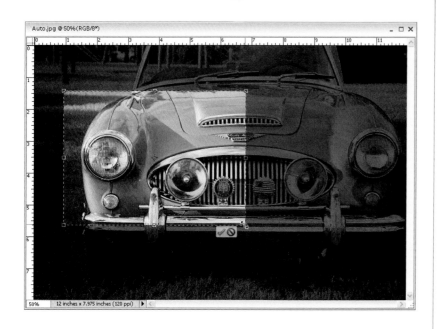

Step Two:
Now click-and-drag the Crop tool over the portion of the photo that you want to be 5x7" (or if your image is horizontal, Elements will automatically adjust your border to 7x5", as it did here). While dragging, you can press-and-hold the Spacebar to adjust the position of your border. Once it's set, press the Enter key and the area inside your cropping border will become 5x7".

Before

After

Cropping to an Exact Custom Size

Okay, now you know how to crop to Elements' built-in preset sizes, but how do you crop to a nonstandard size—a custom size that you determine? Here's how:

Step One:
Open the photo that you want to crop in the Elements Editor. (I want to crop this image to 8x6".) First, press C to get the Crop tool. In the Options Bar, you'll see fields for Width and Height. Enter the size you want for Width, followed by the unit of measure you want to use (e.g., enter "in" for inches, "px" for pixels, "cm" for centimeters, "mm" for millimeters, etc.). Next, press the Tab key to jump over to the Height field and enter your desired height, again followed by the unit of measure.

TIP: You can swap the figures in the Height and Width fields by clicking on the Swaps icon between the fields in the Options Bar.

©SCOTT KELBY

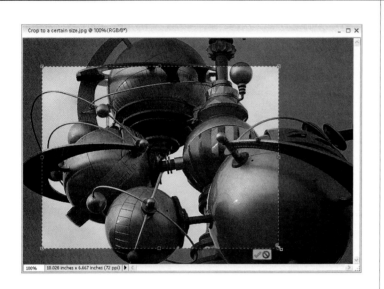

Step Two:
Once you've entered these figures in the Options Bar, click within your photo with the Crop tool and drag out a cropping border. You'll notice that as you drag, the border is constrained to an 8x6" aspect ratio; no matter how large of an area you select within your image, the area within that border will become your specified size. When you release your mouse button, no side handles are visible along the border—only corner handles.

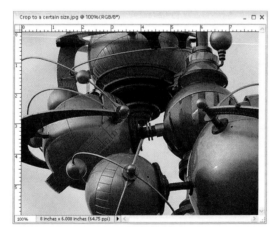

Step Three:
Once your cropping border is onscreen, you can resize it using the corner handles or you can reposition it by moving your cursor inside the border. Your cursor will change to a Move arrow, and you can now click-and-drag the border into place. You can also use the arrow keys on your keyboard for more precise control. When it looks right to you, press Enter to finalize your crop or click on the checkmark icon in the bottom-right corner of your cropping border. (I made the rulers visible [Control-Shift-R] so you could see that the image measures exactly 8x6".)

TIP: Once you've entered a Width and Height in the Options Bar, those dimensions will remain there. To clear the fields, just choose No Restriction from the Aspect Ratio pop-up menu. This will clear the Width and Height fields, and now you can use the Crop tool for freeform cropping (you can drag it in any direction—it's no longer constrained to your specified size).

Continued

COOLER TIP: If you already have a cropping border in place, you can change your dimensions without re-creating the border. All you have to do is enter the new sizes you want in the Width and Height fields in the Options Bar, and Elements 4.0 will resize your cropping border.

Before

After

Elements 4.0 has a cool feature that lets you crop your photo into a pre-designed shape (like putting a wedding photo into a heart shape), but even cooler are the edge effects you can create by cropping into one of the pre-designed edge effects that look like old Polaroid transfers. Here's how to put this feature to use to add visual interest to your own photos (of course, you can use the Heart Shape and do the whole wedding photo thing, but that's so "five-minutes-ago").

Cropping into a Shape

Step One:
In the Elements Editor, open the photo you want to crop into a pre-designed shape, and press the letter Q to get the Cookie Cutter tool.

Step Two:
Now, go up to the Options Bar and click on the down-facing arrow to the right of the word "Shape." This brings up the Custom Shape Picker, which contains the default set of 30 shapes. To load more shapes, click on the right-facing arrow at the top right of the Picker and a list of built-in shape sets will appear. From this list, choose Crop Shapes to load the edge-effect shapes, which automatically crop away areas outside your custom edges.

Continued

Step Three:

Once you find the custom edge shape you want to use from the Custom Shape Picker, just click-and-drag it over your image to the size you want it. When you release the mouse button, your photo is cropped to fit within the shape. *Note:* I like Crop Shape 10 (which is shown here) for something simple, and Crop Shape 21 for something a little wilder. The key thing here is to experiment and try different crop shapes to find your favorite.

Step Four:

You'll see a bounding box around the shape, which you can use to resize, rotate, or otherwise mess with your shape. To resize your shape, hold the Shift key to keep it proportional while you drag a corner point. To rotate the shape, move your cursor outside the bounding box until your cursor becomes a double-sided arrow, and then click-and-drag. As long as you see that bounding box, you can still edit the shape. When it looks good to you, press Enter and the parts of your photo outside that shape will be permanently cropped away.

TIP: If you want your image area tightly cropped, so it's the exact size of the shape you drag out, just turn on the Cookie Cutter's Crop checkbox (up in the Options Bar) *before* you drag out your shape. Then when you press Enter to lock in your final shape, Elements will tightly crop the entire image area to the size of your shape. *Note:* The checkerboard pattern you see around the photo is letting you know that the background around the shape is transparent. If you want a white background behind the shape, click on the Create a New Layer icon at the top of the Layers palette, and then drag your new layer below the Shape layer. Press D then X to set your Foreground to white, then press Alt-Backspace to fill this layer with white.

Before

After

Cropping without the Crop Tool

Sometimes it's quicker to crop your photo using some of Elements' other tools and features than it is to reach for the Crop tool every time you need a simple crop. This is the method I probably use the most for cropping images of all kinds (primarily when I'm not trying to make a perfect 5x7", 8x10", etc.—I'm basically just "eyeing" it).

Step One:
Start by opening a photo in the Elements Editor that you need to crop, and press M to get the Rectangular Marquee tool from the Toolbox. (I use this tool so much that I usually don't have to switch to it—maybe that's why I use this method all the time.) Drag out a selection around the area you want to keep (leaving all the other areas outside the selection that you want cropped away).

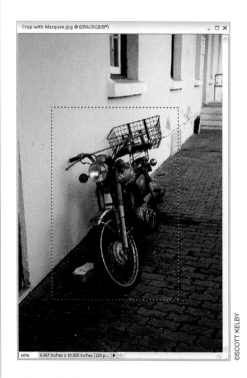

Step Two:
Choose Crop from the Image menu. When you choose Crop, the image is immediately cropped. There are no crop handles, no dialogs—bang—it just gets cropped—down and dirty, and that's why I like it. Just press Control-D to deselect.

TIP: One instance of where you'll often use the Crop command from the Image menu is when you're creating collages. When you drag photos from other documents onto your main document and position them within your collage, any parts of the images that extend beyond the document borders are actually still there. So to keep your file size manageable, choose All from the Select menu or press Control-A, then choose Crop from the Image menu. This deletes all the excess layer data that extends beyond the image border and brings your file size back in line. To deselect, press Control-D.

Before   *After*

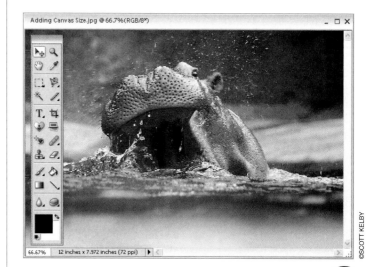

Using the Crop Tool to Add More Canvas Area

I know the heading for this technique doesn't make much sense—"Using the Crop Tool to Add More Canvas Area." How can the Crop tool (which is designed to crop photos to smaller sizes) actually make the canvas area (white space) around your photo larger? That's what I'm going to show you.

Step One:
In the Elements Editor, open the image to which you want to add additional blank canvas area. Press the letter D to set your Background color to its default white.

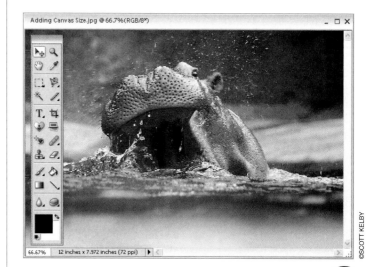

Step Two:
If you're in Maximize Mode, press Control-Minus to zoom out a bit (so your image doesn't take up your whole screen). If you're not in Maximize Mode, click-and-drag out the bottom corner of the document window to see the gray desktop area around your image. (To enter Maximize Mode, click the Maximize Mode icon in the top-right corner of the image window or go under the Window menu, under Images, and choose Maximize Mode.)

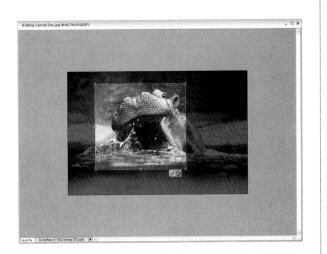

Step Three:
Press the letter C to switch to the Crop tool and drag out a cropping border to any random size (it doesn't matter how big or little it is at this point).

Step Four:
Now, grab any one of the side or corner points and drag outside the image area, out into the gray area that surrounds your image. The cropping border extending outside the image is the area that will be added as white canvas space, so position it where you want to add the blank canvas space.

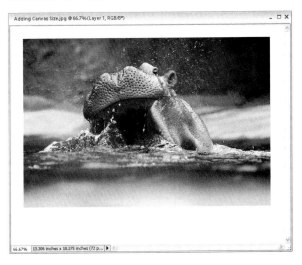

Step Five:
Now, just press the Enter key to finalize your crop, and when you do, the area outside your image will become white canvas area.

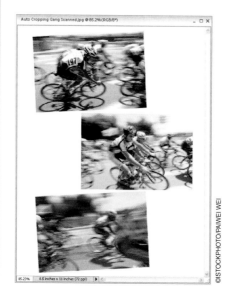

Auto-Cropping Gang-Scanned Photos

A lot of photographers scan photos using a technique called "gang scanning." That's a fancy name for scanning more than one picture at a time. Scanning three or four photos at once with your scanner saves time, but then you eventually have to separate these photos into individual documents. Here's how to have Elements 4.0 do that for you automatically.

Step One:

Place the photos you want to "gang scan" on the bed of your flatbed scanner, and scan the images into Elements using the Organizer (they'll appear in one Elements document). You can access the scanned images by clicking on the Get Photos button in the Organizer's Options Bar. Choose From Scanner in the submenu, and in the dialog that appears, select where and at what quality you want to save your scanned image.

©ISTOCKPHOTO/PAIWEI WEI

Step Two:

Once your images appear as one document in the Editor, go under the Image menu and choose Divide Scanned Photos. It will immediately find the edges of the scanned photos, straighten them if necessary, and then put each photo into its own separate document. Once it has "done its thing," you can close the original gang-scanned document, and you'll be left with just the individual documents.

In Elements 4.0 there's a new way to straighten photos, but it's knowing how to set the options for the tool that makes your job dramatically easier. Here's how it's done:

Straightening Photos with the Straighten Tool

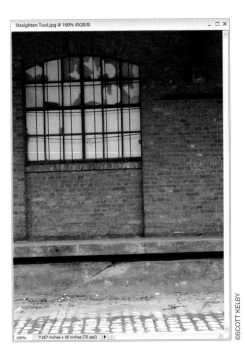

Step One:
Open the photo that needs straightening. The photo shown here looks like the building is tipping to the left.

Step Two:
Choose the Straighten tool from the Toolbox (or just press the P key).

Continued

Step Three:

Take the Straighten tool and drag it along an edge in the photo that you think should be perfectly horizontal, like a horizon line (although in this case, we dragged out the tool along the top of the step).

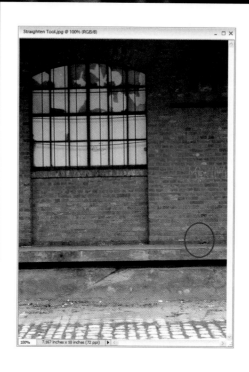

Step Four:

When you release the mouse button, the image is straightened, but as you can see here, the straightening created a problem of its own—the photo now has to be re-cropped because the edges are showing a white background (as the image was rotated until it was straight). That's where the options (which I mentioned in the intro to this technique) come in. You see, the default setting does just what you see here—it rotates the image and leaves it up to you to crop away the mess. However, you can have Elements do the work for you (as you'll see in the next step).

Step Five:
Once you click on the Straighten tool, go up to the Options Bar, and in the Canvas Options pop-up menu, choose Crop to Remove Background.

Step Six:
Now when you drag out the tool and release the mouse, not only is the photo straightened, but the annoying white background is automatically cropped away, giving you the clean result you see here.

TIP: In this example, we used the Straighten tool to straighten our image along a horizontal plane, but if you wanted to straighten the photo using a vertical object instead (like a column or light pole), just press-and-hold the Control key before you drag the Straighten tool, and that will do the trick.

Straightening Crooked Photos

If you hold your digital camera by hand for most of your shots rather than using a tripod, you can be sure that some of your photos are going to come out a bit crooked. Well, I have good news and bad news. First, the good news: Elements has a built-in function for straightening crooked images. Now, the bad news: It doesn't always work. That's why I included a pretty slick workaround for when the auto-straighten function doesn't work.

Automated Straightening
Step One (The Only One):

Open the photo that needs straightening. To use Elements' automated straightening (which works fairly well in many cases), simply go under the Image menu, under Rotate, and choose Straighten Image. If it can find a straight edge, it'll straighten your image (well, most of the time). *Note:* Oftentimes when the image is rotated, you'll see white canvas area around the image, so if you want to straighten and crop at the same time, choose (do I even have to say it?) Straighten and Crop Image from the Image menu, under Rotate. That does it (there is no Step 2).

Manual Straightening
Step One:

Open the photo that needs straightening. Go under the Window menu and choose Info to bring up the Info palette.

Step Two:
Next choose the Line tool from Elements' Toolbox. (It's in the Custom Shape tool's flyout menu just below the Gradient tool. You can press the letter U to cycle through the Custom Shape tools until you get the Line tool.)

Step Three:
Find a straight edge in your photo that is supposed to be horizontal (such as the horizon, a table, a window, etc.—anything that you think should be horizontal). Click-and-drag the Line tool along this straight edge in your photo, starting from the left and extending right, but don't let go of the mouse button (that's important).

Step Four:
While you're still holding down the mouse button, look over on the right side of the Info palette, and third from the top is the letter "A" representing "Angle." Look at the amount and remember that number. Now you can release the mouse button.

Continued

Step Five:

Using the Line tool in this fashion creates a Shape layer, so press Control-Z to undo this layer (it's no longer needed). Next, go under the Image menu, under Rotate, and choose Custom to bring up the Rotate Canvas dialog. Recall that angle you were supposed to remember? That goes in the Angle field in this dialog. You also have to click on the radio button for whether it should rotate to the Right or Left, then click OK and whammo! (whammo! being a technical term); your image is straightened. *Note:* If the rotation leaves white space near the image's corners, you can crop your image with the Crop tool (C). Click-and-drag the tool avoiding the white space and press Enter to finalize the crop.

Resizing Digital Camera Photos

If you're more familiar with resizing scanned images, you'll find that resizing images from digital cameras is a bit different, primarily because scanners create high-resolution scans (usually 300 ppi or more), but the default setting for most digital cameras usually produces an image that is large in physical dimension, but lower in ppi (usually 72 ppi). The trick is to decrease the physical size of your digital camera image (and increase its resolution) without losing any quality in your photo. Here's the trick:

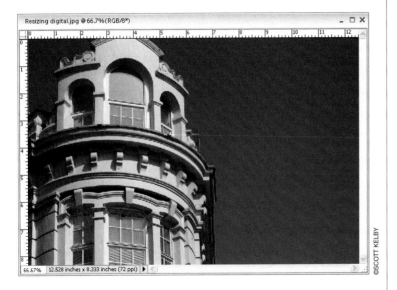

©SCOTT KELBY

Step One:
Open the digital camera image that you want to resize. Press Control-Shift-R to make Elements' rulers visible. Check out the rulers to see the approximate dimensions of your image. As you can see from the rulers in the example here, this photo is around 12x8".

Step Two:
Go under the Image menu, under Resize, and choose Image Size to bring up the Image Size dialog. Under the Document Size section, the Resolution setting is 72 pixels/inch (ppi). A resolution of 72 ppi is considered "low resolution" and is ideal for photos that will only be viewed onscreen (such as Web graphics, slide shows, etc.). This res is too low to get high-quality results from a color inkjet printer, color laser printer, or for use on a printing press.

Continued

Step Three:

If we plan to output this photo to any printing device, it's pretty clear that we'll need to increase the resolution to get good results. I wish we could just type in the resolution we'd like it to be in the Resolution field (such as 200 or 300 ppi), but unfortunately, this "resampling" makes our low-res photo appear soft (blurry) and pixelated. That's why we need to turn off the Resample Image checkbox (it's on by default). That way, when we type in the setting that we need in the Resolution field, Elements automatically adjusts the Width and Height fields for the image in the exact same proportion. As your Width and Height decrease (with Resample Image turned off), your Resolution increases. Best of all, there's absolutely no loss of quality. Pretty cool!

Step Four:

Here I've turned off Resample Image, then I typed 150 in the Resolution field (for output to a color inkjet printer— I know, you probably think you need a lot more resolution, but you usually don't). At a resolution of only 150 ppi, I can actually print a photo that is about 6 inches wide by 4 inches high.

Step Five:
Here's the Image Size dialog for my source photo, and this time I've increased the Resolution setting to 212 ppi (for output to a printing press; again, you don't need nearly as much resolution as you'd think). As you can see, the Width and Height fields for my image have changed.

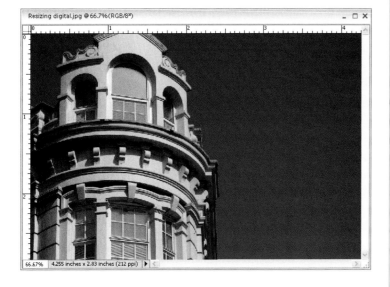

Step Six:
When you click OK, you won't see the image window change at all—it will appear at the exact same size onscreen. But now look at the rulers—you can see that your image's dimensions have changed. Resizing using this technique does three big things: (1) It gets your physical dimensions down to size (the photo now fits on an 8x10" sheet); (2) it increases the resolution enough so you can even output this image on a printing press; and (3) you haven't softened or pixelated the image in any way—the quality remains the same—all because you turned off Resample Image. *Note:* Do not turn off Resample Image for images that you scan on a scanner—they start as high-res images in the first place. Turning off Resample Image is only for photos taken with a digital camera.

Resizing and How to Reach Those Hidden Free Transform Handles

What happens if you drag a large photo onto a smaller photo in Elements? (This happens all the time, especially if you're collaging or combining two or more photos.) You have to resize the photo using Free Transform, right? Right. But here's the catch—when you bring up Free Transform, at least two (or, more likely, all four) of the handles that you need to resize the image are out of reach. You see the center point, but not the handles you need to reach to resize. Here's how to get around that hurdle quickly and easily.

Step One:

Open two photos in the Elements Editor. Use the Move tool (V) to drag-and-drop one photo on top of the other (if you're in Maximize Mode, drag one image onto the other image's thumbnail in the Photo Bin). To resize a photo on a layer, press Control-T to bring up the Free Transform command. Next, hold the Shift key (to constrain your proportions), grab one of the Free Transform corner points, and (a) drag inward to shrink the photo, or (b) drag outward to increase its size (not more than 20%, to keep from making the photo look soft and pixelated). But wait, there's a problem. The problem is—you can't even see the Free Transform handles in this image.

Step Two:

To instantly have full access to all of Free Transform's handles, just press Control-0 (zero), and Elements will instantly zoom out of your document window and surround your photo with gray desktop, making every handle well within reach. Try it once, and you'll use this trick again and again. *Note:* You must choose Free Transform first for this trick to work.

There are a different set of rules we use for maintaining as much quality as possible when making an image smaller, and there are a couple of different ways to do just that (we'll cover the two main ones here). Luckily, maintaining image quality is much easier when sizing down than when scaling up (in fact, photos often look dramatically better—and sharper—when scaled down, especially if you follow these guidelines).

Making Your Photos Smaller (Downsizing)

Downsizing photos where the resolution is already 300 ppi:
Although earlier we discussed how to change image size if your digital camera gives you 72-ppi images, with large physical dimensions (like 24x42" deep), what do you do if your camera gives you 300-ppi images at smaller physical dimensions (like a 10x6" at 300 ppi)? Basically, you turn on Resample Image (in the Image Size dialog under the Image menu, under Resize), then simply type the desired size (in this example, we want a 4x6" final image size), and click OK (don't change the Resolution setting, just click OK). The image will be scaled down to size, and the resolution will remain at 300 ppi. IMPORTANT: When you scale down using this method, it's likely that the image will soften a little bit, so after scaling you'll want to apply the Unsharp Mask filter to bring back any sharpness lost in the resizing (look at the sharpening chapter to see what settings to use).

Continued

Making one photo smaller without shrinking the whole document:

If you're working with more than one image in the same document, you'll resize a bit differently. To scale down a photo on a layer, first click on that photo's layer in the Layers palette, then press Control-T to bring up Free Transform. Pressing-and-holding the Shift key (to keep the photo proportional), grab a corner point and drag inward. When it looks good to you, press the Enter key. If the image looks softer after resizing it, apply the Unsharp Mask filter (again see the sharpening chapter).

Resizing problems when dragging between documents:

This one gets a lot of people, because at first glance it just doesn't make sense. You have two documents, approximately the same size, side-by-side onscreen. But when you drag a 72-ppi photo (of a building, in this case) onto a 300-ppi document (Untitled-1), the photo appears really small. Why is that? Simply put: resolution. Although the documents appear to be the same size, they're not. The tip-off that you're not really seeing them at the same size is found in the title bar of each photo. For instance, the building image is displayed at 100%, but the Untitled-1 document is displayed at only 25%. So, to get more predictable results, make sure both documents are at the same viewing size and resolution (check in the Image Size dialog under the Image menu, under Resize).

This is a resizing technique I learned from my friend (and world-famous nature photographer) Vincent Versace. His poster-sized prints (24x36") always look so sharp and crisp—but we're both shooting with the same 6-megapixel camera—so I had to ask him his secret. I figured he was using some scaling plug-in, but he said he does the whole thing when editing his images. My thanks to Vinny for sharing his simple, yet brilliant technique with me, so I could share it with you.

Rule-Breaking Resizing for Poster-Sized Prints

Step One:
Open the photo you want to resize, then go under the Image menu, under Resize, and choose Image Size. By the way, in Elements 4.0 there's finally a keyboard shortcut to get to the Image Size dialog: Control-Alt-I.

Step Two:
Type in the dimensions you want as your final print size. My original width for my 6-megapixel image is just a hair over 10", so when I type 36" for the Width, the Height field will automatically adjust to around 24" (the Width and Height are linked proportionally by default—adjust one and the other adjusts in kind). Of course, not all images scale perfectly, so depending on how many megapixels your camera is, you may not be able to get exactly 24" (and in fact, you may not want to go that big, but if you do, you might need to enter more than 36" to make your Height reach 24", and then you can go back and crop your Width down to 36" [see the "Cropping to a Specific Size" technique earlier in this chapter]).

Continued

Step Three:

Once your size is in place, you'll need to adjust your resolution upward, so go to the Resolution field and enter 360. Now, you know and I know that this goes against every tried-and-true rule of resolution, and breaks the "never-just-type-in-a-higher-number-with-the-Resample-Image-checkbox-turned-on" rule that we all live and die by, but stick with me on this one—you've got to try it to believe it. So, type it in, grit your teeth, but don't click OK yet.

Step Four:

Adobe introduced some new sampling algorithms for resizing images, and according to Vincent's research, the key to this resizing technique is to not use the sampling method Adobe recommends (which is Bicubic Smoother). Instead, choose Bicubic Sharper in the Resample Image pop-up menu, which actually provides better results—so much so that Vincent claims the printed results are not only just as good, but perhaps better than those produced by the expensive, fancy-schmancy upsizing plug-ins.

Step Five:

I've tried this technique numerous times, and I have to say—the results are pretty stunning. But don't take my word for it—click OK, print it out, and see for yourself. Here's the final image resized to 36x24" (you can see the size using the rulers by pressing Control-Shift-R).

Automated Saving and Resizing

Elements 4.0 introduces a pretty slick little utility that lets you take a folder full of images and do any (or all) of the following automatically at one time: (1) rename them; (2) resize them; (3) change their resolution; (4) color correct and sharpen them; and (5) save them in the file format of your choice (JPEG, TIFF, etc.). If you find yourself processing a lot of images, this can save a ton of time. Better yet, since the whole process is automated, you can teach someone else to do the processing for you, like your spouse, your child, a neighbor's child, passersby, local officials, etc.

Step One:
In the Elements Editor, go under the File menu and choose Process Multiple Files.

Step Two:
When the Process Multiple Files dialog opens, the first thing you have to do is choose the folder of photos you want to process by clicking on the Browse button, then navigating to the folder you want and clicking OK. If you already have some photos open in Elements, you can choose Opened Files from the Process Files From pop-up menu (or you can choose Import to import files). Then, in the second field, you decide whether you want the new copies to be saved in the same folder (by clicking the Same as Source checkbox), or copied into a different folder (in which case, click on the Browse button and choose that folder).

Continued

Step Three:

The third section is File Naming. If you want your files automatically renamed when they're processed, turn on the Rename Files checkbox, then in the fields directly below that checkbox, type the name you want these new files to have and choose how you want the numbering to appear after the name (a two-digit number, three-digit, etc.). Then, choose the number with which you want to start numbering images. You'll see a preview of how your file naming will appear just below the Document Name field.

Step Four:

In the Image Size section, you decide if you want to resize the images (by turning on the Resize Images checkbox), and you enter the width and height you want for your finished photos. You can also choose to change the resolution if you like. Then, if you want to change their file type (like from RAW to JPEG High Quality), you choose that in the bottom section—File Type. Just turn on the Convert Files To checkbox, and then choose your format from the pop-up menu. On the right side of the dialog, there is a list of Quick Fix cosmetic changes you can make to these photos as well, including Auto Levels (to adjust the overall color balance and contrast), Auto Contrast (this is kind of lame if you ask me), Auto Color (it's not bad), and Sharpen (it works well). Click OK and it does its thing, totally automated based on the choices you made in this dialog. How cool is that!

Exposure: 1/4   Focal Length: 270mm   Aperture Value: ƒ/2.8

Color Me Badd
color correction for photographers

The subtitle for this chapter is "Color Correction for Photographers," which invites the question "How is color correction for photographers different from color correction for anybody else?" Actually, it's quite a bit different, because photographers generally work in RGB or black and white. And in reality, digital photographers mostly work in RGB because, although we can manage to build reusable spacecraft and have GPS satellites orbiting in space so golfers here on earth know how far it is from their golf cart to the green, for some reason creating a color inkjet printer that prints a decent black-and-white print is still apparently beyond our grasp. Don't get me started. Anyway, this chapter isn't entirely about black-and-white

prints, and now that I think about it, I'm sorry I brought it up in the first place. So forget I ever mentioned it, and let's talk about color correction. Why do we even need color correction? Honestly, it's a technology thing. Even with traditional film cameras, every photo needs some sort of color tweaking (either during processing or afterward in Elements), because if it didn't need some correction, we'd have about 20-something pages in this book that would be blank, and that would make my publisher pretty hopping mad. So, for the sake of sheer page count, let's all be glad that we don't live in an ideal world where every photo comes out perfect and 6-megapixel cameras are only 200 bucks and come with free 1-GB memory cards.

Before You Color Correct Anything, Do This First!

Before you color correct even a single photo, you need to consider a couple of settings that can affect the results you'll get. It's important to note that the changes you make will remain as your defaults until you change them again, and that (particularly with Color Settings) you may change your settings from time to time based on individual projects.

Step One:
From the Edit menu, choose Color Settings (or press Control-Shift-K).

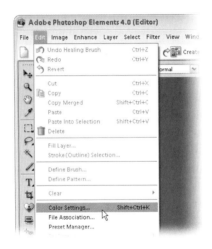

Step Two:
In the Color Settings dialog, choose from the four options: No Color Management, Always Optimize Colors for Computer Screens, Always Optimize for Printing, or Allow Me to Choose. To a large degree, your choice will depend on your final output; but for photographers, I recommend using Always Optimize for Printing because it reproduces such a wide gamut of colors using the Adobe RGB profile (if your photos don't already have a profile assigned), and it's ideal if your photos will wind up in print. *Note:* Unfortunately, color management is beyond the scope of this book. In fact, entire books have been dedicated to the subject. So for now, just switch your Color Settings to Always Optimize for Printing and let's move on.

Step Three:

Now we're moving to a completely different area. Press the letter I to switch to the Eyedropper tool. In the Options Bar, the Sample Size setting for this tool (Point Sample) is fine for using the Eyedropper to steal a color from within a photo and making it your Foreground color. However, Point Sample doesn't work well when you're trying to read values in a particular area (such as flesh tones), because it gives you the reading from just one individual pixel, rather than an average reading of the surrounding area under your cursor.

Step Four:

For example, flesh tones are actually composed of dozens of different colored pixels (just zoom way in and you'll see what I mean); and if you're color correcting, you want a reading that's representative of the area under your Eyedropper, not just a single pixel within that area, which could hurt your correction decision-making. That's why you need to go to the Options Bar, under the Sample Size pop-up menu, and choose 3 by 3 Average. This changes the Eyedropper to give you a reading that's the average of 3 pixels across and 3 pixels down in the area that you're sampling. Once you've completed the changes on these two pages, it's safe to go ahead with the rest of the chapter and start correcting your photos.

Photo Quick Fix

If you have a photo that has some serious problems (bad color, bad lighting, bad everything, etc.), and you have no experience with color correction or repairing other color or lighting nightmares, you'll love Elements 4.0's Quick Fix. It's where you go when you're not experienced at color correcting or fixing tonal problems, but you can see something's wrong with your photo and you want it fixed fast with the least amount of sweat. You'll eventually outgrow Quick Fix and want to use Levels and Unsharp Mask and all that cool stuff, but if you're new to Elements, Quick Fix can do a pretty decent job for ya.

Step One:
Open the photo that needs color correcting (in this example, our photo [shown below] needs the works—color correction, more contrast, and some sharpening). Then, click on the Quick Fix button at the top-right side of the Options Bar to enter the Quick Fix mode.

Step Two:
The Quick Fix dialog shows you side-by-side before-and-after versions of the photo you're about to correct (before on the left, after on the right). If you don't see this view, go to the View pop-up menu in the bottom left of the Quick Fix window and select Before and After (Portrait or Landscape). To the right of your side-by-side preview is a group of nested palettes offering tonal and lighting fixes you can perform on your photo. Start with the General Fixes palette at the top. The star of this palette is Smart Fix. Click the Auto button and Smart Fix will automatically analyze the photo and try to balance the overall tone (adjusting the shadows and highlights), fixing any obvious color casts while it's at it. In most cases this feature does a surprisingly good job. There's an Amount slider under Smart Fix that you can use to increase (or decrease) the effect of the Smart Fix.

©SCOTT KELBY

TIP: By the way, you can also access the Auto Smart Fix command without entering Quick Fix mode by going under the Enhance menu and choosing Auto Smart Fix (or just press the keyboard shortcut Control-Alt-M). However, there are two advantages to applying the Smart Fix here in Quick Fix mode: (1) You get the Amount slider, which you don't get by just applying it from the menu or the shortcut; and (2) you get a side-by-side, before-and-after preview so you can see the results before you click OK. So if it turns out that you need additional fixes (or Smart Fix didn't work as well as you'd hoped), you're already in the right place.

Step Three:
If you apply Smart Fix and you're not happy with the results, don't try to stack more "fixes" on top of that—instead, click the Reset button that appears over the top-right corner of the After preview to reset the photo to how it looked when you first entered Quick Fix mode. If the color in your photo looks a little flat and needs more contrast, try the Auto button in the Levels category, found in the Lighting palette (the second palette down). I generally stay away from Auto Contrast, as Auto Levels seems to do a better job.

Continued

Step Four:

Besides Auto Contrast, there's another very powerful tool—the Lighten Shadows slider. Drag it to the right a bit, and watch how it opens up the dark shadow areas in your photo. Now, on to more Quick Fixing.

Step Five:

The next palette down, Color, has an Auto button that (surprisingly enough) tries to remove color casts and improve contrast like Smart Fix and Levels do, but it goes a step further by including a midtones correction that can help reduce color casts in the midtone areas of your photo. Hit the Reset button to remove any corrections that you've made up to this point, and then try the Auto button in the Color palette. See if the grays in the photo don't look grayer and less reddish. The sliders in the palette are mostly for creating special color effects (move the Hue slider and you'll see what I mean). You can pretty much ignore these sliders unless you want to get "freaky" with your photos.

Step Six:

After you've color corrected your photo (using the Auto buttons and the occasional slider), the final step is to sharpen your photo (by the way, to maintain the best quality, this should be the final step—the last thing you do in your correction process). Just click the Auto button in the Sharpen palette and watch the results. If the photo isn't sharp enough for you, drag the Amount slider to the right to increase the amount of sharpening, but be careful—oversharpening can ruin the photo by becoming too obvious, and it can introduce color shifts and "halos" around objects.

Step Seven:

There are a few other things you can do while you're here (think of this as a one-stop shop for quickly fixing images). Along the bottom of the dialog are icons you can click to rotate your photo (this photo doesn't need to be rotated, but hey, ya never know). In the General Fixes palette, there's an Auto Red Eye Fix if your photo needs it. If you don't like the results, try using the Red Eye Removal tool from the Toolbox on the left side of the dialog. Just click-and-drag over the problem area in your After preview for more red-eye control. Also, there are other tools: You know what the Zoom and Hand tools do (they zoom you in, and then move you around once you're zoomed in), but you can also crop your photo by using the Crop tool within the After preview, so go ahead and crop your photo down a bit.

Continued

Step Eight:

Okay, you've color corrected, fixed the contrast, sharpened your image, and even cropped it down to size. So how do you leave Quick Fix mode and return to regular Elements 4.0? Go to the right-hand corner of the Options Bar and click on the Standard Edit button. That's basically the OK button—it applies all the changes to your photo and returns you to the normal editing mode.

Before

After

In previous versions of Elements, there were two ways to see a histogram. (A histogram is a graph showing the tonal range of your photo.) You could either view it when using Levels, or you could open a dialog that would display a histogram. But you could only view it in this dialog—it wasn't updated live as you made tonal adjustments. Starting in Elements 3.0, Adobe made the Histogram its own floating palette, so now you can have it open as you apply adjustments while in Standard Edit mode. Plus, it shows you before-and-after readings before you click the OK button in a tonal adjustment dialog, such as the Adjust Smart Fix dialog.

Getting a Visual Readout (Histogram) of Your Corrections

©SCOTT KELBY

Step One:
Open the photo that needs a tonal adjustment. Now, go under the Window menu and choose Histogram to open the Histogram palette. (By the way, this palette is only available in Elements 4.0's Standard Edit mode—not in Quick Fix mode.)

Step Two:
Go under the Enhance menu and choose Auto Color Correction. Take a look in the floating Histogram palette and you'll see how the Auto Color Correction command affected the photo's histogram. *Note:* If you see a small symbol in the upper right-hand corner of the graph that looks like a tiny yellow yield sign with an exclamation point in it, that's a warning that the histogram you're seeing is not a new histogram—it's a previous histogram cached from memory. To see a fresh histogram, click directly on that warning symbol and a new reading will be generated based on your current adjustment.

Color Correcting Digital Camera Images

As far as digital technology has come, there's still one thing that digital cameras won't do—give you perfect color every time. In fact, if they gave us perfect color 50% of the time, that would be incredible, but unfortunately, every digital camera (and every scanner that captures traditional photos) sneaks some kind of color cast into your image. Generally, it's a red cast, but depending on the camera it could be blue. Either way, you can be pretty sure there's a cast. (Figure it this way—if there wasn't, the term "color correction" wouldn't be used.) Here's how to get your color in line:

Step One:
Open the digital camera photo you want to color correct. (The photo shown here doesn't look too bad, but as we go through the correction process, you'll see that, like most photos, it really needed a correction.)

Step Two:
Go under the Enhance menu, under Adjust Lighting, and choose Levels (or press Control-L). The dialog may look intimidating at first, but the technique you're going to learn here requires no previous knowledge of Levels, and it's so easy, you'll be correcting photos using Levels immediately.

Step Three:

First, we need to set some preferences in the Levels dialog so we'll get the results we're after when we start correcting. We'll start by setting a target color for our shadow areas. To set this preference, in the Levels dialog, double-click on the black Eyedropper tool (it's on the lower right-hand side of the dialog, the first Eyedropper from the left). A Color Picker will appear asking you to "Select Target Shadow Color." This is where we'll enter values that, when applied, will help remove any color casts your camera introduced in the shadow areas of your photo.

Step Four:

We're going to enter values in the R, G, and B (red, green, and blue) fields of this dialog.

For R, enter 10
For G, enter 10
For B, enter 10

TIP: To move from field to field, just press the Tab key.

Then click OK. Because these figures are evenly balanced (neutral), they help ensure that your shadow areas won't have too much of one color (which is exactly what causes a color cast—too much of one color).

Continued

Step Five:
Now we'll set a preference to make our highlight areas neutral. Double-click on the highlight Eyedropper (the third of the three Eyedroppers in the Levels dialog). The Color Picker will appear asking you to "Select Target Highlight Color." Click in the R field, and then enter these values:

For R, enter 240
For G, enter 240
For B, enter 240

Then click OK to set those values as your highlight target.

Step Six:
Finally, set your midtone preference. You know the drill—double-click on the midtones Eyedropper (the middle of the three Eyedroppers) so you can "Select Target Midtone Color." Enter these values in the R, G, and B fields (if they're not already there by default):

For R, enter 128
For G, enter 128
For B, enter 128

Then click OK to set those values as your midtone target.

Step Seven:

Okay, you've entered your preferences (target colors), so go ahead and click OK in the Levels dialog (without making any changes to your image). You'll get an alert dialog asking you if you want to "Save the new target colors as defaults." Click Yes, and from that point on, you won't have to enter these values each time you correct a photo, because they'll already be entered for you—they're now the default settings.

Step Eight:

You're going to use these Eyedropper tools that reside in the Levels dialog to do most of your correction work. Your job is to determine where the shadow, mid-tone, and highlight areas are, and click the right Eyedropper in the right place (you'll learn how to do that in just a moment). So remember your job—find the shadow, midtone, and highlight areas and click the right Eyedropper in the right spot. Sounds easy, right? It is.

You start by opening Levels and setting the shadows first, so you'll need to find an area in your photo that's supposed to be black. If you can't find something that's supposed to be the color black, then it gets a bit trickier—in the absence of something black, you have to determine which area in the image is the darkest. If you're not sure where the darkest part of the photo is, you can use the following trick to have Elements tell you exactly where it is.

Step Nine:

Go to the top of the Layers palette and click on the half-black/half-white circle icon to bring up the Create Adjustment Layer pop-up menu. When the menu appears, choose Threshold, which brings up a dialog with a histogram and a slider under it.

Continued

Step Ten:

When the Threshold dialog appears, drag the Threshold Level slider under the histogram all the way to the left. Your photo will turn completely white. Slowly drag the slider back to the right, and as you do, you'll start to see some of your photo reappear. The first area that appears is the darkest part of your image. That's it—that's Elements telling you exactly where the darkest part of the image is. Now that you know where your shadow area is, make a mental note of its location, but don't click OK yet. Now to find a white area in your image.

Step Eleven:

If you can't find an area in your image that you know is supposed to be white, you can use the same technique to find the highlight areas. With the Threshold dialog still open, drag the slider all the way to the right. Your photo will turn black. Slowly drag the slider back toward the left, and as you do, you'll start to see some of your photo reappear. The first area that appears is the lightest part of your image. Make a mental note of this area as well (yes, you have to remember two things, but you have to admit, it's easier than remembering two PIN numbers). You're now done with Threshold so just click Cancel because you don't actually need the adjustment layer anymore.

Step Twelve:

Press Control-L to bring up the Levels dialog. First, select the shadow Eyedropper (the one half filled with black) from the bottom right of the Levels dialog. Move your cursor outside the Levels dialog into your photo and click once in the area that Elements showed you was the darkest part of the photo (in Step 10). When you click there, you'll see the shadow areas correct. (Basically, you just reassigned the shadow areas to your new neutral shadow color—the one you entered earlier as a preference in Step 4.) If you click in that spot and your photo now looks horrible, you either clicked in the wrong spot or what you thought was the shadow point actually wasn't. Undo the setting of your shadow point by clicking the Reset button in the dialog and try again. If that doesn't work, don't sweat it; just keep clicking in areas that look like the darkest part of your photo until it looks right.

Step Thirteen:

While still in the Levels dialog, click on the highlight Eyedropper (the one filled with white). Move your cursor over your photo and click once on the lightest part (the one you committed to memory in Step 11) to assign that as your highlight. You'll see the highlight colors correct.

Continued

Step Fourteen:

Now that the shadows and highlights are set, you'll need to set the midtones in the photo. It may not look as if you need to set them, because the photo may look properly corrected, but chances are there's a cast in the midtone areas. You may not recognize the cast until you've corrected it and it's gone, so it's worth giving it a shot to see the effect (which will often be surprisingly dramatic). Unfortunately, there's no Threshold adjustment layer trick that works well for finding the midtone areas, so you have to use some good old-fashioned guesswork (or try "Dave's Amazing Trick for Finding a Neutral Gray" in this chapter). Ideally, there's something in the photo that's gray, but not every photo has a "gray" area, so look for a neutral area (one that's obviously not a shadow, but not a highlight either). Click the middle (gray) Eyedropper in that area. If it's not right, click the Reset button and repeat Steps 12-14.

Step Fifteen:

There's one more important adjustment to make before you click OK in the Levels dialog and apply your correction. Under the Histogram (that's the black mountain-range-looking thing), click on the center slider (the Midtone slider—that's why it's gray) and drag it to the left a bit to brighten the midtones of the image. This is a visual adjustment, so it's up to you to determine how much to adjust, but it should be subtle—just enough to bring out the midtone detail. When it looks right to you, click OK to apply your correction to the highlights, midtones, and shadows, removing any color casts and brightening the overall contrast.

Before   *After*

Dave's Amazing Trick for Finding a Neutral Gray

Finding a neutral midtone during color correcting has always been kind of tricky. Well, it was until Dave Cross, who works with me as Senior Developer of Education for the National Association of Photoshop Professionals (NAPP), came into my office one day to show me his amazing new trick for finding right where the midtones live in just about any image. When he showed me, I immediately blacked out. After I came to, I begged Dave to let me share his very slick trick in my book, and being the friendly Canadian he is, he obliged.

Step One:
Open any color photo and click on the Create a New Layer icon at the top of the Layers palette to create a new blank layer. Then, go under the Edit menu and choose Fill Layer. When the Fill Layer dialog appears, in the Contents section, under the Use pop-up menu, choose 50% Gray, and then click OK to fill your new layer with (you guessed it) 50% gray.

Step Two:
Now, go to the Layers palette and change the blend mode pop-up menu to Difference. Changing this layer's blend mode to Difference doesn't do much for the look of your photo (in fact, it rarely does), but just remember—it's only temporary.

Step Three:
Choose Threshold from the Create Adjustment Layer pop-up menu at the top of the Layers palette. When the dialog appears, drag the slider all the way to the left (your photo will turn completely white). Now, slowly drag the slider back to the right, and the first areas that appear in black are the neutral midtones. Take a mental note of where those gray areas are, and then click Cancel in the dialog, because you no longer need the adjustment layer. (In the example shown here, the neutral midtones are in the center of the building near the lantern.)

Step Four:
Now that you know where your midtone point is, go back to the Layers palette and drag both the Threshold adjustment layer and the 50% gray layer onto the Trash icon (they already did their job, so you can get rid of them). You'll see your full-color photo again. Now, press Control-L to open Levels, get the midtones Eyedropper (it's the middle Eyedropper), and click directly on one of the neutral areas. That's it; you've found the neutral midtones and corrected any color within them. So, will this work every time? Almost. It works most of the time, but you will run across photos that just don't have a neutral midtone, so you'll have to either not correct the midtones or go back to what we used to do—guess.

Studio Portrait Correction Made Simple

If you're shooting in a studio—whether it's portraits or products—there's a technique you can use that makes the color-correction process so easy that you'll be able to train laboratory test rats to correct photos for you. In the back of this book, I've included a color swatch card (it's perforated so you can easily tear it out). After you get your studio lighting set the way you want it, and you're ready to start shooting, just put this swatch card into your shot (just once) and take the shot. What does this do for you? You'll see.

Step One:
When you're ready to start shooting and the lighting is set the way you want it, tear out the swatch card from the back of this book and place it within your shot (if you're shooting a portrait, have the subject hold the card for you), and then take the shot. After you've got one shot with the swatch card, you can remove it and continue with the rest of your shoot.

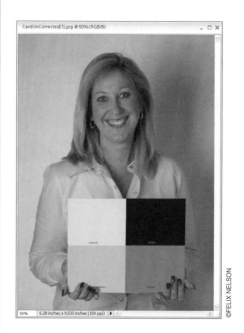

Step Two:
When you open the first photo taken in your studio session, you'll see the swatch card in the photo. By having a card that's pure white, neutral gray, and pure black in your photo, you no longer have to try to determine which area of your photo is supposed to be black (to set the shadows), which area is supposed to be gray (to set the midtones), or which area is supposed to be white (to set the highlights). They're right there in the card. *Note:* I've even included a Camera Raw White Balance swatch if you're working with RAW files. See "Editing Your RAW Images in Camera Raw" in Chapter 2 for more info.

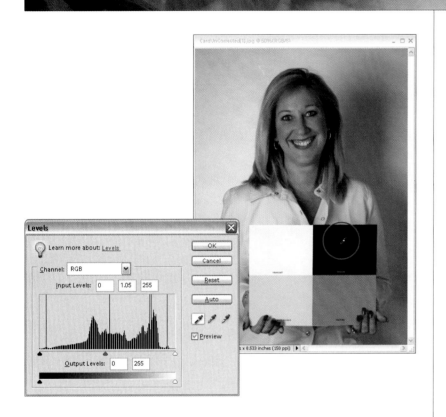

Step Three:
Press Control-L to bring up the Levels dialog. Click the black Eyedropper on the black panel of the card (to set shadows), the middle Eyedropper on the gray (for midtones), and the white Eyedropper on the white panel (sets the highlights), and the photo will nearly correct itself. No guessing, no Threshold adjustment layers, no using the Info palette to determine the darkest areas of the image—now you know exactly which part of that image should be black and which should be white.

Step Four:
Press C to get the Crop tool, crop the card out of the image, and you're set. Best of all, now that you have the Levels setting for the first image, you can correct the rest of the photos using the same settings: Just open the next photo and press Control-Alt-L to apply the exact setting to this photo that you did to the swatch card photo. Or, you can use the "Drag-and-Drop Instant Color Correction" method that appears in this chapter.

TIP: If you want to take this process a step further, many professionals use a Macbeth color-swatch chart (from GretagMacbeth; www.gretagmacbeth. com), which also contains a host of other target colors. It's used exactly the same way: Just put the chart into your photo, take one shot, and then when you correct the photo, each color swatch will be in the photo, just begging to be clicked on.

Drag-and-Drop Instant Color Correction

This is a wonderful timesaving trick for quickly correcting an entire group of photos that have similar lighting. It's ideal for shots where the lighting conditions are controlled, but works equally well for outdoor shots, or really any situation where the lighting for your group of shots is fairly consistent. Once you try this, you'll use it again and again and again.

Step One:
First, here's a tip-within-a-tip: If you're opening a group of photos, you don't have to open them one by one. Just go under the File menu and choose Open. In the Open dialog, click on the first photo you want to open, then hold the Control key and click on any other photos you want to open. Then, when you click the Open button, Elements will open all the selected photos. (If all your photos are contiguous, hold the Shift key and click on the first and last photos in the list to select them all.) So now that you know that tip, go ahead and open at least three or four images, just to get you started.

Step Two:
At the top of the Layers palette, click on the Create Adjustment Layer pop-up menu and choose Levels. *Note:* An adjustment layer is a special layer that contains the tonal adjustment of your choice (such as Levels, Brightness/Contrast, etc.). There are a number of advantages to having this correction applied as a layer, as you'll soon see, but the main advantage is that you can edit or delete this tonal adjustment at any time while you're working, plus you can save this adjustment with your file as a layer.

Step Three:
When you choose this adjustment layer, you'll notice that the regular Levels dialog appears, just like always. Go ahead and make your corrections using Levels (see "Color Correcting Digital Camera Images" earlier in this chapter), and when your correction looks good, click OK. In the Layers palette, you'll see that a new Levels adjustment layer is created.

Step Four:
Because you applied this correction as an adjustment layer, you can treat this adjustment just like a regular layer, right? Right! And Elements lets you drag layers between open documents, right? Right again! So, go to the Layers palette, click on the Levels adjustment layer thumbnail, and drag-and-drop this layer right onto one of your other open photos. That photo will instantly have the same correction applied to it. This technique works because you're correcting photos that share similar lighting conditions. Need to correct 12 open photos? Just drag-and-drop it 12 times (making it the fastest correction in town!).

Continued

Step Five:

Okay, what if one of the "dragged corrections" doesn't look right? That's the beauty of these adjustment layers. Just double-click directly on the adjustment layer thumbnail for that photo, and the Levels dialog will reappear with the last settings you applied still in place. You can then adjust this individual photo separately from the rest. Try this "dragging-and-dropping-adjustment-layers" trick once, and you'll use it again and again to save time when correcting a digital roll that has similar lighting conditions.

Adjusting Flesh Tones

So what do you do if you've used Levels to properly set the highlights, midtones, and shadows, but the flesh tones in your photo still look too red? You can try this quick trick for getting your flesh tones in line by removing the excess red. This one small adjustment can make a world of difference.

Step One:
Open a photo that needs red removed from the flesh tones. If the whole image appears too red, skip this step and move on to Step 3. However, if just the flesh-tone areas appear too red, press L to switch to the Lasso tool and make a selection around all the flesh-tone areas in your photo. (Hold the Shift key to add other flesh-tone areas to the selection, such as arms, hands, legs, etc.)

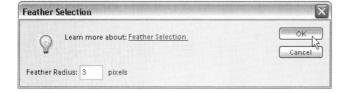

Step Two:
Go under the Select menu and choose Feather. Enter a Feather Radius of about 3 pixels, then click OK. By adding this feather, you're softening the edges of your selection, preventing a hard, visible edge appearing around your adjustments.

Continued

Step Three:

Go under the Enhance menu, under Adjust Color, and choose Adjust Hue/Saturation. When the dialog appears, click on the Edit pop-up menu and choose Reds so you're only adjusting the reds in your photo (or in your selected areas if you put a selection around the flesh tones).

Step Four:

The rest is easy—you're simply going to reduce the amount of saturation so the flesh tones appear more natural. Drag the Saturation slider to the left to reduce the amount of red. With the Preview checkbox turned on, you'll be able to see the effect of removing the red as you lower the Saturation slider.

TIP: If you made a selection of the flesh-tone areas, you might find it easier to see what you're correcting if you hide the selection border from view by pressing Control-H while the Hue/Saturation dialog is open.

Step Five:

When the flesh tones look right, just click the OK button and you're set. But don't forget that your selection is still in place, so press Control-D to deselect.

Before

After

Warming Up (or Cooling Down) a Photo

Back in the day, when we needed to adjust our camera to a particular lighting situation (let's say the image would come out too blue or too warm because of the lighting), we would use color filters that would screw onto the end of our lens. Now we "warm up" or "cool down" a photo digitally using Elements 4.0's Photo Filter adjustment layer. Here's how:

Step One:
Open the photo that needs cooling down (or warming up). In the example shown here, the photo is too warm and has a yellowish tint, so we want to cool it down and make it look more natural. Go to the Layers palette and choose Photo Filter from the Create Adjustment Layer pop-up menu at the top of the palette (its icon looks like a half-black/half-white circle).

Step Two:
When the Photo Filter dialog appears, choose Cooling Filter (82) (or choose a Warming Filter if your image is too cool) from the Filter pop-up menu (this approximates the effect of a traditional screw-on lens filter). If the effect isn't cool enough for you, drag the Density slider to the right to cool the photo some more. Then click OK.

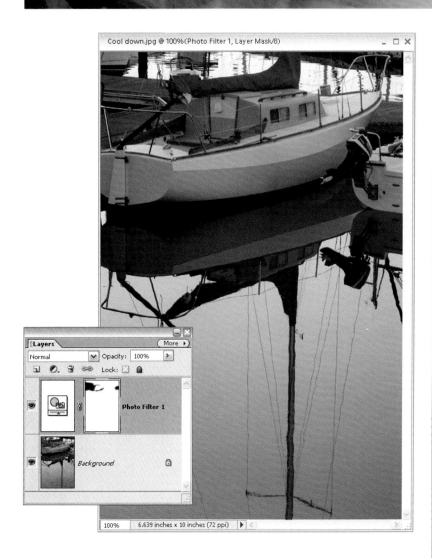

Step Three:
Because this Photo Filter is an adjustment layer, you can edit where the cooling is applied, so press B to switch to the Brush tool, and in the Options Bar, click on the down-facing arrow next to the Brush thumbnail and choose a soft-edged brush in the Brush Picker. Then, press X until you have black as your Foreground color, and begin painting over any areas that you don't want to be cool (for example, if you wanted parts of the boat or the dock to stay warm, you'd paint over those areas). The original color of the image will be revealed wherever you paint.

Color Correcting One Problem Area Fast!

This technique really comes in handy when shooting outdoor scenes because it lets you enhance the color in one particular area of the photo, while leaving the rest of the photo untouched. Real-estate photographers often use this trick because they want to present a house on a bright sunny day, but the weather doesn't always cooperate. With this technique, a blown-out sky shot at daybreak can become a beautiful blue sky in just seconds.

Step One:
Open the image that has an area of color you would like to enhance, such as the sky.

Step Two:
Go to the top of the Layers palette and choose Hue/Saturation from the Create Adjustment Layer pop-up menu (it's the half-black/half-white circle icon). A new layer named "Hue/Saturation 1" will be added to your Layers palette and the Hue/Saturation dialog will appear.

Step Three:
From the Edit pop-up menu at the top of the Hue/Saturation dialog, choose the color that you want to enhance (Blues, Reds, etc.), then drag the Saturation slider to the right. You might also choose Cyans, Magentas, etc., from the Edit pop-up menu and do the same thing—drag the Saturation slider to the right, adding even more color. In the example here, I increased the saturation of the Blues to 35. When your image's area looks as enhanced as you'd like it, click OK.

Step Four:
Your area is now colorized, but so is everything else. That's okay; you can fix that easily enough. Press the letter X until your Foreground color is set to black, then press Alt-Backspace to fill the Hue/Saturation layer mask with black. Doing this removes all the color that you just added, but now you can selectively add (actually paint) the color back in where you want it.

Step Five:
Press the letter B to switch to the Brush tool. In the Options Bar, click the down-facing arrow to the right of the Brush thumbnail, and in the Brush Picker choose a large, soft-edged brush. Press X again to toggle your Foreground color to white, and begin painting over the areas where you want the color enhanced. As you paint, the version of your enhanced photo will appear. For well-defined areas, you may have to go to the Brush Picker again in the Options Bar to switch to a smaller, hard-edged brush.

Continued

TIP: If you make a mistake and paint over an area you shouldn't have—no problem—just press X again to toggle your Foreground color to black and paint over the mistake—it will disappear. Then, switch back to white and continue painting. When you're done, the colorized areas in your photo will look brighter.

Before

After

If you've ever converted a color photo to black and white, chances are you were disappointed with the results. That's because Elements simply throws away the color, leaving a fairly bland black-and-white photo in its wake. In the full version of Adobe Photoshop, there's a feature called Channel Mixer that lets you custom create a better black-and-white image. Unfortunately, that feature isn't in Elements 4.0, but I figured out a way to get similar control using a little workaround. Here's how:

Getting a Better Conversion from Color to Black and White

Step One:
Open the color photo you want to convert to black and white. Press D to set your Foreground and Background to the default black and white.

Step Two:
To really appreciate this technique, it wouldn't hurt if you went ahead and did a regular conversion to black and white, just so you can see how lame it is. Go under the Image menu, under Mode, and choose Grayscale. When the "Discard Color Information?" dialog appears, click OK, and behold the somewhat lame conversion. Now that we agree it looks pretty bland, press Control-Z to undo the conversion, so now you can try something better.

Continued

Step Three:
Go to the top of the Layers palette and choose Levels from the Create Adjustment Layer pop-up menu (it's the half-black/half-white circle icon). When the Levels dialog appears, don't make any changes, just click OK. This will add a layer to your Layers palette named "Levels 1."

Step Four:
Press X until your Foreground color is set to black, then go to the top of the Layers palette and choose Gradient Map from the Create Adjustment Layer pop-up menu. This brings up the Gradient Map dialog.

Step Five:
All you have to do here is click OK, and it gives you a black-and-white image. (And doing just this, this one little step alone, usually gives you a better black-and-white conversion than just choosing Grayscale from the Mode submenu. Freaky. I know.) Clicking OK will add another layer to the Layers palette (above your Levels 1 layer) named "Gradient Map 1."

Step Six:
In the Layers palette, double-click directly on the Levels thumbnail in the Levels 1 layer to bring up the Levels dialog again. In the Channels pop-up menu at the top of the dialog, you can choose to edit individual color channels (kind of like you would with Photoshop's Channel Mixer). Choose the Red color channel.

Step Seven:
You can now adjust the Red channel, and you'll see the adjustments live onscreen as you tweak your black-and-white photo. (It appears as a black-and-white photo because of the Gradient Map adjustment layer above the Levels 1 layer. Pretty sneaky, eh?) You can drag the shadow Input Levels slider to the right a bit to increase the shadows in the Red channel, but don't click OK.

Continued

Step Eight:
Now, switch to the Green channel in the Channels pop-up menu in the Levels dialog. You can make adjustments here as well. Try increasing the highlights in the Green channel by dragging the highlight Input Levels slider to the left. Don't click OK yet.

Step Nine:
Now, choose the Blue channel from the Channels pop-up menu in the Levels dialog. Try increasing the highlights quite a bit and the shadows just a little by dragging the Input Levels sliders. These adjustments are not standards or suggested settings for every photo; I just experimented by dragging the sliders, and when the photo looked better, I stopped dragging. When the black-and-white photo looks good to you (good contrast and good shadow and highlight details), click OK in the Levels dialog.

Step Ten:
To complete your conversion, go to the Layers palette, click on the More flyout menu, then choose Flatten Image to flatten the adjustment layers into the Background layer. Although your photo looks like a black-and-white photo, technically, it's still in RGB mode, so if you want a grayscale file, go under the Image menu, under Mode, and choose Grayscale.

Before (lame grayscale conversion)

After (awesome adjustment layers conversion)

Exposure: 1/250   Focal Length: 70mm   Aperture Value: ƒ/4.0

The Big Fixx
digital camera image problems

Okay, did you catch that reference to the band The Fixx in the title? You did? Great. That means that you're at least in your mid-30s to early 40s. (I myself am only in my mid- to early 20s, but I listen to oldies stations just to keep in touch with baby boomers and other people who at one time or another tried to break-dance.) Well, The Fixx had a big hit in the early '80s (around the time I was born) called "One Thing Leads to Another" and that's a totally appropriate title for this chapter because one thing (using a digital camera) leads to another (having to deal with things like digital noise, color aliasing, and other nasties that pop up when you've finally kicked the film habit and gone totally digital). Admittedly, some of the problems we bring upon ourselves (like leaving the lens cap on; or forgetting to bring our camera to the shoot, where the shoot is, or who hired us; or we immersed our flash into a tub of Jell-O, you know—the standard stuff). And other things are problems caused by the hardware itself (the slave won't fire when it's submerged in Jell-O, you got some Camembert on the lens, etc.). Whatever the problem, and regardless of whose fault it is, problems are going to happen, and you're going to need to fix them in Elements. Some of the fixes are easy, like running the "Remove Camembert" filter, and then changing the blend mode to Fromage. Others will have you jumping through some major Elements hoops, but fear not, the problems you'll most likely run into are all covered here in a step-by-step format that will have you wiping cold, congealed water off your flash unit faster than you can say, "How can Scott possibly be in his mid-20s?"

Compensating for "Too Much Flash" or Overexposure

Don't ya hate it when you open a photo and realize that (a) the flash fired when it shouldn't have; (b) you were too close to the subject to use the flash and it's totally "blown out"; or (c) you're simply not qualified to use a flash at all, and your flash unit should be forcibly taken from you, even if that means ripping it from the camera body? Here's a quick fix to get your photo back from the "flash graveyard" while keeping your reputation, and camera parts, intact.

Step One:

Open the photo that is suffering from "flashaphobia," meaning the entire subject is washed out. Make a copy of the photo layer by dragging-and-dropping your Background layer on the Create a New Layer icon at the top of the Layers palette. This will create a layer titled "Background copy."

Step Two:

Next, change the layer blend mode of the Background copy from Normal to Multiply from the pop-up menu at the top left of the Layers palette. This blend mode has a "multiplier" effect and brings back a lot of the original detail the flash "blew out."

Step Three:
If the photo still looks washed out, you may need to make duplicates of the Background copy layer. Just press Control-J a few times to duplicate this layer. These additional copies of the Background copy layer will already be in Multiply mode.

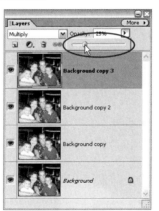

TIP: Incidentally, because of the immutable laws of life, chances are that creating one layer with its blend mode set to Multiply won't be enough, but adding another layer (in Multiply mode) will be "too much." If that's the case, just go to the Layers palette and lower the Opacity setting of the top layer to 50% or less—this way, you can "dial in" just the right amount of flash.

Before

After

Removing Digital Noise

If you're shooting in a low-lighting situation or shooting with a high ISO, chances are you're going to get some amount of "digital noise" (also referred to as "color aliasing"). You generally can't remove all this noise, but you usually can reduce it—and Elements has a feature to help you do just that. However, remember this is one of those "the-cheaper-the-digital-camera-the-more-noise-it-creates" situations, so if you're shooting with an "el cheapo" digital camera, this is a technique you'll be using a lot.

Step One:
Open the photo that was taken in low lighting (or using a high ISO setting) and has visible digital noise. This noise will be most obvious when viewed at a magnification of 100% or higher. *Note:* If you view your photos at smaller sizes, you may not notice the noise until you make your prints.

©SCOTT KELBY

Step Two:
Go under the Filter menu, under Noise, and choose Reduce Noise. The default settings really aren't too bad, but if you're having a lot of color aliasing (dots or splotchy areas of red, green, and blue), drag the Reduce Color Noise slider to the right (try 65% and see how that works).

Step Three:
One thing to watch out for when using this filter is that although it can reduce noise, it can also make your photo a bit blurry, and the higher the Strength setting and the higher the amount of Reduce Color Noise, the blurrier your photo will become. If the noise is really bad, you may prefer a bit of blur to an incredibly noisy photo, so you'll have to make the call as to how much blurring is acceptable, but to soften the noise a bit, drag the Preserve Details slider to the right.

TIP: To see an instant before/after of the Reduce Noise filter's effect on your photo without clicking the OK button, click your cursor within the Reduce Noise's preview window. When you click-and-hold within that window, you'll see the before version without the filter (zoom in if you need to). When you release the mouse, you'll see how the photo will look if you click the OK button.

Before: Although it's difficult to see, look for the digital noise along the side of the ship.

After: Noise removed using a slight blur from the Reduce Noise filter.

Focusing Light with Digital Dodging and Burning

If you've ever used Elements' Dodge and Burn tools, you already know how lame they are. That's why the pros choose this method instead—it gives them a level of control that the Dodge and Burn tools just don't offer, and best of all, it doesn't "bruise the pixels." (That's digital retoucher-speak for "it doesn't mess up your original image data while you're editing.")

Step One:
In this tutorial, we're going to dodge areas to add some highlights, then we're going to burn in the background a bit to darken some of those areas. Start by opening the photo you want to dodge and burn.

Step Two:
Go to the Layers palette, and from the More flyout menu choose New Layer (or just Alt-click on the Create a New Layer icon). This accesses the New Layer dialog, which is needed for this technique to work.

Step Three:
In the New Layer dialog, change the Mode to Overlay, then right below it, choose "Fill with Overlay-neutral color (50% gray)." This is normally grayed out, but when you switch to Overlay mode, this choice becomes available. Click the check-box to make it active, then click OK.

Step Four:
This creates a new layer, filled with 50% gray, above your Background layer. (When you fill a layer with 50% gray and change the Mode to Overlay, Elements ignores the color. You'll see a gray thumbnail in the Layers palette, but the layer will appear transparent in your image window.)

Step Five:
Press B to switch to the Brush tool, and choose a medium, soft-edged brush in the Brush Picker (which opens when you click the Brush thumbnail in the Options Bar). While in the Options Bar, lower the Opacity to approximately 30%.

Continued

Step Six:

Press D then X to set your Foreground color to white. Begin painting over the areas that you want to highlight (dodge). As you paint, you'll see white strokes appear in the thumbnail of your gray transparent layer, and in the image window you'll see soft highlights.

Step Seven:

If your first stab at dodging isn't as intense as you'd like, just release the mouse button, click again, and paint over the same area. Since you're dodging at a low opacity, the highlights will "build up" as you paint over previous strokes. If the highlights appear too intense, just go to the Layers palette and lower the Opacity setting until they blend in.

Step Eight:

If there are areas you want to darken (burn) so they're less prominent (such as the background), just press D to switch your Foreground color to black and begin painting in those areas. Okay, ready for another dodging-and-burning method? Good, 'cause I've got a great one.

Alternate Technique:

Open the photo that you want to dodge and burn, then just click the Create a New Layer icon in the Layers palette and change the blend mode in the Layers palette to Soft Light. Now, set white as your Foreground color and you can dodge right on this layer using the Brush tool set to 30% Opacity. To burn, just as before—switch to black. The dodging and burning using this Soft Light layer appears a bit softer and milder than the previous technique, so you should definitely try both to see which one you prefer.

Before

After

Opening Up Shadow Areas That Are Too Dark

If you have a problem with your photo, there's a pretty good chance it's in the shadow areas. Either you shot the photo with the light source behind the subject, or the lighting in the room put part of the subject in the shadows, or...well...you just messed up (hey, it happens). Luckily, you can open up just the shadows by moving one simple slider. Of course, you have to know where to look.

Step One:
Open the photo that needs to have its shadow areas opened up to reveal detail that was "lost in the shadows."

Step Two:
Go under the Enhance menu, under Adjust Lighting, and choose Shadows/ Highlights. When the dialog appears, it already assumes you have a shadow problem (sadly, most people do but never admit it), so it automatically opens up the shadow areas in your document by 25% (you'll see that the Lighten Shadows slider is at 25% by default [0% is no lightening of the shadows]). If you want to open up the shadow areas even more, drag the Lighten Shadows slider to the right. If the shadows appear to be opened too much with the default 25% increase, drag the slider to the left to a setting below 25%. When the shadows look right, click OK. Your repair is complete.

Before

After

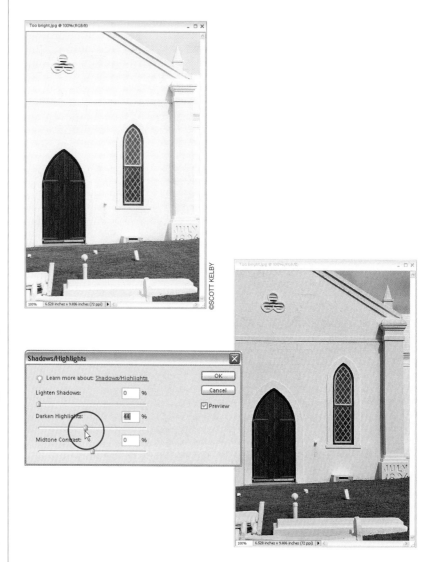

Fixing Areas That Are Too Bright

Although most of the lighting problems you'll encounter are in the shadow areas of your photos, you'll be surprised how many times there's an area that is too bright (perhaps an area that's lit with harsh, direct sunlight, or you exposed for the foreground but the background is now overexposed). Luckily, this is now an easy fix, too!

Step One:
Open the photo that has highlights that you want to tone down a bit. *Note:* If it's an individual area (like the sun shining directly on your subject's hair), you'll want to press the L key to switch to the Lasso tool and put a loose selection around that area. Then go under the Select menu and choose Feather. For low-res, 72-ppi images, enter 2 pixels and click OK. For high-res, 300-ppi images, try 8 pixels.

Step Two:
Now go under the Enhance menu, under Adjust Lighting, and choose Shadows/Highlights. When the dialog appears, drag the Lighten Shadows slider to 0% and drag the Darken Highlights slider to the right, and as you do, the highlights will decrease, bringing back detail and balancing the overall tone of your (selected) highlights with the rest of your photo. Sometimes when you make adjustments to the highlights (or shadows), you can lose some of the contrast in the midtone areas (they can become muddy or flat looking, or they can become oversaturated). If that happens, drag the Midtone Contrast slider (at the bottom of the dialog) to the right to increase the amount of midtone contrast, or drag to the left to reduce it. Then click OK. *Note:* If you made a selection, you'll need to press Control-D to deselect when you're finished.

Before

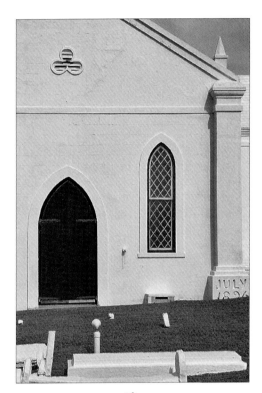

After

Fixing Photos Where You Wish You Hadn't Used the Flash

There's a natural tendency for some photographers to react to their immediate surroundings, rather than what they see through the lens. For example, at an indoor concert, there are often hundreds of lights illuminating the stage. However, some photographers think it's one light short—their flash—because where they're sitting, it's dark. When they look at their photos later, they see that the flash lit everyone in front of them (which wasn't the way it really looked—the crowd is usually in the dark), ruining an otherwise great shot. Here's a quick fix to make it look as if the flash never fired at all.

Step One:
Open a photo where shooting with the flash has ruined part of the image.

Step Two:
Press the letter L to get the Lasso tool, and draw a loose selection around the area where the flash affected the shot.

Step Three:

In the next step, we're going to adjust the tonal range of this selected area, but we don't want that adjustment to appear obvious. We'll need to soften the edges of our selection quite a bit so our adjustment blends in smoothly with the rest of the photo. To do this, go under the Select menu and choose Feather. When the Feather Selection dialog appears, enter 25 pixels to soften the selection edge. (By the way, 25 pixels is just my guess for how much the selection might need. The rule of thumb is the higher the resolution of the image, the more feathering you'll need, so don't be afraid to use more than 25 if your edge is visible when you finish.) Click OK.

Step Four:

It will help you make a better adjustment if you hide the selection border (I call it "the marching ants") from view. We don't want to deselect—we want our selection to remain intact—but we don't want to see the annoying border, so press Control-H to hide the selection border. Now, press Control-L to bring up the Levels dialog. At the bottom of the dialog, drag the right Output Levels slider to the left to darken your selected area. Because you've hidden the selection border, it should be very easy to match the selected area to its surroundings when you drag this slider to the left.

Continued

Step Five:

When the photo looks about right, click OK to apply your Levels adjustment. Then, press Control-H to make your selection visible again (this trips up a lot of people who, since they don't see the selection anymore, forget it's there, and then nothing reacts as it should from that point on). So now press Control-D to deselect and view your repaired "flash-free" photo.

Before

After

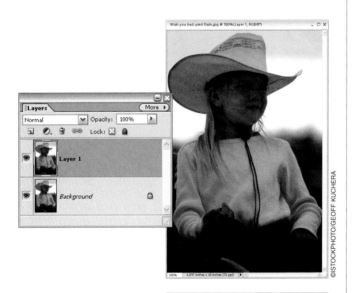

Wouldn't it be great if Elements had a "Fill Flash" brush, so when you forgot to use your fill flash, you could just paint it in? Well, although it's not technically called the Fill Flash brush, you can use a brush to achieve the same effect. I predict you'll like this technique. Hey, it's just a prediction.

When You Forget to Use Fill Flash

Step One:
Open a photo where the subject of the image appears too dark. Make a copy of the Background layer by pressing Control-J. This will create a layer titled "Layer 1."

Step Two:
Go under the Enhance menu, under Adjust Lighting, and choose Levels. Drag the middle Input Levels slider (the gray one) to the left until your subject looks properly exposed. (*Note:* Don't worry about how the background looks—it will probably become completely blown out, but you'll fix that later—for now, just focus on making your subject look right.) If the midtones slider doesn't bring out the subject enough, you may have to increase the highlights as well, so drag the far-right Input Levels slider to the left to increase the highlights. When your subject looks properly exposed, click OK.

Continued

Step Three:

Hold the Control key and click on the Create a New Layer icon at the top of the Layers palette. This creates a new blank layer beneath your duplicate layer. In the Layers palette, click on the top layer (Layer 1), then press Control-G to group this photo layer with the blank layer beneath it. This removes the brightening of the photo from Step 2.

Step Four:

In the Layers palette, click on the blank layer beneath your grouped, top layer. Press B to switch to the Brush tool and click the Brush thumbnail in the Options Bar to open the Brush Picker, where you'll choose a soft-edged brush. Press D to set black as your Foreground color, and then begin to paint (on this blank layer) over the areas of the image that need a fill flash with your newly created "Fill Flash" brush. The areas you paint over will appear lighter, because you're "painting in" the lighter version of your image on this layer.

Step Five:
Continue painting until it looks as if you had used a fill flash. If the effect appears too intense, just lower the Opacity of the layer you're painting on by dragging the Opacity slider to the left in the Layers palette.

Before

After

Fixing Underexposed Photos

This is a tonal correction for people who don't like making tonal corrections (more than 60 million Americans suffer from the paralyzing fear of MTC [Making Tonal Corrections]). Since this technique requires no knowledge of tonal corrections (like using Levels), it's very popular; and even though it's incredibly simple to perform, it does a pretty incredible job of fixing underexposed photos.

Step One:
Open an underexposed photo that could've used either a fill flash or a better exposure setting.

Step Two:
Make a copy of the Background layer by pressing Control-J. This will create a layer titled "Layer 1." In the Layers palette, change the blend mode of this new layer from Normal to Screen to lighten the entire photo.

Step Three:
If the photo still isn't properly exposed, press Control-J again to duplicate this Screen layer, and keep duplicating it until the exposure looks about right (this may take a few layers, but don't be shy about it—keep going until it looks good).

Step Four:
There's a good chance that at some point you'll duplicate the Screen layer again and the image will look overexposed. What you need is "half a layer"—half as much lightening. Here's what to do: Lower the Opacity of your top layer to "dial in" the perfect amount of light, giving you something between the full intensity of the layer (at 100%) and no layer at all (at 0%). For half the intensity, try 50%. (Did I really even have to say that last line? Didn't think so.) Once the photo looks properly exposed, click the More flyout menu at the top right of the Layers palette and choose Flatten Image.

Before

After

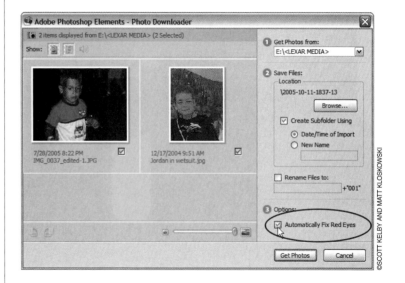

Automatic Red-Eye Removal

Photoshop Elements 4.0 brought some serious new red-eye removal features to the table by automating the entire process. Sure, you still have the old Red Eye Removal tool, but this might be even better, especially if you know in advance that you've got a lot of photos that need a red-eye fix (you shot photos of people in low-light situations using your on-camera flash). You can actually set up Elements 4.0 to automatically remove red eye as the images are imported into the Organizer, or you can do it on a case-by-case basis. Either way—life is good.

Step One:
First, we'll start with the fully automatic version, which you can use when you're importing photos into the Organizer. Here's how it works: When importing photos, the Adobe Photoshop Elements Photo Downloader dialog appears. On the right side of the dialog, under number 3 (Options), there's a checkbox for Automatically Fix Red Eyes. This checkbox (shown circled here) is on by default, so if you think some of the photos you're about to import will have red eye, just click the Get Photos button to start the importing—and the red-eye correction.

Step Two:
Once you click the Get Photos button, the Auto Red Eye Fix Photos dialog will appear, indicating how many photos are being "fixed." Then, it shows you a preview of which photos it determined have red eye as they're being corrected.

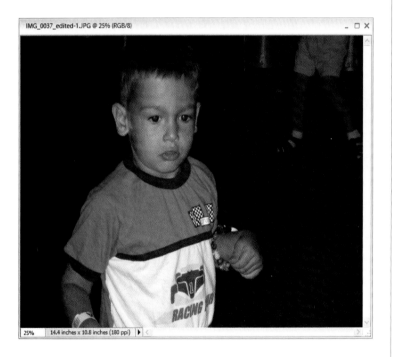

Step Three:
Once the process is complete, it gives you an onscreen report of how many it actually fixed, and it automatically groups the original with the fixed version (in a Version Set), so if you don't like the fix (for whatever reason), you still have the original. You can see both versions of the file by Right-clicking on the photo (in the Organizer) and in the contextual menu, under Version Set, choosing Reveal Items in Version Set.

Step Four:
Here is one of the photos with the red eye automatically removed.

Step Five:
This really isn't a step; it's another way to get an Auto Red Eye Fix, and that's by opening an image in the Editor or even in Quick Fix, and then going under the Enhance menu and choosing Auto Red Eye Fix. You can also use the keyboard shortcut Control-R. Either way, it senses where the red eye(s) is and removes it automatically. See, I told you life was good.

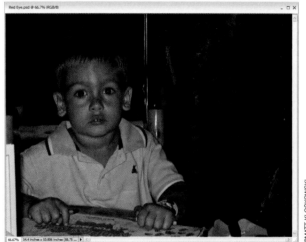

Instant Red-Eye Removal

When I see a digital camera with the flash mounted directly above the lens, I think, "Hey, there's an automated red-eye machine." In studio situations, you don't have to deal with this as much, because your flash probably wouldn't be mounted directly above your lens—you're using bounce flash, holding the flash separately, you've got studio strobes, or one of a dozen other techniques. Elements has had instant red-eye removal for a while now, but the red-eye removal in this version gives significantly better results.

Step One:
Open a photo where the subject has red eye.

Step Two:
Press Z to switch to the Zoom tool (it looks like a magnifying glass in the Toolbox) and drag out a selection around the eyes (this zooms you in on the eyes). Now, press the letter Y to switch to the Red Eye Removal tool (its Toolbox icon looks like an eye with a tiny crosshair cursor in the left corner). There are two different ways to use this tool: click or click-and-drag. We'll start with the most precise: which is click. Take the Red Eye Removal tool and click it once directly on the red area of the pupil. It will isolate the red in the pupil and replace it with a neutral color. Instead, now you have "gray" eye, which doesn't look spectacular, but it's a heck of a lot better than red eye.

Step Three:
If the gray color that replaces the red seems too "gray," you can adjust the darkness of the replacement color by going to the Options Bar and adjusting the Darken Amount. To get better results, you may have to adjust the Pupil Size setting so that the area affected by the tool matches the size of the pupil. This is also done in the Options Bar when you have the Red Eye Removal tool selected. Now, on to the other way to use this tool (for really quick red-eye fixes).

Step Four:
If you have a lot of photos to fix, you may opt for this quicker red-eye fix—just click-and-drag the Red Eye Removal tool over the eye area (putting a square selection around the entire eye). The tool will determine where the red eye is within your selected area (your cursor will change to a timer), and it removes the red. Use this "drag" method on one eye at a time for the best results.

Before

After

Removing Red Eye and Recoloring the Eye

This technique is a little more complicated (not hard, it just has a few more steps) but the result is more professional. After you remove the red eye and replace it with the more pleasing "gray eye" (like in the previous "Instant Red-Eye Removal" trick), you're going to restore the eye to its original color.

Step One:
Open a photo where the subject has red eye.

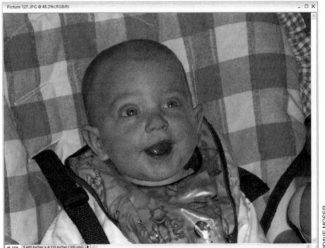

Step Two:
Zoom in close on one of the eyes using the Zoom tool (the magnifying glass, which you access by pressing the Z key). Use the technique shown on the previous pages, which removes the red eye and replaces it with "gray eye," then repeat this step on the second eye. *Note:* You might not want to do this late at night if you're home alone, because seeing a huge, scary eye on your screen can really give you the willies.

Step Three:
Press the L key to switch to the Lasso tool, and draw a very loose selection around one entire eye. The key word here is loose—stay well outside the iris itself, and don't try to make a precise selection. Selecting the eyelids, eyelashes, etc., will not create a problem. Once one eye is selected, hold the Shift key, and then use the Lasso tool to select the other eye in the same fashion (giving you both eyes as selections).

Step Four:
Once you have loose selections around both eyes, press Control-J to instantly copy-and-paste them onto a new layer in the Layers palette. This does two things: (1) It pastes the copied eyes on this layer in the exact same position as they are on the Background layer, and (2) it automatically deselects for you. Now you have just a pair of eyes on this layer.

Step Five:
While you're on this "eyes" layer, go under the Enhance menu, under Adjust Color, and choose Adjust Hue/Saturation. In the dialog, click on the Colorize checkbox (in the bottom right-hand corner). Now you can choose the color you'd like for the eyes by dragging the Hue slider. Don't worry about the color being too intense at this point; you can totally adjust that later. So if you want blue eyes, choose a deep blue and you'll "dial in" the exact shade later. Click OK to apply the color to the irises and the area around them as well. (Don't let this freak you out that other areas around the iris appear blue. We'll fix that in the next step.)

Continued

Step Six:

Press the E key to switch to the Eraser tool. Press D to make sure your Background color is white. Choose a small, hard-edged brush (from the Brush Picker up in the Options Bar), and then simply erase the extra areas around the iris. This sounds much harder than it is—it's actually very easy—just erase everything but the colored iris. Don't forget to erase over the whites of the person's eyes. Remember, the eyes are on their own layer, so you can't accidentally damage any other parts of the photo.

Step Seven:

If the eye color seems too intense (and chances are, it will), you can lower the intensity of the color by simply adjusting the opacity of this layer (using the Opacity slider in the upper right-hand corner of the Layers palette) until the eyes look natural.

Step Eight:
To finish the red-eye correction and recoloring, press Control-E to merge the colored eye layer with the Background layer, completing the repair.

Before

After

Repairing Keystoning

Keystoning is often found in photos with tall objects such as buildings, where the objects appear as if they're falling away from the viewer (giving the impression that the tops of these tall objects are narrower than their bases). Here's how to use Elements' Free Transform function, and one simple filter, to fix the problem fast.

Step One:
Open an image that has a keystoning problem, where a tall object seems to be leaning away from the viewer.

Step Two:
Make sure you're in Maximize Mode by going under the Window menu, under Images, and choosing Maximize Mode. Now we're going to create a guide that we can use to help us align our building. Click on the Foreground color swatch (at the bottom of the Toolbox) to bring up the Color Picker. In the R (red) field enter 74, for G (green) enter 132, and in the B (blue) field enter 244, then click OK to set your Foreground color to a light blue.

Step Three:
Switch to the Line tool (press U to cycle through the Shape tools until you get the Line tool). Go up in the Options Bar and set the Weight to 2 pixels. Then, hold the Shift key and draw a vertical, blue, 2-pixel line from the top of your image down to a corner at the base of your tall object. This will add a Shape layer in your Layers palette. (*Note:* If it's not positioned where you want it, you can drag it with the Move tool [V]. If this layer is locked, click on the Lock icon near the top center of the Layers palette to unlock it.) This blue line will act as your visual guide. Now, in the Layers palette, click back on the Background layer. Press Control-A to put a selection around your entire photo, and then press Control-Shift-J to cut your image from the Background layer and put it on its own separate layer.

Step Four:
With your image's layer active, press Control-T to bring up the Free Transform bounding box.

Step Five:
Go to the Options Bar and you'll see a grid that represents the bounding box around the photo. Click the bottom-center box so any transformation you apply will have the bottom center locked in place.

Continued

Step Six:
Hold Control-Alt-Shift and drag either the top-left and/or top-right corner points of the bounding box outward until the top corner of the object aligns with your guide.

Step Seven:
Making this correction can sometimes make your object look a bit "smushed" and "squatty" (my official technical terms), so release the Control-Alt-Shift keys, grab the top-center point, and drag upward to stretch the photo back out to fix the "squattyness" (another technical term).

Step Eight:
When your object looks right, press Enter to lock in your transformation. Now you can go to the Layers palette, click on your blue-line Shape layer, and drag it onto the Trash icon at the top of the Layers palette to delete it. Then click on your image's layer and press Control-E to merge your image layer with the Background layer. There's still one more thing you'll probably have to do to complete this repair job.

Step Nine:

If after making this adjustment the object looks "round" and "bloated," you can repair that problem by going under the Filter menu, under Distort, and choosing Pinch. Drag the Amount slider to 0%, and then slowly drag it to the right (increasing the amount of Pinch), while looking at the preview in the Pinch dialog, until you see the roundness and bloating go away. When it looks right, click OK to complete your keystoning repair.

Before: In the original photo, the building appears to be "falling away."

After: The same photo after repairing the keystoning and bloating.

Exposure: 1/800 Focal Length: 190mm Aperture Value: ƒ/4.8

The Mask
selection techniques

One of the problems with people is you can't always get them to stand in front of a white background so you can easily select them and place them on a different background in Elements 4.0. It's just not fair. If I were elected president, one of my first priorities would be to sign an executive order requiring all registered voters to carry with them a white, seamless roll at all times. Can you imagine how much easier life would be? For example, let's say you're a sports photographer and you're shooting an NFL *Monday Night Football* game with one of those Canon telephoto lenses that are longer than the underground tube for a particle accelerator; and just as the quarterback steps into the pocket to complete a pass, a fullback comes up from behind, quickly unfurls a white, seamless backdrop, and lets you take the shot. Do you know how fast you'd get a job at *Sports Illustrated*? Do you know how long I've waited to use "unfurl" in a sentence and actually use it in the proper context? Well, let's just say at least since I was 12 (three long years ago). In this chapter, you'll learn how to treat everyone, every object, every thing, as though it were shot on a white, seamless background.

Selecting Square, Rectangular, or Round Areas

Selections are an incredibly important part of working in Elements 4.0. That's because without them, everything you do, every filter you run, etc., would affect the entire photo. By being able to "select" a portion of your image, you can apply these effects only to the areas you want, giving you much greater control. Believe it or not, the most basic selections (squares, rectangles, circles, and ovals) are the ones you'll use the most, so we'll start with them.

Step One:
To make a rectangular selection, choose (big surprise) the Rectangular Marquee tool by pressing the M key. Adobe's word for selection is "marquee." (Why? Because calling it a marquee makes it more complicated than calling it what it really is—a selection tool—and giving tools complicated names is what Adobe does for fun.)

Step Two:
We're going to start by selecting a rectangle shape, so click your cursor in the upper left-hand corner of the left shutter and drag down and to the right until your selection covers the entire shape, then release the mouse button. That's it! You've got a selection, and anything you do now will affect only the area within that selected rectangle (in other words, it will only affect the green shutter on the left).

Step Three:
To add another area to your current selection, just press-and-hold the Shift key, and then draw another rectangular selection. In our example here, you'll want to select the shutter on the right side as well, so hold the Shift key, drag out a rectangle around it, and release the mouse button. Now both shutters are selected.

Step Four:
Now let's make an adjustment and you'll see that your adjustment will only affect your selected areas. Go under the Enhance menu, under Adjust Color, and choose Adjust Hue/Saturation. When the dialog appears, drag the Hue slider to the left (or right), and you'll see the color of the shutters change as you drag. More importantly, you'll see that nothing else changes color—just the shutters. This is why selections are so important—it's how you tell Elements you only want to adjust a specific area. To deselect (making your selection go away), just press Control-D.

Continued

Step Five:

Okay, you've got rectangles, but what if you want to make a perfectly square selection? It's easy—the tool works the same way—but before you drag out your selection, you'll want to hold the Shift key down. Let's try it: Open another image, get the Rectangular Marquee tool, hold the Shift key, and then draw a perfectly square selection (around the black area inside of this fake Polaroid frame, in this case).

Step Six:

While your selection is still in place, open a photo that you'd like to appear inside your selected area and press Control-A (this is the shortcut for Select All, which puts a selection around your entire photo at once). Then press Control-C to copy that photo into Elements' memory.

Step Seven:

Switch back to the Polaroid image, and you'll notice that your selection is still in place. Go under the Edit menu and choose Paste Into Selection. The image held in memory will appear pasted inside your square selection. If the photo is larger than the square you pasted it into, you can reposition the photo by just clicking-and-dragging it around inside your selected opening with the Move tool (V).

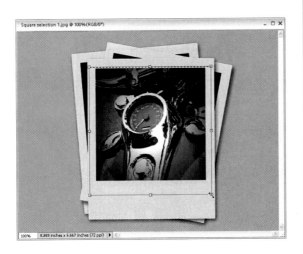

Step Eight:
You can also use Free Transform (press Control-T) to scale the pasted photo in size. Just grab a corner point, press-and-hold the Shift key, and drag inward or outward. When the size looks right, press the Enter key and you're done. (Well, sort of—you'll need to press Control-D to deselect, but only do this once you're satisfied with your image, because once you deselect, Elements flattens your new image into your Background layer, meaning there's no easy way to adjust this image.) Now, on to oval and circular selections...

Step Nine:
Open an image with a circle shape you want to select, and then press M to switch to the Elliptical Marquee tool (pressing M toggles you between the Rectangular and Elliptical Marquee tools by default). Now, just click-and-drag a selection around your circle. Press-and-hold the Shift key as you drag to make your selection perfectly round. If your round selection doesn't fit exactly, you can reposition it by moving your cursor inside the borders of your round selection and clicking-and-dragging to move it into position. If you want to start over, just press Control-D to deselect, and then drag out a new selection. *Hint:* With circles it helps if you start dragging before you reach the circle, so try starting about ¼" to the top left of the circle.

Continued

Step Ten:
We'll change the circle's color (like we did in the previous rectangle project), so go under the Enhance menu, under Adjust Color, and choose Adjust Hue/Saturation. Move the Hue slider to the right until it reads +111, which should give you a dark pink sign. Now press Control-D to deselect.

Step Eleven:
This isn't really a step; it's more of a recap: To make rectangles or ovals, you just grab the tool and start dragging. However, if you need to make a perfect square or a circle (rather than an oval), you hold the Shift key before you start dragging. You're starting to wish you'd paid attention in geometry class now, aren't you? No? Okay, me either.

If you've spent 15 or 20 minutes (or even longer) putting together an intricate selection, once you deselect it, it's gone. (Well, you might be able to get it back by choosing Reselect from the Select menu, as long as you haven't made any other selections in the meantime, but don't count on it. Ever.) Here's how to save your finely-honed selections and bring them back into place anytime you need them.

Saving Your Selections

Step One:
Open an image and then put a selection around an object in your photo using the tool of your choice. To save your selection once it's in place (so you can use it again later), go under the Select menu and choose Save Selection. This brings up the Save Selection dialog. Enter a name in the Name field and click OK to save your selection.

Step Two:
Now you can get that selection back (known as "reloading" by Elements wizards) at any time by going to the Select menu and choosing Load Selection. If you've saved more than one selection, they'll be listed in the Selection pop-up menu—just choose which one you want to "load" and click OK. The saved selection will appear in your image.

How to Select Things That Aren't Round, Square, or Rectangular

By now you know that selecting squares, rectangles, circles, ovals, etc., is a total no-brainer. But things get a little stickier when the area you want to select isn't square or rectangular or, well…you get the idea. Luckily, although it's not quite the no-brainer of the Marquee tools, making those selections isn't hard—if you don't mind being just a little patient. And making these "non-conformist" selections can actually be fun. Here's a quick project to get your feet wet:

Step One:
Open a photo with an odd-shaped object that's not rectangular, square, etc. This is what the Lasso tool was born for, so press the L key to access it from the Toolbox.

Step Two:
Click-and-hold the Lasso tool on the object you want to select (in this case, you'll be selecting my son's orange sweatshirt) and slowly (the key word here is *slowly*) drag the Lasso tool around the object, tracing its edges. If, after you're done, you've missed a spot, just hold the Shift key and click-and-drag around that missing area—it will be added to your selection. If you selected too much, hold the Alt key and click-and-drag around the area you shouldn't have selected.

Step Three:
When the object is fully selected, go under the Select menu and choose Feather (we're doing this to soften the edges of the selected area). Enter 2 pixels (just a slight bit of softening), and then click OK. Now that our edges are softened, we can make adjustments to the object without "getting caught."

Step Four:
In the example here, we're going to remove all the color from his sweatshirt, making it appear gray. Press Control-U to bring up the Adjust Hue/Saturation command. Drag the Saturation slider (the middle one) all the way to the left. This removes all the color, and when you do this, you'll quickly see if you made an accurate selection or not. If you see little slivers of orange, you missed those spots when you were doing your tracing with the Lasso tool. If you want to try again, just press Control-D to deselect, and then press Control-Z (undo) a few times until the original color comes back. Now you can try again, making sure you've got his entire sweatshirt accurately selected.

Step Five:
Click OK in the dialog and press Control-D to deselect. Remember, these adjustments affect only his sweatshirt, not the whole photo, because you selected it with the Lasso tool *before* you removed the color.

Softening Those Harsh Edges

When you make an adjustment to a selected area in a photo, your adjustment stays completely inside the selected area. That's great in many cases, but when you deselect, you'll see a hard edge around the area you adjusted, making the change look fairly obvious. However, softening those hard edges (thereby "hiding your tracks") is easy—here's how:

Step One:

Let's say you want to brighten the area around the lamp, so it looks almost like you shined a soft spotlight on it. Start by drawing an oval selection around the lamp using the Elliptical Marquee tool (press M until you have it). Make the selection big enough so the entire lamp and the surrounding area appear inside your selection. Now, we're going to darken the area around the lamp, so go under the Select menu and choose Inverse. This inverses the selection so you'll now have everything *but* the lamp selected (you'll use this trick often).

Step Two:

Now press Control-L to bring up Levels. When the dialog appears, drag the bottom right-hand Output slider to the left until it reads 140 and click OK. Now press Control-D to deselect. You can see the harsh edges around the oval, and it looks nothing like a soft spotlight—it looks like a bright oval. That's why we need to soften the edges so there's a smooth blend between the bright oval and the dark surroundings.

©SCOTT KELBY

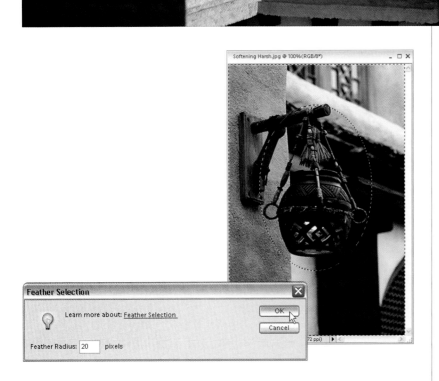

Step Three:

Press Control-D two times so your photo looks like it did at the end of Step 1 (your inversed selection should be in place—if not, drag out another oval and inverse it). With your selection in place, go under the Select menu and choose Feather. When the Feather Selection dialog appears, enter 20 pixels (the higher the number, the more softening effect on the edges) and click OK. That's it—you've softened the edges. Now, let's see what a difference that makes.

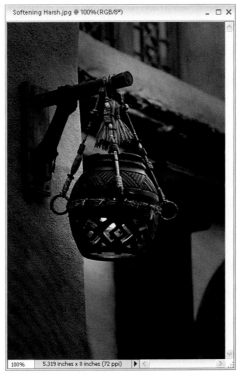

Step Four:

Press Control-L to bring up Levels again, drag the bottom-right Output slider to 140, and click OK. Deselect by pressing Control-D, and you can see that the edges of the area you adjusted are soft and blending together smoothly so it looks more like a spotlight. Now, this comes in really handy when you're doing things like adjusting somebody with a face that's too red. Without feathering the edges, you'd see a hard line around your person's face where you made your adjustments, and it would be a dead giveaway that the photo had been adjusted. But add a little bit of feather (with a face, it might only take a Feather amount or 2 or 3 pixels), and it will blend right in, hiding the fact that you made an adjustment at all.

Selecting Areas by Their Color

So, would you select an entire solid-blue sky using the Rectangular Marquee tool? You probably wouldn't. Oh, you might use a combination of the Lasso and Rectangular Marquee tools, but even then it could be somewhat of a nightmare (depending on the photo). That's where the Magic Wand tool comes in. It selects by ranges of color, so instead of clicking-and-dragging to make a selection, you click once and the Magic Wand selects things in your photo that are fairly similar in color to the area you clicked on. The Magic Wand tool is pretty amazing by itself, but you can make it work even better.

Step One:
Open a photo that has a solid-color area that you want to select (in this case, it's a red door). Start by choosing the Magic Wand tool from the Toolbox (or press the W key). Then, click it once in the solid-color area in your photo. You can see that much of the door is selected, but probably not all of it (because, although the door is red, there are all different shades of red on the door, caused by shadows and bevels. That's why this is such a good example—sometimes one click is all it takes and the whole object will be selected, but more often than not, you'll need to do a little more Magic Wanding to get the full door).

Step Two:
As you can see here, the first click didn't select the entire area (you can see all sorts of little rectangular areas that it missed), so to add these areas to what you already have selected, just press-and-hold the Shift key, and then click on those parts of the door that aren't selected. Keep holding down the Shift key and clicking on all the areas that you want to select until the entire door is selected (don't select the two door handles of course—just the red parts), as shown here. It took about 15 Shift-clicks with the Magic Wand for me to get this entire door selected.

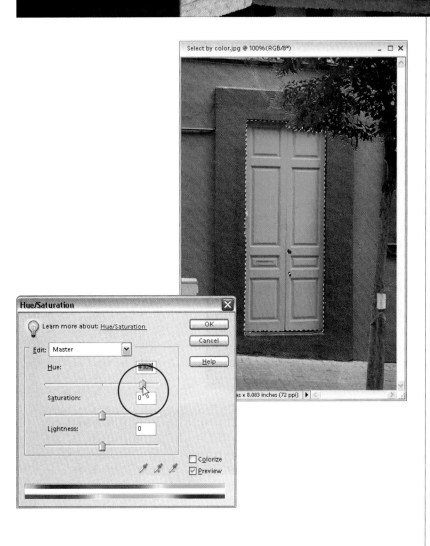

Step Three:
Now you can use the Adjust Hue/Saturation command (Control-U) to change the color of the door, just like you did in previous techniques, by dragging the Hue slider until the door looks the way you want it. Press Control-D to deselect and see your final change.

TIP: If you click in an area with the Magic Wand and not all of that area gets selected, then deselect (Control-D), go to the Options Bar, increase the Tolerance setting, and try again. The higher the setting, the wider the range of colors it will select; so as a rule of thumb: If the Magic Wand doesn't select enough, increase the Tolerance amount. If it selects too much, decrease it.

Making Selections Using a Brush

A lot of people are more comfortable using brushes than using Marquee tools. If you're one of those people (you know who you are), then you're in luck—you can make your selections by painting over the areas you want selected. Even if this sounds weird, it's worth a try—you might really like it (it's the same way with sushi). A major advantage of painting your selections is that you can choose a soft-edged brush (if you like) to automatically give you feathered edges. Here's how it works:

Step One:
Choose the Selection Brush tool from the Toolbox (press the A key). Before you start, you'll want to choose your brush size by clicking on the Brush thumbnail in the Options Bar to open the Brush Picker. If you want a soft-edged selection (roughly equivalent to a feathered selection), choose a soft-edged brush in the Picker or change your brush's Hardness setting in the Options Bar: 0% gives a very soft edge, while 100% creates a very hard edge.

Step Two:
Now you can click-and-drag to "paint" the area you want selected. When you release the mouse, the selection becomes active. *Note:* You don't have to hold down the Shift key to add to your selection when using this brush—just start painting somewhere else and it's added. However, you can press-and-hold the Alt key while painting to deselect areas.

Once you have one or more objects on a layer, putting a selection around everything on that layer is a one-click affair. What's especially great about this ability is that not only does it select the hard-edged areas in a layer, but it also selects the soft-edged areas, such as drop shadows. It'll make sense in a moment.

Selecting Everything on a Layer at Once!

Step One:
Open a layered image in which one layer contains elements you want to select and alter. To instantly put a selection around everything on that layer, just Control-click on that layer's thumbnail in the Layers palette (not its name; its thumbnail).

Step Two:
For one example of why you might want to do this, go to the top of the Layers palette while your selection is still in place and click the Create a New Layer icon. Now, choose a Foreground color and press Alt-Backspace to fill your selected area with that color. Next, change the blend mode of this new layer (at the top of the Layers palette) to Color, so now you have colored the layer's object(s). Lower the Opacity in the Layers palette to add a slight colored cast to your layer. Press Control-D to deselect.

Getting Elements to Help You Make Tricky Selections

If you've tried the Lasso tool for making selections, then you know two things: (1) It's pretty useful, and (2) tracing right along the edge of the object you're trying to select can be pretty tricky. But you can get help in the form of a tool called (are you ready for this?) the Magnetic Lasso tool! If the edges of the object you're trying to select are fairly well defined, this tool will automatically snap to the edges (as if they're magnetic), saving you time and frustration (well, it can save frustration if you know this technique).

Step One:
Click-and-hold for a moment on the Lasso tool in the Toolbox and a menu will pop up where you can choose the Magnetic Lasso tool (or just press the L key until you have it). Then, open an image in which you want to make a selection. Click once near the edge of the object you want to select. Without holding the mouse button, move the Magnetic Lasso tool along the edge of the object, and the selection will "snap" into place. Don't move too far away from the object; stay close to it for the best results.

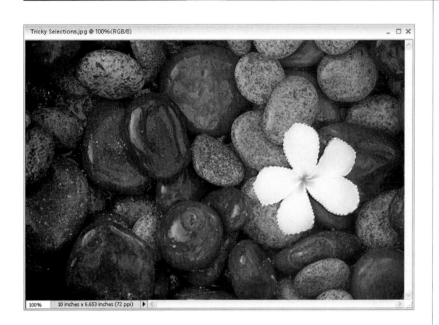

Step Two:
As you drag, the tool lays down little points along the edge. If you're dragging the mouse and it misses an edge, just press Backspace to remove the last point and try again. If it still misses, hold the Alt key and then hold down the mouse button, which temporarily switches you to the regular Lasso tool. Drag a Lasso selection around the trouble area, then release the Alt key and the mouse button, and BAM—you're back to the Magnetic Lasso tool to finish up the job. *Note:* You can also click the Magnetic Lasso tool to add selection points if needed.

Easier Selections with the Magic Selection Tool

This is another one of those tools Adobe added in Photoshop Elements 4.0 that makes you think, "What kind of math must be going on behind the scenes?" because this is some pretty potent mojo for selecting an object (or objects) within your photo. What makes this even more amazing is that I was able to inject the word "mojo" into this introduction, and you didn't blink an eye. You're one of "us" now…

Step One:
Open the photo that has an object you want to select (in this example, we want to select the phone booth). Go to the Toolbox and choose the Magic Selection Brush tool (or just press the F key).

Step Two:
By default, the Magic Selection Brush tool "paints" in red, and since the object we're trying to select is also red, we'd better choose a different color for our brush, so up in the Options Bar click on the down-facing arrow to the right of the Color swatch. A palette of colors will appear, so choose a color that will contrast well with what you're trying to select to make it easier to see.

Step Three:
Take the Magic Selection Brush tool and simply paint a "squiggly" line around what you want to select. You don't have to be precise, and that's what's so great about this tool—it digs squiggles. It *longs* for the squiggles. It *needs* squiggles. So squiggle.

Step Four:
Once you release the mouse button, the Magic Selection Brush makes your selection for you, based on the area that you squiggled over.

Step Five:
Now that we've got it selected, we might as well do something to it, eh? How about this: let's leave the phone booth red, and make the background black and white. You start by going under the Select menu and choosing Inverse (which inverses your selection so you've got everything selected but the phone booth). Go under the Enhance menu, under Adjust Color, and choose Remove Color. That's it. Now you can deselect by pressing Control-D.

Removing Backgrounds

One of the most requested selection tasks is how to remove something (or someone) from a background. Luckily, this task has been made dramatically easier in Elements 4.0 thanks to a fairly amazing tool called the Magic Selection Brush tool (and you know if they use the word "magic" it must be true, thanks to rigid enforcement of the truth in advertising laws).

Step One:
You'll find the Magic Selection Brush tool in the Toolbox (as you might expect) nested with the Selection Brush tool (or you can press F to get it).

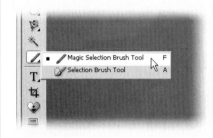

Step Two:
Here's how it works: Just take the brush and drag it over the object you want to select (in this case, I wanted the door and ornamental entry around it, so I dragged from the bottom-left corner diagonally to the top-right corner). The first time I tried it, it almost selected the entire object. The key word here is "almost." Sometimes, it does a perfect job (and the title "magic" is appropriate), and other times, well… magic might not come to mind, but more often than not, it really works wonders. Now, if you paint a line over an area, and it doesn't get the entire door, just hold the Shift key and paint over (or just click on) any area it missed the first time. So, be prepared to Shift-drag one or more lines to get the whole door.

Step Three:

Here the doorway is selected after just two little strokes (my initial stroke, then I held the Shift key and painted over the step on the bottom). *Hint:* You can paint a line, paint a squiggle (you know—a squiggle), or click with the tool, and it'll do the rest. Just don't freak out if it doesn't work perfectly the first time; take a deep breath, hold the Shift key, and paint another stroke. If it selects too much, just undo (Control-Z) and try a slightly different area to stroke.

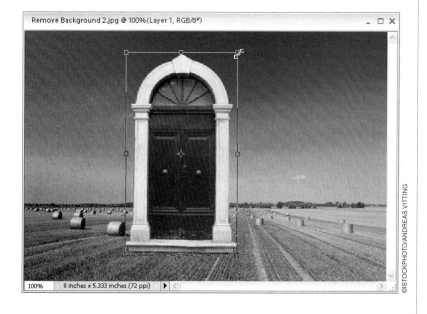

Step Four:

Well, now that we've got a selection, we might as well have some fun with it. Open a different image (in this case, a field with lots of blue sky), then go back to your selected door image (make sure you're in Cascade viewing mode by going under Window, under Images). Press V to get the Move tool, and drag your selected door right over onto the field photo. If the door is too big, press Control-T to bring up the Free Transform bounding box, then hold the Shift key, grab a corner handle, and drag inward to scale it down to size. Then press Enter to lock in your resizing. *Note:* If you can't see the corner handles, press Control-0 (zero).

Continued

©ISTOCKPHOTO/ANDREAS VITTING

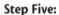

Step Five:
Press Control-J to duplicate your door layer (so now you have a door, then a duplicate right on top of it in the Layers palette). We're going to turn this duplicate into a cast shadow, and to do that we have to start by filling the duplicate door layer with black. So, press the letter D to set your Foreground color to black, and then press Alt-Shift-Backspace to fill your duplicate door with black.

Step Six:
Now we're going to turn this layer into a cast shadow. Start by pressing Control-T to bring up Free Transform again. When the Free Transform bounding box appears, press-and-hold the Control key, and then drag the top-center point down and to the right so the door looks like it's lying down. When it looks like the one shown here, press Enter to lock in your transformation.

Step Seven:
Go to the Layers palette and click-and-drag this shadow layer directly below the door layer, so the shadow appears behind the door (not in front of it).

Step Eight:
To soften the shadow (so the edges aren't so harsh), go under the Filter menu, under Blur, and choose Gaussian Blur. When the dialog appears, enter 4.0 for the Radius (the higher the number, the blurrier the edges will be), and then click OK.

Step Nine:
Your shadow is solid black, so to make it look more realistic, we're going to lower the Opacity so you can see through the shadow a bit. Go to the Layers palette, click on the shadow layer, and then lower the Opacity to around 65% (actually, you can choose any Opacity setting you want—if you want the shadow lighter, choose something less than 65%).

Continued

Step Ten:

Since you're a photographer, you've probably already noticed a problem. The entryway around the door looks "too red" for the surroundings, so we'll have to remove some red to make it look like the door is really in the field. Click on the door image layer in the Layers palette. Press Control-U to bring up the Adjust Hue/Saturation command. Up at the top in the Edit pop-up menu, choose Reds and then drag the Saturation slider almost all the way to the left. This removes the red from the photo, and the reddish entryway now looks white again. Click OK.

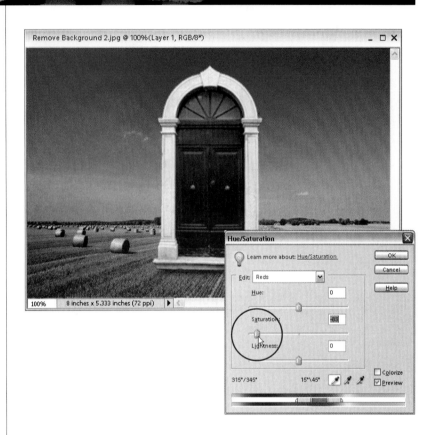

Step Eleven:

Here's the final image, and as I look at it now, I wish I had used only 3.0 or 2.5 for my Gaussian Blur on the shadow, because it looks a little too soft. But hey, that's just me.

Head Games
retouching portraits

This should be called "The Kevin Ames Chapter." Actually, it really should be called the "I Hate Kevin Ames Chapter" because I already had this entire chapter written, until I stopped by Kevin's studio in Atlanta one night to show him the rough draft of the book. What should have been a 15-minute visit went on until after midnight with him showing me some amazing portrait retouching tricks. So I had to go back home and basically rewrite, update, and tweak the entire chapter. Which, I can tell you, is no fun once you think a chapter is done and you're about a week from deadline. But the stuff he showed me was so cool, I literally couldn't sleep that night because I knew his techniques would take this chapter to the next level. And even though

Kevin was incredibly gracious to let me share his techniques with my readers (that's the kind of guy Kevin is), there was no real way I was going to name this chapter "The Kevin Ames Chapter." That's when it became clear to me—I would have to kill him. But then I remembered Kevin had mentioned that Jim DiVitale had developed some of the techniques that he had showed me, so now it was going to be a double murder. I thought, "Hey, they both live in Atlanta, how hard could this be?" but the more I thought about it, what with having to fly back up there and having to fly on Delta (stuffed in like human cattle), I figured I'd just give them the credit they deserve and go on with my life. Thus far, it's worked out okay.

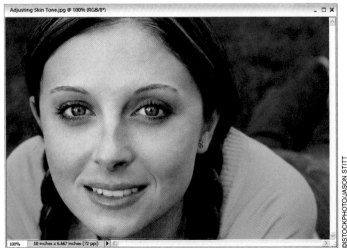

Quick Skin Tone Fix

In photos of people, the most important thing is that the skin tone looks good. That's because it's really hard for someone looking at your photo to determine if the grass is exactly the right shade of green or if the sky is the right shade of blue; but if the skin tone is off, it sticks out like a sore thumb (which would be red if it were really sore). Here's a quick fix to get your skin tones patched up in a hurry:

Step One:
Open an image in which the flesh tone looks like it needs adjusting. In the example shown here, the skin tone looks bluish and a little bit pale, so it definitely needs a fix to look right.

Step Two:
Go under the Enhance menu, under Adjust Color, and choose Adjust Color for Skin Tone.

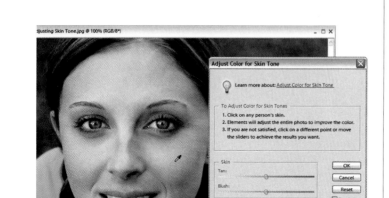

Step Three:
When the Adjust Color for Skin Tone dialog appears, move your cursor over an area of skin tone and click once to set the skin tone for the image. If you don't like your first results, click in a different area of skin tone until you find a skin-tone adjustment you're happy with.

Step Four:
You can also manually tweak the skin tone by using the Tan and Blush sliders, and you can control the overall tint of the light by dragging the Temperature slider to the left to make the skin tones cooler or to the right to make them warmer. *Note:* This skin-tone adjustment affects more than just skin—it usually warms the entire photo. If that creates a problem, use one of the selection tools (even the Lasso tool) to put a selection around the skin-tone areas first, add a 2-pixel Feather (under the Select menu), and then use the Adjust Color for Skin Tone command.

Before

After

Removing Blemishes

When it comes to removing blemishes, acne, or any other imperfections on the skin, our goal is to maintain as much of the original skin texture as possible. That way, our retouch doesn't look pasty and obvious. Here are three techniques I use that work nicely.

TECHNIQUE #1

Step One:
Open a photo containing some skin imperfections you want to remove.

Step Two:
Choose the Clone Stamp tool from the Toolbox (or press the S key). From the Brush Picker (which you access by clicking on the Brush thumbnail in the Options Bar), choose a soft-edged brush that's slightly larger than the blemish you want to remove.

TIP: Once you're working, if you need to quickly adjust the brush size, use the Bracket keys on your keyboard: the Left Bracket key ([) makes your brush smaller; the Right (]) larger.

Step Three:
In the Options Bar, change the Mode pop-up menu of the Clone Stamp tool to Lighten. With its Mode set to Lighten, the Clone Stamp will affect only pixels that are darker than the area you're going to sample. The lighter pixels (the regular flesh tone) will pretty much stay intact, and only the darker pixels (the blemish) will be affected.

Step Four:
Press the letter Z to access the Zoom tool and zoom in if needed, and then switch to the Clone Stamp tool. Find an area right near the blemish that's pretty clean (no visible spots, blemishes, etc.), hold the Alt key, and click once. The Clone Stamp will now sample the skin from that area. Try to make sure this sample area is very near the blemish so the skin tones will match. If you move too far away, you risk having your repair appear in a slightly different color, which is a dead giveaway of a repair.

Step Five:
Now, move your cursor directly over the blemish and click just once. Don't paint! Just click. The click will do it—it will remove the blemish instantly, while leaving the skin texture intact. But what if the blemish is lighter than the skin, rather than darker? Simply go to the Options Bar and change the Mode of the Clone Stamp tool to Darken instead of Lighten—it's that easy. On to Technique #2.

Continued

TECHNIQUE #2
Step One:
Press L to switch to the Lasso tool. Find a clean area (no blemishes, spots, etc.) near the blemish that you want to remove. In this clean area, use the Lasso tool to make a selection that is slightly larger than the blemish. (*Note:* If you make a mistake and need to add to your selection, press-and-hold the Shift key while selecting with the Lasso tool; if you need to remove parts of your selection, press-and-hold the Alt key.)

Step Two:
Once your selection is in place, go under the Select menu and choose Feather. When the Feather Selection dialog appears, enter 2 pixels as your Feather Radius and click OK. Feathering blurs the edges of our selected area, which will help hide the traces of our retouch. Feathering (softening) the edges of a selection is a very important part of facial retouching, and you'll do this quite a bit to "hide your tracks," so to speak.

Step Three:
Now that you've softened the edges of the selection, hold Control-Alt, and you'll see your cursor change into two arrowheads—a white one with a black one overlapping it. This is telling you that you're about to copy the selected area. Click within your selection and drag this clean skin area right over the blemish to completely cover it. When the clean area covers the blemish, release the keys (and the mouse button, of course) to drop this selected area down onto your photo. Now, press Control-D to deselect. The blemish is gone. Best of all, because you dragged skin over from a nearby area, the full skin texture is perfectly intact, making your repair nearly impossible to detect.

TECHNIQUE #3
Step One:
Get the Spot Healing Brush tool from the Toolbox (or just press the J key). We'll use it on the blemishes—and you'll see it works brilliantly.

Step Two:
Just click the tool in a clean area of skin, move over the blemish, and click once. That's it. You've got to love a technique that only has two steps.

Before

After, using all three techniques

Lessening Freckles or Facial Acne

This technique is popular with senior class portrait photographers who need to lessen or remove large areas of acne, pockmarks, or freckles from their subjects. This is especially useful when you have a lot of photos to retouch and don't have the time to use the methods shown previously, where you deal with each blemish individually.

Step One:

Open the photo that you need to retouch. Make a duplicate of the Background layer by going to the Layer menu, under New, and choosing Layer via Copy (or just press Control-J). We'll perform our retouch on this duplicate of the Background layer, named "Layer 1."

©ISTOCKPHOTO/KATERYNA GOVORUSHCHENKO

Step Two:

Go under the Filter menu, under Blur, and choose Gaussian Blur. When the Gaussian Blur dialog appears, drag the slider all the way to the left, then drag it slowly to the right until you see the freckles blurred away. The photo should look very blurry, but we'll fix that in just a minute, so don't let that throw you off—make sure it's blurry enough that the freckles are no longer visible. Click OK.

Step Three:
Hold the Control key and click once on the Create a New Layer icon at the top of the Layers palette. This creates a new blank layer (Layer 2) directly beneath your current layer (the blurry Layer 1).

Step Four:
Now, in the Layers palette, click back on the top layer (the blurry Layer 1), then press Control-G to group the blurry layer with the blank layer beneath it (Layer 2). Doing this removes all the blurriness from view (and that's exactly what we want to do at this point).

Step Five:
In the Layers palette, click on the middle layer (the blank Layer 2), as you're going to paint on this layer. Press the letter D to set your Foreground color to black. Press the letter B to switch to the Brush tool, then click on the Brush thumbnail in the Options Bar, and from the Brush Picker choose a soft-edged brush.

Continued

Step Six:
Lower the Opacity setting of your brush in the Options Bar to 50%, and change the Mode pop-up menu from Normal to Lighten. Now when you paint, it will affect only the pixels that are darker than the blurred state. Ahhh, do you see where this is going?

Step Seven:
Now you can paint over the freckle areas, and as you paint you'll see them diminish quite a bit. If they diminish too much, and the person looks "too clean," undo (Control-Z), then lower the Opacity of the brush to 25% and try again.

Before

After

Here's a quick technique for removing the dark circles that sometimes appear under a person's eyes—especially after a hard night of drinking. At least, that's what I've been told.

Removing Dark Circles under Eyes

Step One:
Open the photo that has the dark circles you want to lessen. Select the Clone Stamp tool in the Toolbox (or press the S key). Then, click on the Brush thumbnail in the Options Bar to open the Brush Picker and choose a soft-edged brush that's half as wide as the area you want to repair. *Note:* Press the letter Z to switch to the Zoom tool and zoom in if needed.

Step Two:
Go to the Options Bar and lower the Opacity of the Clone Stamp tool to 50%. Then, change the Mode pop-up menu to Lighten (so you'll only affect areas that are darker than where you'll sample from).

Continued

Step Three:
Press-and-hold the Alt key and click once in an area near the eye that isn't affected by the dark circles. If the cheeks aren't too rosy, you can click there, but more likely you'll click (sample) on an area just below the dark circles under the eyes.

Step Four:
Now, take the Clone Stamp tool and paint over the dark circles to lessen or remove them. It may take two or more strokes for the dark circles to pretty much disappear, so don't be afraid to go back over the same spot if the first stroke didn't work. *Note:* If you want the dark circles to completely disappear, try using the Healing Brush tool (J) from the Toolbox. Simply Alt-click the Healing Brush in a light area under the dark circles, and then paint the circles away.

Before

After

This is a great trick for removing wrinkles, with a little twist at the end (courtesy of my buddy Kevin Ames) that helps make the technique look more realistic. His little tweak makes a big difference because (depending on the age of the subject) removing every wrinkle would probably make the photo look obviously retouched (in other words, if you're retouching someone in their 70s and you make them look as if they're 20 years old, it's just going to look weird). Here's how to get a more realistic wrinkle removal:

Removing or Lessening Wrinkles

©ISTOCKPHOTO/OLGA VASILKOVA

Step One:
Open the photo that needs some wrinkles or crow's-feet lessened or removed.

Step Two:
Duplicate the Background layer by going to the Layer menu, under New, and choosing Layer via Copy (or press Control-J). You'll perform your "wrinkle removal" on this duplicate layer, named "Layer 1" in the Layers palette.

Step Three:
Get the Healing Brush tool from the Toolbox (or press the J key). Then, choose a soft-edged brush from the Brush Picker (which opens when you click the Brush thumbnail in the Options Bar). Choose a brush size that's close to the size of the wrinkles you want to remove.

Continued

Step Four:

Find a clean area that's somewhere near the wrinkles (perhaps the upper cheek if you're removing crow's-feet, or if you're removing forehead wrinkles, perhaps just above or below the wrinkle). Hold the Alt key and click once to sample the skin texture from that area. Now, take the Healing Brush tool and paint over the wrinkles. As you paint, the wrinkles will disappear, yet the texture and detail of the skin remains intact, which is why this tool is so amazing.

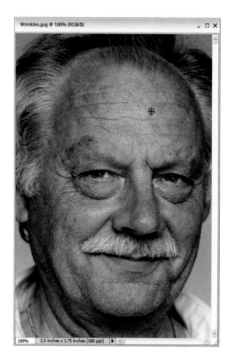

Step Five:

Now that the wrinkles are gone, it's time to bring just enough of them back to make it look realistic. Simply go to the Layers palette and reduce the Opacity of this layer to bring back some of the original wrinkles. This lets a small amount of the original photo (the Background layer, with all its wrinkles still intact) show through. Keep lowering the Opacity until you see the wrinkles, but not nearly as prominent as before.

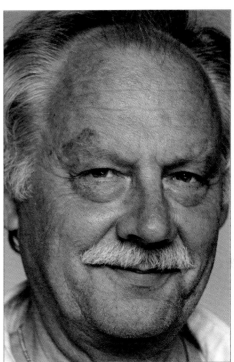

Before *After*

Whitening the Eyes

This is a great little technique for quickly whitening the whites of the eyes, and it has the added benefit of removing any redness in the eye along the way. *Note:* By redness, I mean the "bloodshot-I-stayed-up-too-late" type of redness, not the "red-eye-from-a-flash-mounted-above-the-lens" type of redness, which is addressed in Chapter 5.

Step One:
Open the photo where the subject's eyes need whitening. Press the letter Z to switch to the Zoom tool and zoom in if needed.

Step Two:
Choose the Lasso tool from the Toolbox (or press the L key) and draw a selection around one side of whites in one of the eyes. Press-and-hold the Shift key and draw selections around the other area of whites in the same eye and the whites of the other eye, until all the whites are selected in both eyes.

Step Three:
Go under the Select menu and choose Feather. You'll need to use Feather to soften the edges of your selection so your retouch isn't obvious. In the Feather Selection dialog, enter 2 pixels and click OK.

Step Four:
Go under the Enhance menu, under Adjust Color, and choose Adjust Hue/Saturation. When the Hue/Saturation dialog appears, choose Reds from the Edit pop-up menu at the top (to edit just the reds in the selection). Now, drag the Saturation slider to the left to lower the amount of saturation in the reds (which removes any bloodshot appearance in the whites of the eyes).

Step Five:
While you're still in the Hue/Saturation dialog, from the Edit menu switch back to Master. Drag the Lightness slider to the right to increase the lightness of the whites of the eyes. Click OK in the Hue/Saturation dialog to apply your adjustments, and then press Control-D to deselect and complete the enhancement.

Continued

Before   *After*

This is another one of those 30-second miracles for enhancing the eyes. This technique makes the eyes seem to sparkle by accentuating the catch lights, and generally draws attention to the eyes by making them look sharp and crisp (crisp in the "sharp and clean" sense, not crisp in the "I-burned-my-retina-while-looking-at-the-sun" sense).

Making Eyes that Sparkle

Step One:
Open the photo that you want to retouch. Make a duplicate of the Background layer by going under the Layer menu, under New, and choosing Layer via Copy (or press Control-J), which creates a new layer named "Layer 1." *Note:* Press the Z key to switch to the Zoom tool and zoom in if needed.

Step Two:
Go under the Filter menu, under Sharpen, and choose Unsharp Mask. (It sounds like this filter would make things blurry, but it's actually for sharpening photos.) When the Unsharp Mask dialog appears, enter your settings. (If you need some settings, go to the first technique, named "Basic Sharpening," in Chapter 11, or you can use my favorite all-around sharpening settings of Amount: 85%, Radius: 1, and Threshold: 4 for now.) Then click OK to sharpen the entire photo.

Continued

Step Three:

After you've applied the Unsharp Mask filter, apply it again using the same settings by pressing Control-F, and then apply it one more time using the same keyboard shortcut (you'll apply it three times in all). The eyes will probably look nice and crisp at this point, but the rest of the person will be severely oversharpened, and you'll probably see lots of noise and other unpleasant artifacts.

Step Four:

Hold the Control key and click once on the Create a New Layer icon at the top of the Layers palette. This creates a new blank layer directly beneath your sharpened layer. Now, in the Layers palette, click back on the top layer (the sharpened layer), then press Control-G to group the sharpened layer with the blank layer beneath it. This removes all the visible sharpness (at least for now). In the Layers palette, click on the middle layer (the blank layer), as you're going to paint on this layer.

Eyes that Sparkle.jpg @ 100%(Layer 2, RGB/8*)

Layers

Normal | Opacity: 100%

Lock:

Layer 1

Layer 2

Background

Step Five:
Press the letter D to set your Foreground color to black. Then, press B to switch to the Brush tool. Click on the Brush thumbnail in the Options Bar to open the Brush Picker, and choose a soft-edged brush that's a little smaller than your subject's eyes. Now paint over just the irises and pupils of the eyes to reveal the sharpening, making the eyes really sparkle and completing the effect.

Before

After

Enhancing Eyebrows and Eyelashes

Let's face it—not every face is perfect, so we sometimes resort to using makeup to enhance our facial features. So what happens when the model for your photo shoot forgets to wear mascara—or worse yet—has transparent eyebrows? Well, don't browbeat her (okay, that was lame)—just fix it in Elements.

Step One:
Open the photo that you want to enhance.

Step Two:
Go to the Layers palette and choose Levels from the Create Adjustment Layer pop-up menu (it's the half-white/half-black circle icon at the top of the palette).

Step Three:
When the Levels dialog appears, drag the shadow Input Levels slider to the right to darken the image. The entire image will darken, but don't worry, we'll fix that later—just focus on the eyebrows and eyelashes as you drag the slider. When the eyebrows and eyelashes look good to you, click OK.

Step Four:
Press the letter D to change your Foreground color to black. Then, press Alt-Backspace to fill your adjustment layer mask with black. This hides the Levels adjustment you just made, revealing your original Background layer.

Step Five:
Now, press the letter B to switch to the Brush tool. Click on the Brush thumbnail in the Options Bar and in the resulting Brush Picker choose a small, soft-edged brush that's the same size as the largest area of the eyebrows. Press the X key again to switch your Foreground color to white and begin painting over the eyebrows. As you get to smaller areas of the eyebrows, press the Left Bracket key ([) to decrease the size of your brush.

Continued

Step Six:

If the eyebrows are too dark, don't sweat it—we'll fix that later. Now let's move on to the eyelashes, so press the Left Bracket key ([) to decrease the size of your Brush tool. (You may have to press the Bracket key several times to make the brush the size of the eyelashes.)

Step Seven:

With your small Brush tool, lightly paint over the eyelashes on both eyes. *Note:* If needed, press the Z key to switch to the Zoom tool and zoom into the image for a better look. Then, press the B key to switch back to the Brush tool and begin painting.

Step Eight:
Now the effect may be too intense, so lower the Opacity in the Layers palette to around 65% or until the effect looks natural.

Before

After

Colorizing Hair

This technique (that I learned from Kevin Ames) gives you maximum control and flexibility while changing or adjusting hair color, and because of the use of an adjustment layer, you're not "bruising the pixels." Instead, you're following the enlightened path of "non-destructive retouching."

Step One:
Open the photo you want to retouch. Choose Hue/Saturation from the Create Adjustment Layer pop-up menu at the top of the Layers palette.

Step Two:
When the dialog appears, click on the Colorize checkbox (in the bottom right-hand corner of the dialog) and then drag the Hue slider to the approximate color you'd like for the hair. Doing this will colorize the entire image, but don't let that throw you—just focus on the hair color. You may also have to drag the Saturation slider to the right a bit to make the color more vibrant. Now, click OK and the entire photo will have a heavy color cast over it.

Step Three:
Press the letter D to change your Foreground color to black, and then press Alt-Backspace to fill the layer mask of the Hue/Saturation adjustment layer with black. Doing so removes the colorized tint from the photo.

Step Four:
Press B to switch to the Brush tool. Choose a soft-edged brush from the Brush Picker (by clicking on the Brush thumbnail in the Options Bar). Press X to set your Foreground color to white and begin painting over the hair. As you paint, the tint you added with Hue/Saturation is painted back in. Once the hair is fully painted, change the layer blend mode of your Hue/Saturation adjustment layer to Color, then lower the Opacity in the Layers palette until the hair color looks natural.

Before

After

Whitening and Brightening Teeth

This really should be called "Removing Yellowing, Then Whitening Teeth" because almost everyone has some yellowing, so we remove that first before we move on to the whitening process. This is a simple technique, but the results have a big impact on the overall look of the portrait, and that's why I do this to every single portrait where the subject is smiling.

Step One:
Open the photo you need to retouch. Press Z to switch to the Zoom tool and zoom in if needed.

Step Two:
Press L to switch to the Lasso tool, and carefully draw a selection around the teeth, being careful not to select any of the gums or lips. If you've missed a spot, press-and-hold Shift while using the Lasso tool to add to your selection, or press-and-hold Alt and drag the Lasso to remove parts of the selection.

Step Three:
Go under the Select menu and choose Feather. When the Feather Selection dialog appears, enter 1 pixel and click OK to smooth the edges of your selection. That way, you won't see a hard edge along the area you selected once you've whitened the teeth.

Step Four:
Go under the Enhance menu, under Adjust Color, and choose Adjust Hue/Saturation. When the dialog appears, choose Yellows from the Edit pop-up menu at the top. Then, drag the Saturation slider to the left to remove the yellowing from the teeth.

Continued

Step Five:

Now that the yellowing is removed, switch the Edit pop-up menu back to Master, and drag the Lightness slider to the right to whiten and brighten the teeth. Be careful not to drag it too far, or the retouch will be obvious. Click OK in the Hue/Saturation dialog and your enhancements will be applied. Press Control-D to deselect and see your finished retouch.

Before

After

If you've ever had to deal with hot spots (shiny areas on your subject's face caused by uneven lighting, or the flash reflecting off shiny surfaces, making your subject look as if they're sweating), you know they can be pretty tough to correct. That is, unless you know this trick.

Removing Hot Spots

Step One:
Open the photo that has hot spots that need to be toned down. Press the Z key to switch to the Zoom tool and zoom in if needed. Select the Clone Stamp tool in the Toolbox (or press the S key). Go to the Options Bar and change the Mode pop-up menu from Normal to Darken and lower the Opacity to 50%. By changing the Mode to Darken, we'll only affect pixels that are lighter than the area we're sampling, and those lighter pixels are the hot spots.

Continued

Step Two:
Choose a medium, soft-edged brush from the Brush Picker (found by clicking the Brush thumbnail in the Options Bar), then hold the Alt key and click once in a clean area of skin (an area with no hot spots). This will be your sample area, or reference point, so Elements knows to affect only pixels that are lighter than this.

Step Three:
Start gently painting over the hot spot areas with the Clone Stamp tool, and as you do, the hot spots will fade away.

Step Four:
As you work on different hot spots, you'll have to resample (Alt-click) on nearby areas of skin so the skin tone matches. For example, when you move on to another hot spot, sample an area of skin near the new hot spot that you'll be working on.

Step Five:
It's amazing what you can do in 60 seconds of hot-spot retouching using this technique. Notice how the hot spots are now gone as I paint them away. Much of this was done with brush strokes, but just clicking once or twice with the Clone Stamp tool (as I'm doing here) often works, too.

Before

After

Digital Nose Job

This is a very simple technique for decreasing the size of your subject's nose by 15% to 20%. The actual shrinking of the nose is a breeze and only takes a minute or two—you may spend a little bit of time cloning away the sides of the original nose, but since the new nose winds up on its own layer, it makes this cloning a lot easier. Here's how it's done:

Step One:
Open the photo that you want to retouch. Press the Z key to switch to the Zoom tool and zoom in if needed. Press L to switch to the Lasso tool, and draw a loose selection around your subject's nose. Make sure you don't make this selection too close or too precise—you need to capture some flesh-tone area around the nose as well.

Step Two:
To soften the edges of your selection, go under the Select menu and choose Feather. When the Feather Selection dialog appears, for Feather Radius enter 10 pixels (for high-res, 300-ppi images, enter 22 pixels), then click OK. Now, go under the Layer menu, under New, and choose Layer via Copy. This will copy just the selected area to a new layer (Layer 1).

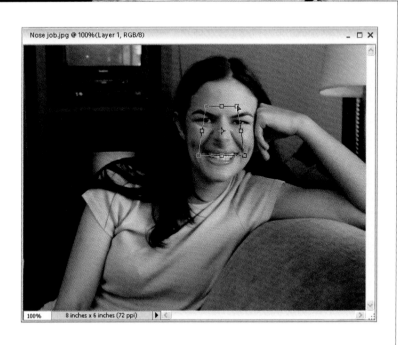

Step Three:
Press Control-T to bring up the Free Transform bounding box. Hold Control-Alt-Shift, then grab the upper right-hand corner point of the bounding box and drag inward to add a perspective effect to the nose. Doing this gives the person a pug nose, so release all the keys, then grab the top-center point and drag straight downward to undo the "pug effect" and make the nose look natural again, but now it's smaller.

Step Four:
When the new size looks about right, press Enter to lock in your changes. If any of the old nose peeks out from behind the new nose, go to the Layers palette, click on the Background layer, and then use the Clone Stamp tool (S) to clone away those areas: Sample an area next to the nose by Alt-clicking, and then clone right over the old nose, completing the effect.

Continued

Before   *After*

Transforming a Frown into a Smile

This is a pretty slick technique for taking a photo where the subject was frowning and tweaking it just a bit to add a pleasant smile—which can often save a photo that otherwise would've been ignored.

Step One:
Open the photo that you want to retouch.

Step Two:
Go under the Filter menu, under Distort, and choose Liquify. When the Liquify dialog appears, choose the Zoom tool (it looks like a magnifying glass) from the Liquify Toolbox (found along the left edge of the dialog). Click it once or twice within the preview window to zoom in closer on your subject's face. Then, choose the Warp tool (it's the top tool in the Liquify Toolbox).

Continued

Step Three:

In the Tool Options on the right side of the dialog, choose a brush size that's roughly the size of the person's cheek. Place the brush at the base of a cheek and click-and-"tug" slightly up. This tugging of the cheek makes the corner of the mouth turn up, creating a smile.

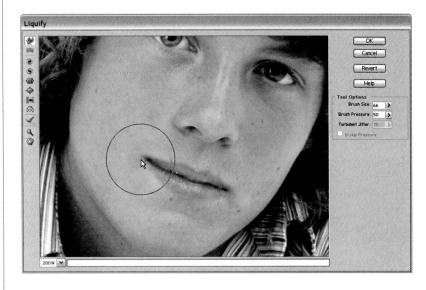

Step Four:

Repeat the "tug" on the opposite side of the mouth, using the already tugged side as a visual guide as to how far to tug. Be careful not to tug too far, or you'll turn your subject into the Joker from *Batman Returns*. Click OK in Liquify to apply the change, and the retouch is applied to your photo.

Before

After

Glamour Skin Softening

This is a technique I learned from Chicago-based retoucher David Cuerdon. David uses this technique in fashion and glamour photography to give skin a smooth, silky look, and it's also popular in shots of female seniors (not high school seniors—the other seniors).

Step One:
Open the photo to which you want to give the glamour skin-softening effect and duplicate the Background layer by going under the Layer menu, under New, and choosing Layer via Copy (or press Control-J).

©ISTOCKPHOTO/MATEUSZ ZAGORSKI

Step Two:
Go under the Filter menu, under Blur, and choose Gaussian Blur. When the dialog appears, enter from 3 to 6 pixels of blur (depending on how soft you want the skin) to put a blur over the entire photo. When it looks good to you, click OK in the dialog.

Step Three:
Next, lower the Opacity of this layer by 50%. At this point, the blurring effect is reduced and now the photo has a soft glow to it. In some cases, you may want to leave it at this, with an overall soft, glamorous effect (you sometimes see portraits of people over 60 with this overall softening), so your retouch is complete. If this is too much softening for your subject, go on to the next steps.

Step Four:
What really pulls this technique together is selectively bringing back details in some of the facial areas. Press E to switch to the Eraser tool, choose a soft-edged brush from the Brush Picker in the Options Bar, and erase over the facial areas that are supposed to have sharp detail, such as eyebrows, lips, and teeth. What you're doing is erasing the blurriness, and thereby revealing the original features on the Background layer beneath your blurry layer.

Continued

Step Five:

David completes his retouch at Step 4, leaving the subject's clothes, hair, etc., with the soft glow. I prefer to switch to a larger, soft-edged Eraser tool and erase over everything else except the skin—so I erase over the hair, the clothes, etc., so everything has sharp detail except the skin. This is totally a personal preference, so I recommend trying both and seeing which fits your particular needs.

Before

After

Slimming and Trimming

This is an incredibly popular technique because it consistently works so well, and because just about everyone would like to look about 10 to 15 pounds thinner. I've never applied this technique to a photo and (a) been caught, or (b) not had clients absolutely love the way they look. The most important part of this technique may be not telling the client you used it.

Step One:
Open the photo of the person that you want to put on a quick diet.

Step Two:
Maximize your view if needed by going under Window, under Images, and choosing Maximize Mode or click the Maximize button in the upper right-hand corner of the image window. Now, press Control-A to put a selection around the entire photo. Then, press Control-T to bring up the Free Transform command. The Free Transform handles will appear at the corners and sides of your photo.

Continued

Step Three:
Grab the right-center handle and drag it horizontally toward the left to slim the subject. The farther you drag, the slimmer the subject becomes.

Step Four:
How far is too far (in other words, how far can you drag before people start looking like they've been retouched)? Use the Width field in the Options Bar as a guide. You're pretty safe to drag inward to around 95%, although I've been known to go to 94% or even 93% once in a while (it depends on the photo).

Step Five:
Press Enter to lock in your transformation and press Control-D to deselect. Now that you've moved the image area over a bit, you'll have to use the Crop tool (C) to crop away the background area that is now visible on the right side of your photo. After you drag out your cropping border over your image, press the Enter key to complete your crop. You can see how effective this simple little trick is at slimming and trimming your subject. Also, notice that because we didn't drag too far, the subject still looks very natural.

Before   *After*

Removing Love Handles

This is a very handy body-sculpting technique, and you'll probably be surprised at how many times you'll wind up using it. It uses Liquify, which many people first dismissed as a "toy for giving people bug-eyes and huge lips," but it didn't take long for professional retouchers to see how powerful this tool could really be.

Step One:
Open the photo that has a love handle repair just waiting to happen.

Step Two:
Go under the Filter menu, under Distort, and choose Liquify. When the Liquify dialog appears, click on the Zoom tool in the Toolbox on the left-hand side of the dialog, and then drag out a selection around the area you want to work on to give you a close-up view for greater accuracy.

Step Three:

Get the Shift Pixels tool from Liquify's Toolbox (it's the seventh tool down or just press S). Choose a relatively small brush size using the Brush Size field near the top-right of the Liquify dialog. With it, paint an upward stroke starting just below and outside of the person's left love handle and continuing upward (as shown here). The pixels will shift back in toward the body, removing the love handle as you paint. (*Note:* When removing love handles on the person's right side, paint downward rather than upward. Why? That's just the way it works.) When you click OK, the love handle repair is complete, and you'll see the difference a quick 30-second retouch can make.

Before

After

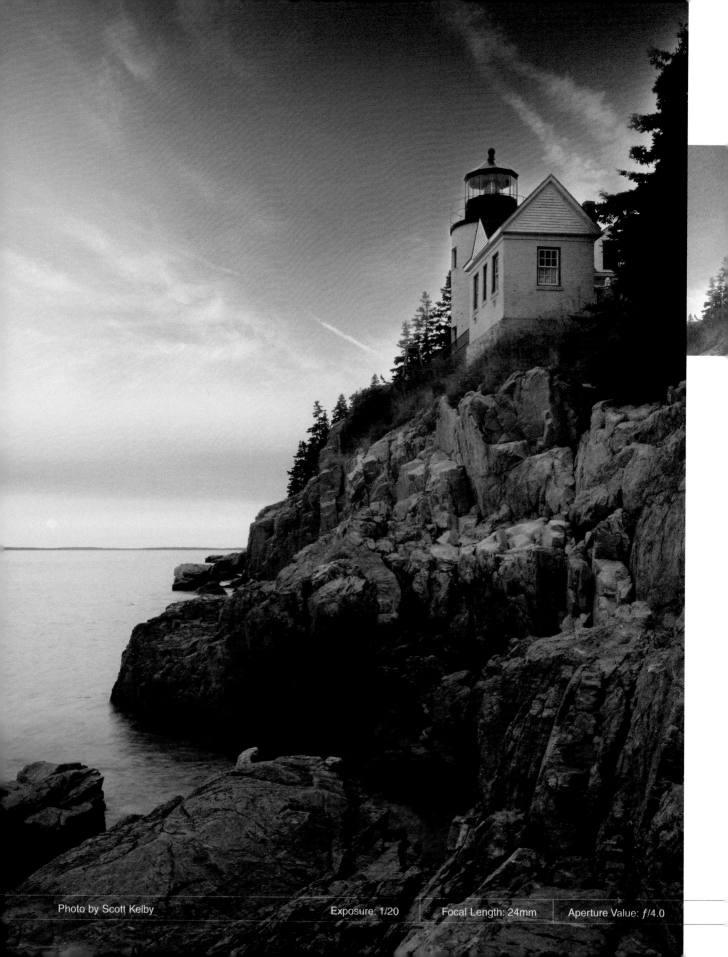

Photo by Scott Kelby

Exposure: 1/20   Focal Length: 24mm   Aperture Value: ƒ/4.0

Take Me Away
removing unwanted objects

Is "Take Me Away" a perfect title for a chapter about removing unwanted objects from your photos or what? I've heard the song (by Christina Vidal from Disney's *Freaky Friday* soundtrack) a couple of thousand times now, because my 8-year-old likes to listen to it (over and over again) on the way to school each morning. Not only have I unconsciously memorized the words, I've actually begun to like the song. It happened around the 13-hundredth time I heard it. By my 14-hundredth listen, I started developing my own background harmonies, and by the 15-hundredth time, I went out and bought the sheet music. This is highly embarrassing stuff, so don't tell any-one. Anyway, this chapter shows you how to remove things that ruin otherwise beautiful photos. For example, let's say you got married, and you've got some great photos from your wedding, but then a year or so later, you get divorced. You looked really great in your wed-ding dress, so you want to keep the photos, but you hate seeing your ex in there. Well, this chapter will show you how to remove him. Well, it doesn't show you exactly that—how to remove your ex from your wedding photos—but it does show you how to remove any annoying thing, so really you could apply these techniques to your wedding photos. But I gotta tell ya, if you spend your time removing your ex from your wedding photos, perhaps learning new Elements techniques shouldn't be your biggest concern.

Cloning Away Unwanted Objects

The Clone Stamp tool has been the tool of choice for removing distracting or other unwanted objects in photos for years now. Although the Healing Brush in many ways offers a better and more realistic alternative, there are certain situations where the Clone Stamp tool is still the best tool for the job. Here's an example of how this workhorse removes unwanted objects:

Step One:
Nothing ruins old-world charm like a screen-printed sign for a restaurant and a utility light from Home Depot. The stain on the street in front of the door doesn't kill the old-world charm that much, but it's distracting, and since we're going to remove the sign and the light (the three offending objects are circled here), we may as well fix the street at the same time, eh? Let's do it.

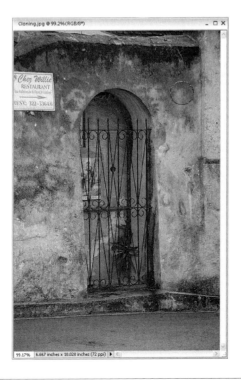

Step Two:
Press S to get the Clone Stamp tool. In the Options Bar, click on the Brush thumbnail to the left of the Size pop-up menu and choose a medium, soft-edged brush in the Picker. Now, hold the Alt key and click once in an area of wall just to the left of the light. This is called "sampling." You just sampled a wall area, and in the next step, you're going to clone that wall area over the light to completely cover it. (By the way, when you sample, a little "target" cursor appears letting you know you're sampling.)

Step Three:
Move directly to your right and begin painting with the Clone Stamp tool. As you paint over the light, the wall you sampled is cloned right over it, so it looks like the light has disappeared. Paint a little in this area to get a feel for how the Clone Stamp works (at least, if it's your first time cloning; if it's not, then you know what to do—start cloning over that light). As you can see here, that light is now gone! The key technique to remember is to sample in an area where the basic light and texture are the same (to the left of the wall), then move straight over to the object. *Note:* The little plus-sign cursor (the area where you sampled) is just to the immediate left of the target cursor (where you're painting now). By keeping them side-by-side, you're making sure you don't pick up patterns or colors from other parts of the photo that would make your cloning look obvious.

Continued

Step Four:

Now, we're going to clone over the sign, and to do that, start by Alt-clicking in an area that has similar tone and texture as the sign. In the example shown here, I Alt-clicked on the right side of the door (near where the light used to be) because both sides of the wall have a similar texture. Normally, you'd Alt-click next to the sign, but in this case, you can get away with Alt-clicking farther away.

Step Five:

Look at the plus-sign cursor (on the right side of the door). That's where I sampled, and now you can start painting over the sign to clone over it (as shown on the left), but it's important to understand why you have to sample from an area that has similar color and texture. For example, try this: Alt-click on the bottom-right side of the door (near the ground), then go up and start cloning over the sign. Look how much lighter (and obvious) the cloning looks (as shown on the right). That's why you usually have to sample very close to where you clone. If not, it's a dead giveaway.

TIP: One of the tricks to removing objects realistically is to sample often (by Alt-clicking) in different but nearby areas so that your cloning appears random, therefore avoiding repeating patterns.

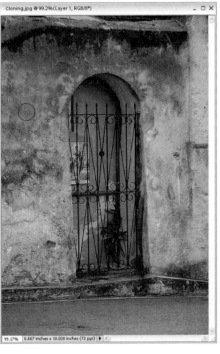

Step Six:
In the example shown here, I've chosen a different spot and Alt-clicked. Then, I started cloning away more of the sign. During the process of removing something as large as the sign, you may want to Alt-click in slightly different areas three or four times, so your cloning looks natural and random. Just keep in mind that wherever you Alt-click, make sure the tone and texture are the same as the area you're cloning into (in other words, it should look the same as the area that currently surrounds the sign).

Step Seven:
Alt-click the Clone Stamp tool in the street to the right of the stains, then paint right over the stains in the street. The clean area of the street that you sampled will hide the stains in the street, completing the technique.

Continued

Before

After

This is an incredibly handy little trick I learned from Rich Harris, who contributes some great tutorials to our magazine, *Photoshop User* (www.photoshopuser.com), and I've found no better way to clone away objects that need to be straight (like horizons, walls, etc.). Thanks to Rich for sharing this technique with us.

Removing Things in a Straight Line

Step One:
Open your image, and then press S to get the Clone Stamp tool. Now press-and-hold the Alt key, and take a look at your cursor (shown here enlarged in the white box). See the horizontal and vertical lines inside the circle? That's the key. You must position the cursor's center "target" line (either horizontal or vertical) on the straight edge that you want to clone in your image (in this case, the horizontal edge of a building). With the Alt key held down, click once when the target (called the "sample cursor") is aligned on the edge in your image.

Step Two:
Drag directly to the right while pressing-and-holding the Alt key, but don't click. With this key held down, align the sample cursor's horizontal center line along the edge in your image.

Continued

Step Three:

With the horizontal line positioned along the edge in your photo, release the Alt key and start cloning. As you clone, paint along the same straight line. It's all about making sure that the cursor's horizontal line is aligned with the edge in your image *before* you start painting.

If there are just one or two annoying things that are messing up your otherwise lovely photo, here's a quick way to get rid of them while maintaining maximum texture and authenticity (because you're using another part of the photo to cover what you don't want visible, so the grain, texture, and well—everything—is right on the money).

Covering Unwanted Elements

©SCOTT KELBY

Step One:
In this example, we have another charming "old-world" door, but the "6" house number pulls the charming "old-world" feel right out of the photo. So...the number has to go. We could use the Clone Stamp tool, but this method makes the removal perfect because you're actually going to cover the "6" with a chunk of the wall close to it, which is an even more realistic fix and is as fast as, if not faster than, the alternative.

Step Two:
Press Z to get the Zoom tool and zoom in on the area with the offensive number. (I bet they got that at Euro-Home Depot.) Now press M to get the Rectangular Marquee tool, and drag out a selection around the "6."

Continued

Step Three:

Click within the selection and drag it directly to the right of the number, so your selection is on the white wall space. You'll need to put a feather on your selection so the edges will be soft and blend in perfectly, hiding the fact that you did anything to the photo at all. So, go under the Select menu and choose Feather. When the Feather Selection dialog appears, enter 1-3 pixels (depending on your percentage of zoom) for the Feather Radius and click OK.

Step Four:

Pressing-and-holding the Alt and Control keys, drag the selected area to the right of the "6." This makes a copy of the selected area, so you're really dragging along a copy of the rectangular chunk of the wall. That area fits perfectly over the number (it fits perfectly because you first created that selection by dragging it over the number, remember?). By the way, you won't see any harsh edges to give you away because you feathered those edges in the previous step.

Before

After

Step Five:
Now, when you press Control-D to deselect, the number will be gone, and your removal will be right on the money. Here's a before and after. You can see what a difference removing that one little area made. I went one step further and zoomed in on the sign in the top-right corner. Then, using the same technique, I removed the sign using chunks of surrounding wall. That way, I removed any hint to the possibility that an area was "cloned."

TIP: If you press-and-hold Alt-Control and the Shift key, your selected area will remain perfectly in line as you drag. Also, you may want to Alt-drag several copies of your selection to cover your object or hide any repeating patterns.

Step Six:
Here's another application of the same technique. On the right side of the photo there's a distracting building, and the easiest fix (without re-cropping and shrinking the width of the photo) is to extend the sky to cover the building. Get the Rectangular Marquee tool, draw a tall, thin rectangular selection around some of the sky, and then feather your selection (under the Select menu).

Before   *After*

Removing Spots and Other Artifacts

In Elements 3.0, Adobe added the Spot Healing Brush tool, which is just about the perfect tool for getting rid of spots and other artifacts. (By the way, the term "artifacts" is a fancy "ten-dollar" word for spots and other junk that wind up in your photos.) Believe it or not, it's even faster and easier to use than the regular Healing Brush, because it's pretty much a one-trick pony—it fixes spots.

Step One:
Open a photo that has spots (whether they're in the scene itself or are courtesy of specks or dust on either your lens or your camera's sensors). In the photo shown here, there are all sorts of distracting little white spots on the building and in the sky.

Step Two:
Press Z to get the Zoom tool and zoom in on an area with lots of spots (in this case, I zoomed in on the top left-hand corner of the image). Now get the Spot Healing Brush tool from the Toolbox (or just press the letter J).

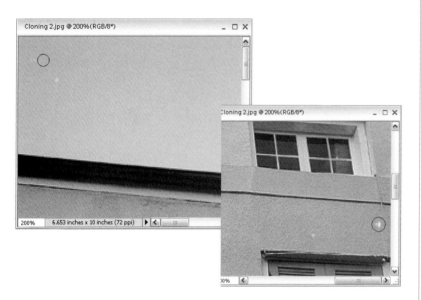

Step Three:
Position the Spot Healing Brush directly over the spot you want to remove and click once. That's it—you don't have to sample an area or Alt-click anywhere first—you just move it over the spot and click—the spot is gone.

Step Four:
You remove other spots the same way— just position the Spot Healing Brush over them and click. I know it sounds too easy, but that's the way it works. So, just move around and start clicking away on the spots. Now you can "de-spot" any photo, getting a "spotless" version in about 30 seconds, thanks to the Spot Healing Brush.

Before

After

Removing Distracting Objects (Healing Brush)

The Healing Brush is ideal for removing spots, little rips, stains, and stuff like that because it keeps more of the original texture and the fixes look more realistic, but it isn't as good as the Clone Stamp tool at removing larger, unwanted objects. For example, if the thing you want to remove is all by itself (it's not overlapping or touching anything else in your photo), then it works great. If not, it "frays" the ends and looks messy. So you'll see how it works, why it doesn't always work, and a great trick for making it work most of the time (with some help from the Clone Stamp tool).

Step One:

In this photo, the distracting object (to me anyway) is the gutter running down the top-right side of the building. So, we're going to use a combination of the Healing Brush and a little bit of the Clone Stamp tool to remove that gutter, while maintaining as much of the original texture and grain as possible.

Step Two:

First we'll look at how the Healing Brush works, and then you'll see what the limitation of the Healing Brush is. Start by pressing Z to get the Zoom tool and zoom into an area you want to remove (in this case, we're going to remove a little spot on the building that appears to the left of the drain). Press J until you get the Healing Brush, and then Alt-click in an area near that spot. At this stage, the Healing Brush works kind of like the regular Clone Stamp tool, so click-and-drag over that little spot. See, it's gone. Piece of cake so far.

Step Three:
Now you're going to find the main limitation of the Healing Brush—and that's when objects touch. Look at the drain pipe. See how the bottom of the pipe touches the roof of the white building? That's trouble. Go ahead and Alt-click near that intersection and try to use the Healing Brush to remove the bottom of the gutter. Ahh, now you see the problem: Where the edge of the gutter meets the rest of the building, it's all smudged. As bad as it looks here, believe it or not, this is pretty mild compared to what often happens when the area you're patching isn't isolated. The Healing Brush only gives you a clean removal if you can paint around the entire object without hitting an edge.

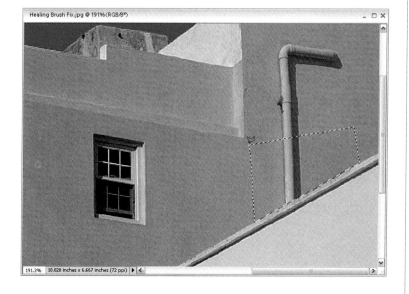

Step Four:
Undo your healing by pressing Control-Z. Now we'll try getting around that limitation: The first thing we want to do is make sure we don't accidentally remove any part of the white roof, so get the Polygonal Lasso tool (press L until you have it). You're going to use it to box in the area with a selection, which will protect your roof because you can only clone inside your selected area. This tool draws straight-line selections, so click it four times to draw a box like the one shown here around the drain pipe.

Continued

Step Five:

Press S to get the Clone Stamp tool from the Toolbox, and then Alt-click once just to the left of the gutter. Now paint a stroke right over the drain pipe to remove it. In the example here, the plus-sign cursor shows where I sampled, and the circular brush cursor shows where I've painted over the gutter. Having that selection in place prevents you from accidentally cloning over any of the white roof, because you can only clone inside the selected area.

Step Six:

Once you've cloned over enough area so the drain pipe is no longer touching the roof, you can press Control-D to deselect. You'll see the bottom of the gutter has been removed, but without all the smudging, thanks to using the Clone Stamp tool.

Step Seven:
Now switch back to the Healing Brush (as shown in the Toolbox), and Alt-click next to the window (unlike the Clone Stamp tool, you don't have to Alt-click right next to the area where you'll be healing—just pick a spot, any spot, that has a similar texture).

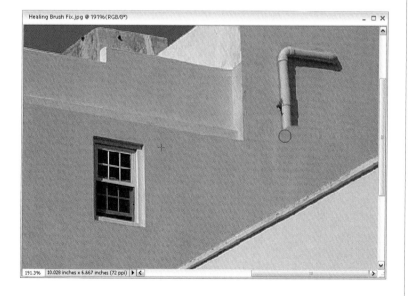

Step Eight:
Begin painting over the gutter to remove it. Don't let it throw you off that the tone looks a bit funny as you're painting. The final healing doesn't take place until you release the mouse button, so there's a second or two where your healing looks bad, but just be patient for a moment.

Continued

Step Nine:
If you can't get the gutter in just one stroke—don't sweat it. Just Alt-click in a different area (again, I'd try somewhere near the window), and paint another stroke until the entire gutter has been removed. So, in short, if you don't mind using the Clone Stamp just a little bit, you can turn the Healing Brush into a real tool for removing larger, unwanted objects.

Before

After

Exposure: 1/500 | Focal Length: 34mm | Aperture Value: ƒ/4.0

38 Special
photographic special effects

This is where the fun begins. Okay, I don't want to discount all the immeasurable fun you've had up to this point, but now it gets really fun. This is where we get to play around in Elements and change reality, and then send the client an invoice for our "playtime." Did the model wear a blouse that was the wrong color? No sweat, change it in Elements. Was it an overcast day when you shot the exterior of your client's house? Just drop in a new sky. Do you want to alter a photo to make it look like you shot it with a soft focus filter on your lens? Now you can do it digitally. Do you want to take your income to the next level? Just shoot a crisp shot of a $20 bill, retouch it a bit, print out a few hundred sheets on your color laser printer and head for Vegas. (Okay, forget that last one, but you get the idea.) This is where the rubber meets the road, where the nose gets put to the grindstone, where the meat meets the potatoes... (Where the meat meets the potatoes? Hey, it's late.)

Creating Drama with a Soft Spotlight

This is a great technique that lets you focus attention by using dramatic soft lighting. The technique I'm showing you here I learned from famous nature photographer Vincent Versace. I had been getting a similar look by filling a layer with black, making an oval selection, feathering the edges significantly, and then knocking a hole out of the layer (as you'll see in the next technique), but Vincent's technique, using the Lighting Effects filter, is so much easier that it's just about all I use now.

Step One:
Open the RGB photo to which you want to apply the soft spotlight effect. In this example, I want to focus attention on the flowers in the center by darkening the area around them. Next, press Control-J to duplicate the Background layer.

Step Two:
Go under the Filter menu, under Render, and choose Lighting Effects. I have to tell you, if you haven't used this filter before, it's probably because its interface (with all its sliders) looks so complex, but luckily there are built-in presets (Adobe calls them "Styles") that you can choose from, so you can pretty much ignore all those sliders. Once you ignore the sliders, the filter is much less intimidating, and you can really have some fun here. The small preview window on the left side of the dialog shows you the default setting, which is a large oval light coming from the bottom right-hand corner.

Step Three:
For this effect, we're going to use a very soft, narrow beam, so go under the Style pop-up menu at the top of the dialog (this is where the presets are) and choose Flashlight.

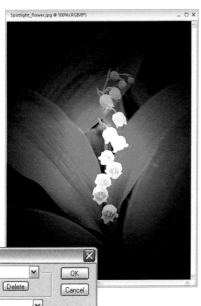

Step Four:
Once you choose Flashlight, look at the preview window and you'll see a small spotlight in the center of your image. Click on the center point (inside the circle) and drag the light into the position where you want it. If you want the circle of light a little bit larger, just click on one of the side points and drag outward. When you click OK, the filter applies the effect, darkening the surrounding area and creating the soft spotlight effect you see here.

Continued

Step Five:

If the Lighting Effect filter seems too intense, you can remedy it immediately after the fact by dragging the Opacity slider in the Layers palette to the left to reduce the effect of the filter. The farther you drag, the less the intensity of the effect. Then, while in the Layers palette, change the blend mode of this layer to Darken, so the flashlight effect doesn't make the colors seem too saturated.

Before

After

If you want to focus attention on something within your image, applying a wide vignette that acts like a soft light is a great way to do this (which is really an alternative to the previous tutorial). What you're really doing is creating a dark border that will burn in the edges of your image. Here's how to do just that:

Burned-In Edge Effect (Vignetting)

Step One:
Open the photo to which you want to apply a burned-in edge effect. Just so you know, what we're doing here is focusing attention through the use of light—we're burning in all the edges of the photo (not just the corners, like lens vignetting, which I usually try to avoid), leaving the visual focus in the center of the image.

Step Two:
Go to the Layers palette and add a new layer by clicking on the Create a New Layer icon at the top of the palette. Press the letter D to set your Foreground color to black, and then fill your new layer with black by pressing Alt-Backspace.

Continued

Step Three:

Press M to get the Rectangular Marquee tool and drag a selection about 1" inside the edges of your photo. Then, to greatly soften the edges of your selection, go under the Select menu and choose Feather. When the dialog appears, enter 50 pixels for a low-res photo (or 170 pixels for a high-res, 300-ppi photo), and click OK.

Step Four:

Now that your edges have been softened, all you have to do is press Backspace, and you'll knock a soft hole out of your black layer, revealing the photo on the Background layer beneath it. Now press Control-D to deselect. *Note:* If the edges seem too dark, you can go to the Layers palette and lower the Opacity of your black layer (in the example shown here, I lowered the Opacity to around 80%).

Before

After

Using Color for Emphasis

This is a popular technique for focusing attention by the use of color (or really, it's more like the use of less color—if everything's in black and white, anything that's in color will immediately draw the viewer's eye). As popular as this technique is, it's absolutely a breeze to create. Here's how:

Step One:
Open a photo containing an object you want to emphasize through the use of color. Go under the Layer menu, under New, and choose Layer via Copy (or just press Control-J). This will duplicate the Background layer onto its own layer (Layer 1).

Step Two:
Press B to get the Brush tool from the Toolbox and choose a medium, soft-edged brush from the Brush Picker in the Options Bar (just click on the arrow next to the Brush thumbnail to open the Picker). Also in the Options Bar, change the Mode pop-up menu to Color for the Brush tool.

Step Three:

Set your Foreground color to black by pressing the letter D and begin painting on the photo. As you paint, the color in the photo will be removed. The goal is to paint away the color from all the areas *except* the areas you want emphasized with color.

TIP: If you make a mistake while painting away the color or later decide that there was something else that you really wanted to keep in color (such as the stem wrapping or necklace in this example), just switch to the Eraser tool by pressing the E key, paint over the "mistake" area, and the original color will return as you paint. (What you're really doing here is erasing part of the top layer, which is now mostly black and white, and as you erase, it reveals the original layer, which is still in full color.)

Before

After

Soft Focus Effect

This is a quick way to emulate the effect of a soft focus filter on your lens. Besides being quick and easy, what I like about this effect is the soft glow it gives your images. Try this technique on a sharp photo of some trees and you'll love what it does for the image.

Step One:
Open the photo to which you want to apply a soft focus effect. Duplicate the Background layer by pressing Control-J. By default, this duplicate layer is named Layer 1.

Step Two:
Go under the Filter menu, under Blur, and choose Gaussian Blur. For low-res images, enter about 6–10 pixels (for high-res images, try 20 pixels instead) and click OK.

Step Three:

That amount of Gaussian Blur will blur the entire image so much that it'll be hard to see any detail. So, to bring back the detail, go to the Layers palette and lower the Opacity setting of this blurred layer to 50%. Lowering the Opacity setting allows the detail to come back, but along with it comes a soft glow that gives the image a dreamy, almost painted look, which completes the effect.

Before

After

Changing an Object's Color

Have you ever wanted to change the color of an object (such as a shirt, a car, etc.) in a photo? You have? Then here's perhaps the fastest, easiest way to change the color of, well…whatever.

Step One:

Open a photo containing an element that needs to be a different color.

Step Two:

Choose the Color Replacement tool, which is found in the Brush tool's flyout menu in the Toolbox (or press the B key until you have it).

TIP: You can adjust the Color Replacement tool's settings by going to the Options Bar, clicking the down-facing arrow next to the word "Brush," and choosing your settings in the Picker that appears.

Step Three:
Open another image that has the color you want to use. Alt-click the Color Replacement tool on the color you want to sample within that image. (In this example, I'm sampling the color from another truck.) Your cursor will temporarily switch to the Eyedropper tool.

Continued

Step Four:

Now return to the photo you want to colorize and start painting with the Color Replacement tool using the sampled color, completing the effect. *Hint:* If you make a mistake, just press Control-Z to undo and try again.

Before

After

When shooting outdoors, there's one thing you just can't count on—the sun. Yet, you surely don't want to take a photo of your house on a dreary day, or shoot a photo of your car on a gray overcast day. That's why it's so important to have the ability to replace a gloomy gray sky with a bright sunny sky. Is it cheating? Yes. Is it easy? You betcha. Do people do it every day? Of course.

Replacing the Sky

Step One:
Open the photo that needs a new, brighter, bluer sky.

Step Two:
You have to make a selection around the sky. Usually, you can click in the sky area with the Magic Wand tool (W) to select most of it, and then choose Similar from the Select menu to select the rest of the sky—but as usual, it likely selected other parts of the image besides just the sky. So use the Lasso tool (L) while holding the Alt key to deselect any excess selected areas on your image. If needed, hold the Shift key while using the Lasso tool to add any unselected areas of the sky. You can use any combination of selection tools you'd like—the key is to select the entire sky area.

Continued

Step Three:

Shoot some nice blue skies and keep them handy for projects like this, or steal a sky from another photo. Simply open one of those "blue sky" shots, and then go under the Select menu and choose All to select the entire photo, or use the Wand or Lasso tools as you did in the previous step to select just the sky you want. Then, press Control-C to copy this sky photo into memory.

Step Four:

Switch back to your original photo (the selection should still be in place). Create a new layer by clicking on the Create a New Layer icon at the top of the Layers palette, then go under the Edit menu and choose Paste Into Selection. The new sky will be pasted into the selected area in your new layer, appearing over the old sky. Press Control-D to deselect.

Step Five:
If the sky seems too bright for the photo, simply lower the Opacity of the layer in the Layers palette to help it blend in better with the rest of the photo. That's it—newer, bluer sky.

Before

After

Neutral Density Gradient Filter

One of the most popular lens filters for outdoor photographers is the Neutral Density filter, because often (especially when shooting scenery, like sunsets) you wind up with a bright sky and a dark foreground. A Neutral Density gradient lens filter reduces the exposure in the sky by a stop or two, while leaving the ground unchanged (the top of the filter is gray, and it graduates down to transparent at the bottom). Well, if you forgot to use your ND gradient filter when you took the shot, you can create your own ND effect in Photoshop Elements.

Step One:
Open the photo (preferably a landscape) where you exposed for the ground, which left the sky too light. Press the letter D to set your Foreground color to black. Then, go to the Layers palette and choose Gradient from the Create Adjustment Layer pop-up menu (it's the half-white/half-black circle icon) at the top of the palette.

Step Two:
When the Gradient Fill dialog appears, click on the little, black downward-facing arrow (it's immediately to the right of the Gradient thumbnail) to bring up the Gradient Picker. Double-click on the second gradient in the list, which is the gradient that goes from Foreground to Transparent. Don't click OK yet.

Step Three:
By default, this puts a dark area on the ground (rather than the sky), so click on the Reverse checkbox to reverse the gradient, putting the dark area of your gradient over the sky and the transparent part over the land. Your image will look pretty awful at this point, but you'll fix that in the next step, so just click OK.

Step Four:
To make this gradient blend in with your photo, go to the Layers palette and change the blend mode of this adjustment layer from Normal to Overlay. This darkens the sky, but it gradually lightens until it reaches land, and then it slowly disappears. So, how does it know where the ground is? It doesn't. It puts a gradient across your entire photo, so in the next step, you'll basically show it where the ground is.

Continued

Step Five:

In the Layers palette, double-click on the thumbnail for the Gradient Fill adjustment layer to bring up the Gradient Fill dialog again. To control how far down the darkening will extend from the top of your photo, just click once on the Gradient thumbnail at the top of the dialog. This brings up the Gradient Editor. Grab the top-right white color stop above the gradient ramp near the center of the dialog and drag the color stop to the left; the darkening will "roll up" from the bottom of your photo, so keep dragging to the left until only the sky is affected, and then click OK in the Editor.

Step Six:

By default, the gradient you choose fills the entire image area, smoothly transitioning from a dark gray at the top center to transparent at the very bottom. It's a smooth, "soft-step" gradient. However, if you want a quicker change from black to transparent (a hard step between the two), you can lower the Scale amount in the Gradient Fill dialog.

Step Seven:
Also, if the photo you're working on doesn't have a perfectly straight horizon line, you also might have to use the Angle control by clicking on the line in the center of the Angle circle and dragging slowly in the direction that your horizon is tilted. This literally rotates your gradient, which enables you to have your gradient easily match the angle of your horizon. When it looks good to you, click OK to complete the effect.

Before: Exposing for the ground makes the sky too light.

After: The ground is the same, but the sky is now bluer and more intense.

Putting One Photo Inside Another

Putting a photo inside another is a fairly popular collaging technique. But in the technique you're going to do here, you'll realistically put one image inside another, matching the angles of the photo. Here's how it's done:

Step One:
Open the photo that you want to put inside another photo. Press Control-A to put a selection around your entire photo, then press Control-C to copy that photo into memory. Next, open the image that you want the copied photo to appear within.

Step Two:
Press the L key until you get the Polygonal Lasso tool from the Toolbox (this tool draws perfectly straight selections; if your object doesn't have straight sides, use another selection tool to create a selection within your image's object). Click the Polygonal Lasso tool once on the bottom-left corner of your object, and then move your cursor up to the top-left corner and click again (a straight line is drawn between your two clicks). Keep clicking at each corner until you have all sides of the object selected (as shown here).

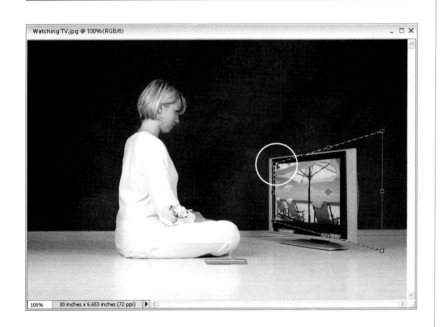

Step Three:
Now go under the Edit menu and choose Paste Into Selection, and the photo you had in memory will be pasted into your selection. Then press Control-D to deselect. But there's a problem—the object is likely angled and your photo probably isn't, so it looks fake. Here's how to fix it: Press Control-T to bring up the Free Transform command. Hold the Control key, grab the bottom-left corner point, and move it to where it touches the bottom-left corner of your object. You'll do the same with the other corners—dragging each one to the corresponding corner of your object.

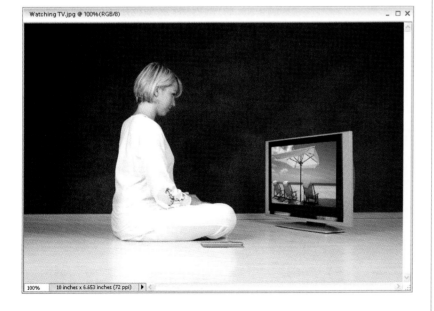

Step Four:
When all four corners are lined up, and your photo has been transformed to fit perfectly within the object, press Enter to lock in your changes, and then press Control-D to deselect, which completes the effect.

Simple Depth-of-Field Effect

If you want to create a quick depth-of-field effect (where the part of the subject closest to the camera is in sharp focus and the background is out of focus), I don't know of a faster, easier way than this.

Step One:

Open the photo that you want to apply the depth-of-field effect to. Press Control-J to duplicate the Background layer to create a new layer that will be named "Layer 1."

Step Two:

Go under the Filter menu, under Blur, and choose Gaussian Blur. When the dialog appears, change the Radius to about 4 pixels (or more if you're using a high-res photo) and click OK to put a blur over the entire image.

Step Three:
Press the E key to switch to the Eraser tool and choose a large, soft-edged brush from the Brush Picker (which is found by clicking the Brush thumbnail in the Options Bar). Start erasing over the parts of the image that appear in the foreground. Erasing on this blurred layer reveals the original, unblurred image on the Background layer. By leaving these areas sharp and the background areas blurry, it creates a simple depth-of-field effect as if you had shot it that way with your camera.

Before

After

Creating Photo Montages

Here's a great way to blend any two (or more) photos together to create a photo montage (often referred to as a collage).

Step One:
Open the photo that you want to use as your base photo—this will serve as the background of your collage. (*Note:* Make sure you're not in Maximize Mode by deselecting it under the Window menu, under Images.) Now open the first photo that you want to collage with your background photo.

Step Two:
Press V to switch to the Move tool, and then click-and-drag the photo from this document right onto your background photo, positioning it where you want it. It will appear on its own layer (Layer 1) in the Layers palette of your background image.

Step Three:
Hold the Control key and at the top of the Layers palette, click on the Create a New Layer icon. This creates a layer directly beneath your current layer (Layer 1). Now, click back on the top layer, then press Control-G to group your photo with the blank layer beneath it. Press the letter D to set your Foreground color to black.

Step Four:
Switch to the Gradient tool by pressing G, and then press Enter to bring up the Gradient Picker (it appears below the Gradient thumbnail in the Options Bar). Choose the second gradient in the Picker (this is the Foreground to Transparent gradient).

Continued

Step Five:

Click on the middle (blank) layer in the Layers palette to make it active. Although you can't see your top photo, try to click the Gradient tool near the center of this photo and drag toward the center of the document. The point where you first clicked on the top layer will be at 100% opacity, and the point where you stop dragging will be totally transparent. Everything else will blend in between. If you want to start over—easy enough—just press Control-Z to undo and click-and-drag again. (Be careful: If you drag beyond the image's border, your Foreground color will appear in the gradient.)

Step Six:

If you want to blend in another photo, click-and-drag that image onto your montage, click on the top layer in the Layers palette, then start again from Step 3. Add as many images as you'd like.

©ISTOCKPHOTO/SEAN LOCKE

Here's how to create the classic soft-edged vignette that was originally made popular decades ago by portrait photographers, and still remains popular for wedding photos and portraits of children. A rectangular version is often used for photos used in print ads of high-priced items such as fine homes, jewelry, perfume, etc.

Creating the Classic Vignette Effect

Step One:
Open the photo to which you want to apply the classic vignette effect.

Step Two:
Press M until you get the Elliptical Marquee tool from the Toolbox and draw an oval-shaped selection around the part of the photo you want to remain visible.

Continued

Step Three:

To soften the edge of your selection, go under the Select menu and choose Feather. When the Feather Selection dialog appears, enter 35 or more pixels (the higher the number, the softer the edge) and click OK.

Step Four:

Here's the thing—you have your subject in a circular selection, and that's the part you want to keep intact. However, you want everything else deleted, so go under the Select menu and choose Inverse. Doing this selects everything except the area you want to keep intact.

Step Five:

Now, press Backspace to remove the background areas, and then press Control-D to deselect. Because you feathered the oval in Step 3, the edges are soft, completing the vignette effect.

TIP: If you'd like to use this soft-edged vignette for collaging with other photos, you'll need the white areas outside the edge to be transparent and not solid white. To do that, just before Step 2, double-click on the Background layer in the Layers palette. A dialog will appear; just click OK to change your Background layer to Layer 0, and then go on to Step 2.

Before

After

Fake Duotone

The duotone tinting look is all the rage right now, but creating a real two-color duotone, complete with curves, that will separate in just two colors on press is a bit of a chore. However, if you're outputting to an inkjet printer, or to a printing press as a full-color job, then you don't need all that complicated stuff—you can create a fake duotone that looks at least as good (if not better).

Step One:

Open the color RGB photo that you want to convert into a duotone (again, I'm calling it a duotone, but we're going to stay in RGB mode the whole time). Now, the hard part of this is choosing which color to make your duotone. I always see other people's duotones, and think, "Yeah, that's the color I want!" but when I go to the Foreground color swatch and try to create a similar color in the Color Picker, it's always hit or miss (usually miss). That's why you'll want to know this next trick.

Step Two:

If you can find another duotone photo that has a color you like, you're set. So I usually go to a stock-photo website (like istockphoto.com) and search for "Duotones." When I find one I like, I return to Elements, press I to get the Eyedropper tool, click-and-hold anywhere within my image area, and then (while keeping the mouse button held down) I drag my cursor outside Elements and onto the photo in my Web browser to sample the color I want. Now, mind you, I did not and would not take a single pixel from someone else's photo—I'm just sampling a color.

Step Three:
Return to your image in Elements. Go to the Layers palette and click on the Create a New Layer icon. Then, press Alt-Backspace to fill this new blank layer with your sampled color. The color will fill your image area, hiding your photo, but we'll fix that.

Step Four:
While still in the Layers palette, change the blend mode of this sampled color layer to Color.

Step Five:
If your duotone seems too dark, you can lessen the effect by clicking on the Background layer, and then going under the Enhance menu, under Adjust Color, and choosing Remove Color. This removes the color from your RGB photo without changing its color mode, while lightening the overall image. Pretty sneaky, eh?

Getting the Polaroid™ Look

This is a quick technique that lets you turn any photo into what looks like a Polaroid snapshot. This is an ideal effect to apply when you really want that "scrapbook" feel, or you're looking for that spontaneous "my-family-on-vacation" feel. Give this one a try—it's much, much easier than it looks.

Step One:
Open the photo you want to turn into a Polaroid. Press Control-A to put a selection around the entire image. Go under the Layer menu, under New, and choose Layer via Cut to remove the photo from the Background layer and put it on a separate layer (Layer 1) above the background. Now press D to set your colors to the default black and white.

Step Two:
To create this effect, you'll need a little more working room around your photo, so go under the Image menu, under Resize, and choose Canvas Size. When the Canvas Size dialog appears, ensure the Relative checkbox is turned on, then add at least 2 inches of space to both the Width and Height. Choose Background in the Canvas Extension Color pop-up menu, and click OK.

Step Three:
Create a new blank layer directly beneath your current layer by Control-clicking on the Create a New Layer icon at the top of the Layers palette (the new layer will be titled "Layer 2"). Press the M key to switch to the Rectangular Marquee tool, and on this layer draw a selection that's about a ½-inch larger than your photo on all sides. This will act as the border for your Polaroid image.

Step Four:
Click on the Foreground color swatch in the Toolbox, choose a very light gray in the Color Picker (I used R=232, G=232, B=232), and then fill your selection with this light gray by pressing Alt-Backspace. Now you can deselect by pressing Control-D. In the Layers palette, click on your top layer (your photo layer) and press Control-E to combine (merge) your photo with the gray rectangle layer below it, creating just one layer.

Step Five:
Make a duplicate of this merged layer by dragging it to the Create a New Layer icon at the top of the Layers palette (this copied layer will be titled "Layer 2 copy"). Press the D key to set your Foreground color to black. Then, press Alt-Shift-Backspace to fill your copied layer with black. Now, in the Layers palette, drag the black layer directly beneath your photo layer. You're going to "bend" this black-filled layer and use it as the shadow for the Polaroid.

Continued

Step Six:
Go under the Filter menu, under Distort, and choose Shear. When the Shear dialog appears, click on the center of the line that appears vertically at the center of the grid. This adds a point to the line. Click-and-drag this point to the left. The bottom of the dialog shows a preview of how your shear will look. When it looks good to you, click OK.

Step Seven:
With the "shadow" layer still active in the Layers palette, press the V key to switch to the Move tool. Then drag this black, sheared layer directly to the right until the corners are peering out, giving the impression that the Polaroid's shadow is bent.

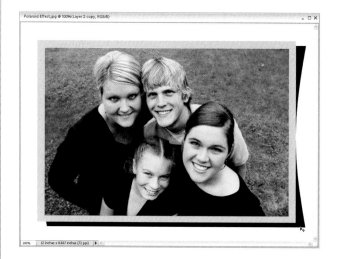

Step Eight:
To soften the edges of your shadow (and make them look, well…shadow-like), go under the Filter menu, under Blur, and choose Gaussian Blur. Enter a Radius of 6 and click OK (enter a Radius of 14 for high-res, 300-ppi images).

Step Nine:
Now that the shadow is soft, you'll need to lower its opacity to make it appear more subtle. Go to the Layers palette and lower the Opacity setting to around 65%. (You can go lower if you like—it's up to you.) Now that your shadow is finished, to make the effect look more realistic, you'll have to bend the edges of the photo itself.

Step Ten:
In the Layers palette, click on your photo layer (Layer 2) to make it active. Then, go under the Filter menu, under Distort, and choose Shear. When the Shear dialog appears, it will still have the last settings you applied in the grid. Click-and-drag the center point on the line to the right to bend your photo in the opposite direction of the shadow. When it looks good to you, click OK. Now use the Move tool to reposition your image above the shadow.

Step Eleven:
Merge the shadow layer and the photo layer into one layer by pressing Control-E. Then, press Control-T to bring up the Free Transform bounding box. Move your cursor outside the bounding box, then click-and-drag upward to rotate the Polaroid. Press Enter to lock in your transformation, giving you the final effect.

Photo to Sketch in 60 Seconds Flat

I learned this technique from Rich Harris, the former creative guru over at Wacom Technologies. He sent me a bunch of PDFs with some special effects he had come up with, and this one just blew me away, so I asked Rich if I could include it in the book. It does the best job I've seen yet of converting a photo into a color pencil sketch.

Step One:

Open the photo you want to convert into a color sketch. Duplicate the Background layer by going to the Layer menu, under New, and choosing Layer via Copy (or by pressing Control-J). Hide this duplicate layer (Layer 1) by going to the Layers palette and clicking on the Eye icon to the left of this layer. Now click on the Background layer.

Step Two:

Press Control-Shift-U to remove the color from the Background layer (technically, this is called "desaturating," but in Elements it's the Remove Color command, which is found under the Enhance menu's Adjust Color submenu). Then press Control-J to duplicate the gray Background layer (this copied layer is titled "Background copy").

Step Three:
With the Background Copy layer active, press Control-I to invert the photo (giving you a photo-negative look).

Step Four:
Go to the Layers palette and change the layer blend mode for the layer to Color Dodge. This turns your photo white (it looks like a blank document, but in the next step, you'll bring back the photo).

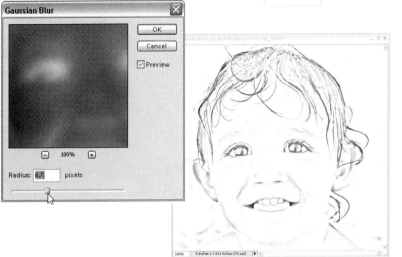

Step Five:
Go under the Filter menu, under Blur, and choose Gaussian Blur. When the dialog appears, drag the Radius slider all the way to the left, and then slowly drag it back to the right, and as you do your sketch will begin to appear. Click OK when the lines look dark, and the photo doesn't look too blurry.

Continued

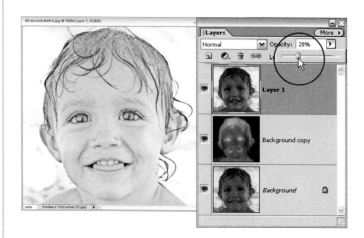

Step Six:
Go to the Layers palette and make the top layer (the color layer) visible again by clicking in the empty box where the Eye icon used to be. Now lower the Opacity of this layer to 20% to bring back a hint of the original color of the photo.

Step Seven:
To add some texture to your sketch, go under the Filter menu, under Texture, and choose Texturizer. When the Texturizer dialog appears, you'll use the default settings (which are: Texture pop-up menu set to Canvas, Scaling set at 100%, Relief at 4, and Light set to Top). Click OK to apply your canvas texture. Now press Control-F to apply the filter again to make the effect a little more intense, completing the technique.

Before

After

If you've taken the time to get your pano set up right during the shoot (in other words, you used a tripod and overlapped the shots by about 15% to 20% each), then you can have Elements 4.0's Photomerge feature automatically stitch your panorama images together. If you handheld your pano shoot, you can still use Photomerge: It's just going to be much more manual with you doing most of the work rather than Elements doing it for you.

Automated Pano Stitching with Photomerge

Step One:
Open the photos that you want Photomerge to stitch together as one panoramic image (you can also open individual images or a folder of images directly from within the Photomerge dialog if you like). In the example shown here, I had four shots already open in Elements.

Step Two:
Go under the File menu, under New, and choose Photomerge Panorama.

Continued

Step Three:

When you choose Photomerge, a dialog appears asking which files you want to combine into a panorama. Any files you have open will appear in the window, or you can click the Browse button and navigate to the photos you need to open. Control-click to select individual files in the Open dialog or if the files are contiguous, click on the first file, press-and-hold the Shift key, then click on the last file. Now click Open and then click OK in the Photomerge dialog.

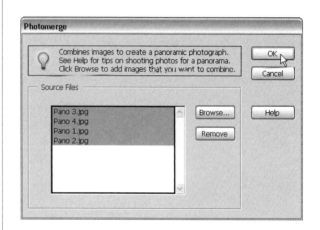

Step Four:

If your pano images were shot correctly (as I mentioned in the introduction of this technique), Photomerge will generally stitch them together seamlessly. If that's the case, click OK and your final panorama will appear as one image. Then you just use the Crop tool (C) to trim away any excess areas in your pano. This is what we call the "best-case scenario," when you've shot the panos on a tripod and overlapped them just like you should so Photomerge had no problems and did its thing right away. It was perfect the first time. But you know, and I know, life just isn't like that.

Step Five:

More likely what you'll get (especially if you handheld your camera or didn't allow enough overlap) is this warning dialog that lets you know that Photomerge "ain't gonna do it for you" (that's a technical phrase coined by Adobe's Alabama tech office). In other words—it's up to you.

Step Six:
Once you click OK in that warning dialog, Photomerge will at least try to merge as many segments together as possible. The segments it couldn't merge will appear in the "Lightbox" (that horizontal row across the top). Although Photomerge didn't do all the work for you, it still can help—just make sure the Snap to Image checkbox on the right-hand side is turned on.

Step Seven:
Get the Select Image tool (it looks like the Move tool) from the Toolbox on the left of the dialog and drag the image's thumbnail from the Lightbox down to your work area near the first image. Slightly overlap the image above the other merged images, release your mouse button, and if Photomerge detects a common overlapping area, it will snap them together, blending any visible edges. It actually works surprisingly well. If you need to rotate a segment to get it lined up, click on it with the Select Image tool first, then switch to the Rotate tool and click-and-drag within the segment to rotate. See, it's not that bad (especially using the Snap to Image option).

Exposure: 1/1250   Focal Length: 70mm   Aperture Value: ƒ/4.0

Get Back
photo restoration techniques

Okay, I know you're thinking, "Hey, this is supposed to be a book for digital photographers. Why are we restoring old damaged photos taken 50 years before digital cameras were invented?" Well, a secret loophole in my book contract enables me, once in every book, to cover a topic that doesn't fall within the general purview of the book. For example, in *The Photoshop CS2 Book for Digital Photographers*, I included a full chapter called "Underrated Breakfast Cereals." So when you're working your way through this chapter, keep thinking to yourself, "Hey, this could be another cereal chapter." Then you'll find not only does this chapter fit, but on some level it fits so well that it makes you want to fix yourself a huge bowl of Kellogg's® Smart Start®. Besides, there's another useful loophole: the theory that once a torn, washed-out, scratched photo of your great-grandfather is scanned, it then becomes a "digital," torn, washed-out, scratched photo of your great-grandfather. And once you open it in Elements 4.0, you'll be engulfed with a burning desire to repair that photo. If I hadn't included this chapter on how to repair and restore these old photos, then where would you be, Mr. "Hey-this-is-supposed-to-be-a-book-for-digital-photographers" frumpy-pants? Don't you feel just a little guilty? I thought so. Now put down your spoon and start restoring some photos.

Colorizing Black-and-White Photos

Once you've restored a black-and-white photo, you might want to consider colorizing (hand tinting) the photo to give it added depth. This particular technique doesn't take a lot of Elements skills; it just takes a bit of patience, because colorizing a photo can take some time.

Step One:
Open the black-and-white photo you want to colorize.

©DAVE GALES

Step Two:
To colorize a photo, your Elements image has to be in a color mode, so if your photo is in Grayscale mode (it will say "Gray" up in your document's title bar), you'll have to convert it to RGB mode by going under the Image menu, under Mode, and choosing RGB Color.

Step Three:
Press L to switch to the Lasso tool and draw a selection around the first area within your photo that you want to colorize. Press-and-hold the Alt key to subtract from your selection or hold the Shift key to add to it. Then, go under the Select menu and choose Feather. When the dialog appears, enter 2 pixels to soften the edge of your selection just a tiny bit, and then click OK.

Step Four:
Now, you could do all of your colorization on the Background layer, but I recommend pressing Control-J to copy your selected area onto its own layer. That way, if a color you've applied winds up looking too intense, you can lower the layer's Opacity to "tone it down" a bit.

Step Five:
Go under the Enhance menu, under Adjust Color, and choose Adjust Hue/Saturation. When the Hue/Saturation dialog appears, click on the Colorize checkbox in the bottom right-hand corner, drag the Hue slider (at the top of the dialog) to the tint you'd like for this selected area, and then click OK.

Continued

Step Six:

In the Layers palette, click on the Background layer to make it active and with the Lasso tool, select the next area to be colorized (in this case, his shirt). Apply a feather to your selection (as you did in Step 3), and press Control-J to copy your selection to its own layer. Now apply your Hue/Saturation adjustment again (like you did in Step 5). When you're applying the color, if it looks too intense, drag the Saturation slider to the left to reduce the color's intensity, giving it a pastel look that's typical of color tinting. When it looks good to you, click OK.

Step Seven:

You'll basically repeat this process to colorize the rest of the photo. Each time you'll go to the Background layer, select an area to be colorized, add a slight feather, copy the selection to its own layer by pressing Control-J, apply the Hue/Saturation command, click the Colorize checkbox, and choose your desired color using the Hue and Saturation sliders. When you're finished, if any of the colors look too intense, just lower the Opacity in the Layers palette. Then choose Flatten Image from the Layers palette's More flyout menu to complete the effect. *Hint:* In this example we're choosing a skin tone. This also tints the whites of her eyes, so you might want to grab the Eraser tool and just erase over the whites to remove that brownish tint.

Before   *After*

Repairing Washed-Out Photos

If you've got an old photo that's washed out, lacking detail, and generally so light that it's just about unusable, try this amazingly fast technique to quickly bring back detail and tone.

Step One:
Open the washed-out photo.

Step Two:
Duplicate the Background layer by dragging it to the Create a New Layer icon at the top of the Layers palette. This creates a layer called "Background copy."

Step Three:
Change the layer blend mode of the Background copy layer by choosing Multiply from the pop-up menu at the top left of the Layers palette. As the name implies, this has a "multiplier" effect that darkens the photo and brings back some of the tonal detail.

Step Four:
If the image is still too blown out, continue making copies of this duplicate layer (which is already set to Multiply mode) by pressing Control-J until the photo no longer looks washed out. If the last layer that you add makes it too dark, just lower the Opacity setting of this layer until it looks right.

Continued

Step Five:

Now you may have a new problem—you've got a bunch of layers. The more layers you have, the larger your Elements file, and the larger your Elements file, the slower Elements goes, so there's no sense in having a bunch of extra layers. It just slows things down. So, once the photo looks good, go to the Layers palette, click on the More flyout menu, and choose Flatten Image to flatten all those layers down into one Background layer.

Before

After

It's amazing how those little spots, specks, and well…junk that winds up on all photos can be so painstaking to remove. In most cases, it's not hard to get rid of spots; it just takes a while. But there is a tool that can greatly speed up the process, so you can spend more time on the important repairs, and less time cleaning up the junk.

Removing Spots and Other Little Junk

Step One:
Open a photo that has some specks, spots, and stuff (if the photo has just a ton of spots all over it, you may want to skip this and turn to the next technique in this chapter, as this one's best suited to situations where you have 30 or 40 spots to remove—not 300). The main offenders in this photo are circled in red.

Step Two:
If needed, use the Zoom tool (Z) to zoom into your document. Then, go to the Toolbox and choose the Spot Healing Brush (or just press J until you have it).

Continued

Step Three:

What's nice about this tool is that you don't have to hold down any keys or do anything special—you just move your cursor over a spot, click once, and it's gone. Best of all, it retains as much of the original texture as possible. So, just move around your photo, position your cursor over a spot, and click. If you come to an area that has a streak or row of specks, you can just paint a stroke right over them, and when you release the mouse button—they're gone.

Step Four:

The Spot Healing Brush doesn't do well when a spot is touching or overlapping another object in the photo. For example, look in the capture in Step 3, and you'll see a white spot that touches the top center of his head. That's when you need to switch to the Clone Stamp tool (S), choose a small, soft-edged brush from the Brush Picker in the Options Bar, and then Alt-click in a clean area near the white spot and clone right over it. These two tools make this a 2-minute repair.

Before

After

Removing Lots of Specks, Dust, and Scratches

If you've used Elements' Dust & Scratches filter, you've probably already learned how lame the filter really is. That is, unless you use this cool workaround that takes it from a useless piece of fluff, to a...well...reasonably useful piece of fluff. This technique works brilliantly for removing these types of artifacts (that's Elements-speak for specks, dust, and other junk that winds up) on the background areas of your photos.

Step One:
Open the photo that needs specks, dust, and/or scratches repaired. Duplicate the Background layer by dragging it to the Create a New Layer icon at the top of the Layers palette. This creates a layer called "Background copy."

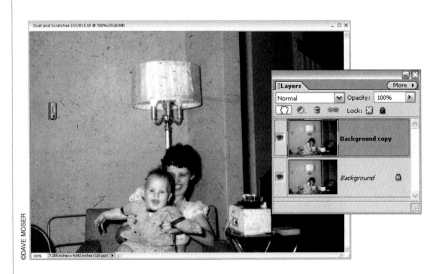

Step Two:
Go under the Filter menu, under Noise, and choose Dust & Scratches. When the Dust & Scratches dialog appears, drag both sliders all the way to the left, then slowly drag the top slider (Radius) back to the right until the specks, dust, and scratches are no longer visible (most likely this will make your photo very blurry, but don't sweat it—make sure the specks are gone, no matter how blurry it looks), and then click OK.

Step Three:
In the Layers palette, hold the Control key and click on the Create a New Layer icon to create a new blank layer beneath your current layer. Now, click back on the top layer and press Control-G to group your blurred layer with the blank layer beneath it. Doing this hides the effect of the Dust & Scratches filter you applied in Step 2.

Step Four:
Press the letter D to set your Foreground color to black. Press B to switch to the Brush tool, click the Brush thumbnail in the Options Bar, and when the Brush Picker appears, choose a medium-sized, soft-edged brush. Now go to the Layers palette, click on your middle, blank layer, and change the layer blend mode pop-up menu from Normal to Lighten. This causes the changes you make with the Brush tool to only affect the pixels that are darker than the area you're painting on this layer. *Note:* Another method for doing this is to change the Brush tool's blend mode to Lighten in the Options Bar. However, I like the layer version better, because you can always change the layer's blend mode later if you don't like how it looks, and you don't get that "after-the-fact" option with the Brush tool.

Continued

Step Five:

With the middle, blank layer active, paint directly over the areas of your photo that have specks. As you paint, the specks and dust will disappear (you're actually revealing the blurred layer above, where you applied the Dust & Scratches filter). Again, this technique works best on background areas, but it can also be useful for cleaning detailed areas. Just use a very small brush to minimize any blurring that may occur, and rather than painting strokes, just move over the speck and click once or twice.

Before

After

If you have an old photo with a serious rip, tear, stain, or other major anomaly, there's a reasonable chance that one of these little nasties could affect a part of your photo's main subject (for example, if it's a photo of a person, a stain could cover a body part or facial feature, leaving you with quite a task). Here's how to repair missing or damaged parts—the easy way.

Repairing Damaged or Missing Parts

Step One:
Open the photo that contains a damaged feature (in this case, part of his arm and his whole elbow are missing because of a tear—plus, part of the rug and the wallpaper are also missing).

Step Two:
Use one of Elements' selection tools (try the Lasso tool if you just need to make a loose selection like the one I did here) to select an undamaged part of the image that you can use to fix the damaged area. For instance, if you're trying to fix a person's left elbow and the right arm is undamaged, select the right arm to use for the repair.

Continued

Step Three:

To keep from having a hard edge around the selected area, you'll need to apply a feather to the edges of your selection. Go under the Select menu and choose Feather. When the dialog appears, enter a Feather Radius. For low-res images, use a 1- to 2-pixel Radius. For high-res, 300-ppi images, you can use as much as 4 or 5 pixels.

Step Four:

You'll need to duplicate the selection, so go under the Layer menu, under New, and choose Layer via Copy (or press Control-J). This creates a new layer with a copy of your selected area on it.

Step Five:

You probably can't just drag this patch over to fill the empty space (because the person would end up with two right arms, leaving him looking slightly freakish). So, you'll need to flip the copied layer by going under the Image menu, under Rotate, and choosing Flip Layer Horizontal, which turns your patch layer into a mirror reflection of the original selection.

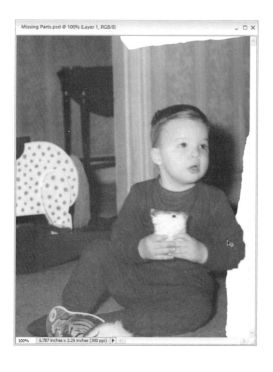

Step Six:

Now, switch to the Move tool by pressing the V key, and with the patch on its own layer, drag it over to where the tear is on the right side of the photo. (*Note:* If you lower the Opacity of the patch layer to about 60%, it may help you precisely position the patch because you'll be able to see some of the original image on the layer beneath it.) If your selection looks a little rough, you can press E to switch to the Eraser tool and erase a little bit along the edge to make it smoother. It probably looks a bit jaggy right now, but once you put some background behind it, you'll be amazed at how it blends right in.

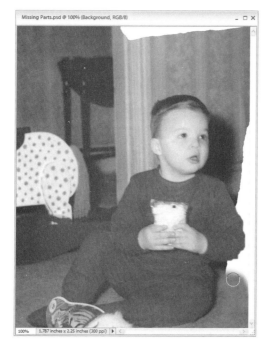

Step Seven:

Go to the Layers palette and click on the Background layer. Now we're going to start fixing the missing carpet to the right of his left knee. Start by pressing S to get the Clone Stamp tool, and then Alt-clicking in the clean area of rug to the left of his right leg (you'll see the plus-sign cursor showing the spot where you Alt-clicked). Then move over to the white area to the right of his left knee and start painting (okay, cloning) over that entire corner of the photo. The carpet on the left will be cloned into that white area on the right. You might have to Alt-click a time or two in different spots so you don't "run out of room" and start cloning other areas.

Continued

Step Eight:

Now you'll want to add that missing dark shadow under his left arm and elbow, so Alt-click in the shadow under his arm, where his left arm and leg first touch (as shown here—look for the plus-sign cursor to see exactly where to Alt-click). Then move along under this arm to clone that shadow.

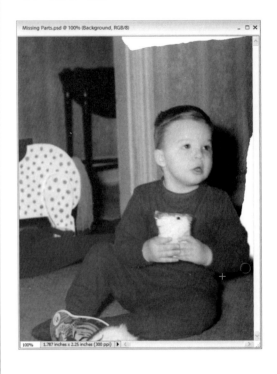

Step Nine:

Now onto the wallpaper fix above his head. Start by pressing M to get the Rectangular Marquee tool and select a clean rectangular area of wallpaper below the tear (make sure you're on the Background layer). To soften the edges of your selection (to help hide any hard edges so your fix won't be a dead give-away), go under the Select menu and choose Feather. When the dialog appears, enter 2 pixels (or higher for high-res, 300-ppi images) and click OK.

Step Ten:

Press Control-J to put that area on its own separate layer. Now get the Move tool, and click-and-drag that copied layer up, positioning it so it covers the white area. Also, make sure the pattern lines up in the wallpaper. Do the same things for the white areas to the left and right of where you just fixed—make a selection on the Background layer, feather it, put it on its own layer, and then click-and-drag it into place. To finish, you'll switch back to the Clone Stamp tool, go to the Layers palette, click on the Background layer, and clone in more areas around his left arm. I cloned down part of the wall to fill in the white areas. The final results are complete in a few quick minutes.

Before

After

Repairing Rips and Tears

There are few things worse than rips, tears, or cracks from a photo being bent, especially when it happens to old family photos you really care about. Here's a simple technique that lets you hide these nasty rips by "covering" them up.

Step One:
Scan a photo that has rips, tears, or bends, and open it in the Elements Editor. The photo here has tears from being bent.

Step Two:
The plan is to clone over the cracks using noncracked, nearby areas. Start by getting the Clone Stamp tool from the Toolbox (or press the S key). Choose a medium to small, soft-edged brush by clicking on the Brush thumbnail in the Options Bar to open the Brush Picker.

Step Three:
Press-and-hold the Alt key and click in a "clean" area near the cracked area. (By clean, I mean Alt-click in an area that has no cracks or other visible problems. To help ensure that your repair doesn't look obvious, it's important to click near the tear, but not too far away from it.)

Step Four:
Move the Clone Stamp tool over the rip and click a few times over the crack. Don't paint strokes—just click. As you click, you'll see two cursors: your brush cursor where you're painting and a crosshair cursor over the area you sampled. This lets you see the area you're cloning from (the crosshair) and the area you're cloning to (the brush cursor). This will be your basic strategy for repairing these rips—Alt-click the Clone Stamp tool in a clean area near the crack, then move your cursor over the crack and click a few times until the crack is covered by the cloned areas. For really large cracks, you can paint some small strokes, but be careful not to pick up any repeating patterns that might give you away.

Continued

Step Five:

Now start working on other areas. Press the Z key to switch to the Zoom tool, zoom in if needed, and then switch back to the Clone Stamp tool. (*Note:* You also might want to try the Healing Brush tool [use it the same way—Alt-click before you start healing] using a similar technique, depending on the photo, as it may work just as well, if not better.) The final result is worth a few minutes of cloning.

Before

After

Exposure: 1/200 | Focal Length: 24mm | Aperture Value: ƒ/3.5

Sharp Dressed Man
sharpening techniques

You're about to learn some of the same sharpening techniques used by today's leading digital photographers and retouchers. Okay, I have to admit, not every technique in this chapter is a professional technique. For example, the first one, "Basic Sharpening," is clearly not a professional technique, although many professionals sharpen their images exactly as shown in that tutorial (applying the Unsharp Mask to the RGB composite—I'm not sure what that means, but it sounds good). There's a word for these professionals—"lazy." But then one day, they think, "Geez, I'm kind of getting tired of all those color halos and other annoying artifacts that keep showing up in my sharpened photos," and they wish there was a way to apply more sharpening, and yet avoid these pitfalls. Then, they're looking for professional sharpening techniques that will avoid these problems—and

the best of those techniques are in this chapter. But the pros are busy people, taking conference calls, getting pedicures, vacuuming their cats, etc., and they don't have time to do a series of complicated, time-consuming steps. So, they create advanced functions that combine techniques. For some unexplainable sociological reason, when pros do this, it's not considered lazy. Instead, they're seen as "efficient, productive, and smart." Why? Because life isn't fair. How unfair is it? I'll give you an example. A number of leading professional photographers have worked for years to come up with these advanced sharpening techniques, which took tedious testing, experimentation, and research, and then you come along, buy this book, and suddenly you're using the same techniques they are, but you didn't even expend a bead of sweat. You know what that's called? Cool.

Basic Sharpening

After you've color corrected your photos and right before you save your files, you'll definitely want to sharpen them. I sharpen every digital camera photo, either to help bring back some of the original crispness that gets lost during the correction process, or to help fix a photo that's slightly out of focus. Either way, I haven't met a digital camera (or scanned) photo that didn't need a little sharpening. Here's a basic technique for sharpening the entire photo:

Step One:
Open the photo that you want to sharpen. Because Elements displays your photo in different ways at different magnifications, it's absolutely critical that you view your photo at 100% when sharpening. To ensure that you're viewing at 100%, once your photo is open, double-click on the Zoom tool in the Toolbox, and your photo will jump to a 100% view (to see the actual percentage of zoom, look up in the image window's title bar or Options Bar, depending on your viewing mode, or look in the image window's bottom-left corner).

Step Two:
Go under the Filter menu, under Sharpen, and choose Unsharp Mask. (If you're familiar with traditional darkroom techniques, you probably recognize the term "unsharp mask" from when you would make a blurred copy of the original photo and an "unsharp" version to use as a mask to create a new photo whose edges appeared sharper.) Of Elements' sharpening filters, Unsharp Mask is the undisputed first choice because it offers the most control over the sharpening process.

Step Three:
When the Unsharp Mask dialog appears, you'll see three sliders. The Amount slider determines the amount of sharpening applied to the photo; the Radius slider determines how many pixels out from the edge that the sharpening will affect; and the Threshold slider determines how different a pixel must be from the surrounding area before it's considered an edge pixel and sharpened by the filter. Threshold works the opposite of what you might think—the lower the number, the more intense the sharpening effect. So, what numbers do you enter? I'll give you some great starting points on the following pages, but for now, we'll just use these settings: Amount: 125%, Radius: 1, and Threshold: 3. Click OK and the sharpening is applied to the photo.

Before

After

Continued

Sharpening Soft Subjects:

Here is an Unsharp Mask setting—Amount: 150%, Radius: 1, Threshold: 10—that works well for images where the subject is of a softer nature (e.g., flowers, puppies, people, rainbows, etc.). It's a subtle application of sharpening that is very well suited to these types of subjects.

Sharpening Portraits:

If you're sharpening a close-up portrait (head-and-shoulders type of thing), try this setting—Amount: 75%, Radius: 2, Threshold: 3—which applies another form of subtle sharpening.

Moderate Sharpening:

This is a moderate amount of sharpening that works nicely on product shots, photos of home interiors and exteriors, and landscapes. If you're shooting along these lines, try applying this setting—Amount: 225%, Radius: 0.5, Threshold: 0—and see how you like it (my guess is you will).

Maximum Sharpening:

I use these settings—Amount: 65%, Radius: 4, Threshold: 3—in only two situations: (1) The photo is visibly out of focus and it needs a heavy application of sharpening to try to bring it back into focus; or (2) the photo contains lots of well-defined edges (e.g., buildings, coins, cars, machinery, etc.).

Continued

All-Purpose Sharpening:

This is probably my all-around favorite sharpening setting—Amount: 85%, Radius: 1, Threshold: 4—and I use this one most of the time. It's not a "knock-you-over the-head" type of sharpening—maybe that's why I like it. It's subtle enough that you can apply it twice if your photo doesn't seem sharp enough after the first application (just press Control-F), but once will usually do the trick.

Web Sharpening:

I use this setting—Amount: 400%, Radius: 0.3, Threshold: 0—for Web graphics that look blurry. (When you drop the resolution from a high-res, 300-ppi photo down to 72 ppi for the Web, the photo often gets a bit blurry and soft.) I also use this same setting on out-of-focus photos. It adds some noise, but I've seen it rescue photos that I would have otherwise thrown away. If the effect seems too intense, try dropping the Amount to 200%.

Coming Up with Your Own Settings:
If you want to experiment and come up with your own custom blend of sharpening, I'll give you some typical ranges for each adjustment so you can find your own sharpening "sweet spot."

Amount:
Typical ranges go anywhere from 50% to 150%. This isn't a rule that can't be broken. It's just a typical range for adjusting the Amount, where going below 50% won't have enough effect, and going above 150% might get you into sharpening trouble (depending on how you set the Radius and Threshold). You're fairly safe to stay under 150%.

Radius:
Most of the time, you'll use just 1 pixel, but you can go as high as (get ready)—2. I gave you one setting earlier for extreme situations, where you can take the Radius as high as 4, but I wouldn't recommend it very often. I once heard a tale of a man in Cincinnati who used 5, but I'm not sure I believe it.

Continued

Threshold:

A pretty safe range for the Threshold setting is anywhere from 3 to around 20 (3 being the most intense, 20 being much more subtle. I know, shouldn't 3 be more subtle and 20 more intense? Don't get me started). If you really need to increase the intensity of your sharpening, you can lower the Threshold to 0, but keep a good eye on what you're doing (watch for noise appearing in your photo).

Before

After

One of the problems we face when trying to make things really sharp is that things tend to look oversharpened, or worse yet, our photos get halos (tiny glowing lines around edges in our images). So, how do we get our images to appear really sharp without damaging them? With a trick, of course. Here's the one I use to make my photos look extraordinarily sharp without damaging the image:

Creating Extraordinary Sharpening

Step One:
Open your image, and then apply the Unsharp Mask filter (found under the Filter menu, under Sharpen) to your image, just as we've been doing all along. (For this example, let's try these settings: Amount 120%, Radius 1, and Threshold 3, which will provide a nice, solid amount of sharpening.)

Step Two:
Press Control-J to duplicate the Background layer. Because we're duplicating the Background layer, the layer will be already sharpened, but we're going to sharpen this duplicate layer even more in the next step.

Continued

Step Three:
Now apply the Unsharp Mask filter again, using the same settings, by pressing Control-F. If you're really lucky, the second application of the filter will still look okay, but it's doubtful. Chances are that this second application of the filter will make your photo appear too sharp—you'll start to see halos or noise, or the photo will start looking artificial in a lot of areas. So, what we're going to do is hide this oversharpened layer, then selectively reveal this über-sharpening only in areas that can handle the extra sharpening (this will make sense in just a minute).

Step Four:
Go to the Layers palette, press-and-hold the Control key, and click on the Create a New Layer icon at the top of the Layers palette (holding the Control key makes the new layer appear below your currently active layer, rather than above it, like usual).

Step Five:
In the Layers palette, click on your oversharpened layer to make it the active layer (it should be your top layer, with that blank layer you just created appearing directly below it in the stack of layers). Now press Control-G. This groups your oversharpened layer with the empty one beneath it; thus it hides the oversharpened layer in that blank layer.

Step Six:

Here's the fun part—the trick is to paint over just a few key areas, which fool the eye into thinking the entire photo is sharper than it is. Here's how: Press B to get the Brush tool, and in the Options Bar, click on the Brush thumbnail to open the Brush Picker and choose a small, soft-edged brush. Press D to set your Foreground color to black. Now, in the Layers palette click on the blank layer, and then start painting on your image to reveal your sharpening. (*Note:* If you make a mistake, press E and erase your black brush stokes with the Eraser tool.) In this image, you'd paint over the center of the daisy and its stem to make them super sharp—and maybe a little on the petals too—but stay away from the edges of each petal, and just paint "inside the lines." That way, the edges don't get halos, but the overall image appears very sharp.

Before

After

Luminosity Sharpening

Okay, you've already learned that sharpening totally rocks, but the more you use it, the more discerning you'll become about it (you basically become a sharpening snob), and at some point, you'll apply some heavy sharpening to an image and notice little color halos. You'll grow to hate these halos, and you'll go out of your way to avoid them. In fact, you'll go so far as to use this next sharpening technique, which is fairly popular with pros shooting digital (at least with the sharpening-snob crowd).

Step One:
Open a photo that needs some moderate to serious sharpening.

Step Two:
Duplicate the Background layer by going under the Layer menu, under New, and choosing Layer via Copy (or press Control-J). This will duplicate the Background layer onto a new layer (Layer 1).

Step Three:

Go under the Filter menu, under Sharpen, and choose Unsharp Mask. (*Note:* If you're looking for some sample settings for different sharpening situations, look at the "Basic Sharpening" tutorial at the beginning of this chapter.) After you've input your Unsharp Mask settings, click OK to apply the sharpening to the duplicate layer.

Step Four:

Go to the Layers palette and change the layer blend mode of this sharpened layer from Normal to Luminosity. By doing this, it applies the sharpening to just the luminosity (lightness details) of the image, and not the color. This enables you to apply a higher amount of sharpening without getting unwanted halos. You can now choose Flatten Image from the Layers palette's More flyout menu to complete your Luminosity sharpening.

Continued

Before

After

This is a sharpening technique that doesn't use the Unsharp Mask filter but still leaves you with a lot of control over the sharpening, even after it's applied. It's ideal to use when you have an image that can really hold a lot of sharpening (a photo with a lot of edges) or one that really needs a lot of sharpening.

Edge Sharpening Technique

Step One:
Open a photo that needs edge sharpening.

Step Two:
Duplicate the Background layer by going under the Layer menu, under New, and choosing Layer via Copy (or press Control-J). This will duplicate the Background layer onto a new layer (Layer 1).

Continued

Step Three:

Go under the Filter menu, under Stylize, and choose Emboss. You're going to use the Emboss filter to accentuate the edges in the photo. You can leave the Angle and Amount settings at their defaults (135° and 100%), but if you want more intense sharpening, raise the Height amount from its default setting of 3 pixels to 5 or more pixels (in the example here, I left it at 3). Click OK to apply the filter, and your photo will turn gray, with neon-colored highlights along the edges.

Step Four:

In the Layers palette, change the layer blend mode of this layer from Normal to Hard Light. This removes the gray color from the layer, but leaves the edges accentuated, making the entire photo appear much sharper.

Step Five:

If the sharpening seems too intense, you can control the amount of the effect by simply lowering the Opacity of this top layer in the Layers palette.

Before

After

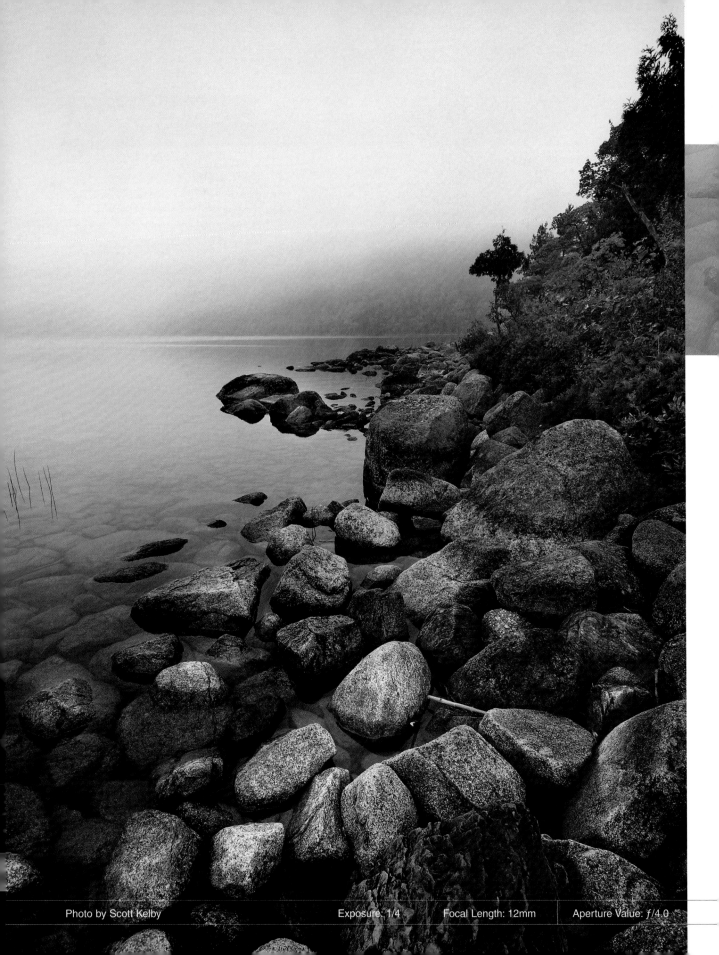

Photo by Scott Kelby

Exposure: 1/4   Focal Length: 12mm   Aperture Value: ƒ/4.0

The Show Must Go On
showing it to your clients

Okay, you've sorted and categorized the photos from the shoot; you've backed up your digital negs to CD; and you've color corrected, tweaked, toned, sharpened, and otherwise messed with your photo until it is, in every sense of the word, a masterpiece. But now it's time to show it to the clients. Hopefully, you'll get to show it to the clients in person, so you can explain in detail the motivation behind collaging a 4x4 monster truck into an otherwise pristine wedding photo. (Answer: Because you can.) There's a good chance they'll see the photo first onscreen, so I included some cool tricks on how to make your presentation look its very best (after all, you want those huge 122" tires to look good), and I even included some techniques on how to provide your own online proofing service using Elements (in case your clients smell bad, and you don't want them coming back to your studio and stinkin' up the place). I want you to really sop up the techniques (like you're using a big ol' flaky biscuit) because once you're done with this chapter, once you've come this far, there's no turning back. At this point, some people will start to scour their studio, searching for that one last roll of traditional print film, probably knocking around at the bottom of some drawer (or hidden in the back of the refrigerator, behind some leftover Moo Shoo Pork), so they can hold it up toward the light, smile, and begin laughing that hysterical laugh that only people truly on the edge can muster. These people are not Kodak shareholders.

Watermarking and Adding Copyright Info

This two-part technique is particularly important if you're putting your photos on the Web and want some level of copyright protection. In the first part of this technique, you'll add a see-through watermark, so you can post larger photos without fear of having someone download and print them. Secondly, you'll embed your personal copyright info, so if your photos are used anywhere on the Web, your copyright info will go right along with the file.

Step One:

We're going to start by creating a watermark template. Create a new blank document in the Elements Editor (go to File, under New, and choose Blank File) in RGB mode in your typical working resolution (72 ppi for low-res, 300 ppi for high-res, etc.). Click on the Foreground color swatch at the bottom of the Toolbox and choose a medium gray color in the Color Picker, then click OK. Now, press Alt-Backspace to fill the Background layer with medium gray. Press the letter D to set your Foreground color to black.

Step Two:

Press T to switch to the Type tool. In the Options Bar, choose a font like Arial Bold from the Font pop-up menu, and then click on the Center Text icon. Click the cursor on the gray background, press-and-hold the Alt key, type "0169" using your numeric keypad, and release the Alt key to create a copyright symbol. (*Note:* On a laptop, press-and-hold the Function key to access your keypad.) Then, press Enter to move your cursor to the next line and type the name you want for the copyright on the photo. If needed, adjust the leading (space between lines) by selecting all your text (Control-A) and choosing a point size in the Set the Leading pop-up menu in the Options Bar. Now hide the Background layer by clicking on its Eye icon in the Layers palette.

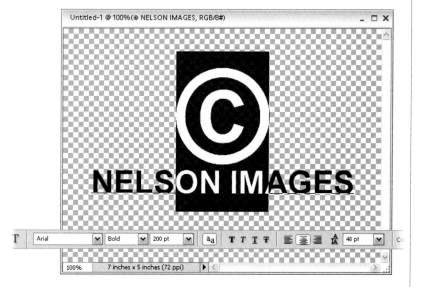

Step Three:

Highlight your name (but not the copyright symbol) with the Type tool and increase the size of your name by using the Set the Font Size pop-up menu in the Options Bar. When it's at the right size, highlight just the copyright symbol, and resize it upward until it's quite a bit larger than your name. Try the type at around 50 points and the copyright symbol at 200 points.

Continued

Step Four:
Go to the Styles and Effects palette (if it's not visible, go under the Window menu and choose Styles and Effects), and in the More flyout menu choose Thumbnail View. In the pop-up menu in the palette's upper left-hand corner, choose Effects. In the second pop-up menu, make sure All is selected. Now scroll down the palette and double-click on the Clear Emboss (type) effect. This applies a beveled effect and makes the fill transparent.

Step Five:
Now you can make the Background layer visible again by going to the Layers palette and clicking in the empty box where the Eye icon used to be. You can now see the Clear Emboss (type) effect clearly (okay, that was pretty lame).

Step Six:
Open the photo you want to contain this transparent watermark. Make sure this photo and the document with your embossed watermark are both visible within Elements (if not, exit Maximize Mode by going under the Window menu, under Images, and choose Cascade).

Step Seven:
Press V to switch to the Move tool, then click-and-drag the large copyright symbol's Type layer from the Layers palette (in the embossed watermark document) and drop it onto your photo (you're dragging a layer between documents). Once the copyright symbol is in your new document, you can resize it as needed. Just press Control-T to bring up Free Transform and click-and-drag one of the corner handles. Add the Shift key to resize the type proportionately. Press Enter to complete your transformation.

Continued

Step Eight:
Now go to the Layers palette and lower the Opacity of your Type layer so it's clearly visible, but doesn't dominate the photo.

Step Nine:
Now for the second part—we'll embed your personal copyright info into the photo file itself. Go under the File menu and choose File Info. This is where you enter information that you want embedded. This embedding of info is supported by all the major file formats on the Windows platform (such as TIFF, JPEG, EPS, PDF, and Elements' native PSD file format).

Step Ten:
In the dialog, change the Copyright Status pop-up menu from Unknown to Copyrighted. In the Copyright Notice field, enter your personal copyright info, and then under Copyright Info URL enter your full Web address. That way, when others open your file in Elements, they can go to File Info, click the Go To URL button, and it will launch their browser and take them directly to your site.

Step Eleven:
Click OK and the info is embedded into the file. Once copyright info has been embedded into a file, Elements automatically adds a copyright symbol before the file's name, which appears in the photo's title bar. That's it—you applied two levels of protection: one visible and one embedded.

Creating Your Own Custom Copyright Brush

If you want a quick way to apply your copyright watermark to an image, check out this trick I learned from portrait photographer (and guru) Todd Morrison. He showed me how to turn your copyright info into a brush, so you're only one click away from applying your mark to any photo. My thanks to Todd for letting me share his ingenious technique.

Step One:

Create a new document in the Elements Editor (go to File, under New, and choose Blank File), and then press U until you get the Custom Shape tool (it's in the flyout menu of Shape tools right below the Gradient tool in the Toolbox). Then, press the Enter key to bring up the Custom Shape Picker onscreen, and from the flyout menu in the top-right corner, choose Symbols. Now choose the Copyright symbol from the shapes in the Picker. Press the letter D to set black as your Foreground color and drag out a copyright symbol in the center of your document.

Step Two:

Press T to switch to the Type tool, and then type your copyright info. The Type tool will create a Type layer above the copyright Shape layer. (*Note:* When you set your type, go up to the Options Bar and make sure your justification is set to Center Text [click on the center of the three Align icons].) Then, type a few spaces between the copyright date and the name of your studio. This enables you to put the large copyright symbol in the center of your type.

Step Three:
Press M to get the Rectangular Marquee tool, and click-and-drag a selection around your type and your copyright symbol. Then, go under the Edit menu and choose Define Brush from Selection. When the Brush Name dialog appears, name your brush and click OK. This adds your type as a custom brush in your Brush Picker. *Note:* Don't worry—the preview of the brush that appears in the Brush Name dialog may look squished, but the brush won't be.

Step Four:
Press B to get the Brush tool. In the Options Bar, click on the Brush thumbnail and in the resulting Brush Picker, scroll to the bottom of the brushes. The last brush in the set is the custom copyright brush you just created.

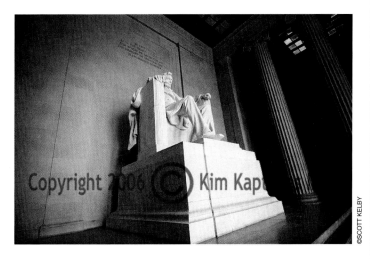

Step Five:
Now that you've created your copyright brush, it's time to put it to use. Open a photo that you want to use as a client proof. Click on the Create a New Layer icon at the top of the Layers palette, and then with the Brush tool, click once where you want your copyright info to appear. Lower the Opacity in the Layers palette so you can see through the copyright. Two things to keep in mind: (1) If the photo is dark, try white as your Foreground color; (2) you can use the Size slider (up in the Options Bar) to change the size of your Brush tool.

Poster Presentation

This technique gives your work the layout of a professional poster, yet it's incredibly easy to do.

Step One:
Open the photo you want to turn into a poster layout.

Step Two:
Go under the Image menu, under Resize, and choose Canvas Size. When the dialog appears, turn on the Relative checkbox, enter 1 inch for both the Width and the Height fields, and choose White in the Canvas Extension Color pop-up menu.

Step Three:
When you click OK, an inch of white canvas space will be added around your photo.

Step Four:
Now you're going to go back to the Canvas Size dialog under the Image menu, under Resize. Add another inch of white canvas but only to the bottom of your image. So, in the Canvas Size dialog enter 1 inch in the Height field, and then in the Anchor grid, click on the top-center anchor (which makes the area you're adding appear below the image).

Continued

Step Five:
Click OK and an additional inch of white canvas area is added below your photo.

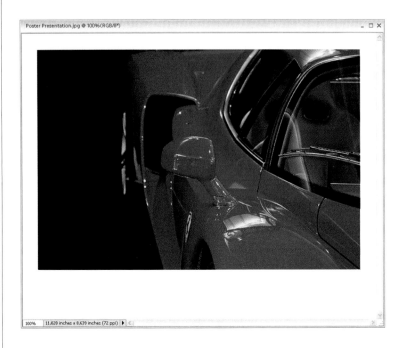

Step Six:
In this extra inch of white space, you'll add some type. Press D set your Foreground to black, and then press T to get the Type tool to add your type (i.e., the name of your studio, the name of the poster, whatever you'd like). I chose the font Gill Sans MT in all caps at a size of 20 points. You'll want to add extra space between the letters, which gives the type an elegant look. To do that, when you're typing in your text, just put an extra space (or two if you like) between each letter using the Spacebar.

Step Seven:
Once your type has been created and you have space between your letters (as mentioned in the previous step), press V to switch to the Move tool and position your type so it's centered below your photo.

Step Eight:
Let's add a thin outside border. Click on the Create a New Layer icon in the top of the Layers palette, and then press Control-A to put a selection around your entire image area. Go under the Edit menu and choose Stroke (Outline) Selection. When the Stroke dialog appears, set black as your stroke Color, set the Width to 1 pixel, set the Location to Center, and click OK. Now you can press Control-D to deselect.

Continued

Step Nine:

To make the outside border thinner and less obtrusive, go to the Layers palette and lower the Opacity setting for this layer to around 30%, giving you the final poster layout shown here.

SCOTT KELBY PHOTOGRAPHY

This is a great technique for displaying your images in online galleries or in PDF presentations for clients. It gives your photos that finished "gallery" look, but without the time or costs involved in framing your prints and then shooting the framed work—it's totally a digital illusion created from scratch in Photoshop Elements 4.0.

Creating a Digital Frame

Step One:
Open the photo you want to frame digitally. Press D to set your Foreground and Background colors to their defaults. Press Control-A to put a selection around your entire photo, and then press Control-Shift-J to cut your photo from the Background layer and put it on its own separate layer (Layer 1).

Step Two:
Go under the Image menu, under Resize, and choose Canvas Size. When the dialog appears, turn on the Relative checkbox, set the Canvas Extension Color pop-up menu to White, and then enter 4 inches for both Width and Height. Click OK to add white space around your photo.

Continued

Step Three:

Press-and-hold the Control key and click on the Create a New Layer icon at the top of the Layers palette. By pressing this key, the new layer you're creating appears below your photo layer, rather than above it.

Step Four:

Press M to get the Rectangular Marquee tool. Draw a selection that's a couple of inches larger than your photo (this will be the edge of your frame, so you'll want to make this selection as big as you want your frame). Next, with your Foreground color still set to black, press Alt-Backspace to fill this selection with black. Do not deselect quite yet.

Step Five:
Now you're going to shrink your selection, so go under the Select menu, under Modify, and choose Contract. When the dialog appears, enter 20 pixels (this will determine the width of your frame, so if you want a thicker frame, use a higher number here) and click OK to shrink your selection.

Step Six:
Press Backspace to knock a hole out of your black rectangle, giving the impression of a black metal frame, and then press Control-D to deselect. Now to add some depth: Go to the Styles and Effects palette (under the Window menu), and from the top-left pop-up menu choose Layer Styles, and from the right pop-up menu choose Drop Shadows. When the shadow icons appear, click on Low to create a soft shadow on the top-left corner and bottom-right corner, which adds some depth.

Continued

Step Seven:
Go back to the Layers palette and click on the Create a New Layer icon. You're going to create a thin mat on this layer, so get the Rectangular Marquee tool again, but this time draw a rectangular selection that's just slightly larger than your image. Fill this selection with black by pressing Alt-Backspace. Don't deselect yet.

Step Eight:
Go under the Select menu, under Modify, and choose Contract. This time, contract just 2 pixels (again, depending on the size of the photo, you might need to make this number a little higher) and click OK, but don't deselect yet.

Step Nine:
Go under the Select menu and choose Feather (this is to soften the edges of your selection). When the dialog appears, enter 2 and click OK to slightly soften the edges. Press Backspace to knock a hole out of this black layer, and press Control-D to deselect. It will now appear as though there's an inner shadow all the way around your layer (as shown here), but that shadow is a little too dark to make a convincing mat.

Step Ten:
Go to the Layers palette and lower the Opacity setting of this thin black layer to around 20%, creating the look of a mat surrounding your photo.

Step Eleven:
Press T to get the Type tool, and choose a script font that looks like handwriting, if possible, from the Font pop-up menu in the Options Bar (I used Fine Hand). Add your signature just below the bottom-right corner of your photo, and then lower the Opacity of your Type layer to around 60% so it looks like you signed the photo in pencil.

Putting Your Photos Up on the Web

Elements has a built-in feature that not only automatically optimizes your photos for the Web, it actually builds a real HTML document for you, with small thumbnail images; links to large, full-size proofs; your email contact information; and more. All you have to do is upload it to the Web and give your friends (or clients) the Web address for your new site. Here's how to make your own:

Step One:
In the Elements Editor, open all the photos that you want to appear on your webpage. (*Note:* You can also Control-click to select images within the Elements Organizer.) Then, go to the task bar above the Options Bar and click on the Create button.

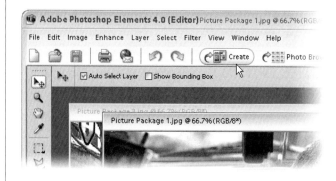

TIP: When you click this, you may get an annoying dialog letting you know that only saved photos will be included in your creation (which in this case is a webpage). If your photos have been saved (if they're named, then they're saved), click OK. If not, click Cancel, then go under the File menu and choose Save. Give them a name and click the Save button. Then click the Create button again.

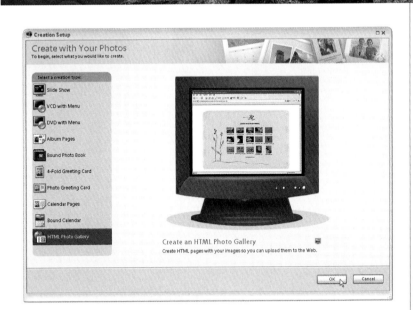

Step Two:
When the Creation Setup dialog appears, you'll see a list of projects you can create on the left side of the dialog. Click on the bottom option, HTML Photo Gallery, and then click the OK button at the bottom-right corner of the dialog.

Step Three:
When you click OK, the Adobe HTML Photo Gallery dialog appears, and all your open photos will be in a column on the left side of the dialog. This dialog is where you make your choices for how your webpage will look. At the top is a pop-up menu of preset webpage layouts (called Gallery Styles). As you choose the different styles in the pop-up menu, a thumbnail preview of each layout appears near the top of the dialog. Choose a style that looks good to you. In the next steps, you'll decide what text will appear on the page, how big the thumbnails and photos will appear on your webpage, and what quality they'll be.

Continued

Step Four:

The first choice you should probably make is determining where your finished webpage will be saved (officially called its "destination"), so click on the Browse button near the bottom-right corner of the dialog to bring up the Browse For Folder dialog. Navigate to the folder in which you want your finished webpage saved, and then click OK. Now you can start customizing your webpage.

Step Five:

Look in the Banner tab in the center section of the dialog. This is where you enter the title and subtitle of your webpage and where you add your email address (if you want people who visit your site to be able to email you). If you're creating this to show your work to clients, you certainly want to include a link for them to email you.

Step Six:
Click on the Thumbnails tab. This is where you choose the size of the small thumbnail images that the people viewing your site will click on to see the full-sized photos. Choose your desired size from the Thumbnail Size pop-up menu. You can also choose captions—such as Filename, Caption (that is, if you already created captions for the images in the Organizer), or Date—to appear under each thumbnail by clicking on the respective checkboxes in the Captions section.

Step Seven:
Click on the Large Photos tab. This is where you choose the final size and quality of the full-size photos displayed on your webpage. Choose your desired size from the Resize Photos pop-up menu, then use the Photo Quality slider to determine their quality. (*Note:* The higher the quality, the longer the photos may take to appear onscreen.) You can again choose titles to appear under each photo in the Captions section by clicking the checkboxes.

Continued

Step Eight:
Enter a name in the Site Folder field in the Destination section and click Save (at the bottom of the dialog). Elements 4.0 will do its thing—resizing the photos, adding your text, making thumbnails, etc.—and a preview of your webpage (complete with live navigation) will appear onscreen. But your page isn't on the Web—it's just a preview within Elements 4.0. To get your photos actually on the Web, you'll have to upload them to a Web server, but before you can do that, you have to find the files to upload.

Step Nine:
Elements automatically creates all the files and folders you'll need to upload your gallery to the Web and saves them in the location you chose earlier in the Destination section of the Adobe HTML Photo Gallery dialog. These are the files and folders you need to put your photo gallery up live on the Web, including your HTML home page (index.html). Now all you have to do is upload them to a Web server and you're live!

I've often joked that we're now one click away from becoming a Sears Portrait Studio since Adobe invented the Picture Package feature, which lets you gang-print the standard, common photo sizes together on one sheet. With Picture Package, Elements does all the work for you. All you have to do is open the photo you want gang-printed, and then Elements will take it from there—except for the manual cutting of the final print, which is actually beyond Elements' capabilities. So far.

Getting One 5x7", Two 2.5x3.5", and Four Wallet-Size Photos on One Print

©SCOTT KELBY

Step One:
Open the photo in the Elements Editor that you want to appear in a variety of sizes on one page, and then go under the File menu and choose Print Multiple Photos.

Step Two:
When the dialog appears, on the right-hand side choose which printer you want to use. Then in section 2, choose Picture Package from the pop-up menu.

Continued

Step Three:
In the third section down, choose the sizes and layout for your Picture Package from the Select a Layout pop-up menu. In this example, I chose Letter (1) 5x7 (2) 2.5x3.5 (4) 2x2.5, but you can choose any combination you like.

Step Four:
Even though you've chosen a layout, only one photo will appear in the layout preview in the center of the dialog. You'll need to click the Fill Page With First Photo checkbox to place your image multiple times.

Step Five:
When you click Print, Elements 4.0 automatically resizes, rotates, and compiles your photos into one printable page that you can then cut. This is a simple use of Picture Package, but it's actually more flexible than it looks, as you'll see in the next step.

Step Six:
Another option you have is to add a custom frame around the photos in your Picture Package. To add a frame, just choose one from the Select a Frame pop-up menu and your choice will be immediately reflected in the preview.

Continued

Step Seven:

If you'd like to create more Picture Package layouts using your same settings, all you have to do is import another photo. You do that by first clicking on the Add button near the bottom left-hand corner of the dialog. This brings up the Add Photos dialog, where you can find the photo you want to import from the Photo Browser, the Catalog, etc. Just click on the checkbox to the left of the image's thumbnail in the dialog, and click Add Selected Photos. Once imported, a small thumbnail of your photo will appear in the list of photos on the left side of the dialog (you can see a second photo has been added in the capture shown here).

Step Eight:

To see the layout with your new photo, click the right-facing arrow button just below the large preview in the center of the dialog. It will toggle you to a layout for your second photo. If you import several photos, you'll be able to toggle to a layout for each photo.

Step Nine:
If you're a more advanced user who understands Color Management options and assigning color profiles, you can click on the More Options button, located directly below the preview, and assign a color space to your photos before printing. But if you're not comfortable making these choices, just skip the More Options button.

Step Ten:
Click Print and here's how your additional Picture Package output will look.

Using Picture Package Layouts with More Than One Photo

Although the Picture Package feature is most often used for printing one photo multiple times on the same page, you can substitute different photos in different positions, and you can customize their location. Here's how:

Step One:
Once you have the Picture Package dialog open (see previous tutorial), click the Add button (near the bottom left-hand corner of the dialog) to add additional photos from the Photo Browser, Catalog, etc., until you have a row of thumbnails appearing down the left side of the dialog. Make sure the Fill Page With First Photo checkbox (found on the right side of the dialog, just below Select a Frame pop-up menu) is turned on.

Step Two:
To add a new photo to your Picture Package layout, just click on the image's thumbnail on the left and drag-and-drop it onto the preview area in the center of the dialog on the position you want it to appear. (*Note:* As you drag, you'll notice a highlight around the preset picture positions in the preview window.)

Step Three:
If you want to move a photo to another position, just click directly on the photo in the preview area and drag it to a new position. It will automatically resize if necessary.

Step Four:
You can have as many different photos as you have positions in your layout, so just continue dragging-and-dropping thumbnails from the left side of the dialog into position within the preview area.

Step Five:
If you'd prefer to just have all your imported photos appear on the page at once (rather than dragging-and-dropping them), turn off the Fill Page With First Photo checkbox and all imported photos on the left of the dialog will automatically flow into place.

Creating a PDF Presentation for a Client

In Elements 4.0 there's a feature that takes a group of images, creates a slide show (complete with transitions), and compresses it into PDF format so you can email it easily to a client for proofing. This is perfect for showing your portfolio to clients, sending clients proofs of wedding shots or portrait sittings, sending friends photos from a party, or one of a dozen other uses, none of which I can think of at this particular moment, but I'm sure it'll come to me later when I'm at the mall or driving to the office.

Step One:
Open the photos you want to use in your PDF presentation in the Editor, and then click on the Create button in the task bar above the Options Bar. (*Note:* You can also Control-click images in the Organizer, and then click the Create button.)

Step Two:
This brings up the Creation Setup dialog with a list of different projects you can create on the left side of the dialog. Click on the top option (Slide Show), and then click the OK button in the bottom-right corner of the dialog.

Step Three:
This brings up the Slide Show Preferences dialog, where you choose various options for your slide show. In this case, let's go with the default settings, so click the OK button near the bottom-right corner of the dialog.

Step Four:
Clicking OK brings up yet another dialog. At the bottom of the dialog are thumbnails of all the photos that will be included in your slide show. The thumbnails are arranged in the order in which they'll appear, but to change the order, just click-and-drag a thumbnail to where you'd like it to appear. If you want to remove an image, Right-click on its thumbnail and choose Delete Slide from the contextual menu. To add an image, click-and-hold on the Add Media button in the top center of the dialog, choose Photos and Videos from Folder, and browse for your image.

Continued

Step Five:

By default, Elements will provide a Fade transition between your slides, but you may want some variety. To choose a different transition, click on the tiny, right-facing arrow to the right of any transition's icon and select a new transition from the pop-up menu that appears. To play it safe, choose something that nearly always works, like Dissolve. To apply this to all of your slides, choose Apply to All from the same menu.

Step Six:

Along the right side of the dialog, in the Properties section, you can customize your active slide by changing its background color, enabling effects, etc. In the Extras section you can add graphics, text, or narration, but since we're doing a simple slide show here, I left the settings at their defaults and clicked the Output button near the top left of the dialog.

Step Seven:

This brings up the Slide Show Output dialog, where you can save your slide show as a PDF. Choose Save As a File from the list of options on the left, and then on the right side of the dialog, turn on the PDF File option. Here's where you choose your slides' settings. I like to use Small (800x600), but you can choose any size you'd like from the Slide Size pop-up menu (or enter your own preferred size by choosing Custom from the menu). Click OK and Elements 4.0 will create a PDF file that's ready for you to email to your client.

Step Eight:
When your client opens your emailed PDF, it automatically launches Adobe Reader in Full Screen mode (your photos appear centered on a black background), and the presentation begins. The capture here shows the first slide in a PDF presentation in Full Screen mode, right before it transitioned to the next photo. (*Note:* If for some strange reason your client/friend doesn't have Adobe Reader installed, he or she can download it free from Adobe's site at www.adobe.com/products/acrobat.)

TIP: Are eight steps just too many for ya? Create a basic PDF slide show by opening your images in the Editor, going under the File menu, and choosing Attach to Email. In the resulting dialog, choose Simple Slide Show (PDF) from the Format pop-up menu, click the Add button in the bottom left-hand corner to navigate to your images, and then choose your images' size and quality (see the following tutorial for recommended settings). When you click the Next button, your default email software will launch with a new message—complete with a PDF slide show—ready for you to send.

How to Email Photos

Believe it or not, this is one of those most-asked questions, and I guess it's because there are no official guidelines for emailing photos. Perhaps there should be, because there are photographers who routinely send me high-res photos that (a) get bounced back to them because of size restrictions, (b) take all day to download, or (c) never get here at all because there are no official guidelines on how to email photos. In the absence of such rules, consider these the "official" unofficial rules.

Step One:
Open the photo that you want to email in the Elements Editor. Go under the File menu and choose Attach to Email. (*Note:* You may get an Email dialog asking you to choose an email client as your default. Choose your email client [Microsoft Outlook, etc.] from the pop-up menu and click Continue.)

Step Two:
This opens your photo in the Attach to Email dialog. The first decision to make is: Who do you want to email this photo to? (Adobe calls this simple task Select Recipients, because that makes it sound significantly more complicated and confusing.) To choose who will receive your photo by email, click in the checkbox beside the contacts (who are in your Contact Book. If a contact isn't in the list, click on the Edit Contacts button at the bottom center of the dialog to add a contact to the list).

Step Three:
In the Choose Format section, leave it set at Individual Attachments. Then, in the Select Size and Quality section, choose the size at which you'd like to send your image. If you choose an image size other than the original size of the photo, you also get to choose a Quality setting. Remember: The higher the quality, the larger your file size will be, so try to find a happy medium. Try a 7 or an 8. Only go higher if you know the person to whom you're emailing this presentation has a high-speed Internet connection.

Step Four:
If you'd like to add a message to your email (like "Here's where I'm on vacation. The weather is here, wish you were beautiful," etc.), enter that in the Message area in the bottom-right corner of the dialog.

Step Five:
Once your options are set, click the Next button in the bottom right-hand corner of the dialog. Clicking Next launches your default email application and your photo and message are automatically attached. All that's left to do now is click the Send button and it's on its way.

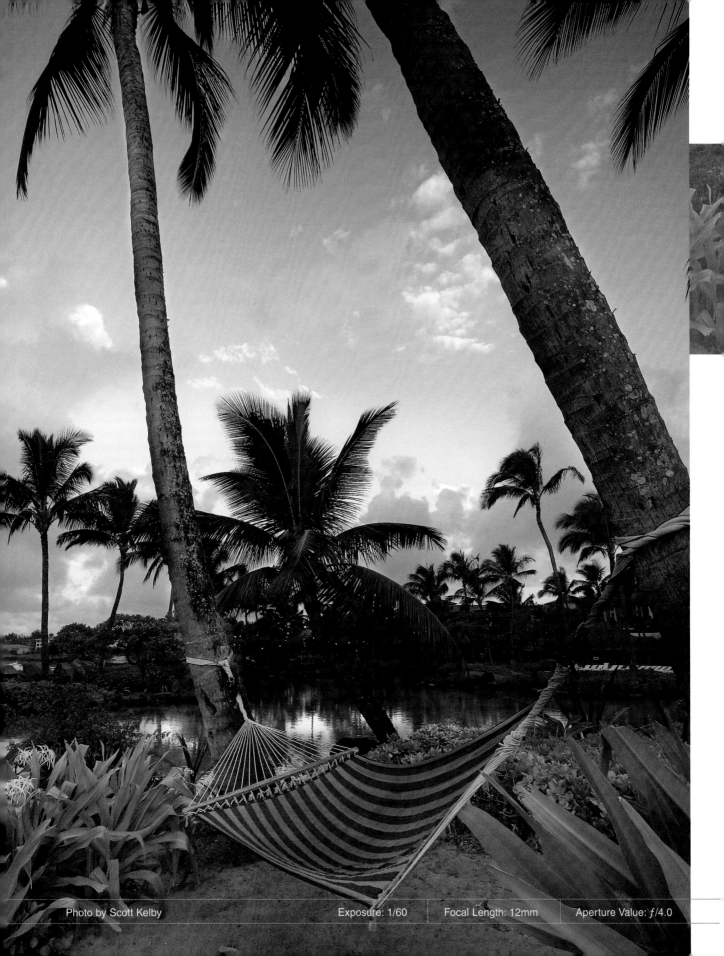

Exposure: 1/60 | Focal Length: 12mm | Aperture Value: ƒ/4.0

Create (or Die)
how to make presentations with your photos

Back in the old days, we'd edit a digital photo and then we'd just print it out. It was a simpler time. If we got the photo centered on the page, it was considered a minor miracle and people would come from local towns and villages just to see our centered prints. But now the young kids have these newfangled contraptions that let you take your photos and turn them into slide shows, webpages, wall calendars, and video CDs. Some folks call this progress, but I say it's just not right! It's not what photos were intended to do.

They're supposed to be still, lifeless, static, and centered on a white piece of paper. But then along comes Photoshop Elements 4.0, with its new "creation" features, and all of a sudden every crackerjack with 2 gigs of RAM thinks he's Dennis Hopper (who coincidentally starred in the documentary *Create [or Die]*, which was released in 2003 to a worldwide audience, many of whom own digital cameras, yet most of whom were not able to adequately center their photos on a page). Leave stuff like centering photos to the pros, I say.

Creating with Your Photos

There is an entire area of Elements 4.0 dedicated to creating projects with your photos. By projects, I mean transforming your photos from just prints into "creations" like full-fledged slide shows, wall calendars, postcards, or Web photo galleries. Here's just one way to access Elements' Create feature:

Step One:

There are about half a dozen ways to get to the Create section of Elements, but the easiest and most visible way to get there is to just click on the Create button that appears above the Options Bar of the Elements Editor or above the Timeline in the Organizer. By the way, if you click the Create button in the Editor, it will just launch the Organizer for you, and then it launches the Create section, so if you're already working in the Organizer, you're halfway there.

Create button in the Editor

Create button in the Organizer

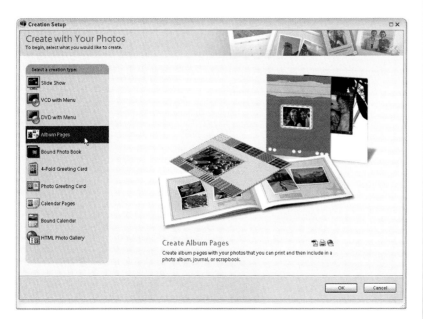

Step Two:
This brings up the Creation Setup dialog with a list of the creation options on your left and a brief description of each creation in the main area of the dialog on the right. To choose one of these creations, first click on the one you want in the list on the left, and then click the OK button on the bottom right.

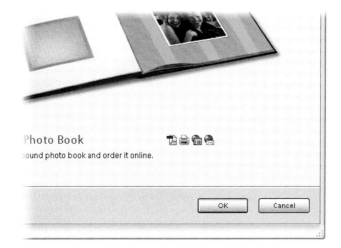

TIP: If you look in the bottom-right corner of the dialog, you'll see a row of tiny icons. These tell you what the final versions of each creation will be. In the screen shot shown here, the Acrobat icon means you can make a PDF of your creation; the printer icon means you can print your creation using your personal printer; the globe with a page icon means you can order your creation online to be custom printed; and the globe with an envelope means it can be emailed. Other icons you might see include the monitor icon, which means it can be viewed onscreen, and the monitor with a disc, which means you can make a video disc of your creation.

Making Full-Blown Slide Shows

Earlier in the book, we looked at how to create a simple slide show from selected photos in the Organizer, but if you really want to create a slide show masterpiece, this is where you come.

Step One:
Once you've clicked on the Create button (in the Organizer or Editor window) and the Creation Setup dialog appears, in the list of Creation types on the left, click on Slide Show, and then click the OK button.

Step Two:
This brings up the Slide Show Preferences dialog, where you choose how you want your slide show set up. For example, at the top you choose how many seconds each slide will appear onscreen. Below that you choose the transition between slides (will it be a soft dissolve or a quick cut between photos), and how long your transition will last. A popular transition effect is called Pan & Zoom (which slowly moves [pans] your images across the screen), and to turn this on, select the checkbox for Apply Pan & Zoom to All Slides.

©SCOTT KELBY

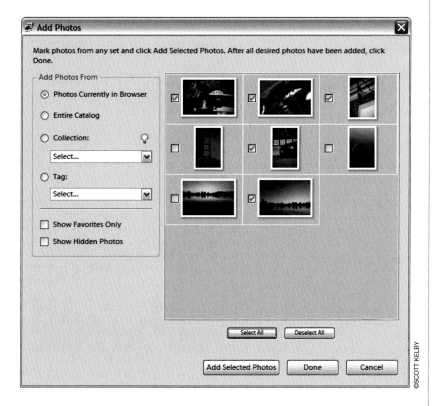

©SCOTT KELBY

Step Three:
Once you click OK, the Slide Show Editor appears, and this is where you'll create your magic (okay, "magic" is probably pushing it a bit, but this is where you'll "do your stuff"). If you selected photos in the Organizer (or Editor) before you clicked the Create button, these photos will appear in the Slide Show Editor's Photo Bin at the bottom, as shown here (which means you can skip Step 4). If not, you'll notice a blank gray screen is staring at you. It's waiting for you to choose which images will appear in your slide show, so click on the Add Media button at the top of the window, select Photos and Videos from Organizer (or Folder), then navigate to the photos you want to use in your slide show.

Step Four:
If you choose to add photos from the Organizer, the Add Photos window will appear. This is where you choose which photos you want to add to your slide show. *Note:* If you selected photos in the Organizer before you clicked Create's Slide Show option, you can skip this step, because photos will already be imported into your slide show—you'll only use Add Photos if either (a) you don't have any photos in your slide show, or (b) you want to add another photo (or more) to your existing slide show. Click the checkbox beside each photo you want in your slide show, then click the Add Selected Photos button at the bottom of the window and click Done.

Continued

Step Five:

To see a quick sample of what your slide show looks like at this point (before you start customizing it), click the Play button beneath the main preview window. You'll see a slide show of your imported photos in the order they were imported, with whichever transitions you chose in the Slide Show Preferences dialog. To stop, click the Pause button (which appears where the Play button used to be). If you're not thrilled with your slide show, it's probably because you're only seeing the default slide show. The slides aren't in order; there's no background music; you haven't customized the slide show your way. Well, that's about to change, because it's time to tweak your slide show.

Step Six:

The first thing to do is put the slides in the order you want them. To do that, just click on a thumbnail in the Photo Bin at the bottom of the dialog and drag it where you want it (the slides play from left to right, so if you want a particular slide to be first, drag that slide all the way to the left). As you drag slides around in the Photo Bin, you'll see a bar indicating where the slide will appear when you release the mouse button.

Step Seven:
With the slides in order, take a look directly beneath your photo thumbnails in the Photo Bin. You'll see "5 sec." That's telling you that this slide will stay onscreen for 5 seconds. If you want it onscreen for a shorter amount of time, just click directly on that number and a contextual menu of duration times will appear. If you want to apply a particular duration to all your slides (for example, you want them all to appear onscreen for 3 seconds), after you choose 3 sec for one slide, click on the time again for that slide and choose Set All Slides to 3 sec.

Step Eight:
Finally, the fun part—choosing your transitions. You can go with the one you originally chose in the Slide Show Preferences, or you can choose a new one. To do that, click directly on the little right-facing triangle that appears to the right of the square transition box (which is between your slides in the Photo Bin). This brings up a pop-up menu of transitions—just choose the one you want and it changes only that transition between those two slides. If you want that transition applied to all your slides, choose Apply to All at the top of the pop-up transition menu. (By the way, if you have no transition between slides, the international symbol for "No!" [a circle with a slash through it] will appear between your slides instead, but you can change that by clicking on the right-facing triangle next to it and choosing a transition from the pop-up list.)

Continued

Step Nine:

If you want to change the duration of one (or more) of your transitions, click on the transition, then in the Properties panel (on the right side of the Slide Show Editor window), change the Transition time (which is measured in seconds) from the pop-up menu (or choose Custom and type in how long you want your transition to be).

Step Ten:

Okay, what's even cooler than transitions? Pan & Zoom (in fact, you can have transitions and Pan & Zoom). Pan & Zoom brings movement to your slides, and this movement makes your slide show feel less static, as the photos move slowly left to right, top to bottom, while they slowly zoom in and out. That's why this effect is so popular. If you clicked the Apply Pan & Zoom to All Slides checkbox in the Slide Show Preferences (when you first opened your slide show), then all you have to do to edit a Pan & Zoom is click on a slide and the Pan & Zoom controls will appear in the Properties panel on the right side of the dialog.

Step Eleven:

If you didn't turn on Pan & Zoom for all slides from the start, it's easy to turn it on. Just click on the slide you want to apply it to, and then in the Properties panel turn on the checkbox for Enable Pan & Zoom. (Needless to say, to turn off the Pan & Zoom for any slide, just click on the slide and turn off the Enable Pan & Zoom checkbox in the Properties panel. I know, I said "needless to say," but then I said it anyway. It's a personality disorder.)

Step Twelve:

Once you've got Pan & Zoom turned on, you can tweak it three very distinct ways: (1) When you turn on Pan & Zoom, a green rectangle appears in the preview window, and the word "Start" appears in the bottom-right corner. You can reposition the location and size of this green square (shown here) to where you'd like the panning and zooming to start. In the Properties panel, if you click on the End thumbnail, you can position the panning end point by moving (and/or resizing) the red square. (2) You can swap the positions of these squares by using the three little buttons between the Start and End thumbnails in the Properties panel. (3) You can add an additional Pan & Zoom, which essentially duplicates your slide, and lets you add another Pan & Zoom segment, so you could have your photo pan from left to right, then in the second segment, zoom from large to small. To do this, click on the Add Another Pan & Zoom to This Slide checkbox at the bottom of the Properties panel.

Step Thirteen:

Now, on to adding titles: If you want to add a title to the beginning of your slide show, click on the first slide in the Photo Bin, and then click the Add Text button at the top of the Slide Show Editor. This brings up the Edit Text dialog, in which you enter your text. As you begin typing, your text appears onscreen.

Continued

Step Fourteen:

Once you click OK in the Edit Text dialog, you can reposition your text by just clicking-and-dragging it where you want it. You can also now choose which font, size, style, opacity, and color you want for your text (and a host of other type tweaks) in the Properties panel on the right side of the dialog. If you need to edit your text, just click on the Edit Text button in the Properties panel or change your font, style, etc., in the bottom of the panel.

Step Fifteen:

If you want your title to appear over a blank slide, rather than over a photo, you can create your title over a blank background by clicking the Add Blank Slide button at the top of the window. This creates an empty black slide. Now you can either click the Add Text button to create the text that will appear over your black slide, or you click on the Text icon in the Extras panel (on the top right of the window), which reveals a list of pre-designed type treatments, including text with shadows (which are about impossible to see over a black background, by the way).

Step Sixteen:

If you want to change the color of your blank slide (from the default black color), you can do that by clicking on the blank slide (in the Photo Bin), and then in the Properties panel you'll see a black color swatch named "Background Color." Click on it to bring up the Color Picker dialog, where you can choose a different color. Once you've chosen a new color, click OK, and your currently selected slide's color will be changed.

Step Seventeen:

All right, the slides are in order, the transitions have been chosen, and the titles have been created. Now, for the finishing touch—music. To add some background music to your slide show, click on the gray bar directly beneath the Photo Bin with the words "Click Here to Add Audio to Your Slide Show." This brings up a dialog prompting you to choose your audio file. You can browse for your own music files or choose from a list of music files in Elements' sample catalog. When you find a song you like, click on its name in the list, and then click the Open button.

Step Eighteen:

Now it's time to preview the finished slide show. Click the Preview button in the top-right corner of the Slide Show Editor, then sit back, relax, and enjoy the "magic." If, while watching your preview, you see something you want to change, just click on the Edit Slide Show button that appears to the right of the Preview button.

Step Nineteen:

When the show is tweaked to perfection (or your personal satisfaction, whichever comes first), it's time to output it into its final form. Click on the Output button on the left side of the Slide Show Editor to bring up the Output options. Now you just click to choose what you want to do with your final show: save it, burn it to CD (or DVD), email your slide show to a friend (in which case, you'll choose either to create a PDF or a very compressed movie), you can post it online, or watch it on TV. This part's up to you, my now accomplished slide show producer.

Creating Postcards or Greeting Cards

If you're interested in cheating Hallmark out of a few bucks, here's a great way to do it—create your own greeting cards. But it's not just about the money—it's about the personalization that can only come from using one of your own photos that makes the card really special (and cheap!). Here's how to do the holidays on a budget (kidding):

Step One:
Start by going to the Organizer and choosing the photo you want to use on the front of your greeting card. Then, click the Create button in the task bar at the top of the Organizer.

Step Two:
When the Creation Setup dialog appears, in the list of creations on the left side of the dialog, click on Photo Greeting Card, and then click OK.

Step Three:
Here's where you choose your layout from the list of styles on the right side of the dialog. If you scroll down a bit, you'll find a variety of pre-made templates (like the one shown here from the section called Season's Greeting), or you can go with more traditional layouts by scrolling back up to the top (hint: go with the traditional). Once you've chosen a layout (please don't choose the one I chose here), click the Next Step button.

Step Four:
Here's where it asks you which photo you want to use. Why don't we use the one we chose earlier? (This is kind of a "Duh!" screen.) Click the Next Step button.

Continued

Step Five:

This section lets you customize the text that will appear on your card, and it also lets you crop your photo within the border by dragging the cropping handles outward (the image will be cropped within the preset photo frame). To add your own text, double-click directly on the words "Double-Click to Insert Title" and the Title dialog will appear. To add more text, double-click on the words "Double-Click to Insert Greeting." After you've entered your text (and chosen your font, color, etc., in the dialog), click on the Done button. Now, click on the Next Step button.

Step Six:

In this screen you simply enter a name in the Photo Greeting Card Name field, and then click the Save button, so if you need to edit it later, you've got the original.

Step Seven:

On the final screen, you'll see a list of things you can do with your greeting card: create a PDF, print it out, or email it. Click on the one you want and it's on its way.

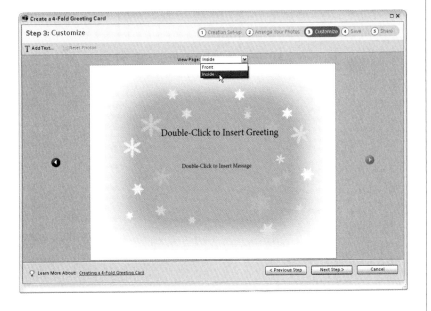

Deluxe Greeting Card:

You can create a four-fold greeting card the same way as creating a photo greeting card, so I won't put you through that whole thing again. Just follow the steps above, except in Step 2 choose 4-Fold Greeting Card. Then, in Step 5, to add text inside your card, choose Inside from the View Page pop-up menu above the card preview area, double-click the placeholder text in the preview, and enter your text in the Greeting dialog.

Creating Photo Album Pages

This is one of my favorite things in Elements 4.0 because Adobe did such a slick job with it. They've created some great-looking templates for photo album pages and digital scrapbooking—and all you have to do is choose which layout you want and it does the rest. Here's how to start using this way-cool feature:

Step One:
Start by going to the Organizer and Control-clicking on the photos you want on your first photo album page. Then, click the Create button (in the task bar above the Timeline) in the top center of the Organizer window.

Step Two:
When the Creation Setup dialog appears, in the list of creations on the left side of the dialog, click on Album Pages, and then click the OK button.

Step Three:

This is where you choose which layout you'd like for your album pages by clicking on one of the styles in the list on the right side of the dialog. As you click on a layout, it gives you a preview of that style on the left. Once you've chosen your layout, then choose how many photos you want to appear on your page from the Photos Per Page pop-up menu in the Options category on the bottom-left side of the dialog. Also choose to include any captions, a title page, etc., and then click the Next Step button.

Step Four:

Now it's time to drag-and-drop the photos into the order you want them to appear. By default, the first photo imported winds up as the photo on the title page (if you chose that option in the previous step), so if you want a different photo on the title page, just click-and-drag it over into the first position. Once you have your photos in the order you want them, click the Next Step button.

Continued

Step Five:

The first page you'll see is the title page, and you can edit the text above your title page if you'd like later, but for now, click the arrow button to the right of the title page preview to jump to your first photo album page.

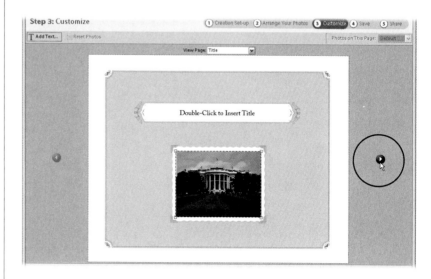

Step Six:

This is where you determine how your photos are cropped into their frames. If you click on one of your photos, you'll see a cropping border around the photo. You can move or resize the photo by grabbing one of the corner points.

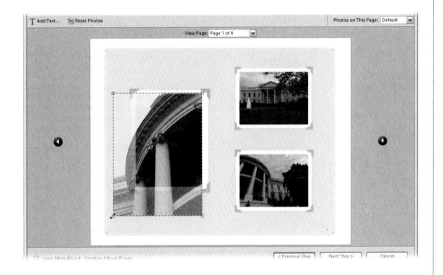

Step Seven:

In the example shown here, I grabbed the bottom-left corner point of the cropping border and dragged outward, which crops the photo in closer. The transparent areas that appear outside the fixed border of your photo will be clipped off when the photo album page is printed. To see how your crop looks, just click on any other photo. If you don't like the order of the photos, then click the Previous Step button and reposition your images (starting with Page 1, just after the title page).

TIP: If you want to edit your title page, now's the time to do it. Just click the Previous Page arrow button to the left of the preview window, double-click the placeholder text that appears, and enter your text in the Title dialog. Just click the right arrow button to return to your album page.

Continued

Step Eight:
Once all the photos are in order on each album page, click the Next Step button. Now it's time to save your album pages, so just give it a name (in the Album Pages Name field on the top-right side of the dialog), and then click the Save button. Just one more step...

Step Nine:
Now you'll see a list of things you can do with your photo album pages: create a PDF, print them out, or email 'em. Click on the one that sounds best to you, and you're done! By the way, if you want to edit or otherwise mess with your album pages, you'll find them in the Organizer window.

Okay, let's say you have 12 really great shots. Now what do you do? That's right—it's calendar time—and using the built-in templates (and auto-dating), it's really so simple that you almost *have* to create your own calendars.

Creating Calendars

Step One:
Open the Organizer and Control-click on all the photos you want to appear in your calendar. (I probably don't have to say this, but open at least 13 so you have one for the cover and then one for every month.) Then, click the Create button in the task bar (above the Timeline) at the top of the Organizer.

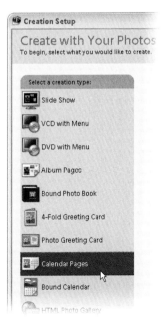

Step Two:
When the Creation Setup dialog appears, in the list of creations on the left side of the dialog, click on Calendar Pages, and then click OK. *Note:* If you want to spend a little money and have your calendar bound professionally, choose Bound Calendar instead. You'll go through the same basic steps mentioned here, except at the end you'll have an option to purchase your calendar online.

Continued

Step Three:

Here you'll do two important things: (1) You'll choose the layout for your calendar from the list of calendar templates on the right side of the dialog, and (2) along the bottom-left corner you'll choose when your calendar starts and ends from the pop-up menus. By choosing those starting and ending dates, Photoshop Elements 4.0 will do the hard part (putting in the dates) for you. When you've made your choices, click on the Next Step button.

Step Four:

Here's where you'll decide which month gets which photo by simply dragging-and-dropping your photos into the order you want (notice the month for each image appears in the top-left corner of the images' thumbnails). When they're in order, click the Next Step button.

Step Five:
The next dialog lets you add captions (if you chose this option in Step 1) and crop your photos, starting with the cover. To add a caption (or title), just double-click on the placeholder text that's already there and a dialog will appear, in which you can add your own text. Next, click the right arrow button to the right of the preview so you can go to and edit individual months. To crop your photos to size, just click on one of the corners of the visible cropping border and drag out until it fits in the preset frame the way you want it to. (*Note:* Transparent areas that fall outside the original border will be clipped away.) When it looks good to you, click the Next Step button.

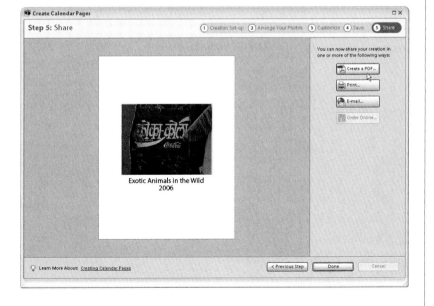

Step Six:
In this next screen, you'll simply enter a name in the Calendar Pages Name field, and then click the Save button at the bottom of the dialog. In the final screen (shown here), you can choose how you want to output your calendar on the right side of the dialog: by creating a PDF of it, printing it out, or emailing it. That's it—your first calendar.

Creating a Video CD

If you've created some slide shows (using the Slide Show feature mentioned earlier in this chapter), you can take those slides shows and transfer them to a video CD, which will play on many DVD players (so you can play them directly on your TV), and you do the whole thing right from within Elements 4.0. Here's how it works:

Step One:
First, you need to create your slide shows, so go ahead and do that, because essentially what you'll create is a CD of slide shows with a default menu that's created by Elements. So if you don't have slide shows first, you can't create a CD, so start there (see the slide show tutorial earlier in this chapter). Once you have your slide shows created, go to the Organizer and click on the Create button.

Step Two:
When the Creation Setup dialog appears, in the list of creations on the left side of the dialog, click on VCD with Menu, and then click OK. *Note:* If you have a DVD burner in your computer, you can choose DVD with Menu and follow the steps here, as the options are basically the same. (I probably don't have to tell you this, but if you have Adobe Premiere Elements 2.0, choose this option and then edit the output file in Premiere.)

Step Three:
This dialog is where you choose which slide shows will comprise your video CD. To add slide shows to your list, click the Add Slide Shows button in the top-left corner and a dialog will appear, where you can choose which of your saved slide shows will appear on your VCD by clicking on their checkboxes. Then, click OK to add them to the main dialog.

Step Four:
Once your slides appear in the main window, you can insert a blank CD into your computer's CD burner, then click the Burn button on the bottom right-hand side of the dialog to burn your slide shows to disc. In the resulting Burn dialog, just click OK, and then Elements will create a WMV file and burn it to an empty disc. (*Note:* Be sure that NTSC is selected in the Video Options section of the Create a VCD with Menu dialog.) Now you can insert your VCD into your DVD player and watch your slide show on your TV.

Creating Your Own Photo Website

If you want to expand the reach of your photos to a wider audience, there's no better way than to create a photo website, and once again Elements 4.0 does all the hard work for you. All you have to do is basically choose which photos you want, which layout you want, and it does the rest. (I covered the HTML Photo Gallery in detail earlier in the book, but I wanted to cover it briefly here as well, since it's one of the "Create" functions, and you'll probably come looking for it in this chapter, too.) Here's how to go global with your photos:

Step One:
Open the Organizer and Control-click on the photos you want to appear on your Web gallery. Then, click the Create button in the task bar at the top of the Organizer.

Step Two:
When the Creation Setup dialog appears, in the list of creations on the left side of the dialog, click on HTML Photo Gallery, and then click OK.

Step Three:
This brings up a dialog where you make all of your most important choices, with the first choice being which layout you want for your gallery. You choose this from the Gallery Style pop-up menu at the top of the dialog. There is a preview of how each gallery looks, but you have to choose it first by name from the list, then when you release the mouse button, the preview of that Gallery Style appears in the dialog.

Continued

Step Four:

If the Banner tab isn't active, click on the word "Banner" to bring up the options. This is where you get to add a title to your site and an email address if you like (this is especially important if you're having clients do their proofing from your website). At the bottom of the Banner tab (in the Destination category) is the location on your hard disk that your HTML file and image folder will be saved to, so click the Browse button and choose that now, so later you'll be able to find your gallery easily for uploading to the Web. Then, enter a name for your gallery's folder in the Site Folder field.

Step Five:

The Thumbnails tab and the Large Photos tabs are where you determine how large the thumbnail images will appear on your website, and how large the full-size photos will appear when a client clicks on one of the thumbnails. You can stick with the default sizes, or click on the Large Photos tab to choose a size and quality setting of your own. You can also choose whether captions will appear below your photos, and if so, you can choose the font and size, too.

Step Six:
Hit the Save button at the bottom of the dialog, and your webpage will be created and saved. Then Elements 4.0 will display a full-size preview of your finished HTML webpage in the HTML Photo Gallery Browser (as shown here). Now look in that folder you specified earlier, and you'll find an HTML document (named "index"), along with folders of your images, thumbnails, pages, etc., ready for you to upload to the Web (providing you have a place to upload them to, of course). *Note:* Everything in that folder gets uploaded: files, folders, and the whole shebang.

Ordering Prints with Just One Click

This is more than just ordering prints with one click; this is setting up your friends and family so you can send them prints directly from Kodak's lab, straight to their house, and you do the whole thing from your computer. You can send yourself prints too, but you already figured that, right?

Step One:

Okay, first let's set up some friends and family members that you'll want to be able to send prints to (direct from Kodak's online service, which is built into Elements 4.0). You see that Order Prints panel (nested in the Organize Bin) in the bottom-right corner of the Organizer window? That's where it all happens. Start by clicking on the New button.

Step Two:

This brings up the New Order Prints Target dialog, which is basically where you're going to enter the contact info for the first family member or friend to whom you want to be able to send "one-click" prints. So, enter a name, mailing address, etc. (so Kodak will know where to ship the prints), then click OK, and that person will be added to your Order Prints panel. Keep clicking the New button and adding contacts until all the people you want to get prints (including yourself) are listed.

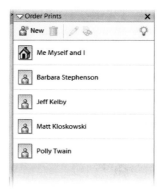

Step Three:
Once you've added some friends and family (and yourself as well), each of you will appear listed in the Order Prints panel. Now, the hard part's over, and the fun can officially begin.

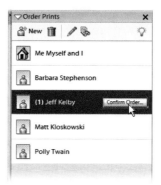

Step Four:
Now, the next time you're looking at a photo and you think, "Ol' Jeff would like a print of this," just click on the photo, and drag-and-drop it right onto Jeff's name in the Order Prints panel. A Confirm Order button will appear next to his name, and once you've dragged over as many photos as you want to send to Jeff, click the Confirm Order button.

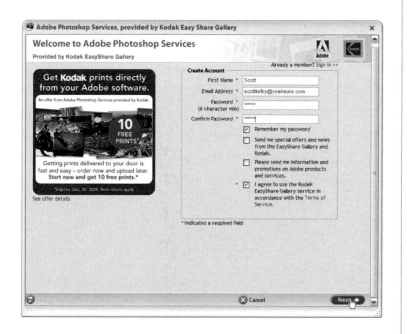

Step Five:
If this is the first time you've ordered prints from within Elements 4.0 (and I'm assuming it is, or you wouldn't be reading this tutorial, right?), then you'll have to create an account with Adobe Photoshop Services, which is partnering with Kodak to provide your prints. To set up your account (registration is free), just go up to the top of the Organizer window, just under the Help menu, and click on Order Prints. This brings up the Adobe Photoshop Services dialog, where you can register for your online printing account. Once you've filled out the form on this page, click the Next button.

Continued

Step Six:

In this screen, you'll choose what style and size prints you want to send. In the example shown here, I'm going to send him one 4x6" single print, which runs me 15 cents (not bad, eh?). If I want more copies or different sizes, I can choose them here as well (as long as my photo has enough resolution to create prints larger than 4x6", of course). Once you've made your choices here, just click the Next button, and it will ask you for some nasty things, like payment information and awful stuff like that.

Step Seven:

After another screen or two you'll reach the Order Prints Confirmation page, and your prints will be processed and sent directly to your friend's address. Although this takes a few steps the first time you register for this service, from now on you just drag-and-drop photos on your friend's or family member's name in the Order Prints panel, and you can bypass almost all of this (of course, you'll still want to choose how many prints and what size), but besides that, it's almost a one-click process and prints are on the way. Try this service once, and you'll find it so easy and convenient, you'll use it again and again until you eventually file for bankruptcy.

Index

Colophon

The book was produced by the author and design team using all Macintosh computers, including a Power Mac G4 733-MHz, a Power Mac G4 Dual Processor 1.25-GHz, a Power Mac G5 1.8-GHz, and a Power Mac G5 Dual Processor 2-GHz. We use LaCie, Sony, and Apple monitors.

Page layout was done using InDesign CS2. The headers for each technique are set in 20 point CronosMM700 Bold with the Horizontal Scaling set to 95%. Body copy is set using CronosMM408 Regular at 10 point on 13 leading, with the Horizontal Scaling set to 95%.

Screen captures were taken with TechSmith SnagIt 7.1.1 on a Dell Precision M60 and a Dell Precision Workstation 650 and were placed and sized within InDesign CS2. The book was output at 150-line screen, and all in-house proofing was done using a Tektronix Phaser 7700 by Xerox.

Additional Resources

ScottKelbyBooks.com
For information on Scott's other books, visit his book site. For background info on Scott, visit www.scottkelby.com.

http://www.scottkelbybooks.com

Photoshop Elements Techniques Newsletter
Photoshop Elements Techniques is a newsletter packed with practical, real-world tips and techniques from some of the leading Photoshop Elements gurus, including Dave Cross, Jan Kabili, Dave Huss, and Scott Kelby. Every issue of Elements will be a valuable resource for digital photographers. Visit the website to view subscription information.

http://www.photoshopelementsuser.com

Photoshop Elements Techniques Website
The ultimate source for Photoshop Elements users features tutorials, downloads, forums, and much more! The site also contains up-to-date Elements news, tips and tricks, and contests.

http://www.photoshopelementsuser.com

KW Computer Training Videos
Scott Kelby and Dave Cross are featured in a series of Adobe Photoshop and Adobe Photoshop Elements training DVDs, each on a particular Photoshop or Elements topic, available from KW Computer Training. Visit the website or call 800-201-7323 for orders or more information.

http://www.photoshopvideos.com

National Association of Photoshop Professionals (NAPP)
The industry trade association for Adobe® Photoshop® users and the world's leading resource for Photoshop training, education, and news.

http://www.photoshopuser.com

Adobe Photoshop Seminar Tour
See Scott live on the Adobe Photoshop Seminar Tour, the nation's most popular Photoshop seminars. For upcoming tour dates and class schedules, visit the tour website.

http://www.photoshopseminars.com

Photoshop World Conference & Expo
The convention for Adobe Photoshop users has now become the largest Photoshop-only event in the world. Scott Kelby is technical chair and education director for the event, as well as one of the instructors.

http://www.photoshopworld.com

PlanetPhotoshop.com
"The Ultimate Photoshop Site" features Photoshop news, tutorials, reviews, and articles posted daily. The site also contains the Web's most up-to-date resource on other Photoshop-related websites and information.

http://www.planetphotoshop.com

Layers magazine
Layers—The How-To Magazine for Everything Adobe—is the foremost authority on Adobe's design, digital video, digital photography, and education applications. Each issue features timely product news, plus the quick tips, hidden shortcuts, and step-by-step tutorials for working in today's digital market. America's top-selling computer book author for 2004, Scott Kelby, is editor-in-chief of *Layers*.

http://www.layersmagazine.com

DOWN
Dirty
TRICKS

Scott Kelby

PHOTOSHOP® ELEMENTS DOWN & DIRTY TRICKS

The Photoshop Elements Down and Dirty Tricks Team

CREATIVE DIRECTOR
Felix Nelson

TECHNICAL EDITOR
Polly Reincheld

COPY EDITOR
Chris Main

PRODUCTION EDITOR
Kim Gabriel

PRODUCTION MANAGER
Dave Damstra

PRODUCTION DESIGNERS
Dave Korman
Taffy Orlowski

COVER DESIGNED BY
Felix Nelson

COVER PHOTOS AND STOCK IMAGES
The royalty-free stock images in this book are courtesy of

Published by
New Riders / Peachpit Press

Composed in Cronos, Helvetica, and Apple Garamond Light by NAPP Publishing

Trademarks
All terms mentioned in this book that are known to be trademarks or service marks have been appropriately capitalized. New Riders / Peachpit Press cannot attest to the accuracy of this information. Use of a term in the book should not be regarded as affecting the validity of any trademark or service mark.

Photoshop is a registered trademark of Adobe Systems, Inc.
Windows is a registered trademark of Microsoft Corporation.

Warning and Disclaimer
This book is designed to provide information about Photoshop Elements. Every effort has been made to make this book as complete and as accurate as possible, but no warranty of fitness is implied.

The information is provided on an as-is basis. The authors and New Riders / Peachpit Press shall have neither liability nor responsibility to any person or entity with respect to any loss or damages arising from the information contained in this book or from the use of the discs or programs that may accompany it.

Printed and bound in the United States of America

www.peachpit.com
www.scottkelbybooks.com

For my close friend
Rod Harlan

"It's the friends that you can
call up at 4 a.m. that matter."
—Marlene Dietrich

ACKNOWLEDGMENTS

I consider myself very, very blessed. Each day I get to work with such a wonderful group of people, and when I'm not working, I'm surrounded by family and friends whom I dearly love, all of whom come together to help and enrich my life in so many ways. There's not a printed acknowledgment I could write that would honor them in the way they deserve, but one of the benefits of writing a book is that at least you get to try.

Kalebra: My wonderful, beautiful, amazing, hilarious, fun-filled, loving wife. You're the greatest thing that's ever happened to me, and asking you to marry me 15 years ago was clearly the single best decision I've ever made. Your spirit, warmth, beauty, patience, and unconditional love continue to prove what everybody always says—I'm the luckiest guy in the world.

Jordan: Little buddy—you're just the greatest. A father couldn't ask for a more fun, more crazy, more lovable, or more loving son than you. I'm so thrilled and proud of the little man you're becoming, and you're so blessed to have your Mom's heart, compassion, and spirit. You're a very special little boy, and you've already touched so many people that I can't imagine all the wonders, adventure, and happiness life has in store for you.

Jeff: I can't tell you what a blessing it's been having you as a brother, and how thrilled I am that for the past three-and-half years, you've been part of our team (plus, I love getting to sneak out for lunch with you every day). You've had an amazing, wonderful, and important impact on my life, and just hearing your voice puts a smile on my face. I love you, man.

Dave Moser: I truly value our friendship all these many years, and I'm thrilled with all the fun and exciting things we're able to do together. There are few people with your passion, guts, integrity, vision, unflinching dedication to quality, and who always insist on raising the bar. I have to thank you for totally sharing my "what-we-do-next-has-to-be-better-than-what-we-did-before" credo. It sometimes annoys the hell out of everyone around us, but it is who we are, and "it is what it is."

Felix Nelson: I don't know how you do it, but you always do. If you had nothing but your amazing Photoshop talents, you'd be in the top one-quarter of one percent of Photoshop designers in the world, but your creativity, talent, ideas, discipline, and humor put you in a league all by yourself. I remember Jack Davis asking me: "Where in the world did you find Felix?" I can only figure God sent you our way. Thanks for everything you do, here in the book, in leading our creative team, and for your friendship and dedication. You da man!

Chris Main: You were there from just about the very beginning and I'm honored to still have you on our team, and I'm delighted I get to work and hang out with you doing lots of very fun stuff. Plus, you have a really cool home cinema. Well done, Mr. Main!

Dave Damstra: If they ever have a competition for best page layout guy in the business, I'm sending you to steal the show. Having you lay out my books is definitely a strategic advantage, and you set the standard, not only in your work, but in your amazing attitude in life as well.

Polly Reincheld: You've only been working with us a short time, but you've already become such a valued member of our team. Your tech-editing skills are absolutely top-notch, but your attitude, sense of humor, and personality put you over the top. We're very lucky to have found you, and I'm really delighted to have you tech-editing my books.

Kathy Siler: Despite the fact that the Redskins are at the bottom of their division, you seem to keep a great attitude (but I know that it's only because my Bucs are near the bottom of the NFC South, too). Okay, Redskins jokes aside (Hey, where's Champ Bailey?), I can't thank you enough for all the things you do—you make my job so much easier (partially because you do so much of it for me), and you do it with such great ease and such a great attitude, and you really look out for me (and believe me, that's no easy job). In short—you rock, kid!

Jim Workman and Jean A. Kendra: I'm very fortunate to have business partners who understand what it takes to do what we do. I can't thank you enough for your constant support, understanding, freedom, and help in accomplishing my goals.

Kim Gabriel: I don't have to tell you—it ain't easy putting together one of these books, but you keep a lot of plates in the air, you keep the trains running on time, and you do a marvelous job of keeping it all moving ahead. I can't thank you enough.

Nancy Ruenzel: My heartfelt thanks to you for helping me through the transition, and for placing such a high value on integrity and always striving to do "the right thing." It's the core reason why our partnership works so well, and I'm honored to have you as my publisher. My thanks to everyone at Peachpit Publishing who works so hard, who shows such loyalty, who is willing to take chances and try new things, yet remains solely focused on just making great books.

Adobe: Thanks to all my friends at the mother ship, including Addy Roff, Mark Delman, Julieanne Kost, Rye Livingston, Russell Brown, Terry "T-bone" White, Kevin Connor, Karen Gauthier, Deb Whitman, Russell Brady, and John Nack. Also, a special thanks to Mark Dahm for his invaluable help with this book.

My personal thanks go to Jeffrey Burke at Brand X Pictures for enabling me to use some of their wonderful stock images in this book.

Kudos and continued thanks to my home team: Julie Stephenson, Barbara Thompson, Fred Maya, Ronni O'Neil, Melinda Gotelli, Pete Kratzenberg, Dave "Kid Rock" Korman, Margie "From New York" Rosenstein, Dave Gales, Dave Cross, and Daphne Durkee. Gone but not forgotten: Stacy Behan, Barbara Rice, Chris Smith, Steve Weiss, Sarah Hughes, and Jill Nakashima.

Thanks to my mentors whose wisdom and whip-cracking have helped me immeasurably, including: John Graden, Jack Lee, Judy Farmer, Dave Gales, and Douglas Poole.

Most importantly, I want to thank God, and His son Jesus Christ, for leading me to the woman of my dreams, for blessing us with such a special little boy, for allowing me to make a living doing something I truly love, for always being there when I need Him, and for blessing me with a wonderful, fulfilling, and happy life, and such a warm, loving family to share it with.

ABOUT THE AUTHOR

Scott Kelby

Scott is Editor-in-Chief and co-founder of *Photoshop User* magazine, Editor-in-Chief of Nikon's digital software magazine, Executive Editor of the *Photoshop Elements Techniques* newsletter, and Publisher of *Layers* magazine (the how-to magazine for everything Adobe).

He is President of the National Association of Photoshop Professionals (NAPP), the trade association for Adobe® Photoshop® users, and he's President of KW Media Group, Inc., a Florida-based software education and publishing firm.

Scott is the best-selling author of more than 30 books, which have been translated into more than a dozen languages, including *The Photoshop Elements Book for Digital Photographers, Photoshop Down & Dirty Tricks, Photoshop Classic Effects,* and *The Photoshop Book for Digital Photographers,* and co-author of *Photoshop Killer Tips,* all from New Riders.

Scott is Training Director for the Adobe Photoshop Seminar Tour, Conference Technical Chair for the Photoshop World Conference & Expo, and a speaker at graphics trade shows and events around the world. He is also featured in a series of Adobe Photoshop and Photoshop Elements training DVDs and has been training Photoshop users since 1993.

For more background info on Scott, visit www.scottkelby.com.

TABLE OF CONTENTS www.scottkelbybooks.com

2005 SUNCOAST GOLF CLASSIC

WITWORTH KEADING GALLERY

THIS IS NOT THE INTRODUCTION

Every book has an introduction, and virtually nobody reads it. That's why, instead of including a boring introduction that nobody will read anyway, this is actually the "preamble" to the book. That's right, baby—a preamble. This is more important than it may sound at first, because as you're probably aware, not many printed documents these days have a preamble (though this could certainly start a trend). In fact, the only document I can think of that has a preamble is the U.S. Constitution (and it's done pretty well thus far). So I'm following in the footsteps of our forefathers by trying to create a piece that will endure for more than 200 years (or until the next version of Elements is released—whichever comes first).

When you break it down, the word "preamble" is really ideal because, as you know, the prefix "pre" means "before the fix" (which in layman's terms means "this all occurred before something was broken"), and the word "amble" is the root of the Latin word "ambulance," which is what you'd need if you were to break your foot while reading this book. So, in short, this preamble is what to read before you break your foot. Ah, it all makes perfect sense now, doesn't it?

So now that we've established that this is clearly NOT an introduction, what will reading this do for you (you being the wonderful, multifaceted, truly unique, genius-type person who bought this book)? Reading this will help you "get inside my head." (Don't worry. I've got a huge bobble-head with more than 120,000 square feet of contiguous air-conditioned warehouse space, so climb right in.)

All kidding aside, taking a quick moment to read this preamble will make using this book much easier and much more enjoyable for you. Primarily because you'll then understand how and why it was written, why I did certain things the way I did, and then how to get the most from this book. Plus, it says something about you and the kind of person you are (the kind of person who will continue reading this preamble, knowing full well that it's really the introduction, simply because you don't want to hurt my feelings. I dig you, man). Now, on to how to use this book.

How to use this book

Think of this as a "Photoshop Elements special effects cookbook." Need to apply a depth-of-field effect to a photo? No sweat. It's in here. Want to make it look like you took your shot in a studio with a full lighting setup? It's in here, too. Need to do cool stuff right now, for a project that's due tomorrow? Just turn to the page that has the effect you need, and follow the step-by-step instructions.

You'll be able to re-create every technique in this book, regardless of your level of Photoshop Elements experience, and you'll unlock the secrets for creating today's hottest photographic effects—the same ones used by the top pros—and the same ones you see every day in magazines, on TV, in Hollywood, and on the Web. Techniques that would otherwise have taken years to learn, but are easy—once you know the secrets. You'll be absolutely amazed at how simple these tricks really are, and they're all here, including those closely guarded, insider, "down-and-dirty" tricks of the trade. It doesn't require years of study—there are no complex mathematical concepts to master—in short, there's no baloney. It's (as we say) "just the funk and not the junk!"

Okay, so now you know what the book is all about—special photographic effects and cool tricks—but you probably have some other questions. Probing, lingering personal questions whose answers may be too uncomfortable for our studio audience, so instead I thought I'd do something safer—a simple Q&A (Quebec & Albatross) section where I make up the questions I'd like to have answered if I were the person buying this book, and then I answer them, as if I'd written this book (which coincidentally, I did). If this sounds at all confusing, it should. Here we go:

Q. Where should I start in the book?
A. Honestly, it doesn't matter. This book isn't designed to be read like a novel, starting with Chapter 1, then Chapter 2, etc. This is a "jump-in-anywhere" book, so jump in at the technique that interests you most. Wherever you start, you'll be able to do the technique right on the spot, because everything is spelled out.

...you'll be able to re-create every single effect in this book, regardless of your previous Photoshop Elements experience.

Q. Do I have to be really good at Photoshop Elements?

A. When I wrote this book, I wrote it so any user, at any level of Photoshop Elements experience, could jump right in and create these effects. For most people this is a blessing, but if you've been using Photoshop Elements since version 1.0, there's something you should know: I spell everything out (at least the first time, in every tutorial). And just because I do that (making the book accessible to everyone), you shouldn't let it "get to you." For example, in a tutorial, the first time I have you make a new blank layer, I write: "Create a new blank layer by clicking on the Create a New Layer icon at the top of the Layers palette." If you've been creating layers since *Roseanne* was a top-rated TV show, you're going to be like, "Oh, this is for beginners." I had to do it that way. Since this isn't a "Start at Chapter 1 and read it cover to cover" book (you can jump in anywhere), someone who's new to Photoshop Elements (like a professional photographer who's now shooting digital) might not know how to create a new layer. There is no "Here's how Photoshop Elements works" chapter at the beginning, like you get in every other Photoshop Elements book. Because of that, the first time a command appears in a technique, I write the whole darn thing out. Again, it's just a few extra words, and you can bounce right by it if you already know how to do it, so don't let it slow you down.

…I wrote this book so any user, at any level of Photoshop Elements experience, could jump right in and create these same effects.

Q. So is this book full of advanced techniques?

A. Well, in a way, yes, in a way, no. Here's the thing: The techniques you're going to learn in this book are the very same techniques used by today's leading digital photographers, Web wizards, and designers. They use these effects on a daily basis, and you can be sure that if they're working for some major TV network, a Hollywood studio, or a worldwide ad agency, these people are definitely advanced. But although these techniques were created and are used daily by advanced users, that doesn't mean they're hard or overly complicated. In fact, my goal was to make these advanced techniques as easy as humanly possible. That's because I want every reader of this book to be able to easily pull off every single technique in the book. That's my goal. It's supposed to *look* like it was hard to create; it's not supposed to *be* hard to create. That's the beauty of it, and that's why I call the book *Down & Dirty Tricks*. There is nothing I love more than finding out that the effect that I thought would be so complex is actually a 60-second quick trick. I love that, and sharing those secrets is what I love even more, and that's exactly, precisely, what this book is all about.

Think of it this way: This book is packed cover to cover with stuff that makes it look like you really broke a sweat. Like you spent weeks crafting the effect (because after all, you're going to charge your client like you worked on it for weeks, right?), but most of it requires you to just follow the simple steps. That's it.

Here's an example: In this book, I'm going to show you what is probably the most popular technique used in Hollywood movie posters today. You know, and I know, that the Hollywood studio hired some big muckety-muck designer to do its posters, but absolutely, without a doubt, if you follow the instructions, you'll be able to create the exact same effect. Does that make it a beginner's book—because a beginner can "pull off" the same technique used by the top pros? Or does this make it an advanced book, because you're learning techniques used by some very advanced users? So basically, you're going to learn advanced techniques that are so easy to pull off, it's going to make you look advanced (even if you're not). If you're already an advanced user, the benefit to you is you'll be able to pull these mini-miracles off even faster, by skipping the extra descriptive copy and jumping right in and getting your hands dirty. It's all how you look at it.

Q. Can I get the photos used in the book?

A. You're kind of pushy. I like that. Actually, thanks to the wonderful people at Brand X Pictures (www.brandxpictures.com), you can download low-res versions of all the photos used in the book, so you can practice right along using the same photos.

Q. Okay, where do I download the photos from the book?

A. Go to the book's companion website at www.scottkelbybooks.com/ddelements3.

Q. So why Brand X?

A. Because, in my humble opinion, they've got the best, coolest, most relevant royalty-free stock images in the market today. I came across them when their catalog came in the mail. I looked at it for about 30 seconds and I knew right then: "These are the images I want in my next book." We called them out of the blue, and convinced (okay, we begged) them to let us (and you) use their amazing stock imagery for the book, and I am absolutely thrilled that they did. They offer more than 20,000 images, and best of all, they're totally not the schlocky "two-men-shaking-hands" standard stock photos that permeate the stock agencies. Their stuff rocks because it's so usable, so "non-stock," and I encourage you to visit their site at www.brandxpictures.com and see for yourself. I know this sounds like a big plug for Brand X (and it is, and they deserve it), but I can assure you that outside of their graciously letting me (and you) use their photos, it's not a paid plug. I don't get a kickback—not a nickel, whether you buy 1 or 1,000 of their images (and CDs, did I mention they sell collections?), but I am indebted to them, especially since they didn't know me from Adam (apparently, they know Adam). I just wanted to let them (and you) know how much better this book is because of their generous contribution. Okay, now I'm "un-plugging."

There is nothing I love more than finding out that the effect that I thought would be so complex is actually a 60-second trick.

Q. What's the volumetric conversion of 7 cubic yards to liters?

A. Glad you asked. Seven cubic yards equals 5351.99 liters. Other Photoshop Elements books just don't give you this kind of in-depth, seemingly useless information. See, I care.

Q. I noticed you mentioned Felix in the book. Who's Felix?

A. Felix is Felix Nelson (yes, that Felix Nelson), and he's about the best, most creative, most talented Photoshop artist in the known universe, and I'm about the luckiest guy in the world to get to work with him every day. He's the Creative Director for *Photoshop User* magazine, he co-authored my *Photoshop Killer Tips* books, and honestly, I learn more from Felix than any other person on the planet. He's just brilliant at taking techniques to the next level, and coming up with inventive and creative new ideas.

For example, I'd ask him to look at a new technique I'd come up with for the book, and he'd look at it and say, "Hey, that looks slick. Ya know, if you added a..." and then he'd mention that one little thing that takes the tutorial from a pretty cool technique to a totally awesome technique. I can't thank him enough for his many tweaks, ideas, and insights that have made this book much better than it would have been.

Q. What's the capital of South Dakota?

A. Pierre.

Q. How many fingers am I holding up?

A. Three. No, four!

This book is packed cover-to-cover with stuff that makes it look like you really broke a sweat. Like you spent weeks crafting the effect...

Q. Is the rest of the book as down-to-earth and straight-to-the-point as this introduction (I mean, preamble)?
A. Sadly, no. The rest of the book is pretty much written like this: Step One: Go under the Filter menu, under Blur, and choose Gaussian Blur. It's all step-by-step from here, giving the exact steps necessary to complete the effect, so there's not much interference, uh, I mean, ancillary instruction, from me. Well, except I am able to share some carefully crafted insights during the intro of each chapter, so please take a moment to read them if you want the full Zen-like experience that comes from reading chapter intros that are as meaningful and thought-provoking as those found in the opening paragraphs of this preamble.

Q. Hey, I just realized something.
A. What's that?

Q. If this is the preamble, the rest of the book must then be the "Amble," right?
A. That's right, my friend. You are indeed worthy of this book. I mean, this "Amble."

Q. So, is it safe to continue on to the "Amble" now?
A. Wow, you've really bought into that whole Amble thing—I'm proud of you. Well, you've done your duty. You've read the preamble, you know what the book's about, how it was written, what to look for (what you're in for), and how to make the most of it. Armed with that knowledge, go forth and follow in the footsteps of our forefathers, who once wrote, "We, the Village People…"—no, that's not it. Anyway….

Turn the page, my young apprentice. It's time for you to "effect" the world.

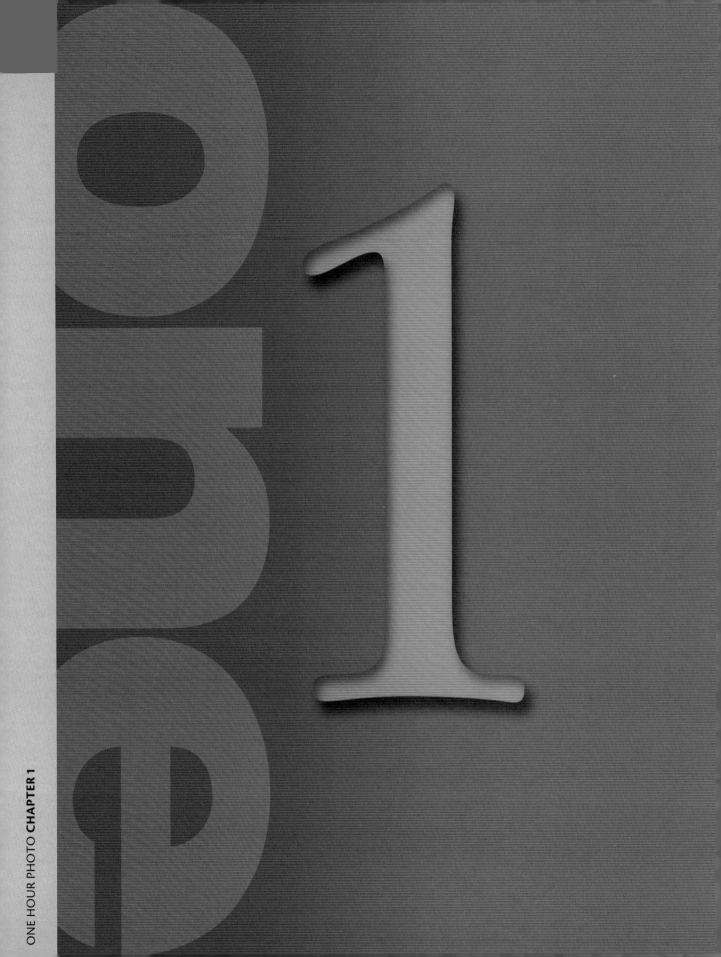

Don't let the title of this chapter fool you; the photographic special effects here don't take one hour.

One Hour Photo
Portrait and Studio Effects

Most take like 3 minutes. Well, 4 if you're editing images with one hand and eating a sandwich with the other. If you charge by the hour, this is the last thing you want to hear, but there's a way around that: If the photo effect you want to use has 12 steps, do only the first 10 steps. Then, drive to your client's office and present it as your "initial proof." Then, drop off your dry cleaning, go to a museum, have some dinner, catch a movie, etc. Then, go back to your office, complete Steps 11 and 12, and return to your client with your "second round of proofs." The effect will look like you worked on it for weeks. Give the client your invoice (include the movie and dinner receipts) and you're a hero—you delivered the effect that knocked his socks off in just one day (but it only took you 3$^1/_2$ minutes to create it). Ahh, now you have a moral dilemma. You feel bad. Guilty even. So you go back to your client and refund everything but a pro-rated 3$^1/_2$ minutes of your hourly charge. Ya know, looking back, if you charge by the hour, you should probably skip this chapter altogether.

Sharp Foreground, Blurred Background

This is a technique that's usually done with a camera, but it doesn't have to be. Basically, you're blurring a copy of the photo, then erasing the blurred areas where you want to retain detail, giving a simple depth-of-field effect that focuses on an object.

STEP ONE: Open the photo that you want to apply the effect to. Go under the Layer menu, under New, and choose Layer via Copy (or press Control-J) to duplicate the Background layer in the Layers palette.

STEP TWO: Go under the Filter menu, under Blur, and choose Gaussian Blur. When the dialog appears, increase the Radius to 4 pixels and click OK to put a blur over the entire image.

STEP THREE: Press the letter E to switch to the Eraser tool. In the Options Bar, click on the down-facing arrow next to the brush thumbnail and choose a medium, soft-edged brush from the Brush Picker. Start erasing over the parts of the image that you want to appear in focus in the foreground. Erasing on this blurred layer reveals the original, unblurred image on the Background layer. By making these areas sharp and leaving the background areas blurry, it creates a simple depth-of-field effect that focuses on an object.

TIP: Press the Left Bracket key ([) to decrease your brush size to erase over any smaller details in the foreground of the photo. You can also lower the Opacity of your duplicate layer to help you see these smaller areas as you erase.

Before

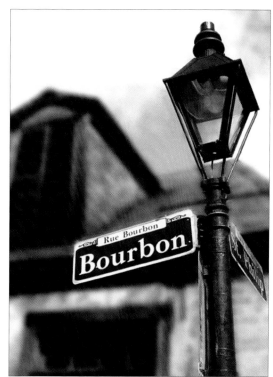

After

Depth-of-Field Effect

As in the previous tutorial, this effect imitates a shot taken with a camera very close to the subject, where the area closest to the lens is in very sharp focus. But with this technique, the image gradually goes out of focus as the depth of field changes.

STEP ONE: Open the image you want to apply the effect to.

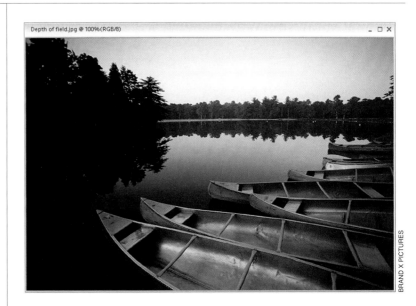

STEP TWO: Go to the Layers palette and choose Levels from the Create Adjustment Layer pop-up menu. When the Levels dialog appears, don't do anything, just click OK. This will create a layer mask that we can use for this effect. Press the G key to switch to the Gradient tool, and in the Options Bar, click on the down-facing arrow next to the gradient swatch and choose the Black to White gradient (the third one in the Picker).

STEP THREE: Click on the layer mask thumbnail of the Levels adjustment layer in the Layers palette to make it active. Now with the Gradient tool active, click on the area that you want to be in focus and drag toward the area that you want to be out of focus. When you do this, a black-to-white gradient will appear in the layer mask thumbnail.

STEP FOUR: Press-and-hold the Control key and click on the layer mask thumbnail. This will put a selection around the gradient you just created. In the Layers palette, click on the Background layer to make it active, then go under the Filter menu, under Blur, and choose Gaussian Blur. As you drag the Radius slider to the right, you'll see your selected area starts to blur. Choose the amount of blur that looks good to you and click OK. Deselect by pressing Control-D, to complete the effect.

Before

After

Creating Gallery Prints

This is a really slick technique for turning a regular photograph into what looks like a gallery print. In the project shown here, you'll start by transforming a color photograph into an Ansel Adams–like black-and-white photo, but we're only doing that because the photo is a mountainous landscape. You can use a regular, less "contrasty" conversion to grayscale for other photos you'll apply this effect to.

STEP ONE: Open the photo you want to turn into a gallery print. Go under the Select menu and choose All. Then, go under the Layer menu, under New, and choose Layer via Cut (or press Shift-Control-J) to put your image on its own layer (Layer 1).

BRAND X PICTURES

STEP TWO: Rather than just going under the Image menu, under Mode, and choosing Grayscale, choose Levels from the Create Adjustment Layer pop-up menu at the top of the Layers palette. When the Levels dialog appears, just click OK.

STEP THREE: Then, choose Hue/Saturation from the Create Adjustment Layer pop-up menu at the top of the Layers palette. When the dialog appears, drag the Saturation slider all the way to the left, and you'll see your photo turn black and white. Click OK.

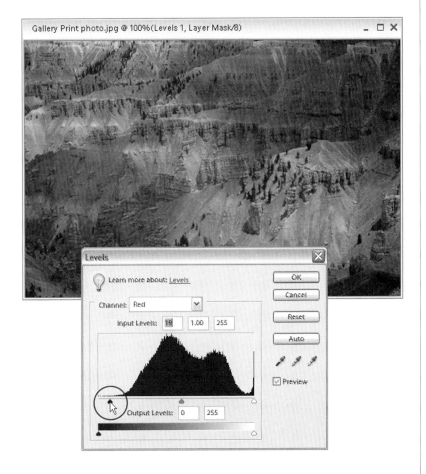

STEP FOUR: We're going for that Ansel Adams effect, so in the Layers 1 palette, double-click on the Levels 1 thumbnail (it's the one on the left below Hue/Saturation 1) and in the resulting dialog, change the Channel pop-up menu to Red. Now you can adjust the Red channel, and because of the Hue/Saturation adjustment layer above the Levels layer, it appears as a black-and-white photo. You can drag the shadow Input Levels slider to the right slightly to increase the shadows in the Red channel. Don't click OK yet.

Continued

STEP FIVE: Change the Channel pop-up menu to Green, and drag the highlight Input Levels slider to the left to increase the highlights. Then, choose Blue in the pop-up menu. Drag the highlight Input Levels slider to the left to intensify the highlights, and then drag the shadow Input Levels slider slightly to the right to darken the shadows. (What you're doing here is similar to using Photoshop's Channel Mixer, which sadly, is now missing in Photoshop Elements.) These settings are not standards for every photo; I just experimented with the sliders until the photo looked better.

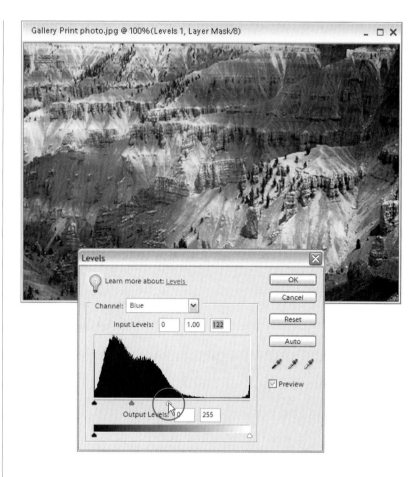

STEP SIX: Now you'll need to add some white space around your photo, so click on the Background layer to make it active, then go under the Image menu, under Resize, and choose Canvas Size. In the Canvas Size dialog, ensure the Relative checkbox is on, then enter 2 inches for Width and 2 inches for Height.

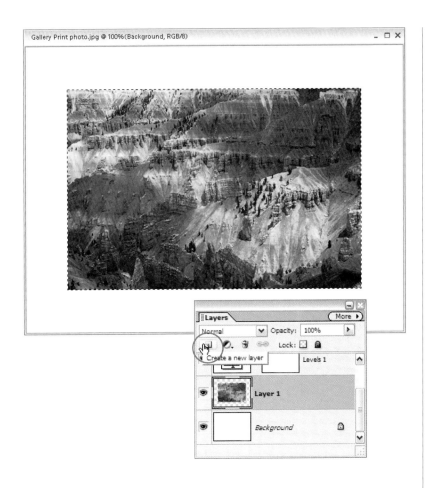

STEP SEVEN: When you click OK, 2 inches of white space is added around your photo. Click on the image layer (Layer 1) in the Layers palette to make it active, then press-and-hold the Control key and click on the image layer's thumbnail, which puts a selection around your photo. Next, click on the Create a New Layer icon at the top of the Layers palette.

STEP EIGHT: On this new layer, you're going to put a very thin stroke around your photo to create a subtle border. Go under the Edit menu and choose Stroke (Outline) Selection. When the Stroke dialog appears, for Width enter 1 pixel, for Color click on the swatch and choose a light gray in the Color Picker, and for Location choose Center.

Continued

STEP NINE: Click OK and the thin gray stroke is applied around your photo. Press Control-D to deselect. Since you applied this stroke on its own layer, if the stroke seems too bold or calls too much attention to itself, you can simply lower the Opacity of the layer in the Layers palette until it looks right to you.

STEP TEN: Press the M key to switch to the Rectangular Marquee tool. Click near the top-left corner of the image and drag out a selection border that's slightly larger than the image. If needed, press-and-hold the Spacebar to reposition your selection as you drag.

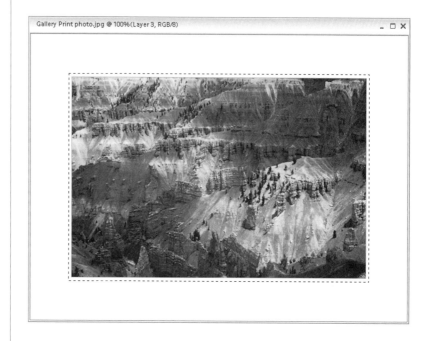

STEP ELEVEN: With your selection in place, click the Create a New Layer icon, then go under the Edit menu and choose Stroke (Outline) Selection. Leave the Width at 1 pixel, but change your stroke color to black by clicking on the gray Color swatch and choosing black in the Color Picker. Leave the Location set to Center.

Gallery Print photo.jpg @ 100% (Witworth Keading Gallery, RGB/8)

STEP TWELVE: Click OK to stroke this outer border with a thin black stroke and press Control-D to deselect. Now, press T to switch to the Type tool, click the Color swatch in the Options Bar, and choose gray in the Color Picker, then "sign" the print (if you indeed took the shot, of course) using a font that looks like handwriting (I used DearJoeItalic set at 22 points). Use the Move tool to position it under the bottom-right corner. Under the left corner, I used the same font to give it that "numbered print" look.

WITWORTH KEADING GALLERY

STEP THIRTEEN: I added the name of a fictitious gallery, using the font Trajan Pro in all caps at 24-point size. However, once I added the type, I left the first letter of each word of the gallery name at 24 points, but I highlighted the rest of the letters and lowered their size to 21 points in the Options Bar, to give a "small caps" feel.

Soft-Edged Portrait Background

This is a technique that I started showing in my live seminars as a 30-second portrait or product-shot background. Basically, it adds a quick "burned in" effect around the edges of your image, and although the background looks pretty bland when complete, as soon as you put an object or person on it, it instantly "makes sense."

STEP ONE: Create a new document in RGB mode by going under the File menu, under New, and choosing Blank File (I created a 4x6" document at 72 ppi). Click the Foreground color swatch in the Toolbox, and when the Color Picker appears, choose the color that you want to appear in the center of your background. Press Alt-Backspace to fill your Background layer with this color.

STEP TWO: Click on the Create a New Layer icon at the top of the Layers palette. Click on the Foreground color swatch again and choose a darker shade of the color you just used (in other words, if you started with a light blue, now pick a dark blue). Then, press Alt-Backspace to fill this new layer with the darker color. Press M to switch to the Rectangular Marquee tool and draw a rectangular selection about 1/2" to 1" inside the edges of your image.

STEP THREE: Go under the Select menu and choose Feather. When the Feather Selection dialog appears, enter 25 pixels for low-res, 72-ppi images (or 60 pixels for 300-ppi, high-res images). Click OK and the feathering will soften the edges of your selection (you'll see the corners of your selection round onscreen). Press the Backspace key to knock out a soft-edged hole in your top (darker) layer.

STEP FOUR: Open the headshot of the person you want to place on this background. Select just the person with no background. (Since my person was on a white background, I clicked the Magic Wand tool [W] on the background and then went under the Select menu and chose Inverse. You could also use the Lasso tool [L] to draw a selection around the person.) Press the V key to switch to the Move tool, and click-and-drag the selected person on top of the new background document to give a studio backdrop look to your headshot, completing the effect.

BRAND X PICTURES

Burning In Portraits

This burned-in edge effect adds an amazing amount of warmth to your portraits, and it's used by professionals everywhere on everything from magazine covers to print ads to the Web. In fact, once you've learned this simple technique, you'll use it again and again. (By the way—once you apply this technique, turn the layer with the effect on/off a couple of times and you'll see what a huge difference it makes.)

STEP ONE: Open the portrait that you want to "burn in."

STEP TWO: Create a new blank layer by clicking on the Create a New Layer icon at the top of the Layers palette. Press the letter D to set your Foreground color to black, and then fill this new layer with black by pressing Alt-Backspace. Press the letter M to switch to the Rectangular Marquee tool and click-and-drag to create a rectangular selection just inside the edges of your image.

STEP THREE: To soften the edges of your selection, go under the Select menu and choose Feather. When the Feather Selection dialog appears, enter 40 pixels (for high-res, 300-ppi images, try 150 pixels), then click OK.

STEP FOUR: Press the Backspace key to knock out a soft-edged hole in this black layer, revealing the photo on the layer beneath. The only problem is the edges are too dark, but you'll fix that in the next step.

Continued

STEP FIVE: Press Control-D to deselect. Then, go to the Layers palette and lower the Opacity of the black layer to around 40% to complete the burned-in effect. To see how effective this technique is, click on the Eye icon to the left of your black frame layer to hide it, revealing just your original image. Now click again in the box where the Eye icon had been. Notice the difference?

Before

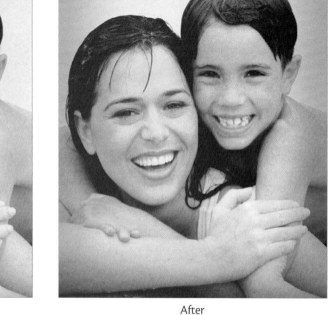

After

Trendy Fashion Blowout Look

This is probably the hottest trend in fashion portrait retouching right now, and you see it everywhere from CD covers (like Madonna's *American Life*), to print ads, to movie posters (like Jet Li's movie *Cradle 2 the Grave*), and everything in between. The effect you're going for is one where the skin tone turns completely white, leaving subtle shadow areas to reveal just the eyes, nostrils, lips, and outline of the face. Here's the trick:

STEP ONE: Open the photo you want to apply the effect to. This technique works best on images with a very light (or white) background (because it usually blows out whatever background is present) and on images of men or women with darker hair. Press Control-J to duplicate the Background layer.

STEP TWO: Press A to switch to the Selection Brush tool. With the duplicate layer active, paint over any areas that have shadow detail, such as the eyes, nostrils, and lips, to select them. (*Note:* To decrease the size of your brush as you paint, press the Left Bracket key on your keyboard, or to increase the size, press the Right Bracket key.) Now, press Control-J again to copy your selection to its own layer. Lower the Opacity of this layer to 40% and change the layer blend mode from Normal to Luminosity.

Continued

STEP THREE: In the Layers palette, click on Layer 1 to make it active. Press D to set your Background color to white, then go under the Filter menu, under Distort, and choose Diffuse Glow. Set the Graininess to 0, the Glow Amount to 10, and the Clear Amount to 15. Click OK to apply the filter. Now, go to the Layers palette and lower the Opacity of this layer to around 80% so you can see some of the original detail from the Background layer.

STEP FOUR: You can see that her skin is considerably lighter, but so is everything else. Press the letter E to switch to the Eraser tool, and in the Options Bar, lower the Opacity of the brush to around 40%. With the duplicate layer active, paint over the eyes, eyebrows, nostrils, and lips (which will reveal the color from the Background layer below). Then, lower the brush Opacity again to around 10% and paint over any shadow detail, such as the side of the nose, around the top of the forehead, and sides of the neck.

STEP FIVE: Return to the Options Bar, change the Opacity of the Eraser tool back to 100%, and paint over the rest of the photo (hair, shirt—everything but the skin) to complete the effect.

Before

After

This chapter is a nice change because you generally get to start each project with a photograph, and then you just

Maximum Exposure
Photographic Effects

add cool effects to it. This is a bigger advantage than it might first seem. I mean, think about it—if you don't start with a photo, you're starting off with a blank canvas. There's nothing more terrifying than staring at a blank page and trying to come up with an awesome effect entirely from scratch. So, in essence, this chapter is kind of like cheating, and that's good. Unless, of course, you live in Las Vegas, where apparently cheating is frowned upon. In fact, if you're caught cheating in a Vegas casino, I've heard they make you use Elements 1 as punishment; so if you live out that way, you don't want to chance it. In fact, in the interest of personal safety, I'd recommend that all Nevada residents skip this chapter entirely, and always start each Photoshop Elements project with a blank page. Hey, the last thing you want is some angry pit boss chasing you around threatening you with outdated products. It's just not worth it.

Adding Objects Behind Existing Objects

Over the years, I've had question after question on how to add a person into an existing image so that it looks as if that person's standing behind other people in that image. Here's a very flexible and visual way to do just that.

STEP ONE: Open the image you want to add another person (or object) into.

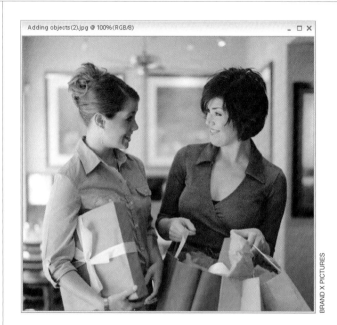

STEP TWO: Use the selection tool of your choice (Lasso tool, Magic Wand tool, etc.) to select the area where you want the additional person to appear in your image. *Note:* When using either of these tools, just press-and-hold the Shift key to add to your selection or press-and-hold the Alt key to subtract from your selection.

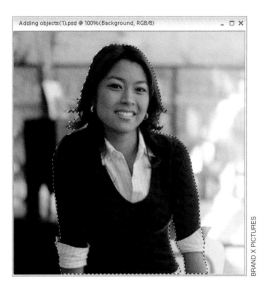

STEP THREE: Open the image you want to add into your original photo. Again, use the selection tool of your choice to select the person (or object). After you make your selection, go under the Edit menu and choose Copy.

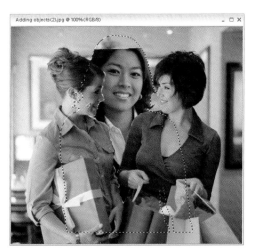

STEP FOUR: Switch back to the main document, go under the Edit menu, and choose Paste Into Selection. This will place your copied selection (in our example, a headshot of a person) into the selection in your main document. Press the letter V to switch to the Move tool. You can now reposition your pasted person within the selected area. Don't deselect yet.

Continued

STEP FIVE: After you've repositioned the pasted image, chances are good that the size won't be correct (it'll either be too large, as in this case, or too small). We'll adjust the size by pressing Control-T to bring up Free Transform. Hold the Shift key, grab one of the top-corner handles, and drag downward (or upward if your image is too small) to resize the object to match the others in the image. You can also reposition the image as you resize: Just click-and-drag inside the Free Transform bounding box. Don't press Enter just yet.

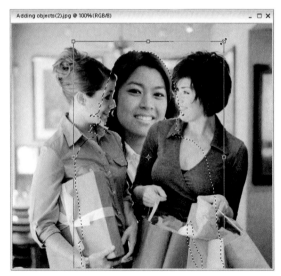

STEP SIX: You'll also notice in our particular image that the light appears on the opposite side of the woman's head than it does on the other subjects in the image. While your Free Transform box is still active, go to the Image window, under Rotate, and choose Flip Horizontal (reposition your image again if necessary). Press Enter to complete the change, and then press Control-D to deselect.

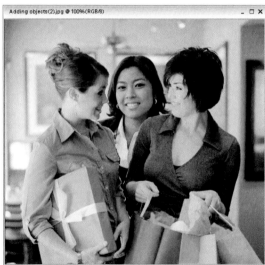

STEP SEVEN: The edges of the pasted image are too sharp and crisp in comparison with the other subjects in the photo. Press the R key to switch to the Blur tool, and in the Options Bar, lower the Strength to around 50%. Using a small, soft-edged brush, paint a slight blur along the edge of the woman's hair and in the space between the two women. This blends the woman into the image.

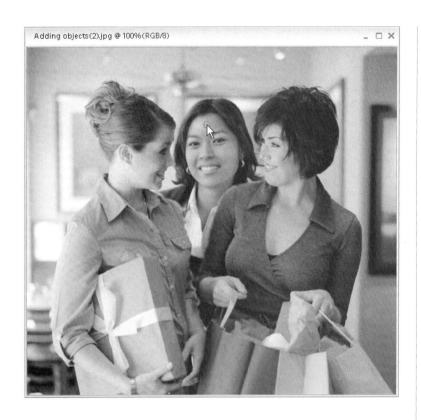

Adding objects(2).jpg @ 100%(RGB/8)

STEP EIGHT: Next, we'll have to deal with the contrast of the pasted image. In this example, she looks too saturated in comparison with the other people. A quick trick for matching contrast is to use the Dodge tool with the Exposure set to around 40% in the Options Bar. When you paint, you'll lighten the dark areas of your pasted image to match more closely with the rest of the image (on areas where your object is too light, paint with the Burn tool using the same low settings), which completes the effect.

Before

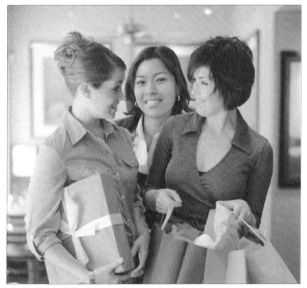

After

Putting an Image in a Monitor

In this technique, we're going to use Free Transform to put an image into a monitor. Now I don't want you to think, "Oh, how often will I need that?" because this technique works just as well for fitting any image into other spaces—a window of a house, a TV screen, a billboard, etc. So it's really a handy one to know.

STEP ONE: Open the image that contains the monitor (TV, etc.) in which you want to place another image.

STEP TWO: Then, open the image you want to place inside the monitor. Press V to switch to the Move tool, and drag this image onto your monitor image. It will appear on its own layer above your Background layer. In the Layers palette, lower the Opacity of this layer to 50%. This will be a big help when you try to position the image within the monitor area—you'll be able to see the monitor through your photo.

STEP THREE: Press Control-T to bring up Free Transform. Click within the bounding box to move the image on top of the monitor, and then press-and-hold the Shift key, grab one of the corner points, and drag inward to scale the image down to a size that's close to the size of the monitor (it doesn't have to be exact, but get it in the ballpark). While still in Free Transform, release the Shift key, press-and-hold the Control key, grab one of the corner points, and drag it to the corresponding corner of the monitor. Pressing the Control key allows you to distort just that one corner. You'll have to do this for all four corners.

STEP FOUR: When you have a perfect fit, press Enter to lock in your transformation, then in the Layers palette, raise the Opacity of this layer back to 100% to complete the effect.

Montage from One Image

This is a technique I saw a few years ago in a print ad in *Entertainment Weekly* for the VH1® original movie *The Way She Moves*. It's very slick, because it lets you create a montage effect using only one image. To get the effect, we need to create an outer glow, and even though Photoshop Elements has an Outer Glow option, you're stuck with a yellow glow that simply won't work for the look we're going for. So here's how to add some quick visual interest to an otherwise static photo:

STEP ONE: Open an image that you want to apply this effect to. Go to the Select menu and choose All (or press Control-A) to put a selection around the Background layer. Then, go to the Layer menu, under New, and choose Layer via Cut (or press Shift-Control-J) to cut your image from the Background layer, and copy it onto its own layer (Layer 1).

STEP TWO: Click on your Background layer in the Layers palette to make it active. Go under the Image menu, under Resize, and choose Canvas Size. When the Canvas Size dialog appears, enter a dimension that's about 25% larger than your current image size for both Width and Height. Choose Black in the Canvas Extension Color pop-up menu, ensure the Relative checkbox is on, and then click OK to add a black canvas area around your image.

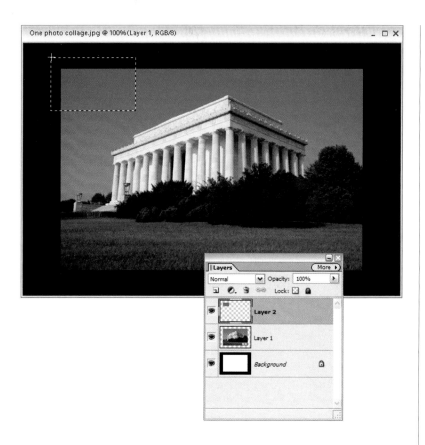

STEP THREE: In the Layers palette, click on your image layer (Layer 1). Press the M key to switch to the Rectangular Marquee tool, and draw a small rectangular selection in one part of your image, but don't select the main focus of the image—choose outer areas for the most part. Copy this selected area from Layer 1 and put it on its own layer by going to the Layer menu, under New, and choosing Layer via Copy (or by pressing Control-J).

STEP FOUR: Press V to switch to the Move tool, and move this new layer either slightly up, down, to the left, or to the right (your choice) about a half inch. When it's where you want it, Control-click on the layer's thumbnail in the Layers palette to load a selection around the rectangle, and then Control-click on the Create a New Layer icon to add a new layer below the rectangle layer.

Continued

STEP FIVE: Go to the Select menu, under Modify, and choose Border. In the Border Selection dialog, enter 4–5 pixels and click OK (use a higher number for high-res, 300-ppi images). Press D to set your Foreground color to black, then press Alt-Backspace to fill your selection with black. Press Control-D to deselect.

STEP SIX: You're going to use this black border for your outer glow, so we need to soften the edges of the border with a Gaussian Blur. With the rectangular border layer still active, go under the Filter menu, under Blur, and choose Gaussian Blur. Enter 2–3 pixels and click OK. In the Layers palette, click on the rectangle layer above the outer glow layer and press Control-E to merge the two layers together.

STEP SEVEN: You'll continue to repeat Steps 3–6 until you've created multiple rectangles with outer glows. Remember to click on your image layer (Layer 1) each time before you create a new rectangular selection, and don't forget to slightly move the rectangle each time.

One photo collage.jpg @ 100%(Layer 33, RGB/8)

WASHINGTON D.C.

STEP EIGHT: Once you've applied the glows to all your layers, you can use the Move tool to drag-and-drop your rectangular layers in the Layers palette, shuffling them into a layout that looks good to you. If you choose, you can then add any type using the Type tool (T) to complete the effect (I used Trajan Pro at 17 points). For more fun, once you've created a rectangular layer, try using the Outer Glow option from the Layer Styles category of the Styles and Effects palette, and you'll see why this method (though it takes longer) looks much better.

Before

After

Blending Images for Instant Collages

This is one of the fastest and most fun ways to blend (or collage) two or more images together. This is so easy to do, yet so effective, that it opens up a whole new way for many people to collage multiple images.

STEP ONE: Open an image that you want to use as the main image in your collage.

STEP TWO: Open a second image that you want to use in your collage. Press the letter V to switch to the Move tool, and drag this image on top of the image in your original document. Make sure this dragged layer (Layer 1) covers or at least significantly overlaps the Background layer in the Layers palette.

STEP THREE: At the top of the Layers palette, Control-click on the Create a New Layer icon. This creates a new layer (Layer 2) directly below the second image layer (Layer 1). Now click on the top image layer (Layer 1), and from the Layer menu, choose Group with Previous (or just press Control-G). Your top image will disappear, and a tiny arrow will appear to the left of the layer letting you know that you just created a layer clipping group.

STEP FOUR: Press the letter D to set your Foreground color to black, then press the G key to switch to the Gradient tool. Press Enter and the Gradient Picker will appear onscreen. Make sure the selected gradient is Foreground to Transparent (the second one in the Picker), and then in the Layers palette, click on the empty layer (Layer 2) to make it active. Click-and-drag the Gradient tool through the layer, stopping before you reach the edge of the top image in the layer stack. You'll notice that the images blend together. To add more images, just start again from Step 2. That's all there is to it.

TIP: If you see the edge of your top image after you draw your gradient, you've dragged too close to the edge or past it. Try pressing Control-Z to undo the gradient, and then click-and-drag again, stopping about 1" before the edge of your image.

Adding Motion Effects

The first technique shown here is very popular for photos taken for editorial purposes (for example, if you're shooting a CEO for a magazine or newspaper article about his company). It's also popular in portraits, because the effect leaves the subject totally in focus but adds movement through the rest of the photo. In the second technique, I'll show you another motion effect that you see everywhere—a massive zoom blur. Both effects are so simple to apply that you're going to wonder, "Is that all there is to it?" Yup, that's all there is to it.

MOTION BLUR
STEP ONE: Open a photo that you want to add movement to. Duplicate the Background layer by going under the Layer menu, under New, and choosing Layer via Copy (or by pressing Control-J).

STEP TWO: Go under the Filter menu, under Blur, and choose Motion Blur. In the Motion Blur dialog, set the Angle to the direction you want to have motion applied (I usually use a horizontal setting, but you can set it so it matches the direction of the object). Use the Distance setting to control the amount of effect (choose between 40–50 for low-res, 72-ppi photos, or try 100 for high-res, 300-ppi images), and click OK.

STEP THREE: Press the letter E to switch to the Eraser tool. Then, go to the Options Bar, click on the down-facing arrow next to the brush thumbnail to get the Brush Picker, and choose a soft-edged brush.

STEP FOUR: Now for the fun part—just erase over the areas that you want to retain detail. As you erase, the original Background layer beneath your motion layer will be revealed. I generally erase the person's face, clothes, etc., but I stop right before the edges.

Continued

Before

After

ANOTHER OPTION: You can use this Motion Blur technique to create a different feel, especially if you use the effect on an action shot like the one shown here. I changed the Angle in the Motion Blur dialog to around −11° and set the Distance to 45.

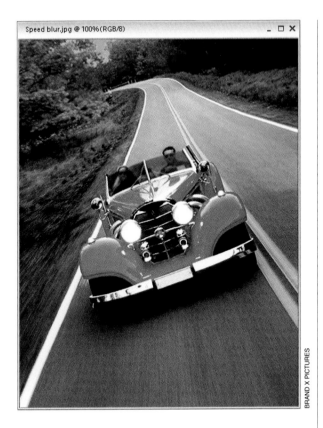

BRAND X PICTURES

ZOOM BLUR

STEP ONE: To create a zoom effect, first open the photo you want to apply the blur effect to.

STEP TWO: Go under the Filter menu, under Blur, and choose Radial Blur. Set the Amount to 100 and the Blur Method to Zoom. Click OK and the classic speed blur effect is applied to your photo.

Adding Motion Step By Step

This is an old trick that I've used for years to make an object look like it's in motion. This is often used for making an object look as if it's coming out of another object, such as an arm moving from off the screen, an object coming out of a box, etc.

STEP ONE: Open the object that you want to give the effect of movement to. Make a loose selection with the Lasso tool (L) (here I selected the man's forearms along with the bat), and go to the Layer menu, under New, and choose Layer via Copy (or press Control-J) to copy the selection onto its own layer.

STEP TWO: Press Control-T to bring up the Free Transform function. Click within the bounding box and drag the layer to move it to the left slightly. Then, move your cursor outside the bounding box to the right and click-and-drag downward to rotate your image just a little. Now, press-and-hold the Shift key, grab a corner point, and drag inward to scale the image down a bit. Press Enter to lock in your transformation.

STEP THREE: Drag this rotated layer to the Create a New Layer icon at the top of the Layers palette to duplicate it. Repeat the same process you did in Step 2: bringing up Free Transform, dragging the object to the left, rotating it, making it smaller, and pressing Enter to lock in your transformation.

STEP FOUR: Repeat the process one more time (making a copy, bringing up Free Transform, moving it, scaling it, etc.) until your Layers palette looks like the one shown here.

Continued

STEP FIVE: In the Layers palette, click on Layer 1 (it should be above the Background layer). Lower the Opacity of this layer to around 50%. Press Alt-Right Bracket to switch to the next layer above it, then lower the Opacity of this layer to around 30%. Press Alt-Right Bracket again and lower the Opacity of the top layer to around 20%.

STEP SIX: In the Layers palette, click on Layer 1 again. Go under the Filter menu, under Blur, and choose Motion Blur. For Distance use 7 pixels or less, leave the Angle set at 0°, and click OK. Press Alt-Right Bracket to switch to the next layer above, then press Control-F to run the same Motion Blur on this layer. Repeat this process again for the remaining layers to complete the effect.

Before

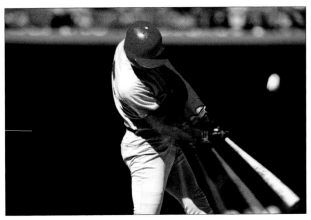

After

Remember that scene in the movie *Dirty Dancing*—the big dance at the end of the movie? At one point,

Dirty Dancing
Focusing Attention

Patrick Swayze comes dancing down the center aisle toward the stage where Baby (yes, parents can be so cruel) stands there waiting for him, while swaying the hem of her skirt to and fro? Do you remember that part? Seriously, did she look incredibly gawky and awkward? I think it was the moment when the director decided to change her name in the movie from Angela to "Baby," as a way of publicly shaming her for not having a cool dance move of her own. Now, you're probably wondering what all this has to do with Photoshop Elements? Plenty—because before you read this chapter, I strongly urge you to go out and rent the *Dirty Dancing* video and tell me if you, as a Photoshop Elements user, would freeze up the way Baby did at one of those "all-eyes-on-you" moments. If you see this movie and feel certain that you could come up with a more compelling "come hither" dance than Baby did, then and only then should you read this chapter.

Backscreening

This is a popular effect in print and multimedia, and it's used when the background image is very busy or very dark (or both) and you want to place ad type over your image that can be read easily. Although we're using the technique with a white-screened effect here, it's just as popular using a dark-screened effect.

STEP ONE: Open a background image that you want to put type over.

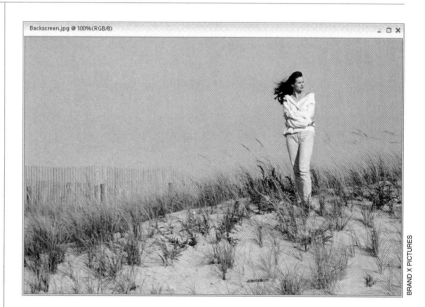

STEP TWO: Press M to switch to the Rectangular Marquee tool, and make a selection where you want your type to appear. While this area is still selected, create a new layer by clicking on the Create a New Layer icon at the top of the Layers palette.

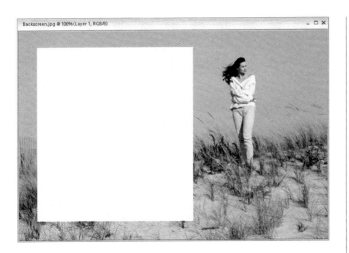

STEP THREE: Press the letter D and then the letter X to set your Foreground color to white. Fill your selection with white by pressing Alt-Backspace, and then deselect by pressing Control-D.

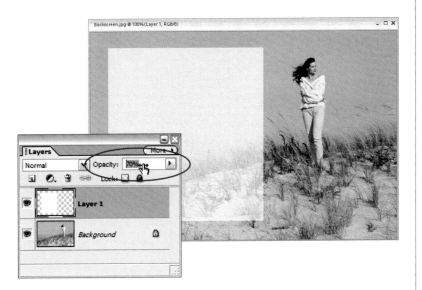

STEP FOUR: Lower the Opacity of this layer to create the amount of back-screen effect you'd like. A 20% screen is a very popular choice for backscreening, so to achieve a 20% screen, you lower the Opacity in the Layers palette to 80% on this layer. In this example, I actually lowered the Opacity to 70%. This lets a bit more of the background show through, as we're going to add very large, black text.

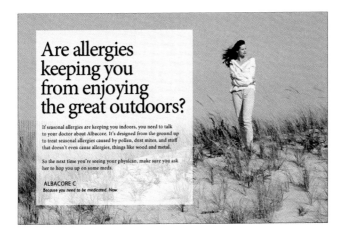

STEP FIVE: Press the T key to switch to the Type tool, and enter your text. The headline and body copy in this example are set in Minion Pro at 50 points and 12 points, respectively. The title of the medication is set at 14 points in Myriad Pro, while the tagline for the medicine is set at 11 points in Gill Sans. Because the black text is so large, it's still very read-able over our white backscreened layer.

Magazine Pop-Up Effect

This effect is inspired by *Sports Illustrated* magazine. It's a technique for focusing attention on one object in an image. Basically, you select an object from the background, put that object on its own layer, lighten the background layer, and add a drop shadow to the object to create depth and focus.

STEP ONE: Open an image that has an element in it that you want to stand out from the background. Press the L key until you have the Magnetic Lasso tool. Click once on the edge of the object to create an anchor point, and slowly drag the tool around the object. The Magnetic Lasso tool will automatically add other anchor points along the edge of the object as you drag. When you get back to where you started, just click on the original anchor point to create the selection. If you need to add to your initial selection, press L again to switch to the regular Lasso tool, press-and-hold the Shift key, and select any additional areas; to subtract from your selection, press-and-hold the Alt key and select any areas you want to remove.

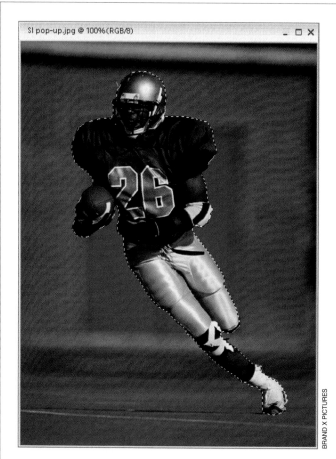

STEP TWO: With your selection in place, go under the Layer menu, under New, and choose Layer via Copy (or just press Control-J) to copy your selection onto its own layer (Layer 1). Now, click on the Background layer in the Layers palette to make it active.

STEP THREE: Press Control-L to bring up the Levels dialog. When it appears, drag the shadow Output Levels slider to the right to lighten the Background layer. Drag the slider until the shadow Output Levels field reads at least 140 (move farther to the right to lighten even more). Click OK when it looks good to you.

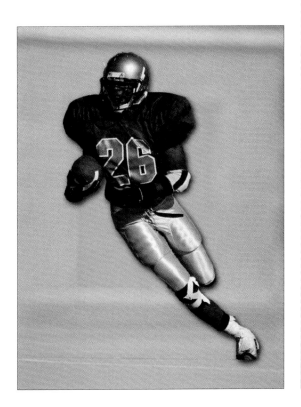

STEP FOUR: To help the object stand off the background even more, you'll add a drop shadow. First, click on Layer 1 in the Layers palette, then go to the Styles and Effects palette (found under the Window menu) and choose Layer Styles in the top-left pop-up menu. In the top-right pop-up menu (where it says Bevels), choose Drop Shadows, and then click on Soft Edge, which completes the effect.

Vignetting Attention

I saw this technique used very effectively on a menu cover for the Olive Garden® restaurant. It's a takeoff on the classic vignette effect, but rather than just softening the edges to focus the attention on the subjects of the image, it adds a soft border technique at the same time.

STEP ONE: Open the image you want to apply the effect to. Press the M key to switch to the Rectangular Marquee tool, and make a selection around the area you want as the focal point of your effect.

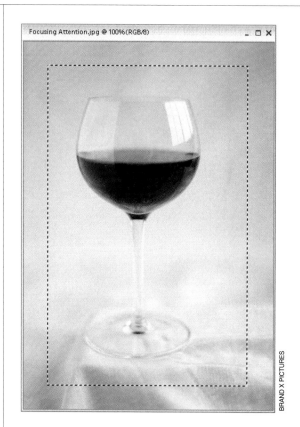

STEP TWO: Go under the Select menu and choose Feather. Enter 5 for the Feather Radius and click OK. (*Note:* For high-res, 300-ppi images, use a Feather Radius of 15 instead.)

STEP THREE: While your selection is still in place, go under the Layer menu, under New, and choose Layer via Copy (or press Control-J) to put the selected area on its own layer above your Background layer.

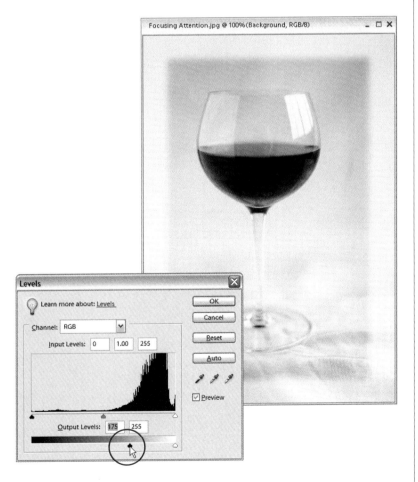

STEP FOUR: In the Layers palette, click on the Background layer to make it active. Press Control-L to bring up the Levels dialog. Click on the shadow Output Levels slider at the bottom of the dialog and drag it to the right about two-thirds of the way (somewhere around 175) to lighten the background image.

Continued

STEP FIVE: To enhance the vignette, click on the Create a New Layer icon in the Layers palette. Now, get the Rectangular Marquee tool again and draw a frame inside the middle of the vignetted border. Go to the Edit menu and choose Stroke (Outline) Selection. In the Stroke dialog, enter 1 pixel for Width, click on the Color swatch and choose black in the Color Picker, choose Inside for Location, and click OK. Press Control-D to deselect. Now, go to the Layers palette and lower the Opacity to around 35%.

STEP SIX: For the final step, you can add type to finish off the design. (The type-face I used for "Ristorante" was Zapfino, and for "BELLA NOTTE" and "WINE LIST" I used Trajan Pro.)

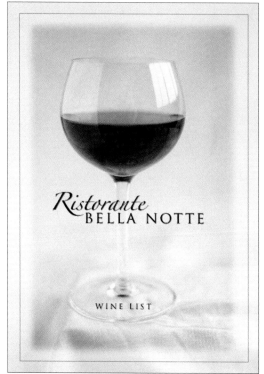

Popping Out of an Image

This is one of those techniques for which I've had so many requests that I wanted to include it here in the book. It's primarily seen in print ads where a person, a body part, a car, etc., extends out from part of the photo and into white space where body copy usually resides. It's kind of as if the object is popping out of the photo, and it not only adds visual interest and movement but it also gives you something to wrap type around.

STEP ONE: Open the photo that has the object or person that you want to extend from part of the image.

STEP TWO: Press the L key to switch to the Lasso tool and draw a selection around the part of the object you want to extend from the photo. If needed, you can hold the Shift key to add to your selection or the Alt key to subtract from your selection. (In this example, we held the Alt key to deselect the area of wall between his right arm and his body.) Once your selection is in place, go under the Layer menu, under New, and choose Layer via Copy (or press Control-J) to put the selected area on its own layer (Layer 1).

Continued

STEP THREE: In the Layers palette, click on the Background layer. Press M to switch to the Rectangular Marquee tool, and draw a selection around the entire left side of your document window, starting near the right edge of where you made your original selection on the object. Press Backspace to erase that part of the background.

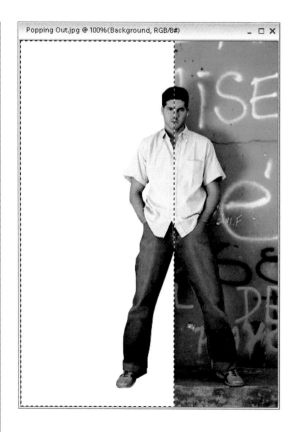

STEP FOUR: Press Control-D to deselect. In the Layers palette, click back on Layer 1 and then go to the Styles and Effects palette (found under the Window menu). With the Layer Styles category selected, choose Drop Shadows from the palette's top-right pop-up menu. Click on the Soft Edge drop shadow. Go under the Layer menu, under Layer Style, and choose Style Settings. When the dialog appears, enter 10 pixels for Shadow Distance and click OK. (*Note:* If the drop shadow creates a visible seam anywhere inside your object, adjust the Lighting Angle in the Style Settings dialog.)

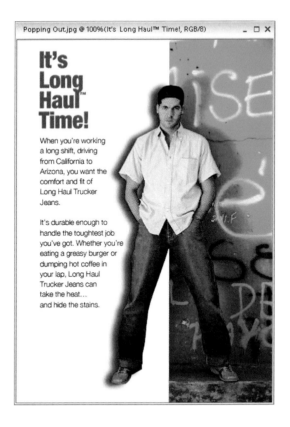

STEP FIVE: Press the T key to switch to the Type tool, and add any additional text. (In my example, I used the typeface Helvetica Condensed for the company name and Helvetica Light for the body copy.)

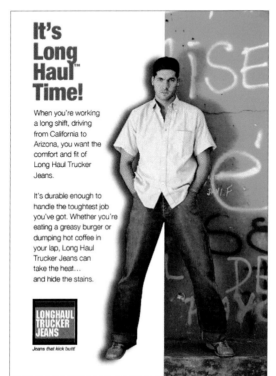

STEP SIX: To complete the effect, you can add a logo as I did here. Draw a square with the Rectangular Marquee tool, choose a dark blue as your Foreground color, and press Alt-Backspace to fill your square selection with blue. Go under the Edit menu, choose Stroke (Outline) Selection, and in the resulting dialog, choose a 5-point black stroke. Then, draw a small rectangular selection inside the square and fill it with red. Add type using the Type tool (I used the typeface Machine for the logo and Helvetica Italic for the tagline under the logo).

Snapshot Focus Effect

I first saw this clever, yet amazingly simple technique used in a brochure for the SeaWorld theme park in Orlando, Florida. It focuses the viewer's eye on one area of the photo by using a snapshot effect, but rather than cropping the photo to fit inside the "Polaroid" snapshot frame, they left the rest of the photo visible and applied a filter to it, creating a very appealing photographic effect. Here's how it's done:

STEP ONE: Open the photo in which you want to have the snapshot focus effect. Press the letter L until you have the Polygonal Lasso tool. You're going to draw a tilted rectangular selection around the area you want to use as the focal point of your photo.

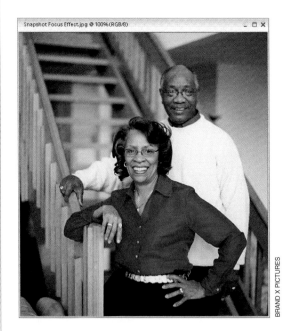

STEP TWO: Start by clicking the Polygonal Lasso tool once where you want the top-left corner of your frame to be, then move your cursor up and to the right and click where you want the top-right corner to be. Continue this until you've created a tilted rectangular selection that has the same basic proportions as a Polaroid photo (like the selection shown here). Then, go under the Layer menu, under New, and choose Layer via Copy (or press Control-J) to copy this selected area onto its own layer above your Background layer in the Layers palette.

STEP THREE: Choose Stroke (Outline) Selection from the Edit menu. In the Stroke dialog, increase the Width to 9 pixels, and then click on the Color swatch and choose white when the Color Picker appears. Change the Location to Inside (which prevents the stroke from having rounded corners by placing it inside the copied photo layer, rather than extending out from it), and click OK.

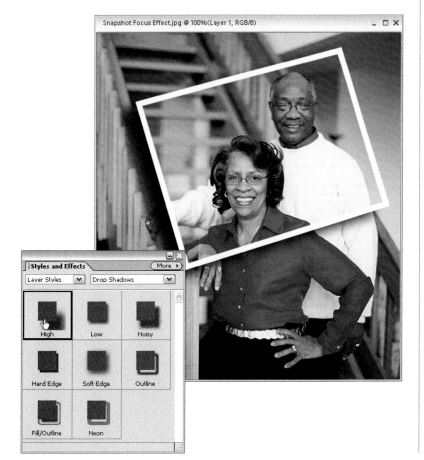

STEP FOUR: Go to the Styles and Effects palette (found under the Window menu), and in the Layer Styles category, choose Drop Shadows from the top-right pop-up menu in the palette. Click directly on the High shadow to give the photo layer a drop shadow. Now, the rest of the tutorial is about adjusting the background to focus more attention on the snapshot you just created.

Continued

OPTION ONE: Here's one way of focusing more attention on the snapshot: In the Layers palette, click on the Background layer to make it active. Press Control-L to bring up Levels, then drag the highlight Output Levels slider at the bottom of the dialog to the left to darken the background. Read on for more options....

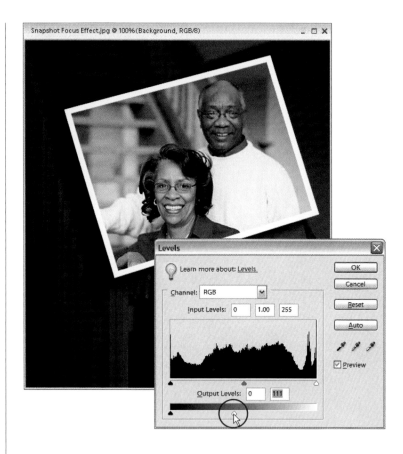

OPTION TWO: Another option is to lighten the background using Levels. Just press Control-Z to undo the darkening of the background from the previous step. Press Control-L to bring up Levels again, but this time, drag the shadow Output Levels slider to the right to lighten the background.

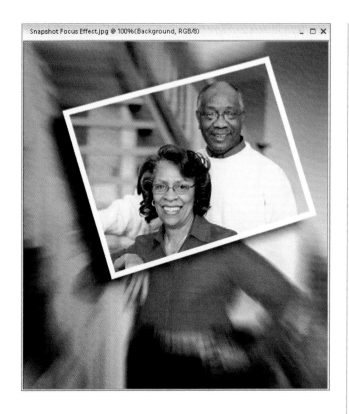

OPTION THREE: Press Control-Z to undo the background lightening. This is the effect SeaWorld's designers used on the background—a zoom blur. To apply a zoom blur, go under the Filter menu, under Blur, and choose Radial Blur. When the dialog appears, choose Zoom under Blur Method, increase the Amount to 35, and click OK.

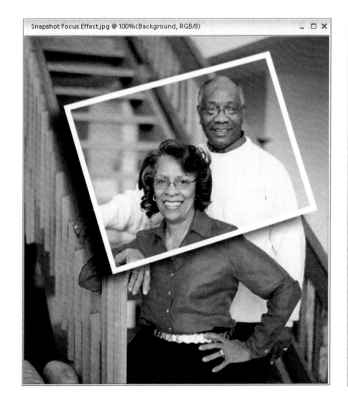

OPTION FOUR: Press Control-Z to undo the zoom blur effect, and try this simple technique that focuses the viewer's eye on the snapshot by removing all color from the Background layer. Just go under the Enhance menu, under Adjust Color, and choose Remove Color.

Magnifying Glass Trick

It's amazing how many times I've seen this particular effect in ads. In this effect, we select and enlarge part of the background, copy it into memory, and then paste it into the circle of a magnifying glass. This makes it look like the magnifying glass is really magnifying what's beneath it.

STEP ONE: Open your background image and open an image of a magnifying glass.

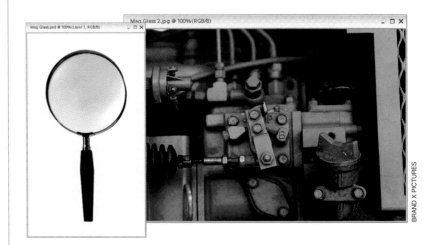

STEP TWO: With the magnifying glass document active, press W to switch to the Magic Wand tool, and click on the white background surrounding the object. Then, go under the Select menu and choose Inverse. With the magnifying glass selected, press V to switch to the Move tool, and drag it onto your background image (it will appear on its own layer in the Layers palette).

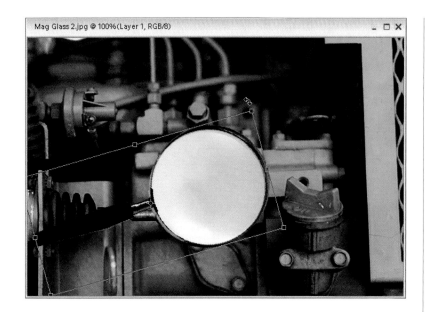

STEP THREE: Press Control-T to bring up the Free Transform function. Press-and-hold the Shift key, grab a corner point, and drag inward to resize the magnifying glass. Click-and-drag outside the bounding box to rotate the magnifying glass, and then click within the bounding box to position it over the part of the image you want to magnify. Press Enter to lock in your transformation.

STEP FOUR: Press the letter W to switch to the Magic Wand tool. Click once inside the round glass area to select it. (*Note:* If the tool doesn't select all of the white space in the glass, go to the Options Bar, increase the Tolerance to around 80, and try again.) In the Layers palette, click on the Background layer, then go under the Layer menu, under New, and choose Layer via Copy (or press Control-J) to put your selection onto its own layer.

Continued

STEP FIVE: Press Control-T to bring up the Free Transform function again. When the bounding box appears, press-and-hold the Shift key, click on a corner point, and drag outward until it gives you the amount of magnification you want. (*Note:* You may want to drag this layer above your magnifying glass layer in the Layers palette as I did here to better see your transformation.) You can reposition the image as you like by clicking-and-dragging within the bounding box. When it looks right, press Enter.

STEP SIX: Press-and-hold the Control key, and in the Layers palette, click on your circular image layer (Layer 2) to select it. Then, press Control-X to cut your selection and save it into memory. Now, delete your current layer by dragging it to the Trash icon at the top of the Layers palette.

STEP SEVEN: In the Layers palette, click on the magnifying glass layer to make it active. Get the Magic Wand tool again and click once inside the round glass area of your magnifying glass to select that area. Go under the Edit menu and choose Paste Into Selection. Your enlarged image will now appear within your magnifying glass.

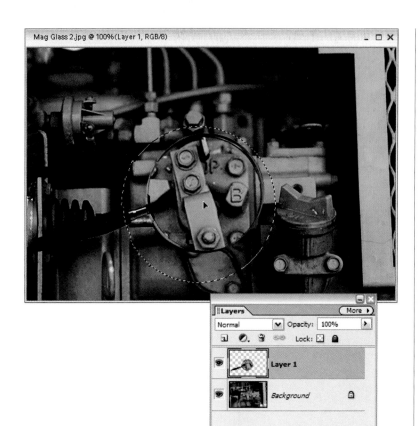

STEP EIGHT: You can switch to the Move tool to reposition this enlarged piece. When it looks good to you, press Control-D to deselect, completing the effect.

Do you have any idea how hard it is for a color effect to be included in this chapter? Sure, by the time a

In Living Color
Color Effects

color effect winds up here, with all the glitz and glamour, it looks like a lot of fun, but believe me, it's a lot of hard work. It starts with an open audition for color effects, which takes place in Houston, L.A., New York, and Atlanta. In each city, a panel of judges then views each aspiring color effect, and from that group they choose only 30 color effects to go compete in the regional semifinals. At the semis, the judges then narrow the color effects down to just 10, who will be vying for the title "Coolest American Color Effect." *Cool American Color Effects*, which airs Wednesday nights on FAUX, is hosted by Ryan Seabiscuit, and…. (Do I even have to keep this up? Seriously, I was pretty sure that you would've stopped reading a hundred words or so ago, and since I was kind of counting on that, I never really developed an ending for this intro. So I'm just kinda going to end it right here. If you don't tell anyone I didn't have an ending, I won't tell anyone you read this far. Deal? Deal.)

Instant Stock Photo Effect

This "wild color" effect is incredibly popular right now. In fact, there are entire collections of royalty-free stock photos that use this technique, and you often see it used in print ads, in magazines, and on the Web. It's ideal for taking an otherwise boring image and using wild colors to make it trendy and interesting.

STEP ONE: Open the photo you want to apply the effect to. In this case, it's a regular RGB photo that looks kinda, well…boring.

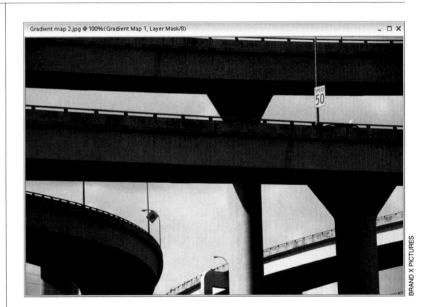

STEP TWO: Go to the Layers palette, and from the Create Adjustment Layer pop-up menu, choose Gradient Map. This will bring up the Gradient Map dialog (seen in the next step).

STEP THREE: Click on the little down-facing triangle to the right of the current gradient swatch to bring up the Gradient Picker. From the Picker's flyout menu (the right-facing arrow), choose Color Harmonies 2 to load this set of gradients; when they appear, choose the "Purple, Green, Gold" gradient (the second one in the Picker).

STEP FOUR: Click OK and this applies a Gradient Map adjustment layer over your photo. This gradient map is usually too intense, and pretty much trashes your photo. To fix that, go to the Layers palette and change the layer blend mode of this layer from Normal to Color. Now the color of the Gradient Map layer blends in more smoothly, and also replicates the wild color effect that's so popular with stock photo collections.

Continued

STEP FIVE: To fine-tune the effect, press the X key until you've set your Foreground color to black, and then press B to switch to the Brush tool. Up in the Options Bar, lower the Opacity for your brush to 50%, then click on the brush thumbnail and choose a large, soft-edged brush from the Brush Picker. Now, paint over areas where you want to have more detail. You're actually painting on the layer mask of the Gradient Map adjustment layer, and as you paint in black, some of the original color will start to reappear.

Before

After

Colorizing Black-and-White Images

This technique for colorizing grayscale images is great for getting that hand-tinted effect. This particular version uses Photoshop Elements' Hue/Saturation command to add color to selected areas.

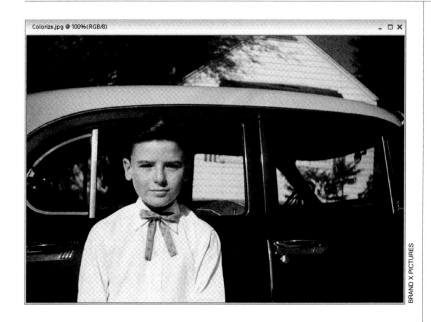

STEP ONE: Open a grayscale image that you want to colorize. You have to be in a color mode to colorize a grayscale image, so go under the Image menu, under Mode, and choose RGB Color.

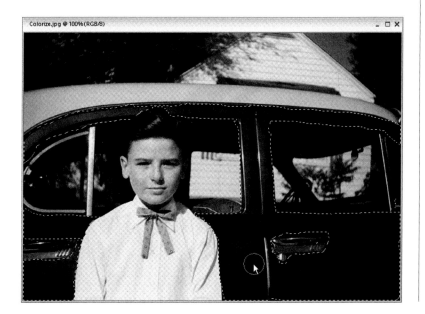

STEP TWO: Using one of the selection tools, select the first area that you'd like to colorize (try pressing A to switch to the Selection Brush tool and painting in your selection). If needed after you make your initial selection, press L to switch to the Lasso tool, press-and-hold the Shift key, and click-and-drag around areas that you want to add to your selection (or press-and-hold Alt as you drag to deselect areas).

Continued

STEP THREE: Now, you'll want to copy your selection to its own layer (in case you want to change colors later), so go under the Layer menu, under New, and choose Layer via Copy (or press Control-J).

STEP FOUR: Go under the Enhance menu, under Adjust Color, and choose Adjust Hue/Saturation (or press Control-U). When the dialog appears, turn on the Colorize checkbox. Now, you can move the Hue slider to choose the color you'd like. If the color seems too intense, drag the Saturation slider to the left.

STEP FIVE: Continue this process of selecting areas, pressing Control-J to copy your selection to its own layer, going to Hue/Saturation, checking the Colorize box, and moving the Hue slider to add color to your image. As I mentioned before, if you change your mind and want to alter the color of an object, just click on its layer in the Layers palette and open Hue/Saturation to select the new color.

Before

After

Painting Away Color

You see this technique widely used in print ads and on TV. It was used very effectively in a print campaign for the Las Vegas nightclub Studio 54 (in the MGM Grand), where everyone in the image was in black and white, but one person appeared in full color, totally drawing the eye to that one person. Here's how it's done:

STEP ONE: Open a color image that you want to apply this effect to. Press the letter D to set your Foreground color to black.

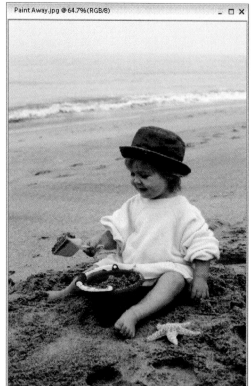

STEP TWO: Press the B key to switch to the Brush tool. Go to the Options Bar and change the Mode pop-up menu from Normal to Color, then click on the brush thumbnail and choose a large, soft-edged brush from the Brush Picker.

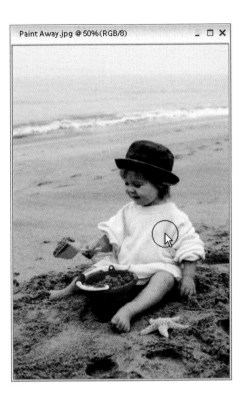

STEP THREE: Start painting. As you paint, the color will disappear, leaving just grayscale in its wake. Paint everything except for the object(s) that you want to remain in color.

Before

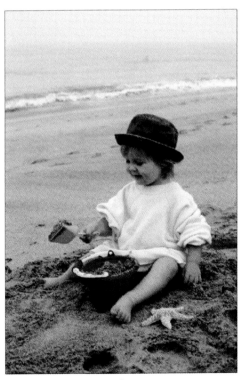

After

Visual Color Change

If there's one thing clients love to do, it's change the color of the products in their product shots. Luckily for you, (a) it's easy, and (b) it creates billable work. Here's one of the easiest ways to change the color of just about anything.

STEP ONE: Open a color image that contains an object or part of an object whose color you want to change.

STEP TWO: Use any selection tool (Lasso, Selection Brush, Magic Wand, etc.) to select the object you want to apply a quick color change to. (In this example, I pressed L to switch to the Lasso tool and selected the woman's blouse. If you use the Lasso tool, after you make your initial selection you can press-and-hold Shift to add to your selection or press-and-hold Alt to deselect areas.)

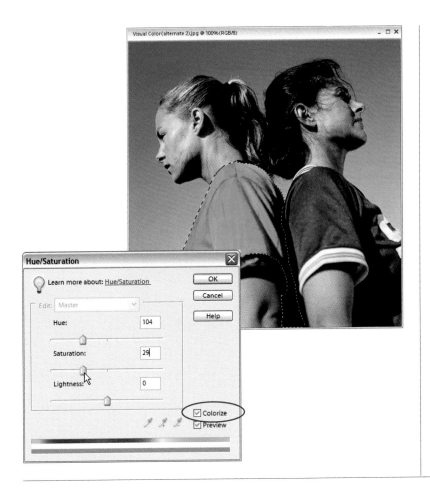

STEP THREE: Go under the Image menu, under Adjust Color, and choose Adjust Hue/Saturation. When the Hue/Saturation dialog appears, check the Colorize box in the lower-right corner. Now, simply grab the Hue slider and drag it until your image changes to a color you like. To soften your color, drag the Saturation slider to the left. When it looks good, click OK.

Before

After

Sepia Tone Effect

The sepia tone effect (popularized many decades ago) has been a staple of many photographers for years. In the project you're going to do here, you get an added twist by using a gradient map to convert your image to grayscale, which gives you a more "contrasty" grayscale conversion.

STEP ONE: Open the image you want to apply the sepia tone effect to.

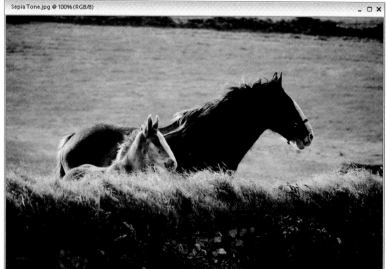

BRAND X PICTURES

STEP TWO: We're going to convert the photo to black and white (okay, grayscale), but we're going to do that using a gradient map so that the conversion has more contrast. Set your Foreground color to black by pressing the letter D. Choose Gradient Map from the Create Adjustment Layer pop-up menu at the top of the Layers palette. When the dialog appears, it immediately makes the photo look black and white, so just click OK. Next, you'll add the sepia tone color over your black-and-white image.

STEP THREE: Go under the Create Adjustment Layer pop-up menu again, but this time choose Solid Color. When the Color Picker appears, click on the color you want for your sepia tone and click OK.

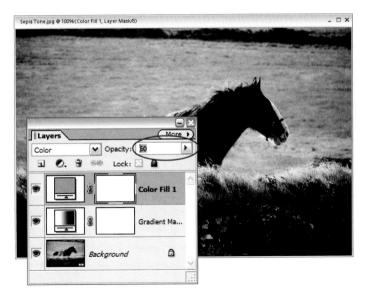

STEP FOUR: Once you click OK, you'll have just a solid block of color, so in the Layers palette, change the layer blend mode of the Solid Color adjustment layer from Normal to Color, and you'll see the sepia tone effect appear. If the color seems too intense, just lower the Opacity in the Layers palette.

Before

After

Photo Tinting

Tinting a color photo with a solid color is very popular and fairly easy—once you know how. What I really like about this technique is that it lets you take a fairly boring photo and turn it into something artistic quickly and easily.

STEP ONE: Open the photo you want to apply a tint effect to.

STEP TWO: Go to the top of the Layers palette and choose Hue/Saturation from the Create Adjustment Layer pop-up menu (it's the second icon from the left). When the dialog appears, click on the Colorize checkbox. Then, move the Hue slider to choose your tint, and if needed, drag the Saturation slider to the left to decrease the color saturation. When it looks good to you, click OK and a tint is applied to the image. Easy enough, eh?

Before   After

This chapter is where you learn to create the effects that will subconsciously force people to purchase products and

Ad-Libbing
Advertising Effects

services they neither want nor need, at prices they can't afford—increasing their personal debt, thereby putting them, and perhaps the entire country, on the verge of a financial collapse that can only be compared to "Black Saturday," when the market *didn't* drop, because it was closed for trading, but had it been open, surely something would've happened, which I would then feel compelled to chronicle here; and that would've made this perhaps the longest run-on sentence in the history of modern literature, rather than the concise, straight-to-the-point introduction that you've come to expect from writers like me, who value your time, yet don't mind using a comma or two (but only when absolutely, positively necessary), like now. Okay, keep breathing, keep breathing. In through the nose, out through the mouth. Or why not try Nasatrin, which provides 12-hour nondrowsy relief from common allergy symptoms, such as....

Backlit Photo Backgrounds

I got the idea for this technique after seeing ABSOLUT VODKA's very slick print ad campaign, and I figured out how to create a similar background in Photoshop Elements—plus, it's easy to do!

STEP ONE: Create a new document in RGB mode (the one shown here is 6x8"). Press the G key to switch to the Gradient tool. In the Options Bar, ensure that the Linear Gradient icon is selected, then click on the Edit button to bring up the Gradient Editor. Click on the third gradient from the left in the top row (Black to White). Double-click on the bottom-left black color stop under the gradient ramp and choose a dark blue in the resulting Color Picker. Then, double-click the bottom-right color stop and choose a light blue in the Picker. Type "Blue" in the Name field, click the New button to save the gradient, and then click OK.

STEP TWO: Click-and-drag the Gradient tool from the top of your image window to the bottom so the lighter shade is on the bottom. Press M until you have the Elliptical Marquee tool, and draw a circular selection in the center of your background. With the selection in place, press Control-L to bring up the Levels dialog. At the bottom of the dialog, drag the shadow Output Levels slider to the right (to around 200), and a soft spotlight effect will appear on your gradient background. Click OK in the dialog, and press Control-D to deselect.

STEP THREE: Go under the Filter menu, under Blur, and choose Gaussian Blur. Enter 30 pixels (65 pixels for high-res, 300-ppi images) and click OK to blur the edges of your spotlight in the gradient layer.

TIP: If you want to change the color of your gradient, press Control-U to bring up the Hue/Saturation dialog while the Background layer is active. Turn on the Colorize checkbox in the lower right-hand corner, and then adjust the Hue slider until you've found the color you like. You can also drag the Saturation slider to the left if your gradient color looks too intense.

STEP FOUR: Open your object image (in this case, a tire). Use any selection tool to select the tire (here I Shift-clicked on the Magic Wand tool [W] in all the white background areas and then went under the Select menu and chose Inverse). With your selection in place, press the letter V to switch to the Move tool, drag this object onto your spotlight document, and position it over your spotlight. Next, go under the Layer menu, under New, and choose Layer via Copy (or press Control-J) to duplicate your object layer.

Continued

STEP FIVE: With your duplicate layer active, go under the Image menu, under Rotate, and choose Flip Layer Vertical. With the Move tool, hold the Shift key, click on the flipped image, and drag straight down (the Shift key will keep the flipped object in the same vertical position as you drag). Keep dragging straight down below the original object so their bottoms are just overlapping. In the Layers palette, lower the Opacity to around 40%, then drag this copied layer below your original object layer (Layer 1).

STEP SIX: Go under the Filter menu, under Blur, and choose Motion Blur. For Angle enter 0°, for Distance enter 13 (try 30 for high-res images), and click OK to blur the reflection a bit and put the focus back on the main object. Press D to set your Foreground color to black, and then click the Create a New Layer icon. With this layer active, press B to get the Brush tool, and in the Options Bar, click on the down-facing arrow next to the brush thumbnail to open the Brush Picker and choose a medium, soft-edged brush. Change the Mode pop-up menu in the Options Bar to Behind and lower the Opacity of the Brush tool to 60%. Press-and-hold the Shift key and draw a straight line under the object to add a soft shadow. If the shadow seems too intense, lower the Opacity of the layer in the Layers palette.

STEP SEVEN: Press M until you have the Rectangular Marquee tool. In the Layers palette, click on the Background layer, and then make a selection around the bottom half of the background. Go under the Layer menu, under New, and choose Layer via Copy (or press Control-J) to copy this selected area onto its own layer. Switch to the Move tool again, hold the Shift key, and drag this layer straight down until the edge of it appears just above the bottom edge of your object.

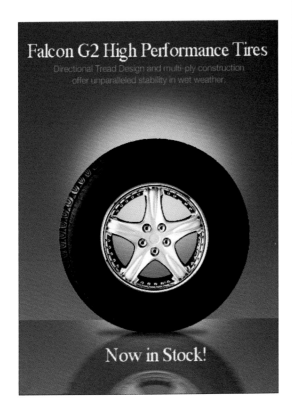

STEP EIGHT: To complete the effect, press T to switch to the Type tool and add some copy. (In this example, for the headline "Now in Stock!" I used the font MS Serif, and for the body copy I used Helvetica Neue.)

Quick, Elegant Product Background

This is a nice way to showcase an elegant product, such as jewelry, watches, etc. It really gives that "shot-in-the-studio" look because it appears as though the red area is created by a soft spotlight. Best of all, this is one of those "create-it-from-scratch-in-60-seconds" effects that appear to have taken hours.

STEP ONE: Create a new document in the size you'd like for your background (the one shown here is a 6x8" document in RGB mode). Press D to set your Foreground color to black, then press Alt-Backspace to fill the Background layer with black. Now, add a new blank layer by clicking on the Create a New Layer icon at the top of the Layers palette.

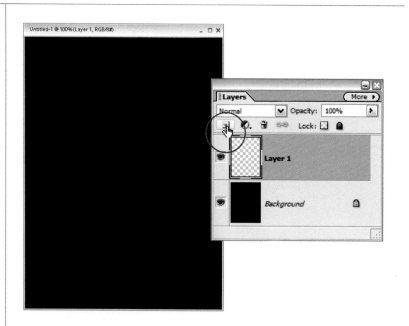

STEP TWO: Press M until you get the Elliptical Marquee tool, and draw a horizontal, oval-shaped selection that extends near the document's left and right edges. If you have to center your selection once you've drawn it, just click the Elliptical Marquee tool within the oval selection area and drag to reposition it.

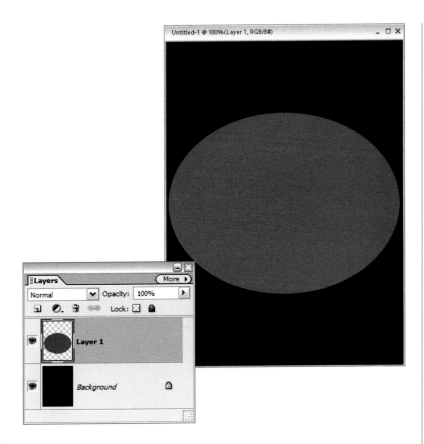

STEP THREE: In the Toolbox, click on the Foreground color swatch to bring up the Color Picker, and then choose red for your Foreground color. Press Alt-Backspace to fill your oval selection with red. Now you can deselect by pressing Control-D.

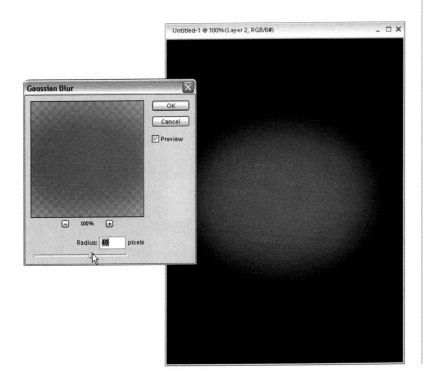

STEP FOUR: To soften the edges of our red oval (and make it look more like a soft, red spotlight), go under the Filter menu, under Blur, and choose Gaussian Blur. When the Gaussian Blur dialog appears, enter 48 pixels (for high-res, 300-ppi images, enter 230 pixels). When you click OK, the edges of your red circle will be softened, creating the effect of a spotlight (this will look more realistic once you add a product to your image, as you'll soon see).

Continued

STEP FIVE: Open an image of the product you want to place on your red spotlight background (in this case, it's a watch). Use any of the selection tools you're comfortable with to put a selection around your product. (In this example, the product is on a white background, so the Magic Wand tool [W] will probably do the trick—just click the Wand on the background, go under the Select menu, and choose Inverse to select just the watch.)

STEP SIX: Once the object is selected, press the letter V to switch to the Move tool, click on the object, and drag it over into your red spotlight document. The watch automatically appears on its own layer in the Layers palette.

STEP SEVEN: To add some depth and to make it look as if the watch is above the background, go to the Styles and Effects palette (found under the Window menu), and with the Layer Styles category selected, choose Drop Shadows from the top-right pop-up menu in the palette. Click on Soft Edge, and then go to the Layers palette and double-click on the Layer Styles icon (it looks like an "ƒ") to the right of the layer's name. When the Style Settings dialog appears, increase the Shadow Distance to 13, change the Lighting Angle to 63°, and click OK.

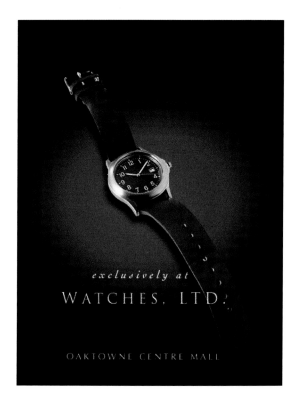

STEP EIGHT: The effect is now complete. To finish things off, you can add some type by pressing T to switch to the Type tool. In the example shown here, the words "exclusively at" are set in the font Cochin Italic. The words "WATCHES, LTD." are set in Trajan Pro, and at the bottom, the words "OAKTOWNE CENTRE MALL" are set in Optima Regular.

Quick Product Shot Background

Here's a very useful photographic background technique that not only looks great, but takes only seconds to create—perfect for catalog shots, magazine ads, and product shots of all kinds. You can even use it as a background for portraits (though you might want to use a less warm combination than yellow and brown).

STEP ONE: Create a new document (the example here is a 6x8" document in RGB mode). Click on the Foreground color swatch at the bottom of the Toolbox and choose a bright yellow in the Color Picker (the build shown here is R: 252, G: 252, and B: 2). Fill your Background layer with this yellow color by pressing Alt-Backspace.

STEP TWO: Click on the Create a New Layer icon at the top of the Layers palette. Change your Foreground color to a very dark brown and fill your new layer with this color by pressing Alt-Backspace. Press the letter M to get the Rectangular Marquee tool, and draw a vertical, rectangular selection in the center of your image area. Then, go under the Select menu and choose Feather. When the Feather Selection dialog appears, enter 50 pixels and click OK. You'll see the edges of your rectangular selection become rounded.

STEP THREE: Now, press Backspace to knock a large, soft-edged hole out of your brown-filled layer, revealing part of your yellow Background layer. Deselect by pressing Control-D.

BRAND X PICTURES

STEP FOUR: Open an image of the product you want to appear on this background and put a selection around the product. (In my example, I switched to the Magic Wand tool [W], clicked on the white background, went under the Select menu, and chose Inverse to select just the makeup cases.) Then, press V to switch to the Move tool, and click-and-drag the product over to your brown/yellow background document. (*Note:* If needed, press Control-T for Free Transform, press-and-hold the Shift key, grab a corner point, and drag to resize your image.) In the Layers palette, drag this layer below your brown-filled layer to soften the effect on the makeup cases.

Continued

STEP FIVE: To add some depth to the image, go to the Styles and Effects palette (found under the Window menu), and with the Layer Styles category selected, choose Drop Shadows from the top-right pop-up menu in the palette. Click Soft Edge, and in the Layers palette, double-click on the Layer Styles icon (it looks like an "*f*") to the right of the layer's name. In the resulting dialog, choose a Lighting Angle of 122°, increase the Shadow Distance to 9, and click OK.

STEP SIX: Finish off your image by pressing the T key to switch to the Type tool, and enter some text. In the example shown here, I entered the word "beautyscape" set in the font Cochin. The store name is set in Gill Sans MT Condensed, and the cities are set in Perpetua.

Fade-Away Reflection

This is a popular technique for products that are displayed on a white background. It makes the product look as if it were shot on a reflective surface, and the reflection just fades away underneath it. Here, we're going to create an ad for a fictitious tennis racket company, and we'll apply the fade-away reflection to the racket.

BRAND X PICTURES

STEP ONE: Open an image of an object that you want to add a fade-away reflection to. Put a selection around the object using any selection tool. In this example, we need to select the racket, so press the letter W to switch to the Magic Wand tool. In the Options Bar, set the Tolerance to 10 and make sure the Contiguous checkbox is on. Shift-click on the white background areas in the image and then choose Inverse from the Select menu to select the racket. Go under the Layer menu, under New, and choose Layer via Cut (or press Shift-Control-J) to cut the object from the Background layer, and copy it onto its own layer.

STEP TWO: In the Layers palette, click on the Background layer to make it active, and then go to the Image menu, under Resize, and choose Canvas Size. In the Canvas Size dialog, enter 2 inches for both Width and Height, ensure the Relative checkbox is on, and click on the top-left square in the Anchor grid. Set the Canvas Extension Color pop-up menu to White and click OK to add white space below and to the right of the racket.

Continued

STEP THREE: Click on Layer 1 in the Layers palette, then go under the Layer menu, under New, and choose Layer via Copy (or press Control-J) to duplicate the layer. Then, from the Image menu, under Rotate, choose Flip Layer Vertical. Press the letter V to switch to the Move tool, press-and-hold the Shift key, then click on the flipped object and drag it straight down until the bottoms of the two objects meet, creating a mirror reflection.

STEP FOUR: With the duplicate layer active, Control-click on the Create a New Layer icon at the top of the Layers palette. This creates a new layer directly below the duplicate layer. Then, click on the duplicate layer, and from the Layer menu, choose Group with Previous (or just press Control-G). Your reflected object will disappear because it's hidden by the empty layer below it. Control-click on the duplicate object layer to load a selection around the reflected object, and then click on the empty layer to make it active.

STEP FIVE: Press the G key to switch to the Gradient tool, and then press Enter to open the Gradient Picker (which will appear in the top-left corner of your screen). Select the Foreground to Transparent gradient (the second one in the Picker), and then click-and-drag from the top of your selection down toward the bottom of the document. Your reflected object will fade away. Press Control-D to deselect, then in the Layers palette, lower the Opacity of the gradient object layer to around 50%.

STEP SIX: To finish off the project, just press the T key to switch to the Type tool, and add some type. (The headline and body copy are set in HelveticaNeue and the name of the fictitious company is set in the typeface Mata. For the red block logo, I created a square selection with the Rectangular Marquee tool (M), set my Foreground color to red, pressed Alt-Backspace to fill the square with the Foreground color, and entered white type set in Mata.)

Classified Ad Effect

You've probably seen this effect used in print ads and on TV a dozen times. It's designed to look like someone tore a classified ad out of a newspaper and highlighted the important points. The effect is easy to pull off—the only thing that takes any time is creating the fake classified ad (but I give you a sample one to download from this book's website, in case you don't feel like doing it yourself).

STEP ONE: This technique starts with a fake classified ad. You can either create your own (as I did here) so that you can customize the text in the center ad (where the focus of the effect will be), or you can download this one from the book's website (check it out at scottkelbybooks.com/ddelements3).

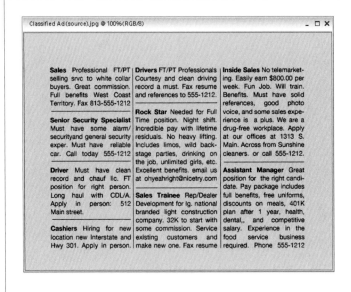

STEP TWO: Press the letter L to get the Lasso tool and draw a loose, rip-like selection around the classified ad that you want the viewer to focus on. This selection should look a little jaggy, as if the section were torn from a newspaper by hand. Then, go under the Layer menu, under New, and choose Layer via Copy (or press Control-J) to copy the selected area up onto its own layer. Press the letter D to set your Background color to white.

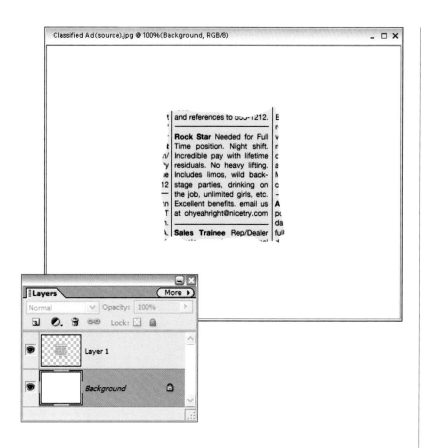

STEP THREE: Go to the Layers palette and click on the Background layer. Go under the Select menu and choose All (or press Control-A) to select the entire background, then press Backspace to delete the excess classifieds, leaving just your ad on the layer above. Deselect by pressing Control-D.

STEP FOUR: Click back on the torn classified layer in the Layers palette to make it active. Go to the Styles and Effects palette (found under the Window menu), and with the Layer Styles selected, choose Drop Shadows from the top-right pop-up menu in the palette. Click on Soft Edge, then go to the Layers palette and double-click on the Layer Styles icon (it looks like an "*f*") to the right of the layer's name. In the resulting dialog, set the Lighting Angle to 20, set the Shadow Distance to 6 pixels (try 40 for high-res, 300-ppi images), and click OK to apply a soft drop shadow to your torn classified ad.

Continued

STEP FIVE: Press-and-hold the Control key and click on the torn newspaper layer to put a selection around it. Then, go under the Select menu, under Modify, and choose Contract. When the dialog appears, enter 3 pixels and then click OK to shrink your selection. Go under the Select menu and choose Inverse, which leaves only the outside edge of your newspaper selected. You'll lighten those edges to help make them look more like they really were torn, so press Control-L to bring up Levels. At the bottom of the dialog, drag the shadow Output Levels slider to the right until the edges look good to you, and then click OK. Deselect by pressing Control-D.

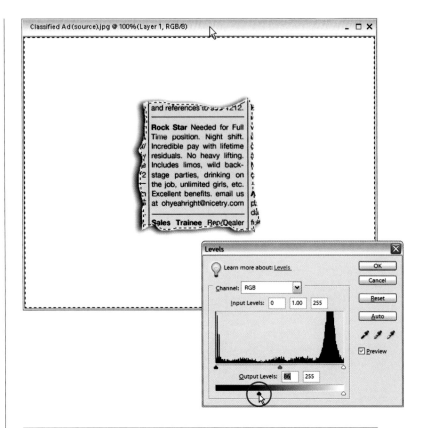

STEP SIX: Next, click on the Create a New Layer icon at the top of the Layers palette. Press B to switch to the Brush tool, then Right-click in the document to bring up the Brush Picker. From the Picker's flyout menu, choose Load Brushes. Navigate to the Photoshop Elements folder, then open the Brushes folder inside the Presets folder. From the list that appears, choose the brush set named Wet Media Brushes and click the Load button. The brushes will appear at the bottom of the Picker. Click on the 19-pixel Light Oil Flat Tip brush, and then press the Left or Right Bracket key until the brush is the same height as a line of your type in the classified. Click on the Foreground color swatch in the Toolbox and set your Foreground color to a highlighter yellow in the Color Picker (I used R: 216, G: 209, and B: 0). Now paint strokes over the lines you want the reader to focus on.

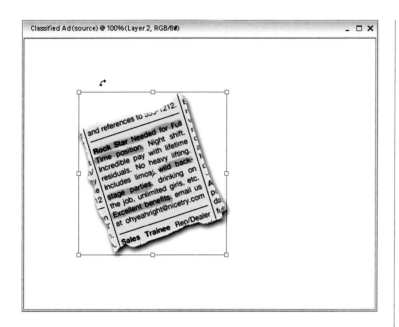

STEP SEVEN: To complete the effect, change the layer blend mode of this layer from Normal to Multiply in the Layers palette, and then you'll be able to see the words through the highlighting. In the ad here, I clicked on the highlight layer and then clicked in the empty box to the left of the classified layer to link them. Then, I pressed Control-T bring up Free Transform to rotate and adjust those layers just a bit.

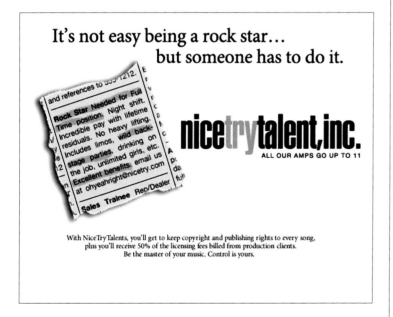

STEP EIGHT: Finally, I pressed T to switch to the Type tool and added text (in the example here, I used the typeface Minion Pro for the headline and body copy, and for the company name I used Helvetica Compressed). *Note:* Make sure you keep a copy of the original with all its layers, because then you can easily update the text for any classified you'll need in the future.

Credit Card from a Photo

In the old days, unless you worked for Visa, MasterCard, or American Express, your chance of designing a credit card was fairly slim, but now there are phone cards, frequent flyer cards, frequent shopper cards, slot club cards, convention badges, and about a hundred other reasons why you may need this effect, primarily as a mockup to show clients.

STEP ONE: Create a new document that's roughly 7x5" set at 72 ppi in RGB. Press D to set your Foreground color to black, and then click on the Create a New Layer icon at the top of the Layers palette. Press the U key until the Rounded Rectangle tool appears in the Toolbox, and then press Shift-Control-R to show the rulers in your document. In the Options Bar, set the Radius for the Rounded Rectangle tool to 10 pixels, then draw your rounded-corner box at the size of a credit card (approximately 3¼ x 2⅛ ", but I'm going to draw mine slightly larger to show the effect better).

STEP TWO: Open the image you want to use in your credit card. Press V to get the Move tool, and drag it into your credit card document. (In the example here, I wanted only the package in the gift card, so I clicked the Magic Wand tool [W] in the white background, went under the Select menu, chose Inverse, and then moved only the package into the card document.) In the Layers palette, lower the image layer's Opacity to 50% to help you see the credit card shape layer when resizing the image. Press Control-T to bring up Free Transform. Press-and-hold the Shift key, grab a corner point, and drag inward to size down your image. Move your cursor outside the bounding box and click-and-drag to rotate the package slightly; then click-and-drag inside the bounding box to position the image.

BRAND X PICTURES

TIP: **TIP:** If you can't see the corner points of the Free Transform bounding box, press Control-0 [zero] to zoom out; when finished, double-click the Zoom tool in the Toolbox to return to 100% zoom.

STEP THREE: Press Enter to lock in your changes, and in the Layers palette, raise the Opacity of this layer back up to 100%. Now, under the Image menu, choose Group with Previous (or press Control-G) to place your photo inside the black credit card shape on the layer below it. The grouping you just created is temporary, so press Control-E to permanently merge your photo layer with the credit card shape layer, leaving just a Background layer and your rounded-corner photo layer.

STEP FOUR: Press T to switch to the Type tool, and add some "credit card type" to your image. Press the letter X to change your Foreground color to white and then add your text, completing the effect. (In this example, I used the font Helvetica Neue Light for "SEFINA" and for the word "card," and I used Helvetica Neue Condensed Bold for the word "gift.")

High-Tech Transparent Info Boxes

I wanted to include an effect that was similar to the high-tech transparent info boxes you see used on nationally televised sports events on ESPN, FOX Sports, etc., for displaying scores, stats, and team info during games. I've used this effect myself when creating the interface for Photoshop training CD-ROMs, but it works just as well over video, as a DVD interface, or even simply in print.

STEP ONE: Open the photo you want to use as your interface background. Then, create a new document at the size you want for your interface (the example here is 8x6"). Create a new blank layer by clicking on the Create a New Layer icon at the top of the Layers palette.

STEP TWO: Press the L key until you have the Polygonal Lasso tool, and draw a selection on the left of the blank document that will later become the navigation area (like the one shown here). To build a selection, press-and-hold the Shift key, click once, move to the next spot, then click again. (The Shift key creates perfectly vertical or horizontal lines and exact 45° angles.) Keep clicking to make these straight-line sections until you have the shape you want. Click on your original starting point to complete the selection.

STEP THREE: Press D to set your Foreground color to black, then press Alt-Backspace to fill the selection with black. Deselect by pressing Control-D.

STEP FOUR: On this same layer, draw another shape using the Polygonal Lasso tool. Again, press-and-hold the Shift key to create perfectly vertical or horizontal lines and exact 45° angles. When the selection is complete, press Alt-Backspace to fill it with black. Deselect by pressing Control-D.

Continued

STEP FIVE: Use the Polygonal Lasso tool to draw another shape selection at the top, fill it with black as well, and deselect by pressing Control-D.

STEP SIX: Press the letter V to switch to the Move tool, press-and-hold the Shift key, and drag-and-drop this shape layer into the photo that you opened in Step One. (The Shift key will center the shapes in the photo.) Now that the main areas of your interface are in place, all you have to do is a little tweaking.

STEP SEVEN: Go to the Layers palette and click on the Create a New Layer icon. Press-and-hold the Control key and click on your shape layer (Layer 1) to put a selection around your shapes. Go under the Edit menu and choose Stroke (Outline) Selection. Set the Width to 1 pixel, click on the Color swatch and choose white in the Color Picker, set the Location to Center, and click OK to put a white stroke around your shape selection. Deselect by pressing Control-D. In the Layers palette, lower the Opacity setting of this white stroke layer to 50%. This makes the stroke appear thinner than its 1-pixel width.

STEP EIGHT: In the Layers palette, click on your shape layer (Layer 1) to make it active. Go to the Styles and Effects palette (found under the Window menu), and with Layer Styles selected, choose Drop Shadows in the palette's top-right pop-up menu. Click on the Soft Edge shadow. Return to the Layers palette and double-click on the Layer Styles icon to the right of the layer. In the resulting dialog, increase the Shadow Distance to 13 pixels and click OK. In the Layers palette, lower the Opacity setting for this layer to 60% to let the image show through your shapes. Now press the letter T to switch to the Type tool, and create the text. (All the type shown here is in the font Helvetica Light.) To highlight any of your interface's menu items, simply select the text with the Type tool, change its color to black, and then draw a selection around it using the Rectangular Marquee tool (M). Create a new layer, and then fill your selection with white. Lower the Opacity of this layer to around 20% and press Control-D to deselect. You can also drag-and-drop an image into the interface as I did here, which completes the effect.

Turning a Logo into a Brush

Tired of importing your client's logo into every little project you do for him? Well, here's a trick for turning his logo into a brush so you can choose it directly from the Brush Picker in the Options Bar and simply paint it into any document.

STEP ONE: Open the document that contains your client's logo.

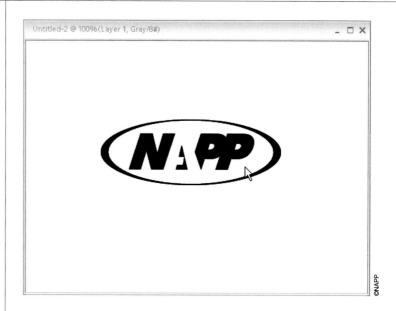

STEP TWO: Press the letter M to switch to the Rectangular Marquee tool, press-and-hold the Shift key, and draw a square selection around the logo. Go under the Edit menu and choose Define Brush from Selection. Name your brush in the New Brush dialog and click OK. As soon as you do, that logo is added as a new brush (with a tiny thumbnail) at the bottom of the Brush Picker.

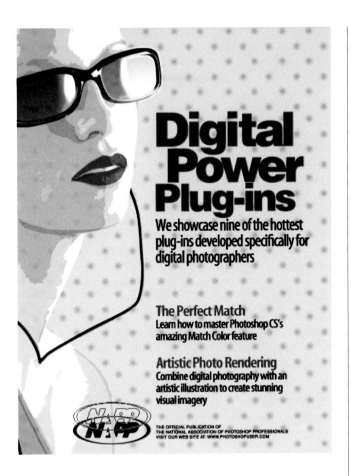

STEP THREE: To use the brush, press the letter B to switch to the Brush tool, then up in the Options Bar, click on the brush thumbnail to open the Brush Picker, and scroll to the bottom to select your new "logo" brush. Click once on a new document to make the logo appear, or click-and-drag for multiple logos. And if you need the logo in a different color, just change your Foreground color before you paint.

I know what you're thinking: "Are the techniques in this chapter really 'cool' effects, or is this just marketing hype?"

Jealous Type
Cool Type Effects

First, I want to point out that there are strict guidelines set in place by a large, scary-sounding government agency to make sure that when a claim is made about a particular product, the claim is true. So, to substantiate the claim that these type effects are indeed worthy of the glitzy marketing term "cool," I formed a blue-ribbon panel that was charged with putting together a crack team of addicts to find Arthur Fonzarelli and get his full endorsement of these effects. Sadly, the panel was not able to locate Mr. Fonzarelli within the allotted time. However, a woman identified only as Pinky Tuscadero, with whom he was once romantically linked, did render her expert opinion in his stead. Her opinion proved beyond reasonable doubt that the effects in this chapter would be considered by Mr. Fonzarelli, or any of the *Happy Days* cast (with the notable exception of Chachi), to be "cool" effects. I think that pretty much settles it.

Instant 3D Type

This technique is so easy and so versatile that I wanted to include it first. The initial few steps of this technique show you how to apply a perspective transformation to your type, while the last few steps show you how to create depth by adding 5,000 type layers (kidding—it's more like 40 or so layers).

STEP ONE: Create a document in RGB mode (the one here is 8x6"). Click on the Foreground color swatch at the bottom of the Toolbox, and in the Color Picker that appears, choose a bright blue. Then, press Alt-Backspace to fill the Background layer with this color. Click on the Foreground color swatch again and choose a bright red in the Picker. Press the T key to switch to the Type tool, and enter your type (the font used here is called Impact).

STEP TWO: You're going to use the Warp Tool feature to add a perspective effect to the type. Click on the Warped Text icon in the Options Bar (it's the third icon from the right and it has the letter "T" with a bent line beneath it). In the Warp Text dialog, choose Flag from the Style pop-up menu. Set the Bend to 0%, the Horizontal Distortion to 60%, and the Vertical Distortion to 0%.

STEP THREE: In the Layers palette, make a copy of your text layer by dragging it to the Create a New Layer icon at the top of the Layers palette. Press D to set your Foreground color to black, then press Alt-Backspace to fill your type with black. Next, in the Layers palette, drag this new black text layer beneath your original text layer.

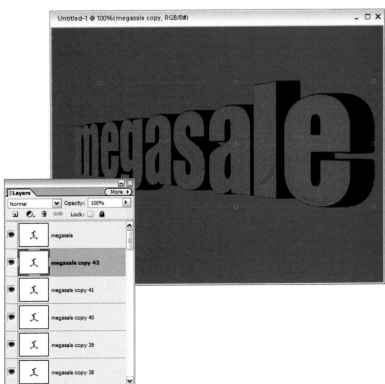

STEP FOUR: Here's where you create the 3D effect. Click on the Move tool. Press-and-hold Alt-Control and press-and-hold the Right Arrow key on your keyboard. As you do this, you'll see the 3D effect emerge. What you're doing is duplicating and simultaneously nudging to the right the black text layer over and over again very quickly. (In the example shown here, I added 42 layers, yet it only took about 15 seconds.) Don't worry about the extra layers; we'll deal with them in the next step.

Continued

STEP FIVE: In the Layers palette, your original red text layer should be on top of the layer stack. Hide this layer from view by clicking once on the Eye icon in the far-left column beside it. Then, scroll down to the bottom of the layer stack and hide the Background layer from view as well, leaving only the 40+ black text layers still visible.

STEP SIX: Go to the Layers palette's flyout menu and choose Merge Visible to combine the 40+ text layers into just one layer. Now, you can make both your Background layer and the top text layer visible again by clicking in the empty box where the Eye icon used to appear, which completes the effect.

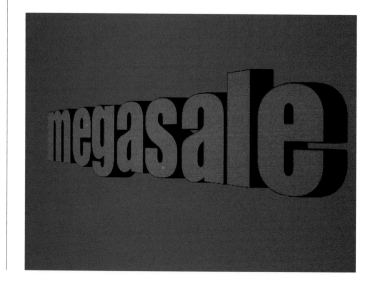

Perspective Type Logo

When the UPN TV network first introduced its current logo, I just assumed it was created in a 3D program, but you can pretty much get the same effect (where it looks like the logo is dropping back, like a one-point perspective effect) from right within Photoshop Elements, thanks to the Free Transform tool's Distort feature.

STEP ONE: Create a new document in RGB mode (the one here is 8x6"). Click on the Foreground color swatch in the Toolbox and choose a bright red in the Color Picker. Fill the background with this red color by pressing Alt-Backspace. Next, press D and then X to set your Foreground color to white. Press the T key to switch to the Type tool, and enter your type (the font shown here is Impact).

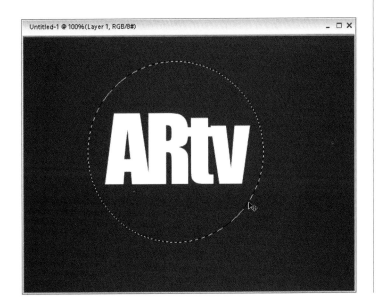

STEP TWO: Create a new blank layer by clicking on the Create a New Layer icon at the top of the Layers palette. Press M until you get the Elliptical Marquee tool. Press-and-hold the Shift key and drag out a circular selection that's larger than your type. (*Note:* If you need to reposition your selection, press-and-hold the Spacebar while you're still dragging with the Elliptical Marquee tool; release just the Spacebar key when you've repositioned the selection where you want it, and finish drawing your selection.)

Continued

STEP THREE: Go under the Edit menu and choose Stroke (Outline) Selection. When the Stroke dialog appears, choose 16 pixels for your Width, set the Location to Center, click on the Color swatch, choose white in the Color Picker, and then click OK. This puts a white stroke around your circular selection. Press Control-D to deselect.

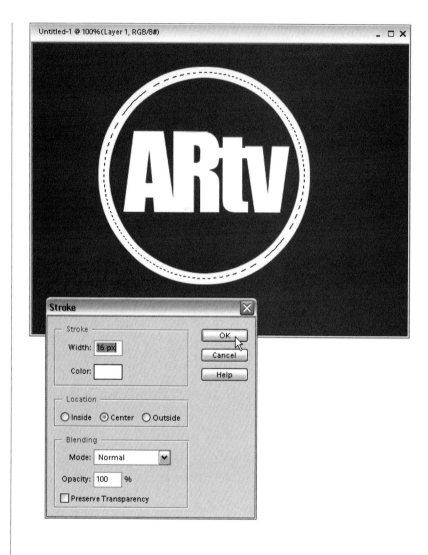

STEP FOUR: In the Layers palette, link your Type layer and your white circle layer together by Shift-clicking on each layer. Then, press Control-E to merge the two layers. (*Note:* Whenever you want to merge an image layer down into a Type layer, you have to link the two layers first in the Layers palette.)

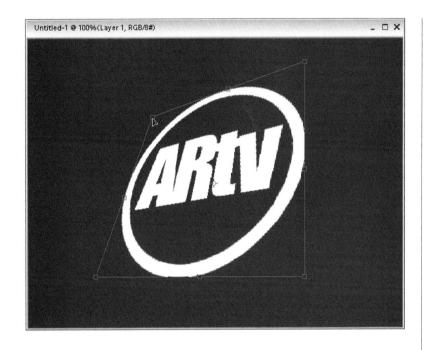

STEP FIVE: Press Control-T to bring up the Free Transform bounding box. Press-and-hold the Control key, click on the top-left corner point of the Free Transform bounding box, and drag down and to the right (you're dragging diagonally inward); the logo will appear to tip backward. Holding the Control key allows you to distort just that one point of the bounding box.

STEP SIX: Press Enter to lock in your transformation and to complete the effect.

Type on a Circle

While this could be a tedious step-by-step technique for wrapping type around a circle, it doesn't have to be. Photoshop Elements' cool Warp Text feature lets you create this effect much faster and easier. Here's how:

STEP ONE: Open the circular image you want to place type around. (*Note:* You can start with a blank document: Just draw a circular selection with the Elliptical Marquee tool; go under the Edit menu, under Stroke [Outline] Selection; and add a 1-pixel black stroke to the selection. You can then use your stroked selection as a guide for the rotation of your text.)

STEP TWO: Press the T key to switch to the Type tool, and then enter your type (the typeface I used here is Copperplate Gothic Bold). Use the Spacebar to add a space between each letter you type (we do this because the next step tends to condense the type, so we need to stretch it out a bit).

STEP THREE: Next, go to the Layers palette and double-click on the "T" thumbnail to highlight your type. (*Note:* It's not necessary to highlight the type to use Warp Text, but I like to use the highlight to help me align the type around the circle.) Click on the Warped Text icon in the Options Bar (it's the third icon from the right and it has the letter "T" with a bent line beneath it) to bring up the Warp Text dialog. From the dialog's Style pop-up menu, choose Arc. While the dialog is open, move your cursor outside the box, click on your type, and drag it into position in your image. Adjust the amount of Bend (dragging the slider to the right in the dialog) until it looks good to you. Click OK to complete the top arc.

STEP FOUR: Make a duplicate of your arced Type layer by dragging it to the Create a New Layer icon at the top of the Layers palette. Next, go to the Layers palette and double-click on the "T" thumbnail to highlight your duplicated type. Once highlighted, type in the word you want for the bottom of the circle (it will replace the highlighted text). Don't forget to add a space between each letter you type. Click outside your duplicate type to temporarily switch to the Move tool, and position the type near the bottom of the circle.

Continued

STEP FIVE: Double-click the "T" thumbnail for the new Type layer in the Layers palette to highlight the text. Click on the Warped Text icon again in the Options Bar. This time, you'll move the Bend slider to the left to arc your type in the opposite direction to match the bottom of the circle. Move your cursor outside the dialog, click on your type, and drag it into position at the bottom of the circle.

STEP SIX: Click OK to complete the bottom arc. Two things to keep in mind when using Warp Text: (1) Longer words require more Bend amount than shorter words; and (2) if your type appears too condensed after using Warp Text, just add spaces between letters.

Putting an Image into Type (Clipping Group)

This technique lets you take any image and place (clip) it inside type that you've set on the layer directly beneath it. This is a pretty flexible effect because you can reposition your image inside the type once it's grouped, and if for some reason you don't like the results, you can easily undo the effect.

STEP ONE: Create a new document in RGB mode (the one here is 8x6"). Press the letter D to set your Foreground color to black, then press the letter T to switch to the Type tool. Create some large display-sized type (tall, thick type-faces, like the Impact font that I used here, work well for this effect).

STEP TWO: Open the image you want to put inside your type. Switch to the Move tool by pressing the letter V, and then click-and-drag this image into your original text document. This should give you three layers: (1) your Background layer, (2) your Type layer, and (3) a layer with the image that you want clipped into your type.

Continued

STEP THREE: With the image layer active in the Layers palette (it should be at the top of the layer stack), choose Group with Previous from the Layer menu (or press Control-G) and your image will appear inside your type. You can now reposition your image within your type by clicking-and-dragging with the Move tool. (*Note:* To undo this effect, press the keyboard shortcut Shift-Control-G.)

STEP FOUR: In most cases, it helps if you add a drop shadow to your Type layer to better define the edges of your letters (plus it looks cool). Click on the Type layer (in the Layers palette), then go to the Styles and Effects palette, and with Layer Styles selected, choose Drop Shadows from the top-right pop-up menu in the palette. Click on the Soft Edge icon to apply a drop shadow.

Untitled-1 @ 100% (Layer 2, RGB/8#)

BRAND X PICTURES

STEP FIVE: Even though we've already created the type effect, let's take it a step further by adding a backscreened background. Open an image that you want to appear in the background, and with the Move tool, drag-and-drop this image into your text document.

STEP SIX: Go to the Layers palette and lower the Opacity of this image layer to around 20% or less. Press U until you have the Line tool, and in the Options Bar enter 1 pixel in the Weight field. Then, draw a line underneath the type. Now add any additional type that you'd like below the line (here I used the typeface Litterbox ICG for the words "ADVENTURE PARK") to complete the effect.

Moving a Background Object in Front of Type

You see this technique used a lot on the covers of major magazines. It's where an object (most often a person's head) appears in front of type. That doesn't sound like that big of a challenge, but once you realize that the person is on a flattened background image, with no layers, it becomes a little trickier. Not hard, just a little trickier.

STEP ONE: Open the background photo that has an object you want to appear in front of some type. Press the letter T to switch to the Type tool, click on the Foreground color swatch at the bottom of the Toolbox to select your color, and create the type you want to appear behind the object. In this example, we're going to put the nameplate of a magazine behind the person's head (the font I used is CronosMM250 Light using two different colors). You create the type now so you'll know how much (or how little) of the object you need to select in the next step.

STEP TWO: Click on your Background layer in the Layers palette and put a selection around the part of the object you want to appear in front of your type. (You can temporarily hide your Type layer by clicking on the Eye icon to the left of the layer in the Layers palette.) I pressed the L key until I had the Magnetic Lasso tool in the Toolbox, and then I clicked once on the right side of her head, released the mouse button, and traced around the top of her head and arms. Once you've traced around the areas you want to select, return to where you first clicked (your cursor will have a circle beside it) and click to complete your selection.

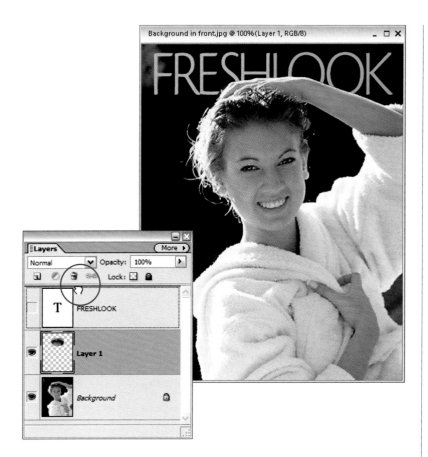

STEP THREE: Once your object is selected, go under the Layer menu, under New, and choose Layer via Copy (or press Control-J) to copy that selected area up onto its own layer. Then, in the Layers palette, drag this layer above your Type layer. Moving that "top-of-the-head" layer in front of the Type layer makes it appear as though the person is in front of the type. (If you hid your Type layer, make it visible again by clicking on the layer's empty Eye icon box to the left of the layer.)

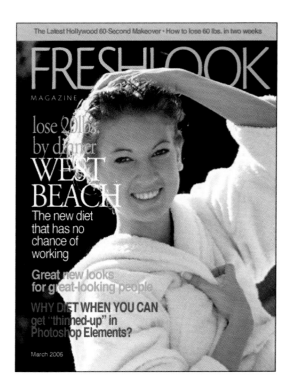

STEP FOUR: To finish this project, add in any other type you want on your cover using the Type tool. You can also use the Rectangle tool to add a colored bar across the top (as I did here), and then enter text over it. (The type at the top is in Helvetica Bold; the main headline, "lose 20 lbs. by dinner," is set in Adobe Garamond Pro; and the rest of the subheads are set in Helvetica Bold.)

Grunge Type

This is probably the most popular effect in Hollywood movie titles, and it's used in a dozen other places as well (in fact, I saw it in a Levi's print ad the evening I was writing this). It uses the technique of "grunging" a photo, but it uses it with type. After you've created the effect, you'll drop it into a movie poster layout (you'll have to do a little work there—mostly formatting type—but it's easy).

STEP ONE: Create a new document in RGB mode (the example here is 8x8"). Press D to set your Foreground color to black, and then fill the background with black by pressing Alt-Backspace. Press X to set your Foreground color to white, and then press the letter T to switch to the Type tool. Now create your white type (the type shown here is in Compacta Bold).

STEP TWO: Open the photo that you'll use to create your grunge. Photos with lots of vertical lines seem to work best; photos that have lots of rounded objects (like palm trees) don't work nearly as well (I know from experience). I had to test the effect on about eight photos before I found this one.

BRAND X PICTURES

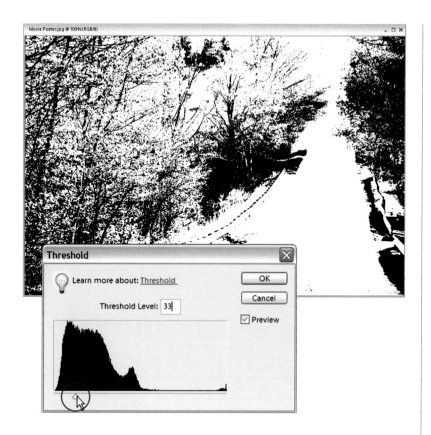

STEP THREE: Go under the Filter menu, under Adjustments, and choose Threshold. Your image will turn into what looks like a black-and-white line drawing. Drag the slider nearly all the way to the left to remove some of the black detail, leaving just broken lines, spots, and smudges. This is the step you'll probably have to try on a number of photos until you find one that looks good. Click OK to apply the Threshold.

STEP FOUR: Press W to switch to the Magic Wand tool, then click directly inside one black area of your photo (it will probably only select a tiny section of your photo). Then, go under the Select menu and choose Similar to select all of the black areas in your photo.

Continued

STEP FIVE: Press V to switch to the Move tool, and drag-and-drop these selected black areas (as one unit) into your white text document. When the "grunged" image appears, press Control-T to bring up Free Transform. Press-and-hold the Shift key, grab a corner point, and drag to adjust the size of the photo until it looks good to you inside the text. (*Note:* If you can't see the corner points of the bounding box, press Control-0 [zero] to adjust your image to fit onscreen.) Click-and-drag inside the bounding box to reposition your "grunged" image. Then, press Enter to lock in your transformation.

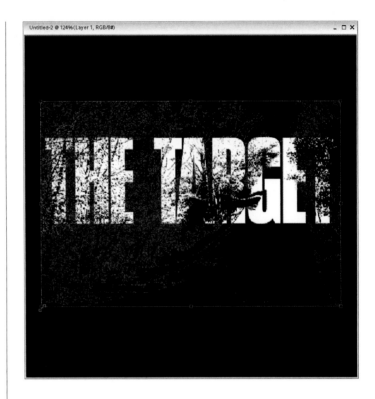

STEP SIX: From the Layer menu, choose Group with Previous (or press Control-G) to clip the black grunge photo inside your white text. You can now use the Move tool if you need to reposition the grunge that's inside the text. At this point the type portion of this effect is now complete.

BRAND X PICTURES

STEP SEVEN: Open the main photo you want to use in your movie poster. (The example here is a shot of a soldier as seen through an infrared scope.) Go back to your grunge text document. You need to merge the grunge layer and Type layer together, but you can't merge an image layer down into a Type layer. The trick is to link the image and grunge layers first, so click on the grunge layer to make it active, and then Shift-click on the Type layer to link it to the grunge layer. Press Control-E to permanently merge them together. Switch to the Move tool and drag this white grunge type over onto your poster document. You can scale the text to size using Free Transform (Control-T).

STEP EIGHT: The final step is to add the rest of the movie poster type, along with any logos you'd like, which completes the effect. (The actors' names at the top are set in Trajan Pro; the subhead above the movie and the descriptive type at the very bottom are set in Helvetica Neue; and the words "SUMMER 2006" are set in Impact.)

Distressed Type

It's not grunge type—it's distressed (damaged) type. This classic effect is as popular as ever, and it shows up in everything from store brands to clothing to movie posters—all using a distressed look based on the technique you're going to do here.

STEP ONE: Create a new document that's 9x7" at 72 ppi in RGB mode. Create a new layer by clicking on the Create a New Layer icon at the top of the Layers palette. Press the letter M to switch to the Rectangular Marquee tool, press-and-hold the Shift key, and draw a square selection. Press the letter D to set your Foreground color to black, then fill your square selection with black by pressing Alt-Backspace. Deselect by pressing Control-D.

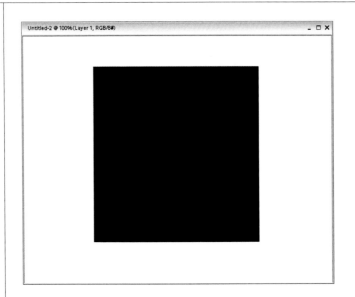

STEP TWO: Press the letter X to set your Foreground color to white, then press the letter T to switch to the Type tool. Click on the black square and enter your white type (I used the font Helvetica Black). Once you've entered your type, with the Type layer active in the Layers palette, press Control-E to merge the Type layer with the black square layer.

STEP THREE: Now to add the distress: Press the letter B to switch to the Brush tool, and click on the brush thumbnail in the Options Bar to bring up the Brush Picker. In the Brush Picker, scroll down until you find the 39-pixel Dry Brush from the default set of brushes. With your Foreground color still set to white, move this brush over black areas in your image and start clicking your mouse button. Don't paint strokes—just click your mouse button a number of times. Try 10 or 12 clicks in one area, then move your cursor to another area, click seven or eight times, and move to another area, keeping your locations and number of clicks random.

STEP FOUR: Now, go back up to the Brush Picker and choose a different brush size and shape. In this case, try the 48-pixel Oil Heavy Flow Dry Edges brush, and do the same thing you did in the previous step—click multiple times over black areas in your logo. Press the D key to set your Foreground to black and click a few times over the white type in the same fashion. The more distressed, the better.

Continued

STEP FIVE: To enhance the type effect, you can add a photo in the background. Simply open an image you want to add, press V to switch to the Move tool, and drag-and-drop the image onto your type document. In the Layers palette, drag the image layer below the distressed text layer, and lower the image layer's Opacity until it looks good to you.

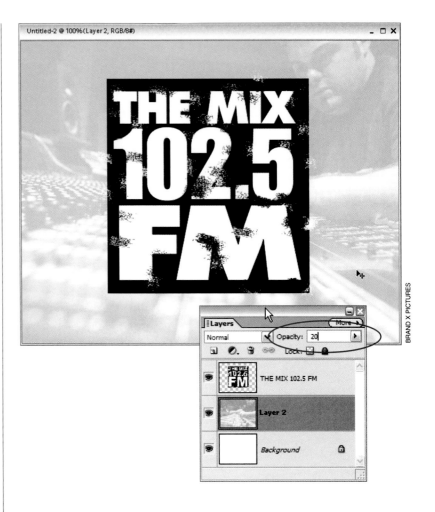

BRAND X PICTURES

STEP SIX: You may notice some brush strokes splattering over onto your back-screened photo. If that's the case, click on the distressed text layer in the Layers palette to make it active, and with the Rectangular Marquee tool, put a selection around the black square. Go to the Select menu, choose Inverse, and then press the Backspace key to delete the excess brush strokes. Press Control-D to deselect, completing the effect.

Carved in Stone

This "carved in stone" technique is more realistic, has more depth, and is basically "more gooder" (as my son would say) than most "carved" type effects out there. Actually, I just think it's "bester."

STEP ONE: We're going to start by opening an appropriate image (this technique will work with almost any background image, but honestly, carving in stone looks best when the background image is, well...stone). Duplicate the Background layer by dragging it to the Create a New Layer icon at the top of the Layers palette.

STEP TWO: Press D to set your Foreground color to black. Then press T to switch to the Type tool, and enter your text at a large size (I used the font Trajan Pro). Control-click on your Type layer in the Layers palette to put a selection around your type. Then, click on the Eye icon next to your Type layer to hide the layer from view.

Continued

STEP THREE: Now, click on the Background copy layer in the Layers palette to make it the active layer. Press Shift-Control-I to *inverse* the selection, meaning it selects everything but the part of the photo you want to keep. Press Backspace to remove the excess background from the Background copy layer. You won't see anything happen really, but what you're doing is creating a layer that contains only the stone in the shape of the text. Press Control-D to deselect.

STEP FOUR: From the Edit menu, choose Stroke (Outline) Selection. In the Stroke dialog, set the Width to 1 pixel, click on the Color swatch and choose white in the Color Picker, set the Location to Inside, and then click OK.

STEP FIVE: From the Styles and Effects palette (found under the Window menu), ensure Layer Styles is selected, and then choose Inner Shadows from the palette's top-right pop-up menu. Click the Low icon to apply an inner shadow. Return to the Layers palette and drag the Type layer to the Trash icon to delete it since you no longer need that layer.

STEP SIX: The final step is to darken the inside of the letters to help "sell" the effect that the type is carved into the background. To do this, press Control-L to bring up the Levels dialog (you should still have the Background copy layer active). At the bottom of the dialog, move the highlight Output Levels slider to the left until you reach approximately 210, then click OK to complete the effect.

Transparent TV Type

I call this "TV Type" because you see a similar effect all the time on network logos in the lower right-hand corner of your TV screen. Although it's ubiquitous on television, I've seen this effect used in print and on the Web over and over again, and I like the fact that you can make it as subtle or powerful as you want simply by adjusting the Opacity slider in the Layers palette.

STEP ONE: Open the image to which you want to add the effect. Press D to set your Foreground color to black, and then press T to switch to the Type tool. Create your type (I used the font Trajan Pro here).

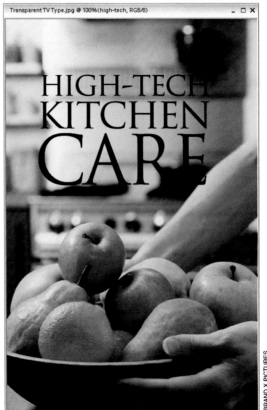

STEP TWO: We now want to run a filter on the text, but we can't run a filter on a Type layer, so we'll first have to convert it to an image layer. Go to the Layer menu and choose Simplify Layer to convert it from a Type layer into an image layer. In the Layers palette, click on the Lock Transparent Pixels icon (it's the first icon next to the word "Lock").

STEP THREE: Go under the Filter menu, under Stylize, and choose Emboss. When the Emboss dialog appears, change the Height to 5 (try 9 for high-res, 300-ppi images) and click OK to apply a hard bevel to your type. Your type will turn gray, with highlights and shadows along the edges. In the Layers palette, change the layer blend mode of this layer from Normal to Hard Light to make the gray fill disappear while leaving the highlights and shadows still visible.

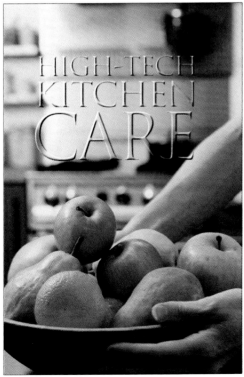

STEP FOUR: To round and smooth out the effect, with Lock Transparent Pixels still turned on in the Layers palette, go under the Filter menu, under Blur, and choose Gaussian Blur. Enter 1–2 pixels (try 6 for high-res images), and click OK to apply soft shading inside the letters, completing the effect. If the effect is too intense, try lowering the Opacity of the text layer in the Layers palette.

Here we are—more than half way through the book—at a chapter subtitled "Special Effects," but I don't

Saturday Night Special
Special Effects

want you to think that I've run out of cool things to share. Au contraire (gratuitous use of French in everyday conversation inspired by *Frasier*). I specifically used the term "Special Effects" because that's just what these effects are—special. Oh sure, I toyed with other names, like "Zowie-Wowie Effects," "Turbo-Mondo Spasmatic Effects," and even "Intergalactic Alien Death-Ray Effects," but those names just weren't special enough for the effects I had planned for this chapter. But before you launch into the chapter and begin creating effects with an unbridled zeal heretofore hidden beneath layers of conformity and years of ingrained neo-conservatism (I'm not sure what any of that means, but my publisher told me to use a lot of big words), I just want to thank you for spending these special moments with me. See, how could I call this chapter anything but "Special Effects"?

Digital Pixel Effect

This is one of those classic effects that's used every time the word "digital" appears on a book cover, a billboard, or a magazine cover or spread. It makes the image (in our example, a person) look like he's becoming "digital" because half of the image is turning into pixels.

STEP ONE: Open the photo you want to apply the effect to (it's usually applied to photos of people, but I've seen it used on product shots as well).

STEP TWO: Duplicate the Background layer by going under the Layer menu, under New, and choosing Layer via Copy (or by pressing Control-J). You'll apply the effect to this duplicate layer.

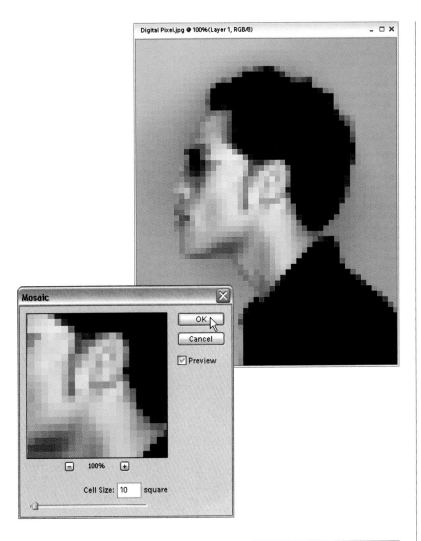

STEP THREE: Go under the Filter menu, under Pixelate, and choose Mosaic. When the dialog appears, for Cell Size enter 10 pixels (this isn't an "official" size, so if you'd like smaller or larger pixels, feel free to experiment), then click OK to pixelate the entire layer.

STEP FOUR: Press-and-hold the Control key and click on the Create a New Layer icon at the top of the Layers palette. This adds a blank layer directly beneath your duplicate image layer. In the Layers palette, click on the duplicate image layer to make it active, then under the Layer menu choose Group with Previous (or press Control-G). This creates a clipping group, which hides the pixelated effect on the duplicate image layer.

Continued

STEP FIVE: In the Layers palette, click on the blank layer to make it active. Press the letter G to switch to the Gradient tool, then press Enter, and the Gradient Picker will appear onscreen. Choose the Foreground to Transparent gradient (it's the second one in the Picker), and then click the Gradient tool on the right side of the document and drag horizontally to the left.

STEP SIX: The photo will then blend gradually from the clean photo on the left to the pixelated photo on the right. What you're really doing here is revealing the clean photo on the Background layer, and then blending to the pixelated image layer at the top of the layer stack, giving the classic pixelated "digital" look.

Attaching a Note to a Photo

If you need to add a caption to a photo, you *could* just backscreen an area or create some reverse type, but with this effect you can create stronger visual interest for your caption, drawing the reader's eye right where you want it to go.

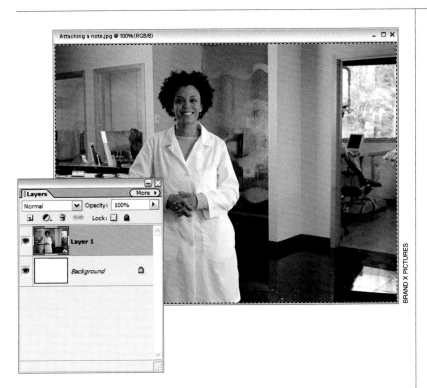

STEP ONE: Open the photo you want to use in the effect. Press Control-A to select the entire photo, then go under the Layer menu, under New, and choose Layer via Cut (or press Shift-Control-J) to cut the photo from the Background layer and copy it onto its own separate layer (Layer 1).

STEP TWO: Go under the Image menu and choose Canvas Size. When the dialog appears, turn on the Relative checkbox, enter 2 inches for both Width and Height, and choose White in the Canvas Extension Color pop-up menu. Click OK to add some white space around your photo.

Continued

STEP THREE: Choose Stroke (Outline) Selection from the Edit menu. Set the Width to 15 pixels (30 pixels for high-res, 300-ppi images), set the Location to Inside (to give your stroke straight corners rather than the default rounded corners), and click on the Color swatch to choose a light gray in the Color Picker. Click OK to apply a gray stroke around your image area.

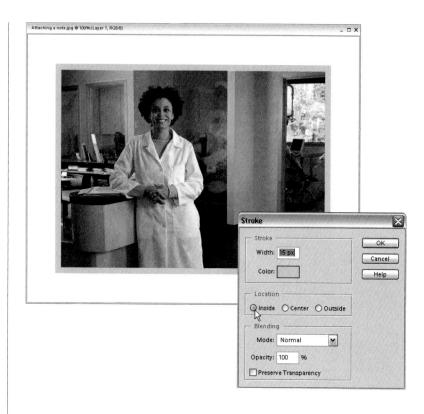

STEP FOUR: Go to the Styles and Effects palette (found under the Window menu) and with Layer Styles selected, choose Drop Shadows from the palette's top-right pop-up menu. Click on the Soft Edge icon, and then in the Layers palette, double-click on the Layer Styles icon (it looks like an "f") to the right of the layer's name. In the Style Settings dialog, increase the Shadow Distance to 10, turn off the Use Global Light checkbox, and click OK.

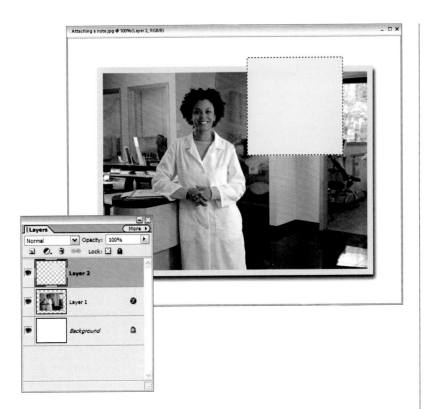

STEP FIVE: Create a new layer by clicking on the Create a New Layer icon at the top of the Layers palette. Press the letter M to switch to the Rectangular Marquee tool, press-and-hold the Shift key, and make a square selection in the area you want your note to appear. In the Toolbox, click on the Foreground color swatch and choose a "Post-it–like" yellow color in the Color Picker (I used R: 255, G: 255, and B: 161). Fill your selection with this yellow by pressing Alt-Backspace, then deselect by pressing Control-D.

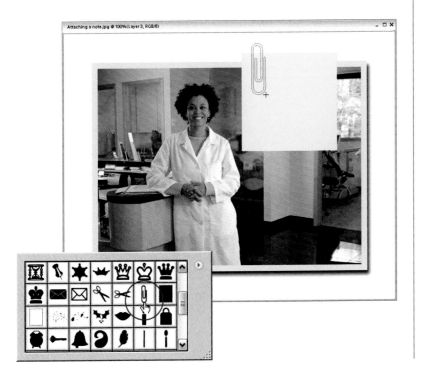

STEP SIX: Press U until you get the Custom Shape tool from the Toolbox, and then press the Enter key to bring up the Custom Shape Picker onscreen. From the Picker's flyout menu, choose Objects to load a new set of custom shapes. Scroll down until you find the Paper Clip shape and select it. In the Toolbox, click on the Foreground color swatch and select gray in the Color Picker. Now, click the Custom Shape tool near the top of your yellow note, then press-and-hold the Shift key and drag the tool to create a paper clip. Press the V key to switch to the Move tool and position the paper clip at the top of your yellow note.

Continued

STEP SEVEN: Click on the Foreground color swatch and choose a dark blue in the Color Picker, then press the letter T to get the Type tool. Add your message to the note (the text here is in the font ITC Bradley Hand). Go to the Layers palette and link the paper clip, note, and Type layers together by pressing the Shift key and clicking on each layer so you can move all three layers as one group.

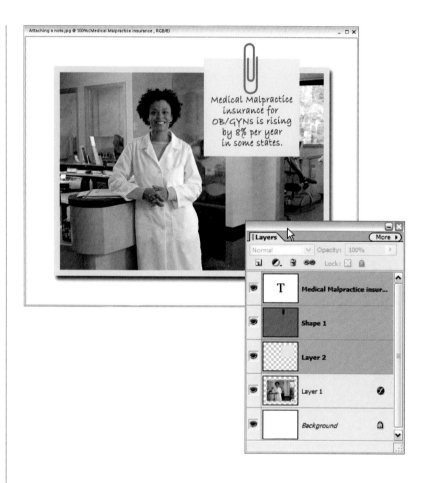

STEP EIGHT: Press Control-T to bring up Free Transform. Move your cursor outside the bounding box and click-and-drag to rotate the note slightly. You can click-and-drag inside the bounding box to reposition the note. Press Enter when it looks about right.

STEP NINE: Next, you'll add a metallic look to the paper clip. Click on the paper clip layer in the Layers palette to make it active, then go to the Styles and Effects palette (found under the Window menu), and with Layer Styles selected, choose Wow Chrome from the palette's top-right pop-up menu. Click on the Wow-Chrome Textured icon and your paper clip will get a metallic look. Now, go under the Layer menu and choose Simplify Layer to change your paper clip Shape layer into a regular image layer.

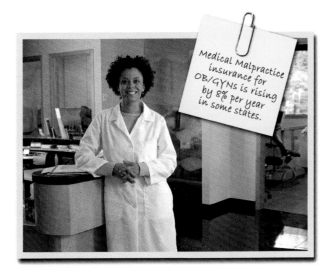

STEP TEN: Press the letter E to switch to the Eraser tool. In the Options Bar, click on the brush thumbnail, and in the resulting Brush Picker, choose a small, soft-edged brush. Erase the inside part of the paper clip (along with some of the shadow areas) to make it appear as if that part of the paperclip is behind the note and photo. Now, click on the yellow note layer, then choose Drop Shadows in the top-right pop-up menu in the Styles and Effects palette and click on the Soft Edge icon. In the Layers palette, double-click the Layer Styles icon, turn off the Use Global Light checkbox in the resulting Style Settings dialog, and click OK to complete the effect.

Mapping a Texture to a Person

You may have heard this effect referred to as a Displacement Map technique because it uses Photoshop Elements' Displace filter to map a texture from one object onto another object. This has become particularly popular in the past couple of years, and fortunately it's quite easy to do, even though it looks as if you worked on the image for hours.

STEP ONE: Open the image that you want to apply a texture to. (In this example, we're using a photograph of a man, and we're going to apply the texture to his skin.)

STEP TWO: Make a duplicate of your image by going under the File menu and choosing Duplicate. Then, go under the Image menu, under Mode, and choose Grayscale. When the warning dialog appears, just click OK to discard the color and convert this duplicate image into a grayscale image.

STEP THREE: Go under the Filter menu, under Blur, and choose Gaussian Blur. Apply a 2-pixel blur to your grayscale image and click OK. (*Note:* Two pixels is okay for low-res, 72-ppi images; for high-res, 300-ppi images, try 4 or 5 pixels.) Now, go under the File menu and choose Save. Name this blurry grayscale image file "Map" and save it in Photoshop's native format (making it a PSD file). This is the file we'll use when we apply the Displace filter in Step 6.

BRAND X PICTURES

STEP FOUR: Open the image you want to use as a texture. Press V to switch to the Move tool, press-and-hold the Shift key, and click-and-drag this texture image on top of your original color image. (Pressing-and-holding the Shift key will center the image above the target image of the person.)

Continued

STEP FIVE: Press Control-A to put a selection around the entire image area. Then, go under the Filter menu, under Distort, and choose Displace. When the Displace dialog appears, enter 10 for both Horizontal Scale and Vertical Scale. Under Displacement Map, choose Stretch To Fit, and for Undefined Areas, choose Repeat Edge Pixels. Click OK.

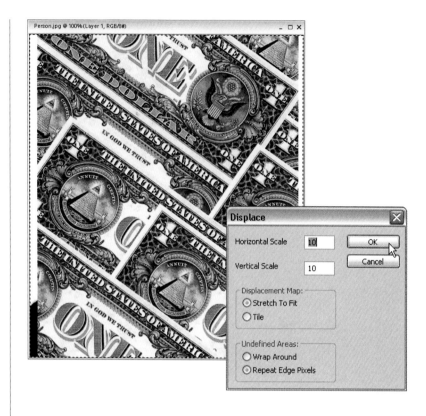

STEP SIX: When you click OK, a dialog appears prompting you to "choose a displacement map." Locate the grayscale file you saved earlier (in Step 3), click the Open button, and the Displace filter will use this map file to "map out" the texture to fit your image. You'll see your image area warp a bit when you apply this filter, but to see the full effect, there's still a little more work to do.

STEP SEVEN: Press Control-D to deselect. In the Layers palette, click on the Eye icon in the far-left column beside the texture layer to hide it. Click on your original image layer (the man) and use your favorite selection tool to select the background area behind him. (*Note:* Since the background behind this man is a solid color and easy to select, I clicked the Magic Wand tool [W] on the background to select it.)

STEP EIGHT: In the Layers palette, click on the texture layer to make it active (your selection should still be in place). Press the Backspace key to leave a silhouette of the texture in the shape of the man's head. Deselect by pressing Control-D. At the top left of the Layers palette, change the layer blend mode of this texture layer to Multiply to make it look as if it were tattooed on his skin. (*Note:* For different effects, try the Overlay or even Soft Light layer blend mode.) Lower the layer's Opacity to around 50%. With the texture layer active, use the Eraser tool (E) with a small, hard-edged brush to erase over his hair, eyes, lips, teeth, tongue, eyebrows, shirt, and chain so that the effect just appears on the skin to complete the effect.

Dividing a Photo into Puzzle Pieces

This effect has been around for a while, but what rekindled my interest was seeing it on Apple's iLife product box. If you had to draw the puzzle pieces, it would be quite a task, but luckily, four puzzle shapes are built right into Photoshop Elements (as custom shapes). The technique can be used to make an editorial statement, a dramatic effect, a fun effect—it's pretty much up to you how you use it.

STEP ONE: Create a new document in RGB mode (for this example, I created an 8x6" document). Press D to set your Foreground color to black, and then press U until you get the Custom Shape tool from the Toolbox. Up in the Options Bar, click on the Shape thumbnail to bring up the Custom Shape Picker. From the Picker's flyout menu, choose Objects to import this set of shapes.

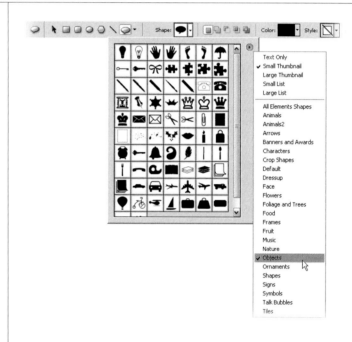

STEP TWO: Once the set is loaded, navigate in the Picker until you see four puzzle shapes. Select the second puzzle shape (Puzzle 2), and then click the Custom Shape tool in the top-left corner of the blank document and start to drag. Now press-and-hold the Shift key after you start dragging. (*Note:* The Shift key constrains the puzzle piece proportionally. But if you press-and-hold the Shift key before you click-and-drag, all of your shapes will be added to the same Shape layer, and we need each puzzle piece on its own layer so we can reposition or resize it as necessary. So make sure you don't press the Shift key until *after* you start dragging.)

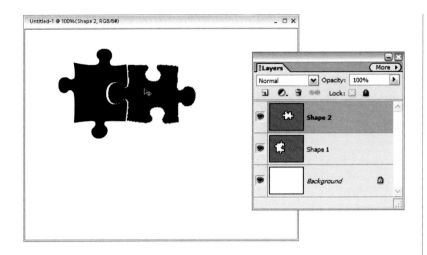

STEP THREE: Return to the Custom Shape Picker in the Options Bar and choose the first of the four puzzle shapes (Puzzle 1). Click the Custom Shape tool to the right of the current shape, then press-and-hold the Shift key once you start dragging out a puzzle piece that is approximately the same size as your first puzzle piece. Press V to switch to the Move tool, then position this piece into the other piece, but make sure you leave a slight gap between the two (let them almost touch, but for this to work correctly, you need a tiny gap—it shouldn't look as if it's one solid piece).

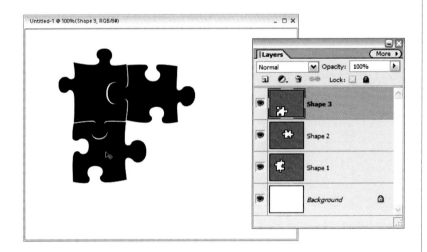

STEP FOUR: Press U until you have the Custom Shape tool again, and from the Custom Shape Picker choose the third of the four puzzle shapes (Puzzle 3). Click below the left puzzle piece, press-and-hold the Shift key once you start dragging out this puzzle shape, which also creates another layer (Shape 3) in the Layers palette. Use the Move tool to position this piece up against the bottom of the left puzzle piece. Again, make them very close, but leave a tiny gap between the pieces.

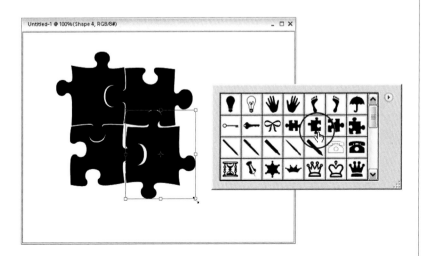

STEP FIVE: Get the Custom Shape tool again. In the Custom Shape Picker, click on the second puzzle piece (Puzzle 2). Click below the far-right puzzle piece and press-and-hold the Shift key after you start to drag out the shape. This shape won't match up without some tweaking: Go under the Image menu, under Rotate, and choose Layer 180°. Switch to the Move tool and press Control-T to bring up Free Transform. Hold the Shift key, grab a corner point, and adjust this puzzle piece so it fits with the others. Press Enter to lock in your transformation.

Continued

STEP SIX: You'll need to save a selection of the bottom-right puzzle piece so you can later pull that piece away from the others, so with the last Shape layer you created still active (Shape 4), go under the Layer menu and choose Simplify Layer to change it into a regular image layer. Now, in the Layers palette, Control-click on this layer to put a selection around the bottom-right puzzle piece. Go to the Select menu and choose Save Selection. Name your selection in the resulting dialog and click OK. Press Control-D to deselect.

STEP SEVEN: Open the photo you want to apply the puzzle effect to. Using the Move tool, click-and-drag this photo into your puzzle document, positioning the photo at the top of the layer stack in the Layers palette. Hide both the Background and photo layers from view by clicking on the Eye icons to the left of those layers in the Layers palette. Then, with any visible layer active, choose Merge Visible from the palette's flyout menu to merge all the puzzle pieces into one single layer. You can make the Background and photo layers visible again by clicking in the empty boxes where the Eye icons used to be.

BRAND X PICTURES

STEP EIGHT: In the Layers palette, click on the photo layer to make it active, and choose Group with Previous from the Layer menu (or just press Control-G) to clip the photo into the puzzle pieces. Now you can use the Move tool to reposition your image within the puzzle pieces.

STEP NINE: In the Layers palette, ensure that your image layer is active, and then press Control-E to merge the image and puzzle layers into one layer. Now remember that selection you saved? You're going to need it, so go under the Select menu and choose Load Selection. Your saved selection should appear in the Selection pop-up menu (if not, click on the down-facing arrow to bring up the Selection pop-up menu and choose it from the list). Once your selection loads, go under the Layer menu, under New, and choose Layer via Cut (or press Shift-Control-J) to cut this selection and copy it onto its own layer in the Layers palette.

STEP TEN: With the Move tool, drag your cut puzzle piece to the right. Then, press Control-T to bring up Free Transform, click outside the bounding box, and rotate the puzzle piece slightly to the left. Press Enter when it looks good to you. Now press Control-E to merge this rotated puzzle piece layer with the other puzzle layer. With this puzzle layer active, go to the Styles and Effects palette (found under the Window menu). With the Layer Styles category selected, choose Bevels from the top-right pop-up menu and click on the Simple Emboss icon. Now select Drop Shadows from the palette's top-right pop-up menu and select the Low shadow icon. From the Layer menu, under Layer Style, choose Style Settings and in the resulting dialog, lower the Shadow Distance to 1 pixel and change the Lighting Angle to 30° to complete the effect.

Brushed Metal

If you're creating interfaces, it's just a matter of time before you say to yourself, "Ya know, I could really use some brushed metal." I know it sounds unlikely, but it happens (more often than I care to admit). Here's how to whip up some brushed metal from scratch (just like grandma used to make):

STEP ONE: Create a new document in RGB mode (this example is 8x6"). Press G to switch to the Gradient tool, and then press Enter to bring up the Gradient Picker onscreen. From the default set of gradients, choose the Copper gradient (it's the fifth gradient in the second row). Click the Gradient tool at the top of the image window and drag to the bottom—but you need to do two things when dragging the gradient: (1) Drag at a slight angle to the right, and (2) start at the top but drag about an inch past the bottom of the image window (it's easier than it sounds). Then release the mouse button to create the gradient shown here.

STEP TWO: Go under the Enhance menu, under Adjust Color, and choose Remove Color (or press Shift-Control-U) to remove the copper color from your gradient. Then, go under the Filter menu, under Noise, and choose Add Noise. When the Add Noise dialog appears, enter 20 for Amount, select Gaussian, turn on the Monochromatic checkbox, and click OK.

STEP THREE: Return to the Filter menu, under Blur, and choose Motion Blur. When the Motion Blur dialog appears, enter 33° for Angle and 75 for Distance. When you click OK, Photoshop Elements applies the Motion Blur to your image.

Brushed metal after cropping away harsh edges

TIP: Take a look at the left and right edges of the image in the previous step, and you can see that these areas don't look as good as the rest of the image. To get around that, we often make our new document about 1/2" wider than we really need so we can crop it down later to remove those harsh edges.

TV Scan Lines

This technique, which simulates the scan lines that a television produces when photographed with a camera, remains one of the most popular effects in print, on TV, and on the Web.

STEP ONE: Open the image in which you want to apply TV scan lines—either RGB or Grayscale will work. Create a new document that's 1 pixel wide by 4 pixels high in the same resolution and color mode as your open image (e.g., if you want to add scan lines to an RGB image, choose RGB).

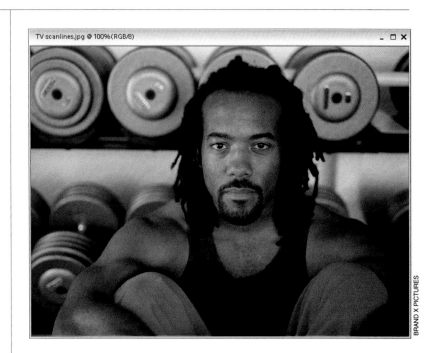

STEP TWO: Press Z to switch to the Zoom tool and zoom in on this tiny document until it's easily seen (you might have to zoom in as much as 1600%). Press D to set your Foreground color to black, then press M to switch to the Rectangular Marquee tool and select the top half of the image. Press Alt-Backspace to fill the selected half of your image with black, and then press Control-D to deselect. Go under the Edit menu and choose Define Pattern (this command will save your black-and-white document as a pattern that we'll use in the next step). A dialog will appear in which you can name your new pattern "Scan Lines." You can now close this file without saving it.

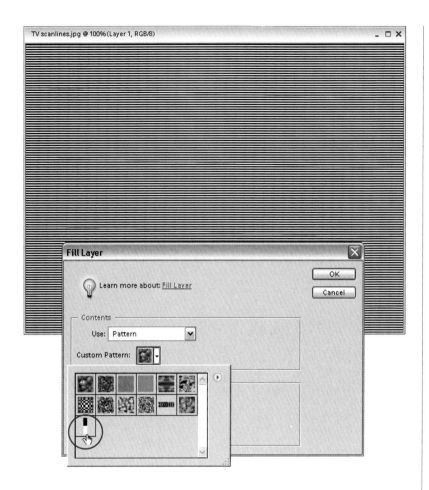

STEP THREE: Go back to your original document and click on the Create a New Layer icon at the top of the Layers palette. Go under the Edit menu and choose Fill Layer. In the Fill Layer dialog, choose Pattern in the Use pop-up menu, then click on the Custom Pattern thumbnail to reveal the Pattern Picker. Click on the last pattern (it will be the Scan Lines pattern you just saved) to choose it. Click OK to fill your new layer with your black-and-white scan lines pattern.

STEP FOUR: In the Layers palette, change the scan lines layer's blend mode from Normal to Overlay. Lower the Opacity so that the effect isn't too strong (in other words, adjust to suit your taste) to complete the effect.

Reflective Chrome Gradient

This technique, a takeoff on the chrome effect created by traditional airbrush artists, uses a gradient that mimics the reflection of the ground and the sky the same way they would be reflected by real chrome. In this example, we'll create a custom gradient to simulate that style of chrome, but the gradient alone isn't enough—it's the other elements you add to it that give the impression of chrome.

STEP ONE: Create a new document in RGB mode at 72 ppi (this example is 8x6"). Press D to choose black as your Foreground color, then press Alt-Backspace to fill the Background layer with black. Add a new blank layer by clicking on the Create a New Layer icon at the top of the Layers palette. Hide the black background by clicking on the Eye icon in the far-left column beside the Background layer.

STEP TWO: Create the shape you want for your metal console. In this example, I clicked on the Foreground color swatch and chose gray in the Color Picker. Then I pressed U until I had the Rounded Rectangle tool and created, well...a simple rounded rectangle. In the Options Bar, I clicked on the Simplify button to change this Shape layer into a regular image layer.

STEP THREE: Next, press G to switch to the Gradient tool, and in the Options Bar, click on the Edit button to bring up the Gradient Editor. When the Gradient Editor appears, click on the Black to White gradient (it's the third gradient in the top row). Using the Black to White gradient as a starting point, double-click on the far-left color stop located directly below the gradient ramp. This brings up the Color Picker. In the RGB fields, enter R: 164, G: 175, and B: 184 to set this first stop to a light "sky" blue. Click OK in the Picker. Next, slide the far-right color stop over to the center of the gradient ramp. Double-click on it to set its color. This time in the RGB fields, enter R: 226, G: 227, and B: 226 to set this middle stop to an almost white color. Click OK in the Picker.

STEP FOUR: Click immediately to the right of your middle color stop under the gradient ramp to add a new color stop. Slide this color stop almost right up against the middle color stop. Double-click on this new color stop, and in the RGB fields of the Color Picker, enter R: 78, G: 73, and B: 67 to set this new stop to a brownish-gray color. We're going to add two more stops: one halfway between the middle and the end (set to R: 224, G: 221, and B: 87 for a dull yellow) and then one at the very right end of the gradient ramp (set to R: 226, G: 225, and B: 198 for a very light, almost white stop). Your gradient should look like the one shown here. Name this gradient "metal sky," click the New button, and then click OK to save it.

Continued

STEP FIVE: Now we add the fluff stuff that helps sell the effect. Press-and-hold the Control key, and in the Layers palette, click on the layer with your rounded rectangle to put a selection around it. Then, go under the Select menu, under Modify, and choose Contract. Enter 6 pixels and click OK to shrink your selection. Hold the Shift key, click the Gradient tool at the top of your selection, and drag it to the bottom. Don't deselect yet.

STEP SIX: While your selection is still in place, add a new blank layer above your current layer by clicking on the Create a New Layer icon at the top of the Layers palette. Go under the Edit menu and choose Stroke (Outline) Selection. When the Stroke dialog appears, make sure the stroke color is set to black, and enter 2 pixels for the stroke Width. Set your Location to Center and click OK to apply a 2-pixel stroke around your selection. Don't deselect yet.

STEP SEVEN: Now press U until you have the Line tool (it's one of the Shape tools in the Toolbox). In the Options Bar, enter 1–2 pixels for Weight. We're going to visually divide our console using lines, so create the lines similar to the ones shown here (make sure to stay within the selected area). Press-and-hold the Shift key, then click-and-drag to create your lines (the Shift key keeps each line perfectly horizontal or vertical and also keeps all the lines on one Shape layer instead of creating a new layer for each line that you draw). Deselect by pressing Control-D.

STEP EIGHT: Make a duplicate of this line Shape layer by dragging it to the Create a New Layer icon at the top of the Layers palette. Press D and then X to set white as your Foreground color, then press Shift-Alt-Backspace to fill your lines with white (adding the Shift key fills just the object on the layer instead of filling the entire layer). Press V to switch to the Move tool, then press the Left Arrow key once and the Down Arrow key once to offset your white lines from your black lines, giving the impression of an indentation. Now, drag your stroked rectangle layer (Layer 1) to the top of the layer stack to ensure your lines appear inside the black stroke.

Continued

STEP NINE: Make your black Background layer visible again (click in the far-left empty box where the Eye icon used to be). Click on the gradient layer, and go to the Styles and Effects palette (under the Window menu), and with Layer Styles selected, choose Bevels from the top-right pop-up menu. Click on the Simple Inner bevel to add a bevel effect to your rounded rectangle.

STEP TEN: Now, just create any buttons to complete the effect. Simply press U until you get the Polygon tool, set its Sides to 3 in the Options Bar, and click-and-drag to add navigation buttons. To give the buttons the "sunken-in" look, choose the Simple Sharp Pillow Emboss from the Bevels section of the Styles and Effects palette.

Building a Video Wall

This technique creates a wall made out of TV monitors, with each monitor containing part of a much larger, single image. You start by creating a single screen, duplicating and stacking it, and pasting an image into a selection of each monitor.

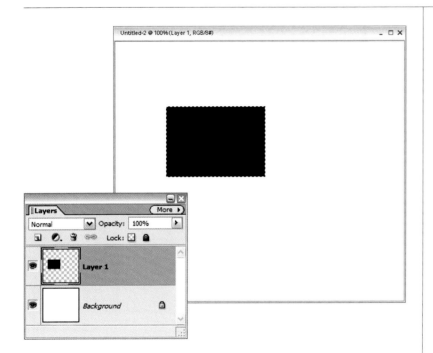

STEP ONE: Create a new document in RGB mode (the one here is 8x7"). Create a new blank layer by clicking on the Create a New Layer icon at the top of the Layers palette. Press M to get the Rectangular Marquee tool, and draw a horizontal rectangular selection. Press D to set your Foreground color to black, and then press Alt-Backspace to fill your selection with black.

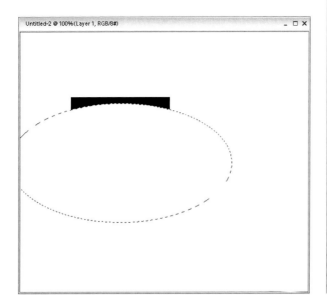

STEP TWO: Press M until you have the Elliptical Marquee tool. Drag out a large oval-shaped selection over the black rectangle. Move your cursor inside the oval, and click-and-drag to position the top edge of the oval near the top of the black rectangle. Press the Backspace key to knock out the bottom section of the black rectangle, then deselect by pressing Control-D. This leaves a narrow rectangle that curves inward on the bottom.

Continued

STEP THREE: Create another new layer by clicking on the Create a New Layer icon. Press M until you have the Rectangular Marquee tool again, and draw a rectangular selection that's wider and a bit higher than the black shape. Press-and-hold the Alt key (which lets you subtract from your selection) and draw a smaller selection that starts at the top-left corner of the thin black shape and extends down and to the right, forming a smaller rectangle. This will become the frame of your video monitor.Click the Foreground color swatch at the bottom of the Toolbox, and in the resulting Color Picker, choose a very dark gray. Fill your selection with gray by pressing Alt-Backspace, and then press Control-D to deselect.

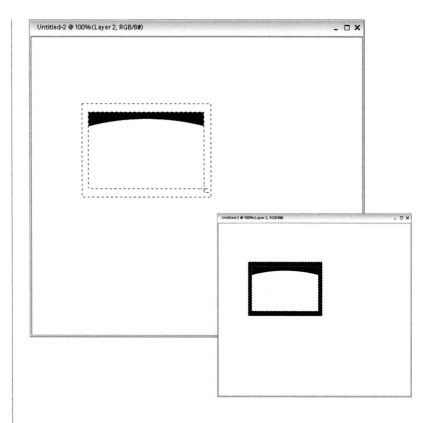

STEP FOUR: Go to the Styles and Effects palette (found under the Window menu), and with Layer Styles selected, choose Bevels from the palette's top-right pop-up menu. Click on the Simple Emboss icon. Now, go to the Layers palette, and with this frame layer active, press Control-E to merge it with the black rectangle layer, creating a white Background layer and your video monitor layer (Layer 1). Although it doesn't look like it at this stage, the first video monitor is complete; but it needs to be resized, so you'll use Free Transform to scale it down in the next step.

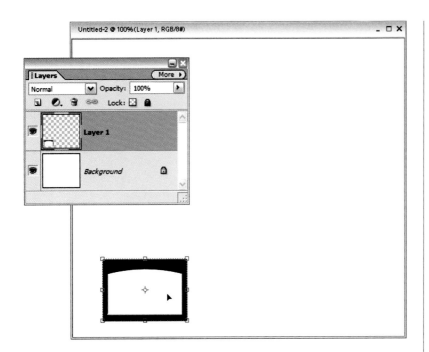

STEP FIVE: Press Control-T to bring up the Free Transform bounding box. Press-and-hold the Shift key, grab a corner point, and drag inward to shrink the size of the video monitor. Once you've scaled it down, move your cursor inside the bounding box and click-and-drag the video monitor down toward the bottom-left corner of the image area. Press Enter to lock in your transformation.

STEP SIX: Press V to switch to the Move tool, then press-and-hold Shift-Alt, click within your monitor, and drag to the right to create a copy of your monitor. Drag the duplicate until its left edge touches the right edge of the original monitor. Release the mouse button. While pressing the same keys, click in the new monitor and drag to the right to create a third image. Now, go to the Layers palette, and with the top monitor layer active, press Control-E two times to merge the three monitor layers into one monitor layer (Layer 1).

Continued

STEP SEVEN: Press-and-hold Shift-Alt again, then click on the monitors and drag upward to create a copy of your three monitors. Repeat this process until you have a stack of monitors four rows high, resembling a video wall. With the top monitor layer active, press Control-E three times to merge all the video monitor layers together into one layer (Layer 1).

STEP EIGHT: Press W to switch to the Magic Wand tool. Click once inside one of the monitor screens to select it. Hold the Shift key and click in every screen until the inside of each monitor is added to the selection. (We used the Magic Wand, but you can use any selection tool you're comfortable with.) When the inside of each screen is selected, open the image you want to add into your screens.

BRAND X PICTURES

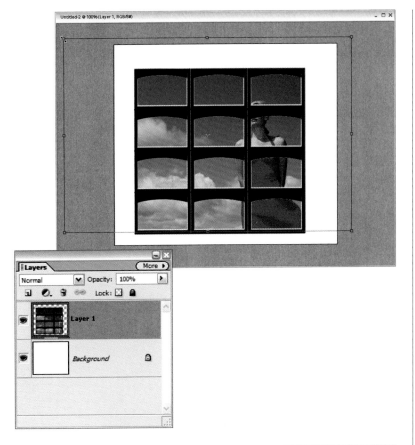

STEP NINE: With the image that you want to add to your video wall active, select the entire image by pressing Control-A, then press Control-C to copy it into memory. Switch back to your video wall image. In the Layers palette, with the video wall layer active, go under the Edit menu and choose Paste Into Selection to put this image into your video wall. Switch to the Move tool and click-and-drag to position your image inside the wall. Press Control-T to bring up Free Transform. (*Note:* If you can't see the bounding box corners, press Control-0 [zero] or just drag out your image window to change your view.) Press-and-hold the Shift key, grab a corner point, and drag to scale your image. When it looks good to you, press Enter, but don't deselect your image just yet.

STEP TEN: Using the Move tool, position your image within the video wall. Press Control-D to deselect, completing the effect. (*Note:* Make sure you have your pasted image where you want it, because once you deselect, your image is "stuck" inside the monitors and you won't be able to move it again.)

Lightning Effect

This is about the quickest, easiest, and most time-tested way to add a lightning effect to your photo without having to draw a bunch of shapes or jump through a lot of time-consuming hoops.

STEP ONE: Open the photo you want to use as your background (in this case, a photo of a creepy house at night). Press D and then X to set your Foreground color to white and your Background color to black. Create a new layer by clicking on the Create a New Layer icon at the top of the Layers palette.

STEP TWO: Press the G key to switch to the Gradient tool and then press Enter to bring up the Gradient Picker. Choose the Foreground to Background gradient (it's the first gradient in the Picker). Click the Gradient tool on the left side of your image area and drag all the way to the right.

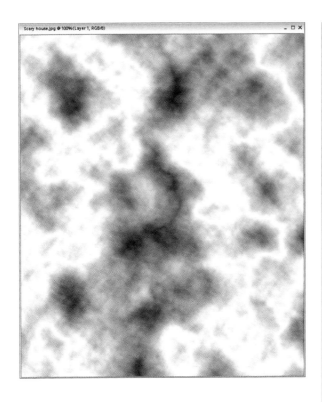

STEP THREE: Now go under the Filter menu, under Render, and choose Difference Clouds to apply a random cloud pattern over your gradient. (*Note:* Each time you apply this filter, you get a different look, so if you don't like the way your lightning appears, just press Control-F to reapply the Difference Clouds, or even try applying it three or four times until you come up with a lightning pattern that looks better.) When the lightning strikes look good to you, press Control-I to invert them.

STEP FOUR: Press Control-L to bring up the Levels dialog. Grab the top-center Input Levels slider (the midtones slider) and drag it to the right. When you're almost all the way to the right, you'll see your lightning appear in your image. Click OK.

Continued

STEP FIVE: To make your lightning blend in with your photo, go to the Layers palette and change the layer blend mode of your lightning layer from Normal to Screen.

STEP SIX: The lightning goes right over everything in the image, but if you don't want that, you can do this: Press E to switch to the Eraser tool, and in the Options Bar, click on the brush thumbnail to open the Brush Picker. Choose a medium, soft-edged brush, and with the lightning layer active in the Layers palette, erase any lightning areas you don't want to appear on your image, which completes the effect. (*Note:* In this example I pressed V to switch to the Move tool and click-and-dragged the lightning strikes to reposition them in my image.)

Gettin' "Gelly" with Buttons

We're in a "gel design age" thanks to the look of Apple's Aqua interface for Mac OS X and the resulting marketing pieces that sprang forth from it. When we first showed this technique in *Photoshop User* magazine, it took literally twice as many steps, but we've since found a way that makes it so easy, you can create your own aqua-like button in about 60 seconds.

STEP ONE: Create a new document that's in RGB mode set at 72 ppi (the one shown here is 7x5"). Click the Foreground color swatch at the bottom of the Toolbox and choose a light blue in the Color Picker, then press U until the Rounded Rectangle tool appears in the Toolbox. Up in the Options Bar, set the Radius to 40 pixels and drag out your shape, which will appear on its own Shape layer (Shape 1) in the Layers palette. Click the Simplify button in the Options Bar to rasterize the Shape layer into an image layer.

STEP TWO: Control-click on your pill layer (Shape 1) to select it. Click the Create a New Layer icon at the top of the Layers palette to create a blank layer. Then, go under the Select menu, under Modify, and choose Contract. Enter 20 pixels and click OK to contract your selection. (*Note:* How much you contract your selection depends on the size of your original pill shape. If your pill shape is really small, contracting 20 pixels may make the selection completely disappear. So play with the setting until you get a selection that looks like the one shown here.) Press the letter D and then X to set your Foreground color to white. Press Alt-Backspace to fill your contracted selection with white, and then press Control-D to deselect.

Continued

STEP THREE: Go under the Filter menu, under Blur, and choose Gaussian Blur. When the dialog appears, enter 10 pixels and click OK to apply a blur to your white layer. Press V to switch to the Move tool, and drag your blurry white layer down to where its bottom edge touches the bottom of the pill shape.

STEP FOUR: Now, Control-click your original pill layer (Shape 1). Create a new blank layer by clicking on the Create a New Layer icon at the top of the Layers palette. Click the Foreground color swatch and choose a darker blue in the Color Picker than the blue that you used for your original pill shape, then fill your selection with this darker blue by pressing Alt-Backspace. Deselect by pressing Control-D.

STEP FIVE: In the Layers palette, press-and-hold the Control key and click once on the white blurry layer to put a selection around it (don't change layers, just get the selection in place; the dark blue pill layer should still be active). Now, press the Backspace key to knock a soft hole out of the dark blue pill shape. Don't deselect yet.

STEP SIX: Press M to switch to the Rectangular Marquee tool, then place your cursor inside the selected area (that you just knocked out) and drag the selection upward a little bit (maybe one-quarter of the way up) and hit Backspace again. Repeat this one or two more times, until you're almost to the top of the pill (make sure you stop just short of the top). Deselect by pressing Control-D.

STEP SEVEN: Click on the white blurred layer (Layer 1) in the Layers palette. Press-and-hold the Control key and click once on the original pill layer (Shape 1) to put a selection around the pill (though the white blurry layer is still active). Press Shift-Control-I to inverse your selection, then press Backspace to remove any spillover onto the background from your white blur. Deselect by pressing Control-D.

STEP EIGHT: In the Layers palette, Control-click on your original pill layer (Shape 1) to select it. Click the Create a New Layer icon and drag this new layer (Layer 3) to the top of the layer stack in the Layers palette. Then, go under the Select menu, under Modify, and choose Contract. Enter 20 pixels (or the same number of pixels that you contracted in Step 2) and click OK to contract your selection. Press the letter D and then X to set your Foreground color to white. Now press G to switch to the Gradient tool and press Enter to make the Gradient Picker visible onscreen. Choose the second gradient from the left (Foreground to Transparent) and drag this gradient from the top of your selection to the bottom. Deselect by pressing Control-D.

Continued

STEP NINE: Press V to switch to the Move tool, and drag your white gradient layer upward to where it's almost at the top, but leave a gap of dark blue between your white gradient and the top of the pill. This creates the highlight area of the pill.

STEP TEN: Press Control-T to bring up Free Transform. Within the bounding box, right-click and choose Perspective in the contextual menu. Then, grab the bottom-left corner point, and click-and-drag to the left just a bit to add a perspective effect to your highlight layer. Press Enter to lock in your transformation.

STEP ELEVEN: Hide the Background layer by clicking on the Eye icon to the left of it in the Layers palette, then choose Merge Visible from the palette's flyout menu. This merges all of the layers that make up the pill into one layer.

STEP TWELVE: Click in the empty Eye icon box to the left of the Background layer in the Layers palette to make it visible again. Then, click on the merged pill layer to make it active. Go to the Styles and Effects palette (found under the Window menu), and with Layer Styles selected, choose Drop Shadows from the palette's top-right pop-up menu. Click on the High drop shadow icon. Press T to switch to the Type tool and add any text you'd like (the font here is Minion Pro). To complete the effect, return to the Styles and Effects palette, and with your Type layer active in the Layers palette, click on the Low drop shadow to enhance your type.

Yummy Metal Web Buttons

In this day and age, if you have to make a Web button, it better be pretty slick. Here's a technique for making a yummy-looking, metallic-like, reflecto-looking, plastic thingy that is…well, pretty slick.

STEP ONE: Create a new document in RGB mode at 72 ppi (the example here is 8x6"). Create a new blank layer by clicking on the Create a New Layer icon at the top of the Layers palette. Press M until you have the Elliptical Marquee tool, hold the Shift key, and draw a circular selection. Press D and then X to set your Foreground color to white.

STEP TWO: Press G to switch to the Gradient tool, and then press Enter to open the Gradient Picker onscreen. Choose the Foreground to Background gradient (it's the first one in the Picker). Then in the Options Bar, click on the Radial Gradient icon (it's the second icon in the set of five). Drag a white-to-black gradient from the left center of the selection to about 1/4" past the right edge. Don't deselect yet.

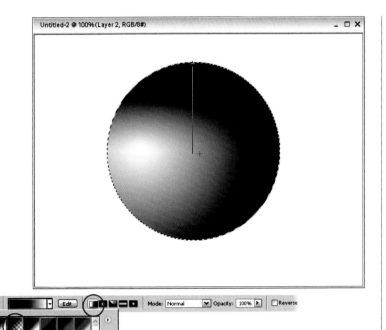

STEP THREE: Click on the Create a New Layer icon at the top of the Layers palette, and then press D to set your Foreground color to black. Press Enter to bring up the Gradient Picker again and choose the Foreground to Transparent gradient (the second one from the left). In the Options Bar, choose the Linear Gradient (the first icon in the set of five). Click the Gradient tool at the top of your selection and drag to the middle to fill the top with black.

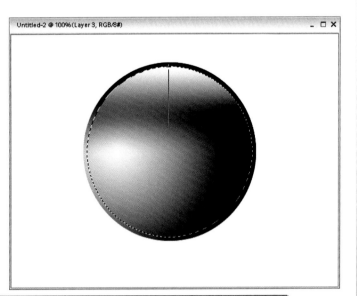

STEP FOUR: In the Layers palette, lower the Opacity of this gradient layer to around 75%. With your selection still in place, click on the Create a New Layer icon again. Go under the Select menu, under Modify, and choose Contract. Enter 6 pixels and click OK. Press X to set your Foreground color to white, then click at the top of your new selection with the Gradient tool and drag down through about one-third of your selected area. Press Control-D to deselect.

Continued

STEP FIVE: Go under the Filter menu, under Blur, and choose Gaussian Blur. Enter 3 pixels and click OK. Duplicate your top layer by dragging it to the Create a New Layer icon at the top of the Layers palette. Go under the Image menu, under Rotate, and choose Layer 180°. Press V to switch to the Move tool, press-and-hold the Shift key, and drag this layer straight down almost to the bottom edge of the circle (pressing the Shift key keeps the layer aligned vertically). In the Layers palette, lower the Opacity of this layer to 60%.

STEP SIX: Click back on Layer 3 (the layer below your current duplicate layer) to make it active and press Control-T to bring up Free Transform. Press-and-hold the Shift key, grab the bottom-right handle, and shrink this white gradient by around 15%. (*Note:* Check out the Width and Height fields in the Options Bar to gauge your percentage.) Press Enter to lock in your transformation.

STEP SEVEN: In the Layers palette, click on the Eye icon to the left of the Background layer to hide it, and from the palette's flyout menu choose Merge Visible to merge all of the layers that make up your button into one layer. Then, go to the Styles and Effects palette, and with Layer Styles selected, choose Drop Shadows from the top-right pop-up menu. Click on the High drop shadow icon. You're going to add color to your Web button, so press Control-U to bring up the Hue/Saturation dialog. Click the Colorize checkbox and move the Hue slider to choose a color for your button. When you've found a color you like, click OK.

STEP EIGHT: You've just created a Web button that you can use over and over again in any project. Here I clicked on the Background layer to make it active and then dragged my button layer to the Create a New Layer icon at the top of Layers palette to duplicate it. Then I used Hue/Saturation to recolor the duplicate button. Now check out those yummy buttons!

THIS SIDE
TOWARD SCREEN

CHAPTER 8
DOWN & DIRTY TRICKS

THIS SIDE
TOWARD SCREEN

CHAPTER 8
DOWN & DIRTY TRICKS

THIS SIDE
TOWARD SCREEN

CHAPTER 8
DOWN & DIRTY TRICKS

Before you try the techniques in this chapter, it's important to understand what glints, reflections, and shadows are.

Shadows of the Night
Glints, Reflections, and Shadows

Many of you may already have a full understanding, but before you go any further, I think it would be wise (for all parties involved) to test your understanding with a few simple questions. If you're able to answer these three simple queries without a single wrong answer, then this chapter is for you. However, if you miss one or more answers, you might want to skip ahead to the chapter on rainbows, puppies, and cuddly little teddy bears. Ready? Begin:

(1) Which of these is the name of a character in the *Star Trek Enterprise* series? (a) Lt. Shaq, (b) Ensign Puff Daddy, (c) First Officer Eminem, or (d) Subcommander T'Pol.

(2) On *Star Trek: The Next Generation*, which of these is NOT a real location within the ship? (a) The Holo Deck, (b) the Bridge, (c) Ten-Forward, or (d) Central Perk.

(3) Which *Star Trek TNG* character wound up on *Deep Space Nine* as well? (a) Commander Waffle, (b) First Officer Sausage, (c) Lt. Eggs'n'bacon, or (d) Lt. Worf.

The answers are (and these are so obvious that I hate to even write them): 1: b, 2: a, 3: b. (They're actually all *d* of course, but you have to admit, it made you stop for just a second, didn't it?)

Perspective Cast Shadow

This twist on the classic drop shadow effect adds realism in two ways: (1) It casts a shadow that's more like what an actual light source would cast; and (2) the shadow has a bit of a harder edge near the object but gets softer as it moves away.

STEP ONE: Open the image of an object that you want to give a perspective cast shadow to. Put a selection around the object (here I Shift-clicked the Magic Wand tool [W] on all the white background areas, went under the Select menu, and chose Inverse to select just the two men). With the object selected, go under the Layer menu, under New, and choose Layer via Cut (or press Shift-Control-J).

STEP TWO: You'll need to add some canvas area to make room for your cast shadow, so click on the Background layer to make it active. Then, go under the Image menu, under Resize, and choose Canvas Size. In the Canvas Size dialog, enter 4 inches for Width, ensure the Relative checkbox is on, click the right-center square in the Anchor grid, and choose White in the Canvas Extension Color pop-up menu. Click OK to add your white canvas area.

STEP THREE: Make a copy of the object layer by dragging it to the Create a New Layer icon at the top of the Layers palette. Press the letter D to change the Foreground color to black, then press Shift-Alt-Backspace to fill your duplicate object with black (holding Shift fills just the object on the layer and not the entire layer). Now, press Control-T to bring up the Free Transform command. Right-click within the bounding box and choose Distort from the contextual menu. You need to make the copy filled with black lie almost flat in the background, so grab the top-center control point and drag it down and to the left. Press Enter to complete your transformation.

STEP FOUR: Switch to the Gradient tool by pressing the letter G. In the Options Bar, click on the down-facing arrow next to the gradient thumbnail to bring up the Gradient Picker, and choose the Black to White gradient (it's the third one in the Picker). At the top of the Layers palette, click on the Lock Transparent Pixels icon for your shadow layer (it's the first icon after the word "Lock"). Drag the Gradient tool from one end of your shadow to the other. You want the gradient to start with black at the base of your object and change to white as the shadow extends away from the object.

Continued

STEP FIVE: Turn off the Lock Transparent Pixels icon on your shadow layer in the Layers palette. Go under the Filter menu, under Blur, and choose Gaussian Blur. When the dialog appears, enter 2 pixels for Radius, and click OK. (*Note:* For high-res, 300-ppi images, you'll need to use higher settings when applying Gaussian Blurs and feathering selections in this and the following steps.) In the Layers palette, drag Layer 1 copy below Layer 1. This puts the shadow behind your object.

STEP SIX: To add more realism, you can create a perspective blur, where the shadow is less blurry near the object and becomes blurrier the farther away it gets (like in real life). To do this, press M to switch to the Rectangular Marquee tool and draw a rectangular selection that covers the top quarter of your cast shadow. Go under the Select menu and choose Feather. Add a 5-pixel feather to soften the transition. Then, go under the Filter menu, under Blur, and choose Gaussian Blur. Add a 2-pixel blur, and then deselect by pressing Control-D.

STEP SEVEN: With the Rectangular Marquee tool, draw another selection that covers the top half of your cast shadow. Feather the selection by 5 pixels again, apply a 3-pixel Gaussian Blur, and then deselect (see previous step). Draw a new selection that covers the top three-quarters of your shadow (almost to the base of the object), apply another 5-pixel Feather (from the Select menu), and then press Control-F to apply a 3-pixel Gaussian Blur again.

STEP EIGHT: When you're finished, you'll have created a 10-pixel blur around the farthest areas of the cast shadow, an 8-pixel blur around the three-quarter mark, a 5-pixel blur one-quarter of the distance away from the base, and only a slight 2-pixel blur up close to the object. To finish the effect, lower the Opacity of the shadow layer in the Layers palette to around 45%.

Reverse Cast Shadow

This shadow effect is widely used in print and on the Web to give the impression that the light source is coming from behind the object, rather than from the front or the side, as Photoshop Elements shadows are usually applied. Most notably, I saw it on the logo for the movie *The Talented Mr. Ripley*.

STEP ONE: Create a new document (the one here is 8x6" in RGB mode). Click on the Foreground color swatch at the bottom of the Toolbox and select a color in the Color Picker that you want to use for the background of the image. Press Alt-Backspace to fill the Background layer with the color you chose.

STEP TWO: Press D and then X to set your Foreground color to white. Press T to switch to the Type tool, and enter your type. (*Note:* I used Minion Pro as the typeface, and then on the Background layer, I made a selection with the Rectangular Marquee tool [M] just below the type and filled the selection with a darker color, but it's not necessary for this technique.)

STEP THREE: After you've created your type, go under the Layer menu, under New, and choose Layer via Copy (or press Control-J) to duplicate your Type layer. Go to the Image menu, under Rotate, and choose Flip Layer Vertical. Press V to switch to the Move tool, and while pressing-and-holding the Shift key, drag the flipped layer downward until the bottom of the duplicate text nearly touches the bottom of the original type.

STEP FOUR: From the Layer menu, choose Simplify Layer to rasterize the duplicate Type layer into a regular image layer. Press Control-T to bring up the Free Transform function. Right-click directly inside the Free Transform bounding box and choose Perspective in the contextual menu. Grab either the bottom-left or the bottom-right corner handle of the bounding box and drag outward to create a perspective effect. (*Note:* If you can't see the bounding box, press Control-0 [zero] to resize the image onscreen.) Next, grab either the top-left or the top-right corner handle and drag inward to accentuate the effect, then press Enter to complete the transformation. (To return to the previous view, go under the Window menu, under Images, and choose Cascade.)

Continued

STEP FIVE: With the reflection layer active, press D to set your Foreground to black, and then press Shift-Alt-Backspace to fill the reflection with black (holding Shift fills just the object on the layer instead of the entire layer). Now, go under the Filter menu, under Blur, and choose Gaussian Blur. Add a slight, 1.5-pixel blur to soften the shadow. (*Note:* For high-res, 300-ppi images, you'll need to use higher settings when applying Gaussian Blurs and feathering selections in this and the following steps.)

STEP SIX: Press M to switch to the Rectangular Marquee tool, and drag a rectangular selection around the center of your shadow. Go under the Select menu, choose Feather, and set the Radius to 10 pixels. Click OK to soften the edges of your selected area. Then, return to the Filter menu, under Blur, and choose Gaussian Blur. Apply a 2-pixel blur. Deselect by pressing Control-D.

STEP SEVEN: Draw another rectangular selection at the bottom of your image window, and feather it by 10 pixels again. Press Control-F to apply the 2-pixel Gaussian Blur again. This makes your shadow appear blurrier as it moves away from the base of the type—just like a shadow would in real life.

STEP EIGHT: Deselect by pressing Control-D, then go to the Layers palette and lower the Opacity of this shadow layer to around 35% to complete the effect.

Glassy Reflections

This is a nice technique for enhancing a logo or Web button by adding small reflections in a couple of areas to make it appear as if the logo were made of glass. In this tutorial, we start with an elliptical logo, but you can apply a similar effect to a round logo.

STEP ONE: Open the logo (or graphic) to which you want to apply the glass-like highlight reflections. (You can practice with this logo by downloading it from the book's companion website at www.scottkelbybooks.com/ddelements3.) The logo needs to be on its own layer, so if it's not, select the logo with any selection tool (Lasso, Magic Wand, etc.) and go under the Layer menu, under New, and choose Layer via Cut (or press Shift-Control-J) to cut the logo from the Background layer and copy it onto its own layer.

STEP TWO: Press-and-hold the Control key, and in the Layers palette, click on the logo layer to put a selection around it. Go under the Select menu, under Modify, and choose Contract. Enter 12 and click OK. (The goal is to shrink the selection so that it's a couple of pixels inside the inner ellipse. You may have to experiment with the amount of contraction.)

STEP THREE: Press L until the Polygonal Lasso tool appears in the Toolbox. Up in the Options Bar, in the set of four icons, click on the third icon from the left so that when you're using the Polygonal Lasso, it will subtract from the current selection. Start by clicking in the white space just outside the bottom-left side of the logo, then click within the logo about a quarter of the way in from the left, and then click near the top-left side just outside the logo to create a V-shaped selection (that will be the area where the reflection will be added). Continue clicking with the Polygonal Lasso tool all the way around the outside of the logo until you reach the point where you started (remember, you're subtracting from your elliptical selection). When you move the Polygonal Lasso tool over the point where you started, a tiny circle will appear next to your cursor, and when you click on the starting point with your Polygonal Lasso, you'll be left with just the left corner area selected.

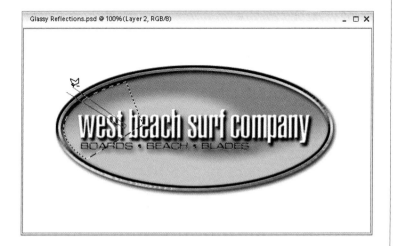

STEP FOUR: We need to knock out a thin triangular hole in the middle of our selection for a more-realistic look. Using the Polygonal Lasso tool, draw a straight line that begins just outside the top-left side of your ellipse and goes down at an angle to about three-quarters of the way inside your selection. Continue drawing until you've created a thin rectangle inside your original selection. When you click on the point were you started, that rectangle will be removed from the selection. Next, create a new blank layer by clicking on the Create a New Layer icon at the top of the Layers palette.

Continued

STEP FIVE: Press the letter D and then X to set your Foreground color to white. Press G to switch to the Gradient tool, and press Enter to bring up the Gradient Picker onscreen. Choose the second gradient from the left (Foreground to Transparent). Now, click the Gradient tool at the top-left side of your selection and drag down at an angle just past the right edge of your selection. Deselect by pressing Control-D to complete the left-side reflective highlight. If the reflection seems too intense, you can lower the Opacity of this layer in the Layers palette to around 75%—but that's totally up to you.

STEP SIX: Now on to the lower-right-side reflection: In the Layers palette, click on the Create a New Layer icon, and then press-and-hold the Control key and click on the logo layer to put a selection around it. Return to the Select menu, under Modify, and choose Contract. Enter a number of pixels to shrink the selection to the very edge of the inner ellipse (12 pixels in this example). Press M until you have the Elliptical Marquee tool, and in the set of four icons in the Options Bar, click on the third icon from the left so the tool will subtract from the current selection. Click near the top-left corner of the document and drag out an ellipse that overlaps the current selection so that just a small portion of the original ellipse remains on the lower-right side.

Glassy Reflections.psd @ 100%(Layer 2, RGB/8)

STEP SEVEN: Press G to switch to the Gradient tool (all your settings should still be in place from Step 5), and this time click just outside the bottom-right part of the logo and drag just past the left side of the selection inside the logo. Your selection will fill with the Foreground to Transparent gradient. Press Control-D to deselect.

STEP EIGHT: If needed, lower the Opacity of this reflection layer in the Layers palette to around 85% to complete the effect.

The Fastest Logo Job in Town

This is another popular method for creating a glassy reflection on a logo, but this time, we'll create the logo as well. This method is so quick, you can complete the effect in less than 60 seconds (if you stop at Step 4). If you decide to take it further, it could take you as long as a whopping 90 seconds to get through Step 6. Either way, it's a minute-and-a-half tops.

STEP ONE: Create a new document in RGB mode (the example here is 8x6"). Create a new blank layer by clicking on the Create a New Layer icon at the top of the Layers palette. Press M until you have the Elliptical Marquee tool, and draw an oval selection in the middle of your image area. Click on the Foreground color swatch in the Toolbox, choose a medium blue in the Color Picker, and then fill your oval with blue by pressing Alt-Backspace. Deselect by pressing Control-D.

STEP TWO: Press D and then X to set your Foreground color to white, then press the letter T to switch to the Type tool, and create your type (in the example shown here, I used the font Showcard Gothic). Go to the Layers palette and Control-click on the oval layer to put a selection around it. Then, go under the Select menu, under Modify, and choose Contract. When the Contract Selection dialog appears, enter 10 pixels and click OK. (*Note:* For high-res, 300-ppi images, contract by 40 pixels instead.)

STEP THREE: With white as your Foreground color, create a new blank layer by clicking the Create a New Layer icon at the top of the Layers palette. Press the letter G to switch to the Gradient tool, and press Enter to bring up the Gradient Picker onscreen. Choose the Foreground to Transparent gradient (it's the second gradient in the Picker), ensure that the Linear Gradient icon is selected in the Options Bar, and then drag your gradient from the top of your selection down about halfway through the logo.

STEP FOUR: Deselect by pressing Control-D. In the Layers palette, lower the Opacity of this layer to around 70%. You could stop at this point and consider the effect complete (and many times I've seen this technique executed only this far), but if you want to add a little more detail (by adding a shadow), go on to the next steps.

Continued

STEP FIVE: In the Layers palette, click the Create a New Layer icon and then Control-click on the oval layer to put a selection around it. Press B to get the Brush tool, click on the brush thumbnail in the Options Bar, and choose a 65-pixel (or larger) soft-edged brush from the Brush Picker. Press D to set your Foreground color to black, then paint a stroke starting at the right side of the oval. Trace along the bottom of your selection, painting down and to the left as you go. Deselect by pressing Control-D.

STEP SIX: After your stroke is drawn, go to the Layers palette and lower the Opacity of this layer to around 50% to complete the effect. (*Note:* This is one of those rare times where I wouldn't add a default drop shadow, because what you just painted acts as a shadow on its own.)

Oscar Starbrights

I call these "Oscar Starbrights" because you see these lens effects used on distant shots of the stage at the Oscar Awards ceremony and a host of other indoor stage events, from boxing matches to rock concerts. The effect is similar to the "star effects" filter used with still cameras.

STEP ONE: Open the image in which you want to apply starbrights. Press the letter D and then X to set your Foreground color to white.

STEP TWO: Now we'll create the brush. Press Control-N to make a new file. Make the Width and Height 60 pixels. The Background Contents should be White. In the Options Bar, click on the Brush preview and from the Brushes pop-up menu, choose Calligraphic Brushes. Select the Flat 28-pixel brush and in the Options Bar, set the size to 5 pixels. Now we'll make an "X" shape: click once in the upper-left corner of the blank document, then press the Shift key and click once in the lower-right corner; do the same with the other corners of the document. With your "X" shape created, choose Define Brush from the Edit menu. Name the brush Star and click OK.

Continued

STEP THREE: Create a new blank layer (Layer 1) by clicking on the Create a New Layer icon at the top of the Layers palette. Press X to make your Foreground color white. Now, click your brush on the first spot where you want a starbright to appear (don't paint, just click one time). Click the Create a New Layer icon again (to create Layer 2). In the Options Bar, change the Size to 30 pixels and then click on the brush icon to the right of the words "More Options." In the palette that appears, change the Angle to 45°. Click once on the center of your original starbright. Now, go up to the Options Bar and click Brushes. Select Default Brushes from the pop-up menu, and choose the round 27-pixel, soft-edged brush from the Brush Picker. Click the Brush tool once again in the center of your original starbright.

STEP FOUR: Create another blank layer (Layer 3). In the Layers palette, Control-click on the original starbright layer (Layer 1) to put a selection around your starbright. Press G to switch to the Gradient tool, and then go to the Options Bar and click on the down-facing arrow next to the gradient thumbnail to bring up the Gradient Picker. Choose the Spectrum gradient (it's the first one in the third row), click on the Radial Gradient icon in the Options Bar, and then drag the Gradient tool from the center of your starbright to the right, just past the edge of the starbright.

STEP FIVE: Deselect by pressing Control-D. In the Layers palette, change the layer blend mode from Normal to Lighten. Then, click on the Eye icon to the left of the Background layer to hide that layer, and choose Merge Visible from the palette's flyout menu. This merges all of the layers that make up the starbright into a single layer.

STEP SIX: Click on the far-left empty box next to the Background layer to make it visible again. Now you can go under the Layer menu, under New, and choose Layer via Copy (or just press Control-J) a few times to create duplicates of your starbright layer. Press V to switch to the Move tool and click-and-drag the starbrights to other locations in your image, completing the effect.

Adding a Lens Flare

This is a nice way to add some visual interest to an image. The sad part about this technique is that photographers go out of their way to avoid lens flare, and here we're about to show you how to add it. It just ain't flare. ;-)

STEP ONE: Open the photo you want to apply a lens flare effect to, making sure it's set to RGB mode by going to the Image menu, under Mode, and choosing RGB Color. In this example, we're going to apply it to a photo of the sun shining through some trees, but this technique also works well with night images or images that are dark (the photo has to be dark enough for the lens flare effect to be seen). Go to the top of the Layers palette and click on the Create a New Layer icon.

STEP TWO: Press D to set your Foreground color to black, then fill this new layer with black by pressing Alt-Backspace. Under the Filter menu, under Render, choose Lens Flare. When the dialog appears, increase the Brightness to 150% and choose 50-300mm Zoom for Lens Type. We're going to want the lens flare to appear as if it's peeking through the trees, and we'll position it using the Move tool in the next step, but we don't want to have to move the lens flare too much once we've applied it. So while you're still in the Lens Flare dialog, click on the little crosshair in the preview area and drag the center of the lens flare to approximately where you want it located in the final image. When it looks good to you, click OK.

STEP THREE: The black lens flare layer completely covers the photo on the Background layer. So you'll need to go to the Layers palette and change the layer blend mode from Normal to Screen. When you change the layer blend mode, the lens flare will then blend in with your image. Press the letter V to switch to the Move tool, and reposition the center of the flare until it's peeking through the tree branches.

STEP FOUR: That's it—you've completed your lens flare effect. If the flare seems too bright, just lower the lens flare layer's Opacity in the Layers palette.

Instant Star Field

This is one of those "create-something-from-nothing" techniques, because within just a few seconds, you go from a blank document to a star field. This makes a great background for collage projects, or you can add it to existing images. Warning: While replicating this technique, you may feel an uncontrollable urge to say things like, "Make it so!" and "To the Transporter room." This will pass.

STEP ONE: Create a new document (the example here is 8x6") in RGB mode at 72 ppi. Press D to set black as your Foreground color, then press Alt-Backspace to fill your background with black. Next, go under the Filter menu, under Noise, and choose Add Noise. Enter approximately 40% for Amount, choose Gaussian for Distribution, check Monochromatic, and click OK.

STEP TWO: Return to the Filter menu again, choose Blur, and select Gaussian Blur. For Radius enter 0.5 (half a pixel) and click OK to apply just a slight blur to your noise. To bring out the star field in your noise, go under the Filter menu again, under Adjustments, and choose Threshold. When the Threshold dialog appears, drag the slider to the left until the "stars come out," then click OK. Press Control-F to apply another 0.5-pixel Gaussian Blur to soften the stars.

STEP THREE: To enhance the "out-in-space" look, I generally add a Lens Flare effect to the star field. Add a new layer by clicking on the Create a New Layer icon at the top of the Layers palette, and fill this new layer with black by pressing Alt-Backspace. Next, go under the Filter menu, under Render, and choose Lens Flare. Use any Brightness setting or Lens Type you like (I used the defaults settings), and click OK.

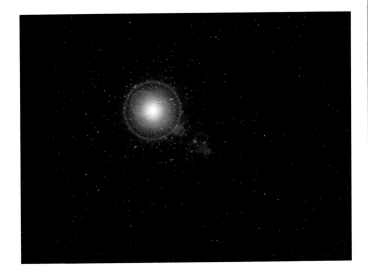

STEP FOUR: To bring the Lens Flare into your star field, just change the blend mode of this layer in the Layers palette from Normal to Screen, which completes the effect.

9

This is the chapter where it all comes together. This is where we dissect some of the most popular product

Show Me the Money
3D and Packaging Effects

and 3D Photoshop Elements effects and expose them for the cheap, tawdry tricks that they are. It's no secret that some big companies spend vast sums of money to find out what motivates people to spend their hard-earned money on a particular product. For example, recent studies have shown that if you use a blue color on the cover of your product, and use a combination of black, blue, and gold on the inside of your product, people will find the product absolutely irresistible, regardless of the content. Further studies have shown that if you're able to work some suggestive words into the name of your product (for example, the word "Dirty"), then overall sales will increase by nearly 32%. If, on top of that, you can somehow apply a grunge effect to the aforementioned word, you'll have a product so compelling that even Hindu priests will abandon their mountaintop spiritual sanctuaries just to buy whatever it is you're selling. This is powerful information. Use it wisely.

3D Magazine Effect

This technique first caught my attention when I saw it in various UK computer magazines (like *Computer Arts*) in their subscription ads, and then it started catching on in the States. It's ideal for giving some depth to a cover design, a page from a newsletter, a magazine, etc.

STEP ONE: Create a new blank document that's slightly larger than the page you're giving depth to (the blank document here is set at 72-ppi in RGB mode, but all you have to make sure of is that your new document is the same resolution as the object to which you want to apply the effect). Then, open your object (in this case, a cover of a newsletter), press V to switch to the Move tool, and click-and-drag the object into your blank document.

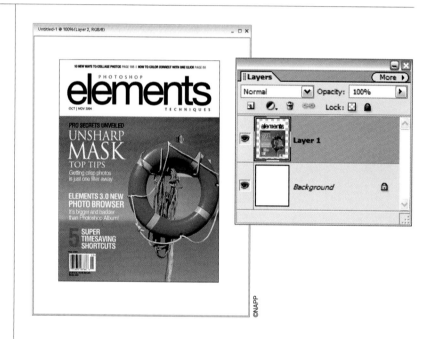

STEP TWO: Press M to switch to the Rectangular Marquee tool, and draw a rectangular selection around the bottom quarter of your cover. Next, create a new blank layer by clicking on the Create a New Layer icon at the top of the Layers palette. Then, go under the File menu, under New, and choose Blank File. When the New dialog appears, enter 1 pixel for Width, 2 pixels for Height, and choose the same resolution and color mode as your original cover document. Click OK to create a very tiny, new document.

STEP THREE: Press Control-+ (Plus Sign) nine times to zoom in on your document. With the Rectangular Marquee tool, select the top half of your document. Press the D key to set your Foreground color to black, then press Alt-Backspace to fill your selection with black. Press Control-D to deselect. Next, go under the Edit menu and choose Define Pattern. Name your pattern and click OK. Close this document without saving it.

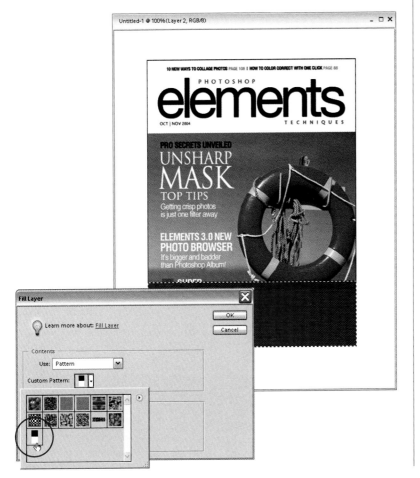

STEP FOUR: Switch back to your original document. Your selection should still be in place, so go under the Edit menu and choose Fill Selection. In the Fill Layer dialog, choose Pattern from the Use pop-up menu. Click on the Custom Pattern thumbnail to bring up the Pattern Picker. Choose the very last pattern in the Picker (it's the one you just created, which is very similar to the TV scan lines effect in Chapter 7, except that we created a smaller scan line). Click OK to fill your selection with horizontal black-and-white lines. Deselect by pressing Control-D.

Continued

STEP FIVE: Press Control-T to bring up the Free Transform bounding box around your black-and-white lines. Drag the top center point downward to shrink your lines. This will act as the book's pages. Next, press-and-hold the Control key, click on the bottom left-hand corner point, and drag upward to pinch the left side of the pages. Press Enter to lock in your changes.

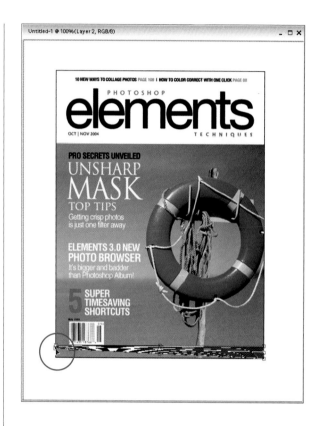

STEP SIX: Press V to switch to the Move tool, and drag the "book pages" down until the top of the pages touches the bottom of your cover. In the Layers palette, drag this layer beneath your cover layer, then click on the cover layer to make it active. Press Control-E to merge the cover with the pages layer directly beneath it.

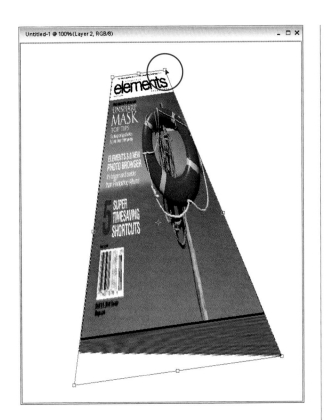

STEP SEVEN: With the cover layer active in the Layers palette, press Command-T to bring up Free Transform. Move your cursor outside the bounding box and click-and-drag up and to the left to rotate the cover a little. Next, press-and-hold Shift-Alt-Control, grab the top-right corner point and drag inward quite a bit to add a perspective effect. The cover will look pixelated and distorted, but don't sweat it; that will go away once you leave Free Transform. Now, grab the top center point, and drag quite a bit downward to remove the "stretched looked" from the book cover. This works well because it maintains the perspective effect, without all the distorted stretching. Press Enter to lock in your transformation.

STEP EIGHT: Go to the Styles and Effects palette, and with Layer Styles selected, choose Drop Shadows in the palette's top-right pop-up menu. Click on the High drop shadow icon to apply a drop shadow to your cover. Then, in the Layers palette, double-click the Layer Styles icon to the right of the cover layer. In the resulting dialog, lower the Shadow Distance to around 5–10 pixels and click OK to complete the effect.

3D Hardcover Book Effect

This technique for creating the pages and spine of a hardcover book makes great use of what is perhaps the lamest filter in all of Photoshop Elements—3D Transform. Any technique that manages to use this filter has got to be worth something.

STEP ONE: Create a new document in RGB mode at 72 ppi (I created an 8x6" document). Create a new layer by clicking on the Create a New Layer icon at the top of the Layers palette. Then, go under the Filter menu, under Render, and choose 3D Transform. Select the Cube tool from the Toolbox on the left-hand side of the dialog and drag out a cube in the dialog preview window.

STEP TWO: Press A to switch to the Direct Selection tool (the hollow arrow), click on the back, bottom-right corner of the cube, and drag slightly down and to the left to shrink the depth of your cube, making it look more like a cereal box. Now, click on the front, top-right corner point and drag to the right to tip the box back a bit (don't worry—it'll tip—it's in 3D).

STEP THREE: In the 3D Transform dialog, click on the Options button. In the resulting dialog, ensure the Display Background checkbox is turned off and click OK. While still in the 3D Transform dialog, press R to switch to the Trackball tool (it's right above the Zoom tool in the dialog's Toolbox), click on the left side of the preview window, and drag to the right. Keep dragging until your shape rotates all the way around to reveal the back side (which appears as a solid color). When it looks like the one shown here, click OK and the shape will appear in the document you created in Step 1.

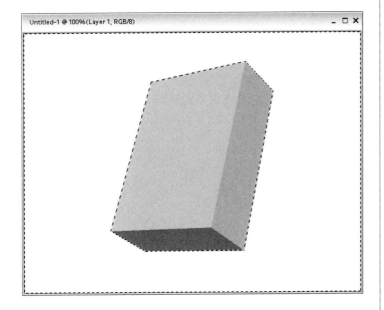

STEP FOUR: In many cases, the edges of your cube will have some fringe or look somewhat jaggy, but that's easy to fix. Press-and-hold the Control key, go to the Layers palette, and click on the cube layer to put a selection around your cube. Then, go under the Select menu, under Modify, and choose Contract. Enter 1 pixel and click OK to shrink your selection slightly. Go under the Select menu and choose Inverse (so now the only thing that's selected on this layer is that 1 pixel, all the way around your cube shape). Press Backspace to remove this 1-pixel edge fringe. Now, you can deselect by pressing Control-D.

Continued

STEP FIVE: Open the image that you've already created for your hardcover book. (The example here is a fictitious book cover, which you can download from this book's companion website, www.scottkelbybooks.com/ddelements3.) Press V to switch to the Move tool, click on this book cover, and drag it into your cube document. In the Layers palette, ensure that this layer appears directly above the cube layer in the layer stack.

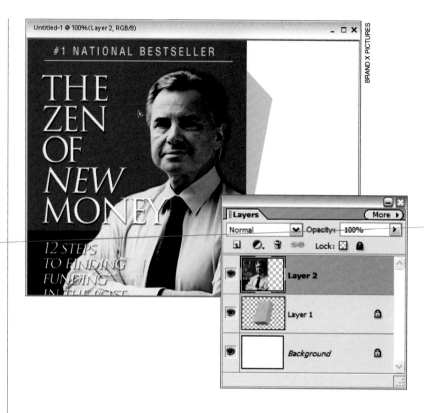

STEP SIX: In the Layers palette, lower the Opacity of the cover layer to 50% so you can see the cube through the cover. Press Control-T to bring up Free Transform. If you can't see the Free Transform handles, press Control-0 (zero) to zoom your image out. Then, press-and-hold the Shift key and drag one of the corner points to scale the photo down until it's just a little larger than the cube. Don't press Enter yet.

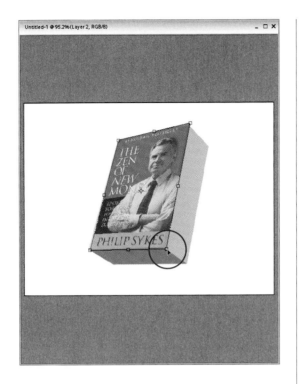

STEP SEVEN: While Free Transform is still active, press-and-hold the Control key, grab the top-left corner point of the cover, and drag it over until it aligns with the top-left corner of the cube. Keep pressing the Control key, grab the bottom-left corner of the cover, and do the same thing—stretch that corner to match the bottom-left corner of the cube. When you're close, drag it down just a tiny bit past the bottom front of the cube, because you want this fake cover to hang below the top part of the pages just a bit. Now do the same to the right side: Grab the top-right corner, align it to the top-right corner of the front face of the cube, and let it extend a little over the edge as well; do the same thing for the bottom-right corner—let a little hang over the edge (like a cover would on a real book). When it looks right, press Enter to lock in your transformation.

STEP EIGHT: Double-click on the Zoom tool in the Toolbox to return your view to 100%, then go to the Layers palette and raise the Opacity of your cover layer back up to 100%. Now you're going to need a tiny drop shadow between your cover and the pages (your cube), so go to the Styles and Effects palette, and with Layer Styles selected, choose Drop Shadows from the palette's top-right pop-up menu. Click on the Low drop shadow icon, and in the Layers palette, double-click on the Layer Styles icon (it looks like an "*f*") to the right of the layer. In the Style Settings dialog, lower the Shadow Distance to 2 pixels and click OK.

Continued

STEP NINE: In the Layers palette, click on your pages layer (the cube layer), go under the Layer menu, under New, and choose Layer via Copy (or press Control-J) to duplicate it. Press the letter I to get the Eyedropper tool, and click on a color within your book cover to sample it for the Foreground color (this will become the color of your spine and back cover, which will be slightly visible behind the pages). Then, press Shift-Alt-Backspace to fill your duplicate cube with your chosen color.

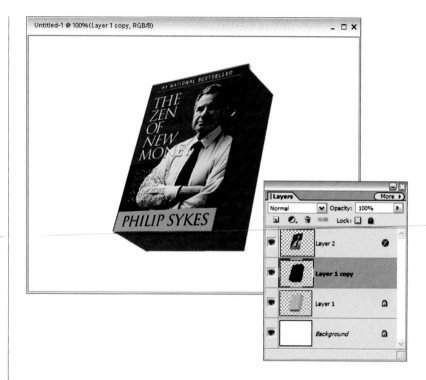

STEP TEN: Go to the Layers palette and drag this layer beneath the original cube layer. Get the Move tool, then press the Down Arrow key on your keyboard two or three times and the Right Arrow key two or three times to reveal the colorized cube, which forms the spine and back cover. To complete the effect, go to the Styles and Effects palette, and with the Drop Shadows section still selected, click on the Soft Edge icon.

Creating 3D Packaging

You can use Photoshop Elements' built-in tools to turn a flat image into an object that has depth (such as product packaging, a video box, etc.). In this tutorial, we'll add perspective to an image using Photoshop Elements' transformation tool, but we'll also add shading and highlights to help "sell" the effect that the image has depth.

STEP ONE: Open the image that you want to use as the cover of your product box. Press Control-A to select the entire image, then go under the Layer menu, under New, and choose Layer via Cut (or press Shift-Control-J) to cut your cover shot from the Background layer and copy it onto its own layer. In the Layers palette, double-click directly on this layer's name to highlight it, and rename it "Front."

STEP TWO: Go under the Image menu, under Resize, and choose Canvas Size. Ensure the Relative checkbox is turned on, and enter 4 inches in both the Width and Height fields. In the Canvas Extension Color pop-up menu choose White, and then click OK. This gives some needed work area around the image. Press the letter V to switch to the Move tool, and click-and-drag your image to the right side of the document window.

Continued

STEP THREE: To build the spine, create a new layer by clicking on the Create a New Layer icon at the top of the Layers palette. Double-click on this layer's name and rename it "Spine." Press M to switch to the Rectangular Marquee tool and draw a vertical rectangular selection to the left of your box front that's the same height as the box front. Click on the Foreground color swatch at the bottom of the Toolbox, and in the resulting Color Picker, choose a color that will complement the colors in your box front. (*Note:* While the Color Picker is open, move your cursor outside the dialog, and when your cursor turns into the Eyedropper tool, click within your image to sample a color.) Fill this selection with your chosen color by pressing Alt-Backspace, and then press Control-D to deselect. Press D to set your Foreground color to black, and with the Rectangular Marquee tool, select the top part of the spine. Press Alt-Backspace to fill the selection with black, and then press Control-D to deselect.

STEP FOUR: Click on the Front layer in the Layers palette to make it active. With the Rectangular Marquee tool, draw a long narrow rectangle across the top of the Front layer that's roughly the same height as the one you drew at the top of the spine in Step 3. Press Alt-Backspace to fill this rectangle with black, and then press Control-D to deselect.

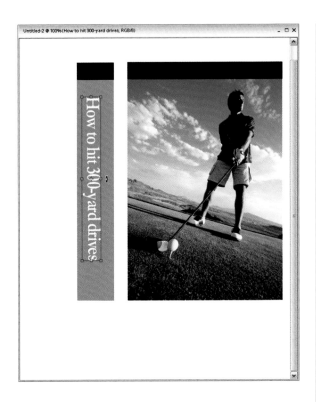

STEP FIVE: I recommend adding some text to the spine to help sell the 3D effect, so press D and then X to set your Foreground color to white, and then press T to switch to the Type tool. Enter your white type (I used the typeface Adobe Garamond Pro). Once you've entered your type, press Control-T to bring up Free Transform. Click outside the bounding box and drag to rotate the type 90° to the right to make it vertical, then click within the bounding box to position your type in the center of the spine. To enlarge your text, grab a corner point and drag outward slightly. When it looks good to you, press Enter.

STEP SIX: You need to merge your Type layer with the Spine layer beneath it, so with the Type layer active in the Layers palette, press Control-E to merge the layers together. Now, click on the merged Spine layer and press Control-T to bring up Free Transform again. Press-and-hold Shift-Alt-Control, then click-and-drag the top-right corner point of the bounding box straight upward about ½" higher than the top of the box front (you'll see the spine stretch both up and down on the right side as you do this). Release the keys, grab the middle-left handle, and drag inward about the same amount as you dragged the top-right corner point to remove the distortion caused by the stretching. Press Enter when it looks good to you.

Continued

STEP SEVEN: Switch to the Type tool again and enter any text that you want on your cover. The title is set in the font Garamond and the golfer's name is in the font Adobe Garamond Pro, while the production company and tagline are set in Myriad Pro. For the title, I went to the Styles and Effects palette (found under the Window menu), and with Layer Styles selected, I chose Drop Shadows from the top-right pop-up menu, and then clicked on the Soft Edge icon. Add any logos (such as the DVD logo I used here) as well. When you've added all the items you want on your cover, go to the Layers palette, click the eye icon next to the Background layer and the Spine layer to hide them. Then, in the Layers palette's flyout menu, choose Merge Visible (Shift-Control-E).

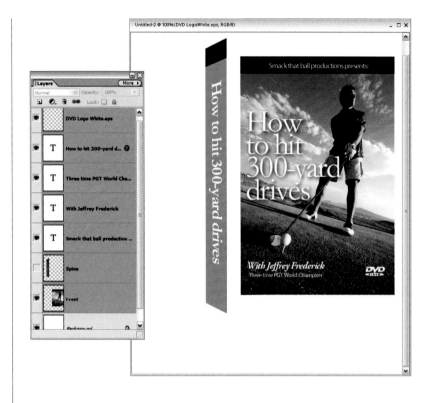

STEP EIGHT: Make sure you still have the Front layer active and press Control-T to bring up Free Transform. Press-and-hold Shift-Control and grab the upper-left corner point and drag straight upward until it matches the height of the spine. Then, grab the lower-left corner point and drag straight downward until it lines up with the bottom of the spine. Release the keys and drag the middle-right handle inward about 1". Press Enter to lock in your transformation.

STEP NINE: Click on the Spine layer in the Layers palette to make it active. Press V to switch to the Move tool, and drag the spine to the right until it touches the left edge of the box. (*Note:* If a corner doesn't align, press Control-T, press-and-hold Shift-Control, grab a corner point, and align it to the front corner. Press Enter when you're done.) Press Control-L to bring up Levels. Move the highlight Output Levels slider to the left a bit to darken the spine, and then click OK.

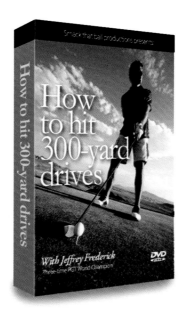

STEP TEN: Next, click on the Front layer in the Layers palette, then press B to switch to the Brush tool. In the Options Bar, lower the Opacity of the Brush tool to 20%, click on the Airbrush icon (it's to the right of the Opacity field), and then click on the brush thumbnail. In the resulting Brush Picker, choose a very small, hard-edged brush. Press D and then X to set your Foreground color to white. Press-and-hold the Shift key and click at the top corner where the spine and cover meet, and drag down between the box front and the spine to add a highlight along the edge. Now, click on the Background layer in the Layers palette, and press D to set your Foreground color to black. In the Options Bar, lower the Opacity of the Brush tool to around 40%, then click on the brush thumbnail, and in the resulting Brush Picker, choose a very large, soft-edged brush. Paint a soft drop shadow below the box with one smooth stroke. That's it!

Creating a DVD Effect

This is a simple version of how to create a DVD. I've seen different gradients used for this effect, but the rainbow one I'm showing here seems to be the most popular. I've seen this technique used mostly on products in which the disc appears as if it's protruding from some DVD packaging, because everybody wants to make it clear that the package contains a DVD, not a VHS tape.

STEP ONE: Create a new document in RGB mode (the one here is 8x8"). Then, create a new blank layer by clicking on the Create a New Layer icon at the top of the Layers palette. Press M until you get the Elliptical Marquee tool, press-and-hold the Shift key, and drag out a circular selection for your disc.

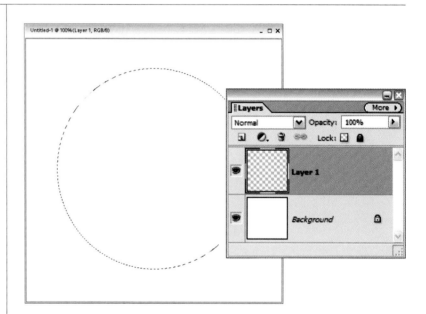

STEP TWO: Press G to switch to the Gradient tool, then up in the Options Bar click on the Edit button to bring up the Gradient Editor. In the Gradient Editor, you'll create a gradient that goes from a medium gray to white to medium gray. Start by clicking on the Orange to Yellow to Orange gradient (it's the last one in the top row of Presets), and under the gradient ramp, double-click on the far-left color stop. Choose a medium gray in the Color Picker. Then, double-click the center color stop and choose white in the Color Picker. Finally, double-click the right color stop and choose a medium gray in the Color Picker. Name this gradient "gray," click the New button, and then click OK.

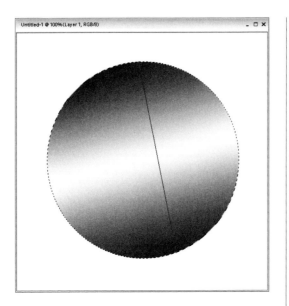

STEP THREE: Click the Gradient tool at the top of the selection and drag downward, at a slight angle to the right, through the circular selection. Don't deselect yet. Click on the Create a New Layer icon in the Layers palette, then go under the Select menu, under Modify, and choose Contract. When the Contract dialog appears, enter 4 pixels and click OK to shrink your selection.

STEP FOUR: You'll build a different gradient for this layer, so get the Gradient tool again, click on the Edit button in the Options Bar to bring up the Gradient Editor, and edit the existing gradient. Double-click the far-left color stop and choose white in the Color Picker. Then, double-click the center color stop, choose a dark gray in the Picker, and drag this color stop closer to the far-left white color stop. Finally, double-click the far-right color stop and choose white in the Picker. Name this gradient "gray white," click the New button, and then click OK.

Continued

STEP FIVE: Click the Gradient tool at the top of the selection and drag downward at a slight angle to the right. The gradient only affects the area within the selected area, and because you contracted the selection by 4 pixels, you can still see part of the original gradient around the edge of the circle just outside of the current selection.

STEP SIX: Choose Stroke (Outline) Selection from the Edit menu. When the Stroke dialog appears, change the Width to 1 pixel, set the Location to Outside, click on the Color swatch and choose black in the Color Picker, lower the Opacity to 50%, and then click OK to put a thin black stroke around your inner circle gradient. Press Control-D to deselect. In the Layers palette, click on the original circle layer (Layer 1), go under the Edit menu, choose Stroke (Outline) Selection again, and just click OK (the settings should be the same as before) to apply the same stroke to the original, larger gradient circle layer.

STEP SEVEN: In the Layers palette, Control-click the smaller circle layer to put a selection around it, then click the Create a New Layer icon. Drag this new blank layer to the top of the layer stack, making it the topmost layer. Get the Gradient tool again and press Enter to bring up the Gradient Picker onscreen. Choose the Transparent Rainbow gradient (it's the second gradient in the bottom row).

STEP EIGHT: Click-and-drag this rainbow gradient through the center of your selection, but don't drag from the top of the selection to the bottom—start just above the middle and drag downward to just below the middle, at a slight angle to the right. Don't deselect yet.

Continued

STEP NINE: With the rainbow gradient layer active in the Layers palette, go under the Filter menu, under Distort, and choose Pinch. Enter 100% for Amount and click OK. Now, go under the Filter menu again, under Blur, and choose Radial Blur. Enter 40 for Amount, choose Spin for Blur Method, Good for Quality, and click OK. Press Control-D to deselect.

STEP TEN: Press-and-hold the Shift key, then with the Elliptical Marquee tool, draw a smaller circular selection in the center of the disc. (*Note:* Press-and-hold the Spacebar as you drag out your selection to reposition it if needed. When you have it where you want it, just release the Spacebar and continue dragging out the selection.) With your selection in place, go under the Select menu and choose Feather. In the Feather Selection dialog, enter 20 pixels for the Radius and click OK to soften the center selection. Press Backspace to knock a soft hole out of the rainbow effect, then press Control-D to deselect.

BRAND X PICTURES

STEP ELEVEN: In the Layers palette, ensure that the top rainbow layer is active and press Control-E two times to merge the three gradient layers into one disc layer. Using the Elliptical Marquee tool, press-and-hold the Shift key, and create another small circular selection in the center of your DVD (this circular selection should be smaller than the one you created in the previous step). Press Backspace to knock out a hole on this disc layer, and then press Control-D to deselect, which completes the DVD effect. But if you want to see your DVD in action, see the option below.

OPTION: You can make your DVD appear to be popping out of a package if you like. Just open your DVD package (this is the one we created earlier in this chapter), and make sure the package is on its own layer (you can click the Magic Wand tool [W] on the white background, go under the Select menu and choose Inverse, then press Shift-Control-J to cut the package from the Background layer and copy it onto its own layer). Switch to your DVD document, press V to switch to the Move tool, and drag-and-drop your disc onto the package document. Drag the disc layer below the package layer in the Layers palette, then press Control-T to bring up Free Transform. Right-click in the bounding box and choose Perspective in the contextual menu. Then grab the bottom-left corner point and drag downward to give the disc the same perspective as the package. Press Enter and you're done!

3D Photo Cubes

I've seen people create these photo cubes before, but it's always been such a long and laborious process that I usually ended up going in a different direction. However, using the 3D Transform filter, it suddenly becomes really simple. Don't let the number of steps fool you—this is a very easy project.

STEP ONE: Create a new document in RGB mode (the one here is 8x8"). Start by creating a new blank layer by clicking on the Create a New Layer icon at the top of the Layers palette. We'll use this layer to create a 3D cube that we'll use as our guide.

STEP TWO: Go under the Filter menu, under Render, and choose 3D Transform. When the 3D Transform dialog appears, click on the Cube tool in the Toolbox on the left and drag out a cube shape in the preview window. Click on the Options button, and in the resulting dialog, turn off the Display Background checkbox and click OK. While still in the 3D Transform dialog, press R to switch to the Trackball tool, click within your preview area, and drag to the right. As you drag, the cube will rotate, exposing its back side, which includes shading on all three sides. (*Note:* You'll have to click-and-drag quite a ways to the right—in fact, your cursor will actually extend outside the 3D Transform dialog as you drag.) When it looks good to you, click OK and your shaded cube will appear on your blank layer.

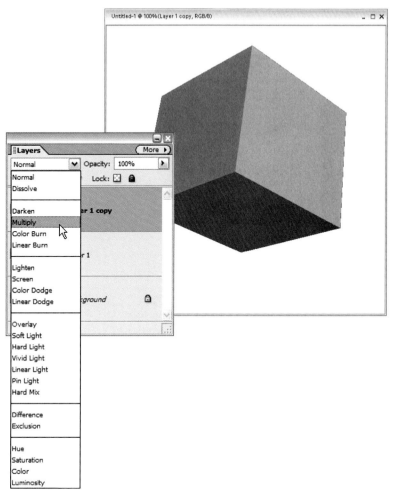

STEP THREE: The shading is somewhat subtle, so to intensify it, duplicate the cube layer by going under the Layer menu, under New, and choosing Layer via Copy (or by pressing Control-J). Then, change the layer blend mode in the Layers palette for this duplicate layer to Multiply. This has a multiplying effect and makes the shading on the cube more pronounced. Now, press Control-E to merge the Multiply cube layer permanently with the original cube layer below (creating just one layer).

STEP FOUR: Open the first photo you want to use on your photo cube. Press V to switch to the Move tool, and click-and-drag this photo over to your cube document. It will appear on its own layer above your cube layer. (*Note:* If needed, press Control-T to bring up Free Transform, press-and-hold the Shift key, grab a corner point, and resize your image so it fits onscreen.) The cube has perfectly square sides, so to keep from distorting your photos as you place them into the cube shape, you'll need to make them perfectly square as well. To do that, press M to switch to the Rectangular Marquee tool, press-and-hold the Shift key, and drag out a square selection over your photo. If you need to reposition your square once it's in place, just click the Rectangular Marquee tool within your selection and drag just the selection.

Continued

STEP FIVE: When your square selection is positioned correctly, go under the Select menu and choose Inverse. This inverses the selection. Press Backspace, and everything on that layer inside your selection is erased, leaving you with a perfectly square photo. Press Control-D to deselect.

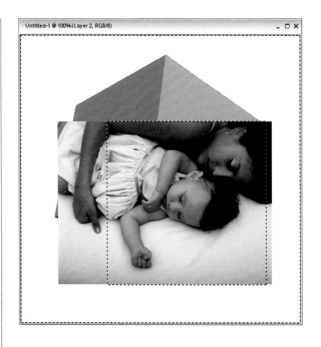

STEP SIX: In the Layers palette, lower the Opacity of this layer to 20% so you can see the cube below (the cube is your guide, so being able to see it is critical). Now, press Control-T to bring up Free Transform. Press-and-hold the Control key, grab the top-left corner of the bounding box, and drag it until it aligns with the top-left corner of the right face of the cube. Because you lowered the opacity of your photo layer, this is very easy. By the way, holding the Control key as you drag invokes Free Transform's Distort feature.

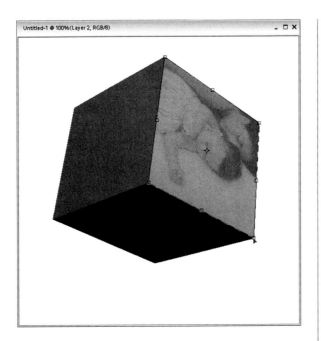

STEP SEVEN: Next, while still holding the Control key, grab the top-right Free Transform point and drag it until it aligns with the top-right corner of the cube. You'll do this for all four corners: Press-and-hold the Control key, grab a corner of your photo's bounding box, and align it with the corresponding corner of your cube face until all four sides match the cube. Then, press Enter to lock in your transformation on the right side of the cube.

STEP EIGHT: Remember how you lowered the opacity of this layer earlier? Well, now that the photo's aligned to the cube, you can go to the Layers palette and raise the Opacity of your photo layer back up to 100%.

Continued

STEP NINE: Now you're going to repeat the process (Steps 4–8) for the left and bottom faces of the cube: Open a photo, drag it over into your cube document, put a square selection around the most important part of the photo, inverse your selection, press Backspace, lower the Opacity of the layer to 20%, bring up Free Transform, hold the Control key, align the corner points to the cube, press Enter to lock in your transformation, and raise the Opacity back to 100%.

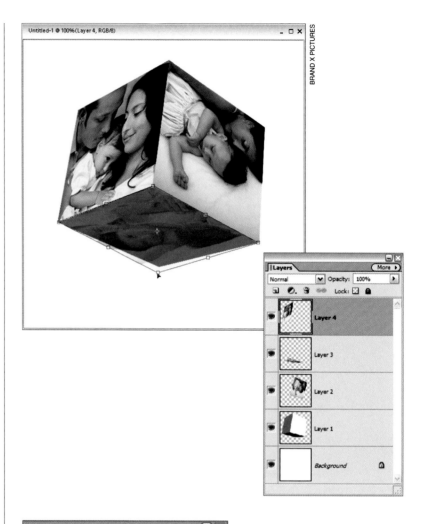

STEP TEN: Once you align all three photos and raise their Opacity settings back to 100%, you'll see the photo cube take shape. The only problem is, we've covered up all the shading from the cube (the photo on the bottom isn't darker, the right side isn't lighter, etc.). So go to the Layers palette, and with the top layer active, press Control-E twice to merge the three photo layers into just one layer, right above the cube layer (don't merge the cube layer with the photo layers).

BRAND X PICTURES

STEP ELEVEN: Now you're going to use the cube itself to add the shading to your photos. In the Layers palette, drag the cube layer above your photo layer, then change the layer blend mode of this cube layer to Soft Light. When you do this, your photo cube will appear subtly shaded, with the bottom photo becoming darker, the right photo lighter, and the left side not as light.

OPTION: The effect is essentially complete, but I thought I'd put it on a background just to show you the final effect. Open a photo you want to use as a background (I opened a photo of some clouds for my background). Now, return to your photo cube layer and press Control-E to merge your shaded cube and photo cube together permanently. Switch to the Move tool and click-and-drag this cube over onto the clouds background to complete the effect. (Notice how the bottom of the cube now appears darker?) This is just one way to use this effect—try creating multiple cubes, with other photos, and slightly rotate each for a different effect.

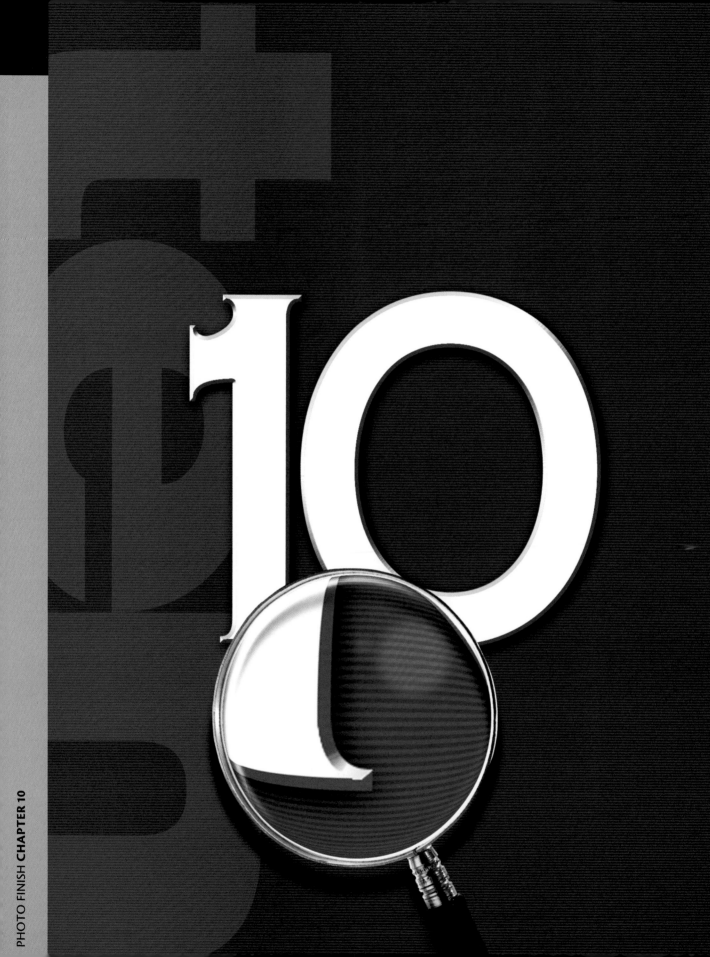

This is where it all pays off. These are the edge effects that you can use when it's time to present your work

Photo Finish
Edge Effects

to the client. This is where you'll learn how to add those little extras that make you and your photos stand out from the crowd. This is where your "click-click" turns into "bling-bling!"; where your "tap-tap" turns into "cha-ching"; where your "pipp-pipp" turns into your "ace-deuce." Okay, I should've stopped with bling-bling. These are the kinds of effects that can transform you from a scrappy kid in the streets, struggling along with some off-brand megapixel point-and-shoot, and turn you into a real playa, poppin' Cristal corks at one of P. Diddy's parties and cranking off shots with your Nikon D2X. That is, provided you actually are a scrappy kid in the streets. If you're not, and instead you're a middle-aged wedding photographer from Grand Rapids, I don't think you'll make it past the bouncers where P. Diddy hangs. But it's certainly worth a try. It's all gravy.

Filmstrip Templates

Photographers use this technique for a host of reasons: displaying client photos (especially modeling shots), high school senior portraits, travel shots, and shots used in online portfolios. There's one great thing about this technique—once you've created one filmstrip, you can save it as a template and apply it to any photo in seconds. Here's how it's done:

STEP ONE: Create a new document in RGB mode at a resolution of 300 ppi (the example here is 6x4"). Click on the Create a New Layer icon at the top of the Layers palette to create a new blank layer. Press D to set your Foreground color to black, then press M to switch to the Rectangular Marquee tool. Create a large rectangular selection, fill it with black by pressing Alt-Backspace, and then deselect by pressing Control-D.

STEP TWO: Inside your black rectangle, draw a smaller rectangular selection with the Rectangular Marquee tool. You're going to need this smaller rectangular selection later in this project, so save it by going under the Select menu and choosing Save Selection. When the dialog appears, enter a name and click OK. Now, press the Backspace key to knock the smaller rectangular selection out of the larger black rectangle. Deselect by pressing Control-D.

STEP THREE: Press the letter X to set white as your Foreground color. Next, go to the Layers palette and create a new blank layer. You'll need to zoom in close for this step, so press Alt-Control-+ (Plus Sign) to zoom in without changing your window size. Press-and-hold the Spacebar key to temporarily access the Hand tool, and click-and-drag within your image area until you're viewing the top-left corner of your black rectangle. Release the Spacebar, then press the U key until you have the Rounded Rectangle tool in the Toolbox. Now, up in the Options Bar, enter 15 pixels in the Radius field (the higher the number, the rounder the corners). On this new layer, draw a small rounded corner shape in the top black border area (you're actually creating the first hole along the top of the filmstrip). Then, click the Simplify button in the Options Bar to convert this Shape layer into an image layer.

STEP FOUR: Once you've got your first shape drawn, press the letter V to switch to the Move tool, then go to the Layers palette and Control-click on this layer to put a selection around your shape. Press-and-hold Shift-Alt, then click-and-drag the shape to the right to create a dupli-cate of your shape (the Shift key keeps your dragged copy aligned horizontally, and the selection ensures that the dupli-cate shape is drawn on the same layer as the original shape instead of a new layer being created for it). Continue dragging copies until you have a whole row across the top, then press Control-D to deselect.

Continued

STEP FIVE: Press Control-0 (zero) to fit your entire filmstrip onscreen. Go back to the Layers palette and Control-click on the "row-of-rounded-rectangles" layer (Shape 1) to select all of the rectangles. Press-and-hold Shift-Alt again, but this time drag straight down to the bottom border to duplicate this row of rectangles, creating the holes along the bottom of the filmstrip. Press Control-D to deselect.

STEP SIX: Return to the Layers palette and Control-click on the little rectangles layer (Shape 1) to put a selection around all the white rounded rectangles at the top and bottom of the filmstrip. Once the selection appears, you can drag-and-drop this layer onto the Trash icon at the top of the Layers palette to delete it (you don't need it anymore—you only needed it to create the selection). In the Layers palette, click on the black rectangle layer (your selection should still be in place) and press Backspace to knock that selection out of your black rectangle. Press Control-D to deselect (we'll now refer to this as our "filmstrip layer").

STEP SEVEN: Click on the filmstrip layer to make it active in the Layers palette. Then, go to the Styles and Effects palette (found under the Window menu), and with Layer Styles selected, choose Drop Shadows from the palette's top-right pop-up menu. Click on the Low drop shadow icon, then return to the Layers palette and double-click on the Layer Styles icon (it looks like an "*f*") to the right of the filmstrip layer. In the resulting Style Settings dialog, decrease the Shadow Distance to 10 pixels and click OK.

STEP EIGHT: Click on the Foreground color swatch at the bottom of the Toolbox, and when the Color Picker appears, choose an olive color (I used R: 141, G: 162, and B: 68) and click OK. Now press Z to switch to the Zoom tool, and zoom into the lower left-hand corner of the filmstrip. Press the letter T to switch to the Type tool, and type the number "21" (as if this were the 21st frame on the roll). I used Adobe's font Copperplate Gothic Bold set at 9 points in the example shown here.

Continued

STEP NINE: Now, create a new blank layer by clicking on the Create a New Layer icon at the top of the Layers palette. Then, press L until you have the Polygonal Lasso tool from the Toolbox. You're going to draw a thin triangle at the bottom of the filmstrip, so click once and drag upward or downward to create a straight vertical line for the left side of your triangle. Click again to the right where you want the point of the triangle to be, then click back where you started (or double-click) to close the selection. Now, go under the Edit menu and choose Stroke (Outline) Selection. When the Stroke dialog appears, for Width choose 3 pixels and click OK to stroke your triangular selection with the olive green color that you chose earlier. Deselect by pressing Control-D. Now, switch back to the Type tool and enter "21A" to the right of your triangle (hold the Alt key and click with the Zoom tool to zoom out if you need to). We're adding this type and the triangle to make the filmstrip look more realistic.

STEP TEN: Open the photo that you want to appear within your filmstrip. Switch to the Move tool and click-and-drag this photo directly into your filmstrip document. In the Layers palette, drag this image layer down in the layer stack until the photo appears directly below your filmstrip layer. If you need to resize the photo, press Control-T to bring up Free Transform, press-and-hold the Shift key, grab any corner point, and resize the photo so that the part that you want to keep appears within the center of the filmstrip. When it looks good to you, press Enter.

STEP ELEVEN: Remember that selection we saved back in Step 2? Well, Bunky, now you need it. With your image layer active in the Layers palette, go under the Select menu and choose Load Selection. Your selection should appear in the dialog (if not, click on the down-facing arrow to open the Selection pop-up menu and choose your selection from the list). Click OK in the Load Selection dialog. Now you're going to remove the excess parts of the image so the image appears completely within the filmstrip. To do that, go under the Select menu again and choose Inverse (or just press Shift-Control-I) to select everything on this layer but the photo in the center (in other words, all the excess photo is selected). Press Backspace to erase those areas. Now, you can deselect by pressing Control-D. Go under the File menu and choose Duplicate, then choose Save As from the File menu to save this "template" as a PSD file with all of its layers intact.

STEP TWELVE: Back in your original filmstrip document, you'll need to link together all the layers that make up your filmstrip in the Layers palette, so click once in the second column of the filmstrip layer, each Type layer, the triangle layer, and your photo layer to link them together. Now press Control-T to bring up Free Transform. Move your cursor outside the bounding box, and click-and-drag to rotate your filmstrip. Press Enter to lock in your rotation, completing the effect. (*Note:* Remember how you saved the file back at Step 11, before the rotation? You did that because it can now act as a template. To use this effect again on a different photo, simply open your saved filmstrip document, trash the photo layer, open a different photo, drag it in, load your saved selection, inverse the selection, delete the excess photo areas, link the layers, rotate, and you're done!)

Photo Mount Effect

Here's a handy technique for creating visual interest by adding photo mounts to the corners of your images. This is popular with wedding and travel photographers, as well as photo retouchers. What's nice about this is that once you've created one set of mounts, you can save the layered file and use them again and again. Plus, at the end of the effect, there's a pretty cool background texture you create from scratch.

STEP ONE: Create a new document in RGB mode (the one here is 6x4"). Create a new blank layer by clicking on the Create a New Layer icon at the top of the Layers palette. Press the letter M to switch to the Rectangular Marquee tool, press-and-hold the Shift key, and draw a square selection in the middle of your image area. Press D to set your Foreground color to black, then fill your square with black by pressing Alt-Backspace. Deselect by pressing Control-D.

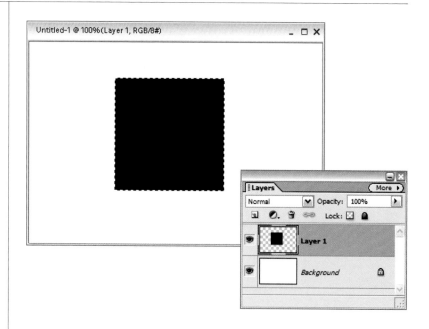

STEP TWO: Press L until you have the Polygonal Lasso tool. You're going to first draw a diagonal line through the center of your square, so click the tool just outside the square's bottom-left corner, drag diagonally beyond the square's top-right corner, and click again. Now, drag to the left beyond the top-left corner of the square and click, and then return to the bottom-left corner where you started and click one last time to complete your selection. Press Backspace to remove that area of the square, then press Control-D to deselect. You'll be left with a black triangle.

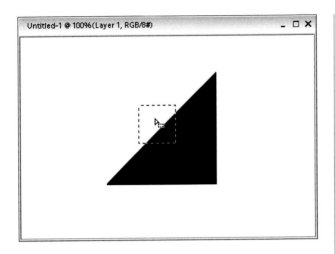

STEP THREE: Switch to the Rectangular Marquee tool again, press-and-hold the Shift key, and drag out a small square selection that's quite a bit smaller than your black triangle. With the Rectangular Marquee tool, click inside the selection and drag it so it overlaps a small section in the center of the black triangle's left side. Press the Backspace key to knock a little triangular chunk out of your black triangle. Deselect by pressing Control-D.

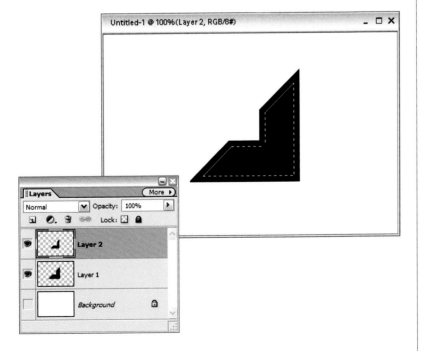

STEP FOUR: Next, press-and-hold the Control key, go to the Layers palette, and click on your shape's layer. This puts a selection around your entire shape. You'll need to shrink your selection, so go under the Select menu, under Modify, and choose Contract. When the Contract Selection dialog appears, enter 8 pixels, then click OK to shrink your selection (depending on the size and resolution of your shape, you may need to experiment with the number of pixels that you contract by). Create a new blank layer by clicking on the Create a New Layer icon at the top of the Layers palette. Fill your selection with black by pressing Alt-Backspace. Deselect by pressing Control-D.

Continued

STEP FIVE: With your new shape layer active in the Layers palette, go to the Styles and Effects palette (found under the Window menu), and with Layer Styles selected, choose Bevels from the palette's top-right pop-up menu. Click on the Simple Pillow Emboss icon, then go to the Layers palette and double-click on the Layer Styles icon (it looks like an "ƒ") to the right of the top shape layer. In the resulting Style Settings dialog, decrease the Bevel Size to around 3 pixels. When you click OK, some soft highlights and shadows are added inside your contracted shape, which help make it appear embedded into the larger shape.

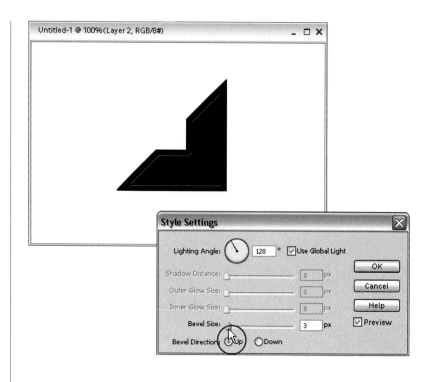

STEP SIX: In the Layers palette, click on the larger black shape layer (Layer 1), then return to the Styles and Effects palette. With Bevels still selected in the palette's top-right pop-up menu, click on the Simple Inner icon. Then, from the Styles and Effects palette's top-right pop-up menu, choose Drop Shadows and click on the Soft Edge icon. In the Layers palette, double-click on the Layer Styles icon to the right of the larger shape layer. In the resulting dialog, change the Lighting Angle to -30°, lower the Bevel Size to around 3 pixels, and click OK. In the following steps, we'll add this mount to the four corners of a photograph.

STEP SEVEN: Open the photo you want to apply the effect to. Then, create a new, larger blank document in RGB mode (the document must be larger than your image). Press V to switch to the Move tool, and then click-and-drag your photo onto this new document. Your photo will show up on its own separate layer. Use the Move tool to center your photo within the image area.

STEP EIGHT: You're going to add a border around your photo, so choose Stroke (Outline) Selection from the Edit menu. In the Stroke dialog, enter 11 pixels for Width, choose Inside for Location, and then click on the Color swatch and choose a light gray in the Color Picker. When you click OK, a Polaroid-like border appears around your photo (which can be seen in the capture in the following step).

Continued

STEP NINE: Go back to your photo mount document and merge your two shape layers together by clicking on the top layer in the Layers palette and pressing Control-E. Then, choose Simplify Layer from the Layer menu. Switch to the Move tool, click on the photo frame mount, and drag-and-drop it onto your photo document. It'll probably be too big, so you'll need to scale it down to size: Press Control-T to bring up Free Transform. Press-and-hold the Shift key, grab a corner point, and drag inward to scale the photo mount down to size. When the size looks right, move your cursor within the bounding box, and click-and-drag it into position at the bottom-right corner of your image. Press Enter to lock in your transformation.

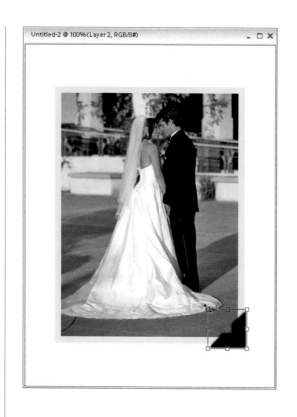

STEP TEN: Duplicate your photo frame mount by going under the Layer menu, under New, and choosing Layer via Copy (or by pressing Control-J). Then, go under the Image menu, under Rotate, and choose Flip Layer Horizontal to flip your duplicate layer (this will become your bottom-left mount). Using the Move tool, click-and-drag to position this mount in the bottom-left corner of the image. Now, you'll need to repeat this process for the other two corners: Duplicate the bottom-left mount layer, choose Layer 90° Right from the Rotate submenu, and position it in the top left-hand corner. Then, duplicate that mount layer, choose Flip Layer Horizontal, and position it in the top right-hand corner.

STEP ELEVEN: Now you're going to add a background texture. In the Layers palette, click on the Background layer and press Control-J to duplicate it. Choose Fill Layer from the Edit menu. In the Fill Layer dialog, choose Pattern from the Use pop-up menu, and then click on the Custom Pattern thumbnail to bring up the Pattern Picker. Click on the Pattern Picker's flyout menu and choose Texture Fill to load that set of texture patterns (click No if Elements asks you to save your current patterns). Return to the flyout menu again and choose Small List so you can see the patterns by name. Choose the pattern named Noise, but don't click OK yet.

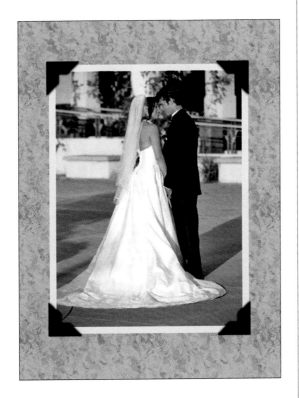

STEP TWELVE: In the Fill Layer dialog, lower the Opacity amount to 29% and click OK to apply this texture to the Background copy layer. Press Control-L to bring up Levels. In the Levels dialog, grab the highlight Output Levels slider and drag it to the left a little to darken the pattern and make it look a bit like marble. Click OK in the Levels dialog and the effect is complete.

Quick Slide Mounts

Several years ago, I wrote a Photoshop tutorial on how to make your own digital slide mounts. The end result looked authentic, but getting there was pretty brutal, because creating rounded corners for your slide took a series of blurs, Levels adjustments, and a host of other "pain-in-the-butt" steps. The original effect took 10 to 15 minutes to create. Now it's down to 60 seconds—thanks to features in Photoshop Elements—and that's good because displaying your photos in slide mounts (for online portfolios, wedding shots, etc.) is becoming popular once again.

STEP ONE: Create a new document in RGB mode at whatever size and resolution you'd like. Click on your Foreground color swatch at the bottom of the Toolbox and choose a light gray in the Color Picker (I used R: 212, G: 212, and B: 212). Press U until you have the Rounded Rectangle tool from the Toolbox. Up in the Options Bar, the Radius setting should be set to 10 pixels by default, which is fine for low-res, 72-ppi images (but enter 40 pixels for 300-ppi, high-res images). Click-and-drag out a rounded rectangle that has the same proportions as a typical slide. You'll notice Elements automatically creates a Shape layer for this rectangle in the Layers palette, but we want this layer to be a pixel-based layer, so in the Options Bar, click on the Simplify button.

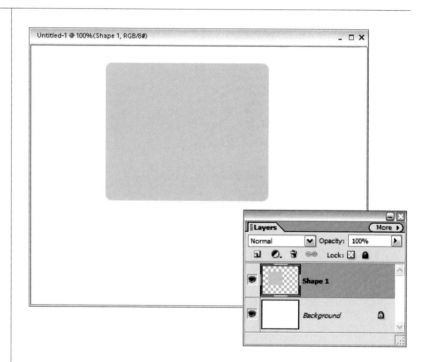

STEP TWO: Press M to switch to the Rectangular Marquee tool and drag out a horizontal selection within the center of the gray, round-cornered rectangle. Once your selection is in place, just press Backspace to knock a hole out of your slide, which creates the basic slide shape. Deselect by pressing Control-D.

STEP THREE: Go to the Styles and Effects palette (found under the Window menu), and with Layer Styles selected, choose Drop Shadows from the palette's top-right pop-up menu. Click on the Low drop shadow icon. Now, go under the Layer menu, under Layer Style, and choose Style Settings. In the Style Settings dialog, decrease the Shadow Distance to 1 pixel and click OK. This shadow will cast onto the photo that you'll place on the layer beneath the slide in the last two steps of this technique, making the photo appear as if it's inside the mount itself.

STEP FOUR: To finish off our slide template, we'll add some text for added realism (I call it a template, because once you've built this one slide, you can use it as a template to create as many slides as you'd like). Press D to set your Foreground color to black, then press the letter T to switch to the Type tool. Add your type (the font used here is Arial in all caps with the Center Text icon selected in the Options Bar). Now, lower the Opacity setting for your Type layers to 50% in the Layers palette to help them blend in with the slide. Then, click on the Eye icon next to the Background layer to hide it, and choose Merge Visible from the Layers palette's flyout menu. This leaves you with a single layer with the completed slide on it. Click on the far-left empty box next to the Background layer to make it visible again.

Continued

STEP FIVE: Now for the fun part: Open a photo you want to appear within your slide, press V to switch to the Move tool, and click-and-drag the image into your slide template. In the Layers palette, drag the photo layer below your slide layer. To get your photo small enough to fit inside the slide window, press Control-T to bring up Free Transform. Press-and-hold the Shift key, grab a corner point, and drag inward to shrink it until it's just slightly larger than the center opening of the slide. Press Enter to lock in your resize.

STEP SIX: Merge the photo layer and the slide layer together by clicking on the top slide layer and pressing Control-E. Then click within the document window and drag your completed slide into a new document. Now you can go back to your template and create more slides: Just press Control-Z to undo the merge, drag the photo layer to the Trash icon at the top of the Layers palette, repeat Step 5 using a different photo, and then repeat this step. In this final piece, I made four slides and rotated each in a different direction using Free Transform.

Painted Edges Technique

This technique, where you essentially hide the photo and then paint it back in, is particularly popular for landscape and portrait photographers; but it works so well, for so many different styles of photos, that you'll be amazed at how many other uses you'll find for it.

STEP ONE: Open the photo you want to apply the effect to.

STEP TWO: Create a new blank layer by clicking on the Create a New Layer icon at the top of the Layers palette. Press D and then X to set your Foreground color to white, then fill this new layer with white by pressing Alt-Backspace (your image will disappear, but we'll get it back in a minute).

Continued

STEP THREE: Press the E key to switch to the Eraser tool. Go up to the Options Bar, and bring up the Brush Picker by clicking on the brush thumbnail. Click on Brushes and choose Thick Heavy Brushes. Select the first brush, the 111-pixel Flat Bristle brush.

STEP FOUR: To help you see what you want to paint back in, lower the Opacity of the top white layer to around 50% in the Layers palette. Now you can paint over the areas you want to be visible. Start painting a few strokes with this brush from left to right across your image area. As you do, the original photo will paint back in. One of the cool things about this brush is that it has some gaps in it (like painting with a real dry brush), which helps give it a realistic, painted look. Take a look at the bottom stroke in particular and you can see the gaps (some upper areas don't have as many gaps because I painted more than one stroke over those areas).

STEP FIVE: Go back to the Brush Picker in the Options Bar and choose the next 111-pixel brush (the Rough Flat Bristle brush) in the Picker. Paint a stroke along the top of the painted effect with only a very small portion of this brush tip extending over the top of the already painted areas. This adds a more random, spattered look along the top edge. Do the same along the bottom. Raise the Opacity of this white layer in the Layers palette back to 100% so you can see your painting effect.

STEP SIX: For the finished piece, you can add a line of text. Press D to set your Foreground color to black, then press T to switch to the Type tool and enter your text (the typeface used here is Minion).

Distressed Edge Effect

For years now, we've all been doing a cheesy "Diffuse filter version" of this technique to create edge effects, but generally, the pros have never used it (instead they've always used third-party frame plug-ins and other stock photo sources for a more realistic edge effect). Well, I came up with a way to create edges that look like the ones the pros use, and although it takes a little more effort than the "Diffuse cheesy version," it looks vastly better.

STEP ONE: Open the photo you want to use in this effect, and press D to set your Background color to white. Press Control-A to select the entire photo, then go under the Layer menu, under New, and choose Layer via Cut (or press Shift-Control-J) to cut the photo from the Background layer and copy it onto its own separate layer (Layer 1).

STEP TWO: To create an edge, you'll need to add a little breathing room around your photo, so go under the Image menu, under Resize, and choose Canvas Size. When the dialog appears, ensure the Relative checkbox is on, enter 2 inches in both the Width and Height fields, choose White from the Canvas Extension Color pop-up menu, and click OK to add some white space around your photo (which can be seen in the following step).

STEP THREE: Now that you've got that white space, you'll need to add a thick black stroke around your photo. Choose Stroke (Outline) Selection from the Edit menu. In the Stroke dialog, set the Width to 10 pixels, set the Location to Inside (to give your stroke straight corners rather than the default rounded corners), and click on the Color swatch and choose black in the Color Picker. Click OK to apply the black stroke around your photo.

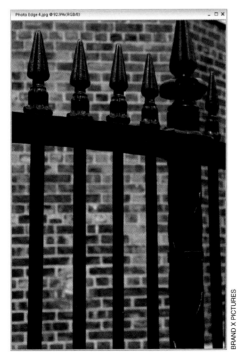

STEP FOUR: We're going to use different photos to help us create our edges, so open a photo that you'd like to use for one of your four distressed edges. Photos that have objects with visible straight edges in them (such as buildings) work best. The lines don't have to be perfectly horizontal or vertical, because you can always rotate it once it's in place.

Continued

STEP FIVE: Go under the Enhance menu, under Adjust Color, and choose Remove Color (or just press Shift-Control-U) to remove the color from your photo. Then, go under the Enhance menu, under Adjust Lighting, and choose Brightness/Contrast. You're going to adjust the Contrast to create an ultra-high-contrast image that's just short of looking bitmapped. In this instance, moving the Contrast slider all the way to the right gives us a good messy edge; but adjust yours until you've created an edge within your image that you like. Now, drag the Brightness slider to the right to remove even more black from the image. When it looks good to you, click OK.

STEP SIX: Switch to any selection tool you're comfortable with (I used the Rectangular Marquee tool in this case, but you could just as easily use the Polygonal Lasso tool) and select the edge you want to use in your main image. Press V to switch to the Move tool, then click within your selection and drag it over into your original photo document, which puts this edge piece on its own separate layer in the Layers palette.

STEP SEVEN: Most likely the edge is too large, so press Control-T to bring up Free Transform. Press-and-hold the Shift key, grab a corner point, and drag inward to scale it down until it fits. (*Note:* If you can't see the corner points of the Free Transform bounding box, press Control-0 [zero] to zoom out.) Click within the bounding box and position the edge on a side of your photo. You may need to click outside the bounding box and drag to rotate the edge, especially when applying it to the left or right side of the photo. When it looks good to you, press Enter to lock in your transformation. In the Layers palette, change the layer blend mode from Normal to Darken (this makes it easier to align the edge and blends it in with the black stroke around your photo).

STEP EIGHT: You'll repeat Steps 4–7 until you've created new edges for the other three sides of your photo: Open a new image, remove the color (Shift-Control-U), bring up Brightness/Contrast, adjust the sliders in the dialog until it looks good to you, select your edge, drag it into your photo, size and position the edge using Free Transform (Control-T), and change the layer blend mode to Darken. Once all the pieces are in place you may need to "clean up" some of the edges, so press the letter E to switch to the Eraser tool, go to the Layers palette and click on the edge layer that you want to erase from, then erase over any chunks along the side that you don't want in the image, which completes the effect.

Ripped Edge Technique

While working on another book, I showed some color proofs to a friend and he asked how we had created the ripped edge effect that we had used on long menus and the Options Bar (we had "ripped" away parts of menus and the Options Bar when they were too long to fit on the page). He thought I should include the technique in a book, so here it is.

STEP ONE: Open the image you want to rip. Press D and then X to set your Background color to white. You need the image cut from the Background layer, so press Control-A to select your image, then go under the Layer menu, under New, and choose Layer via Cut (or press Shift-Control-J) to put the image on its own layer (Layer 1).

STEP TWO: Press L to switch to the Lasso tool, and draw a selection around the part of the image that you want to keep. I started by drawing a jaggy line through the document from top to bottom (this will be the part of the image that's torn), then I dragged outside the image window, going all the way around to the point where I started making my selection. (*Note:* To add to your selection, press-and-hold the Shift key while using the Lasso tool, or to subtract from your selection, press-and-hold the Alt key.)

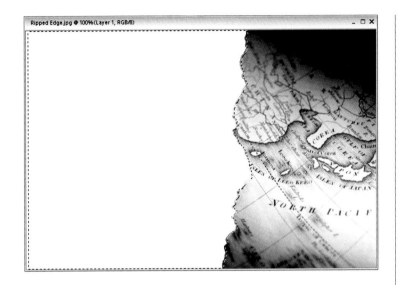

STEP THREE: Go under the Select menu and choose Inverse (or press Shift-Control-I) to inverse your selection, selecting the part of your image that you no longer want visible. Press Backspace to delete this area. Then, press the Right Arrow key (or whichever arrow key matches the direction your tear is in) about four times to nudge your selection over about 4 pixels into your image.

STEP FOUR: Press Control-L to bring up the Levels dialog. At the bottom of the dialog, drag the shadow Output Levels slider to the right until it reads 220, and then click OK. This lightens the 4-pixel selected area to almost white. Press Control-D to deselect.

Continued

STEP FIVE: Go to the Styles and Effects palette (found under the Window menu), and with Layer Styles selected, choose Drop Shadows from the palette's top-right pop-up menu. Click on the Soft Edge icon, then in the Layers palette, double-click on the Layer Styles icon to the right of the image layer. In the resulting dialog, decrease the Shadow Distance to 0 pixels, change the Lighting Angle to 179°, and click OK.

STEP SIX: Now just press T to switch to the Type tool and add any type you'd like to complete the effect. (The typeface used here is Gill Sans Light.)

4x5 FILM

220 EPC SSO

11

This chapter is actually much cooler than its subtitle implies; it's just that I couldn't come up with a cooler

Different Strokes
Artistic Effects

sounding name than "Artistic Effects," so don't hold that against the effects themselves—it's not their fault. I was afraid the name might scare some people away, because they might think, "Oh, that's painting and working with brushes, and I can't paint, so I'll just skip over this chapter and head on over to 'Advertising Effects.'" I don't think the Gary Coleman reference in the chapter head helped sell this chapter much either, but there's a trick in here for taking a photograph and making it look like you really can paint. It's called "The Evil Deceit Trick." Not really, but I bet if it were, that's the first one you'd turn to. Yes, you would. Oh come on, you act like I hardly know you.

Faking Hand-Drawn Silhouette Illustrations

The inspiration for this technique came from a T-shirt I saw for a zoo. You start with objects or people in photographs and convert them into silhouettes, and the final effect looks as if you drew the figures in Adobe Illustrator. In this project, we're going to build a design for a golf competition by converting a photo into a drawing.

STEP ONE: Start by opening the photo that you want to change into a drawing. Use any selection tool you'd like to put a selection around the object (I used the Magnetic Lasso tool). As usual, the Magnetic Lasso tool didn't do a perfect job all by itself, so after it was done, I had to add in some areas to the selection by pressing L until I had the Lasso tool, pressing-and-holding the Shift key, and clicking-and-dragging to select the additional areas. (*Note:* To subtract from your selection, press-and-hold the Alt key while using the Lasso.)

STEP TWO: Once the object is fully selected, go under the Layer menu, under New, and choose Layer via Copy (or press Control-J) to copy the selection onto its own separate layer (Layer 1) above the Background layer.

BRAND X PICTURES

STEP THREE: Open the photo that will serve as a background for the object (in this case, it's a photo of a sunset). Go to the Layers palette and click on the Create a New Layer icon to create a new blank layer. Then, press M to switch to the Rectangular Marquee tool and draw a rectangular selection across the bottom quarter of your photo. Press D to set your Foreground color to black, then press Alt-Backspace to fill this rectangle with black. Press Control-D to deselect.

STEP FOUR: Switch back to the original photo, and with your object's duplicate layer active in the Layers palette, press the letter V to switch to the Move tool. Click on the object and drag it over onto your sunset background. Once it's in your sunset document, you'll probably need to scale it down in size, so press Control-T to bring up Free Transform. Press-and-hold the Shift key, grab a corner point, and drag inward to shrink the object. When it's the size you want, press Enter to lock in your transformation.

Continued

STEP FIVE: Your Foreground color should still be black, so all you have to do is press Shift-Alt-Backspace to fill the object with black, creating a hand-drawn silhouette effect (holding the Shift key fills just the object with black and not the entire layer).

STEP SIX: The final step is simply to add some type with the Type tool (I used the font Copperplate Regular), which completes the effect.

Colorizing Line Art

Colorizing line art is really very simple: Start out by switching to RGB color mode, create selections inside your line art, and then colorize the selections on layers. Sounds easy enough, so let's get started.

STEP ONE: Scan your line art image into Photoshop Elements in RGB mode if possible, because your image has to be in a color mode if you're going to add color to it. If your line art image is already in Grayscale mode, you can simply go under the Image menu, under Mode, and choose RGB Color.

STEP TWO: Your scanned image will appear on the Background layer, but we need to convert it to a regular layer. In the Layers palette, double-click directly on the name "Background" and a dialog will appear in which you can name your new layer. Name it "Lines" and click OK to convert your Background layer into a regular editable layer.

Continued

STEP THREE: Create a new blank layer by clicking on the Create a New Layer icon at the top of the Layers palette. Then, go under the Layer menu, under New, and choose Background From Layer. This converts your just-created blank layer into a Background layer (we need this empty Background layer because it provides a white backdrop to work upon).

STEP FOUR: In the Layers palette, click on your Lines layer to make it active. Change its layer blend mode from Normal to Multiply. This makes the white areas of your Lines layer transparent, leaving only the black lines visible (you can't see this onscreen because of your white Background layer below, but it will all become very "clear" soon—sorry, couldn't help myself). Press W to switch to the Magic Wand tool (and make sure Contiguous is checked in the Options Bar). Click once inside an area you want to colorize and the Magic Wand tool will select that area. In this example, I clicked on the football player's jersey. (*Note:* You can use any selection tool you'd like: Lasso, Selection Brush, etc. Also, you can press-and-hold the Shift key to add to your selection, or press-and-hold the Alt key to subtract from your selection. Both shortcuts work with most selection tools.)

STEP FIVE: Press-and-hold the Control key and click on the Create a New Layer icon. This creates a new layer directly beneath your Lines layer, and this is where you'll add your color for the jersey. Click on the Foreground color at the bottom of the Toolbox, choose your color in the resulting Color Picker, then press Alt-Backspace to fill your selected area with color. Because your Lines layer is in Multiply mode, you can see the color through the white areas on that layer. Press Control-D to deselect.

STEP SIX: You'll continue this same process to colorize the rest of the image—just repeat Steps 4 and 5 to complete the effect. You put each color on its own layer because if you later want to change colors, you can just Control-click on that color layer in the Layers palette, choose your new color from the Foreground color swatch, and fill the selection with the new color. (For the final image here, I pressed B to switch to the Brush tool, chose green as my Foreground color, and on a new layer, I painted in some grass with a medium, hard-edged brush.)

From Photo to Oil Painting

I had heard that Ted LoCascio (our former Senior Associate Designer at *Photoshop User* magazine) had come up with a pretty amazing technique for turning any photo into an oil painting, and as soon as he showed it to me, I asked him (okay, I begged him) to let me share it here in the book. It's without a doubt one of the best-looking, easiest oil techniques I've ever seen.

STEP ONE: Open the photo you want to apply the effect to.

STEP TWO: Go under the Enhance menu, under Adjust Color, and choose Adjust Hue/Saturation (or just press Control-U). When the dialog appears, increase the Saturation to 50 and click OK to make your photo's colors more vivid.

STEP THREE: Go under the Filter menu and choose Filter Gallery. In the middle column of the Filter Gallery dialog, click on the Distort set to expand its set of filters, and then click on the Glass thumbnail. Set the Distortion amount to 3, set the Smoothness to 3, choose Canvas from the Texture pop-up menu, and set the Scaling to 79%. Don't click OK yet.

STEP FOUR: Click on the New Effect Layer icon in the bottom-right corner of the dialog (right next to the Trash icon). Click on the Artistic set, and then click on the Paint Daubs thumbnail. Set the Brush Size to 4, set Sharpness to 1, and choose Simple in the Brush Type pop-up menu. Don't click OK just yet....

Continued

STEP FIVE: Click on the New Effect Layer icon again at the bottom of the dialog. Click on the Brush Strokes set, and then click on the Angled Strokes thumbnail. Set the Direction Balance to 46, Stroke Length to 3, and Sharpness to 1. No, don't click OK yet.

STEP SIX: Click on the New Effect Layer icon one last time at the bottom of the dialog. To add a canvas-like texture, click on the Texture set, then click on the Texturizer thumbnail. Choose Canvas in the Texture pop-up menu, set the Scaling to 65%, set Relief to 2, and choose Top Left for Light. *Now* you can click OK to apply all four filters to your photo.

STEP SEVEN: Duplicate this filter layer by going under the Layer menu, under New, and choosing Layer via Copy (or by pressing Control-J). Then, go under the Enhance menu, under Adjust Color, and choose Remove Color (or press Shift-Control-U) to remove all the color from this layer. In the Layers palette, change the layer blend mode of this layer from Normal to Overlay.

STEP EIGHT: Go under the Filter menu, under Stylize, and choose Emboss. When the Emboss dialog appears, set the Angle to 135°, the Height to 1 pixel, and the Amount to 500%, and click OK. Then, go to the Layers palette and lower the Opacity of this layer to 40%, to give the oil painting effect.

Instant Woodcut Effect

This is a quick effect that allows you to instantly transform a color RGB image into that drawn woodcut effect that's popping up everywhere. We see this effect on the Web quite often where a woodcut object is used as an icon, but the effect works just as well in other projects.

STEP ONE: Open the image that you want to turn into a woodcut, then double-click on the Background layer. In the resulting dialog, just click OK and your Background layer will become a regular layer. Make a copy of this layer by dragging it to the Create a New Layer icon at the top of the Layers palette.

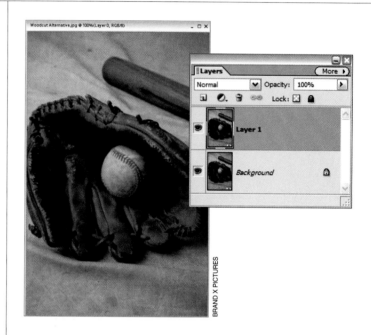

STEP TWO: Go under the Filter menu, under Other, and choose High Pass. In the High Pass dialog, enter a Radius of 2.5 pixels and click OK. Now, go under the Enhance menu, under Adjust Color, and choose Remove Color (or press Shift-Control-U) to remove all the color from your duplicate layer.

STEP THREE: Go to the Filter menu, under Adjustments, and choose Posterize. When the dialog appears, enter 2 in the Levels field and click OK.

STEP FOUR: To see the effect take shape, change the layer blend mode in the Layers palette from Normal to Multiply. Next, click on Layer 0 (the bottom layer) in the Layers palette to make it active and lower the Opacity of this layer to 60% to complete the effect. (You'll have to use your own judgment, but somewhere between 60–70% opacity usually looks about right.)

Photo to Line Art Morph

This is a great little trick that morphs a photograph into line art. I've seen this used numerous times, most recently in a backlit ad on the terminal wall at LAX. Those who remember the award-winning video for the song "Take On Me," by the group a-ha, will experience a momentary 80s flashback when they try this technique.

STEP ONE: Open the image you want to morph into a line drawing. Go under the Layer menu, under New, and choose Layer via Copy (or press Control-J) to create a duplicate of your Background layer.

STEP TWO: While on this duplicate layer, go under the Filter menu, under Stylize, and choose Find Edges (don't worry, there are no dialog options here—Photoshop Elements automatically finds the edges within your document). Then, go under the Enhance menu, under Adjust Color, and choose Remove Color (or press Shift-Control-U) to remove all the color from the duplicate layer. *(Note: Applying the Find Edges filter introduces lots of highly saturated patches of color, so removing the color is a must.)*

STEP THREE: Now that the color is gone, we need to remove some of the leftover "noise" and unnecessary detail created by the Find Edges filter. Press Control-L to bring up the Levels dialog. Drag the highlight Input Levels slider to the left to "blow out" the extra detail, leaving just the most substantial lines. When it looks good to you, click OK.

STEP FOUR: In the Layers palette, ensure your black-and-white line layer is active, then Control-click on the Create a New Layer icon at the top of the palette to create a new blank layer beneath your line layer. Click back on your line layer to make it active and choose Group with Previous from the Layer menu (or press Control-G) to group this line layer with the blank layer below it, which will hide the line layer onscreen.

Continued

STEP FIVE: Press D to set your Foreground color to black. Switch to the Gradient tool by pressing the G key, and then press Enter to bring up the Gradient Picker. Click on the Foreground to Transparent gradient (it's the second one in the Picker). Now, go to the Layers palette and click on the empty layer below your line layer to make it active. With the Gradient tool, click on the right side of your image and drag to the left. After you drag out your gradient, the left side of the top layer will become transparent, revealing the original photo on the layer below, and it will smoothly blend into the line art version of your image on the right.

STEP SIX: If you want to add a little color to your line art, change the layer blend mode of your gradient layer in the Layers palette to Lighten (which I used here), Vivid Light, or (for a lot of color) Overlay; this completes the effect.

COLOPHON

The book was produced by a design team using all Macintosh computers, including a Power Mac G4 733-MHz, a Power Mac G4 Dual Processor 1.25-GHz, a Power Mac G5 1.8-GHz, and a Power Mac G5 Dual Processor 2-GHz. We use Apple, LaCie, and Sony monitors.

Page layout was done using InDesign CS. The headers for each technique are set in 20-point CronosMM700 Bold with the Horizontal Scaling set to 95%. Body copy is set using CronosMM408 Regular at 10 points on 13-point leading, with the Horizontal Scaling set to 95%.

Screen captures were taken with TechSmith SnagIt 7.1.1 on a Dell Precision M60 and a Dell Precision Workstation 650, and were placed and sized within InDesign CS. The book was output at 150-line screen, and all in-house proofing was done using a Tektronix Phaser 7700 by Xerox.

ADDITIONAL RESOURCES

ScottKelbyBooks.com
For information on Scott's other books, visit his book site. For background info on Scott, visit www.scottkelby.com.

http://www.scottkelbybooks.com

Photoshop Elements Techniques
Photoshop Elements Techniques is a newsletter packed with practical, real-world tips and techniques from some of the leading Photoshop Elements gurus, including Dave Cross, Jan Kabili, Dave Huss, and Scott Kelby. Every issue will be a valuable resource for Photoshop Elements users. Visit the website to view subscription information.

http://www.photoshopelementsuser.com

Photoshop Elements Techniques Website
The ultimate source for Photoshop Elements users features tutorials, downloads, forums, and much more! The site also contains up-to-date Elements news, tips and tricks, and contests.

http://www.photoshopelementsuser.com

KW Computer Training Videos
Scott Kelby and Dave Cross are featured in a series of Adobe Photoshop and Adobe Photoshop Elements training DVDs, each on a particular Photoshop or Elements topic, available from KW Computer Training. Visit the website or call 813-433-5000 for orders or more information.

http://www.photoshopvideos.com

The Photoshop Elements 4 Book for Digital Photographers
This book gives you the inside tips and tricks of the trade for correcting, editing, sharpening, retouching, and presenting your photos like a pro. You'll be absolutely amazed at how easy and effective these techniques are—once you know the secrets.

http://www.scottkelbybooks.com

National Association of Photoshop Professionals (NAPP)
The industry trade association for Adobe® Photoshop® users and the world's leading resource for Photoshop training, education, and news.

http://www.photoshopuser.com

Adobe Photoshop Seminar Tour
See Scott live at the Adobe Photoshop Seminar Tour, the nation's most popular Photoshop seminars. For upcoming tour dates and class schedules, visit the tour website.

http://www.photoshopseminars.com

Photoshop World Conference & Expo
The convention for Adobe Photoshop users has now become the largest Photoshop-only event in the world. Scott Kelby is technical chair and education director for the event, as well as one of the instructors.

http://www.photoshopworld.com

PlanetPhotoshop.com
"The Ultimate Photoshop Site" features Photoshop news, tutorials, reviews, and articles posted daily. The site also contains the Web's most up-to-date resources on other Photoshop-related websites and information.

http://www.planetphotoshop.com